CATTLE-LORDS AND CLANSMEN

THE SOCIAL STRUCTURE OF EARLY IRELAND

CATTLE-LORDS AND CLANSMEN

THE SOCIAL STRUCTURE OF EARLY IRELAND

NERYS THOMAS PATTERSON

UNIVERSITY OF NOTRE DAME PRESS
NOTRE DAME   LONDON

Library of Congress Cataloging-in-Publication Data

Patterson, Nerys Thomas.
    Cattle-lords and clansmen : the social structure of early Ireland
/ Nerys Thomas Patterson. — 2nd ed.
        p.   cm.
    Includes bibliographical references and index.
    ISBN 0-268-00800-0 (alk. paper)
    1. Social structure—Ireland—History.   2. Kinship—
Ireland—History.   3. Ireland—Social life and customs—
To 1500.   4. Civilization, Medieval.   5. Civilization, Celtic.
I. Title.
GN585.I7P38   1994
306.83′09415—dc20   93-45597
                                                              CIP

I FY MHLANT

for my children

RHIANNON A BARBARA

Rhiannon and Barbara

CONTENTS

Illustrations

PREFACE TO THE SECOND EDITION

The first edition of this book was published as a library edition by Garland, New York, in the series, *Harvard Studies in Sociology* (A. Sörensen and L. Greenfeld, eds., 1991). It originated in my 1981 dissertation for the Harvard Departments of Sociology and of Celtic Languages and Literatures, but was supplemented by several years of post-doctoral work, undertaken while I taught in the Celtic Department at Harvard.

In the Preface to the first edition I emphasized that Irish sources can be used to consider questions in European cultural history, especially the materialism of early European social values. I still think this is the case and hope to complete a study of the European 'goodliness' complex, in which goods and goodness merged ideologically. However, it now seems to me that a historical sociological study of Irish society needs no justification beyond itself. Ireland was European but differed from the mainstream in several ways, and deserves to be known by all medievalists as part of the range of European social types. For the same reason, anthropologists, archaeologists and sociologists who engage in comparative studies ought also to be more aware of the nature of this society.

In this second edition a new chapter has been added that deals with the seasonal rhythms of social life (Ch. 5). This is intended to breathe some life into the abstract model of social relations that the book as a whole presents. Sociologists familiar with the work of the late Prof. George Homans, my thesis director in Sociology, will recognize his influence here. I am grateful to James Langford, Director of Notre Dame University Press, for giving me the opportunity to present this fresh material. The second edition also takes account of recent contributions to the field of Irish historical research. Another improvement is that this volume includes an index. I have taken the opportunity to correct mistakes in the first edition, though doubtless there remain many imperfections.

A limitation of this book is that it does not discuss monastic estates and communities. This is simply too big a subject to be encompassed alongside a full treatment of secular society. Readers should realize, however, that in addition to the social groups depicted here, there existed monastic estates that in many ways resembled those of the secular clans, but also differed significantly in that the clerical nobility did not devote themselves to warfare, but merely resorted to it when need be. Monastic clans were competitive, but they tended to expand on the heels of military conquest by the secular clans to which they were allied and were also often related through kinship (Charles-Edwards 1984: 128).

I have retained most of the features of the first edition's scholarly *apparatus*. Following standard practice in social anthropology I cite vernacular terms for native institutions, so as not to introduce cultural assumptions into the discussion of textual evidence. Since too much vernacular can daze the reader, however, I sometimes revert to English terms after the meaning of the Irish term has been distinguished. Wherever I have noted that a term is capable of literal translation, my authority is the Royal Irish Academy's *Dictionary of the Irish Language (DIL)*; I have not footnoted such references. A glossary of Irish terms is given at the end of the book. I have kept the use of technical terms for kinship and other social relations to a minimum, but a glossary of these is also provided. To save space, abbreviations of the titles of law-tracts have unfortunately been used frequently. As to the orthography of Irish proper nouns, I confess to an inconsistent approach: where these are simple, or would be familiar to anyone with some knowledge of Irish tradition, I have retained the Irish spelling (e.g. Cú Chulainn), but otherwise I use Anglicized forms (e.g. Moytura for *Mag Tuired*).

For reasons of economy, I have curtailed the quotation of text, giving only short citations from one text of the original Irish printed primary sources, and confining these to the footnotes. Following established usage, canonical text (i.e. original old text), is written in upper case, while commentaries and glosses are in lower case. Where the passage in question is long, I have in many cases cited only the *incipit* or a short quotation. Moreover, where a point is well established, I have given only the line numbers in the modern diplomatic edition of the law-tracts, the *Corpus Iuris Hibernici* (Binchy 1978), or a reference to the source and discussion of the point in Kelly's *Guide to Early Irish Law* or in *Studies in Early Irish Law*. Only where I believe the point or the source has not been widely discussed by specialists in the law-tracts, do I cite whole passages of original text in the notes. My purpose, in general, is to offer convenient references to the printed source in *CIH* or other authoritative editions, rather than exhaustive evidence that the point is supported by the citation. Experts in the Old Irish law-tracts may thus draw their own conclusions as to whether I have mis- or over-interpreted a passage.

As to translations, the Old Irish language of the law-tracts is such a notoriously difficult field of study, that I have as far as possible, depended on established scholarly editions and translations. Where these are available only in German, as is the case with Thurneysen's works, I have offered paraphrases of his translations rather than quotations in German. Where it has been necessary to cite translations from *AL*, I have in some cases modified these, usually by interpolating an explanation between clauses according to how I understand the Irish text. (Needless to say, I do not claim to offer definitive translations.) The interpolations, are intended to indicate the sense of the passage, which the literal translation in *AL* often obscures. Readers wishing to consult the sources should note that the references provided in the footnotes are to the line numbers in *CIH*, to line numbers in the text of *Críth Gablach* (page numbers in references to *CG* indicate the editor's discussion and notes), and to the page and line numbers of the English translation of the passage in *AL*, where the source has been translated in that edition.

My thanks are again owed to those who contributed to the first edition of this book: the members of my thesis committee, the late George Homans, Charles Dunn and Elizabeth Gray; Jack Goody, Jane Guyer, Pauline Peters, and the late Victor Turner, who offered valuable comments during an early stage of the research; former members and affiliates of the Department of Celtic Languages and Literatures at Harvard, notably Bettina Arnold, John V. Kelleher, Proinsias Mac Cana, John Carey, John Koch, Jean Rittmueller, Lionel Joseph, Bill Mahon, Dorothy Africa, and Paul Jefferiss. Margo Granfors and Suzanne Washington made valuable technical contributions to the original MS production. Others who deserve thanks for helpfulness at various times are Thomas Bisson, Wallace MacCaffrey, Robin Chapman Stacey, Fergus Kelly, Steven Ellis, Francis J. Byrne, and D. Ellis Evans. In addition, I wish to thank the following for assistance during the production of the second edition: Bette-Jane Crigger, Margaret Mac Curtain, Maura Herbert, Tim Taylor, and Carol Roos. Needless to say, none of the above are implicated in whatever errors and indiscretions appear in the following pages, which are my sole responsibility.

I am also grateful to the following institutions for support: the Mrs Giles Whiting Foundation; the H. B. Earhart Foundation; the librarians and staff of Widener Library; and the Law and Liberal Arts Fellowship Program at Harvard Law School. Finally, I wish to thank the Prize Committee of the American Conference on Irish Studies for honoring me with the Donald Murphy Prize for the most distinguished first book of 1992 in the field of Irish studies.

But above all, I am grateful to my family and friends for their support during the circumstances that attended the making of this work. In particular Judy Clark and Judy Dowling, my husband, Orlando Patterson, and my daughters, Barbara and Rhiannon, have been constant sources of help, companionship and commiseration.

N.W.T.P.
September, 1993.

ABBREVIATIONS

(For full information see entry, by editor, in the Bibliography)

AL   *Ancient Laws of Ireland* i-iv, ed. and transl., W. Nielsen
Hancock, *et al.* 1848-51.

AM   *Audacht Morainn* ('the testament of Morann'), ed. and transl.,
Fergus Kelly. 1976.

ATH   *Di Chetharshlicht Athgabála* ('the four divisions of
distraint'), ed. and transl., D. A. Binchy. 1973.

BA   *Berrad Airechta: an Old Irish Tract on Suretyship.*, ed. and
transl., Robin Chapman Stacey, in T. M. Charles-Edwards and
Morfydd E. Owen, and D. B. Walters, eds. 1986.

BB   *Bechbretha, an Old Irish law-tract on bee-keeping*, ed. and
transl., T. M. Charles-Edwards and Fergus Kelly. 1983.

CA   *Cáin Aicillne* ('the law of base-clientship'), ed. and German
transl., R. Thurneysen. 1923.

CB   *Córus Bescnai* ('the regulation of proper behavior'): *CIH*
520.1-536.27; 903.37-905.9; 1812.23-1821.27 = *AL* iii 3-79.

CCF   *Cóic Conara Fugill* ('the five paths to judgment'), ed. and
German transl., R. Thurneysen. 1926.

CG   *Críth Gablach*, ed. D. A. Binchy. 1941.

CIH   *Corpus Iuris Hibernici*, ed. D. A. Binchy. 1978.

CL   *Cáin Lánamna* ('the law of marriage'), ed. and German transl.,
R. Thurneysen in *SEIL*.

CS   *Cáin Sóerraith* ('the law of free clientship'), ed. and German
transl., Thurneysen. 1925.

DIL   *Contributions to a Dictionary of the Irish Language*, gen. ed.,
E. G. Quinn. 1913-76.

DRS   *Dliged Raith 7 Somaíne la Flaith* ('right of a fief and
renders of a lord'), ed. and transl. B-J. Crigger.1991.

FF   *Fodla fine* ('*D'Fodlaib Cineoil Tuaithi*'; 'the divisions of the
kin-group of a *tuath*): *CIH* 429.14-432.15 = *AL* iv 283-91.

IR   *Irisches Recht*, ed. and German transl., R. Thurneysen. 1931.

SEIL *Studies in Early Irish Law*, ed. D. A. Binchy. 1936.

SM   The *Senchas Már*.

UB   *Uraicecht Becc* ('the small primer'), ed. and transl. Eóin Mac
Néill. 1923.

CATTLE-LORDS AND CLANSMEN

THE SOCIAL STRUCTURE OF EARLY IRELAND

CHAPTER ONE

Reconstructing Early Irish Society: Sources and Scholarship

Most of the evidence for early Irish[1] social structure is found in a rich, complex and damaged body of writings in Old and Middle Irish, Latin, and combinations of these. Compiled by clerics and members of the secular learned groups, in *scriptoria* both famous and obscure, the manuscripts were copied, glossed, commented upon, and edited by scribes, for over a thousand years. Sometimes they were beautifully illuminated and immensely valuable, as was the celebrated Book of Kells, and were the product of sophisticated *scriptoria* in wealthy monasteries (Hughes 1958). In other cases, the penmanship was untidy, and the MS grubby and stained by ink-blots. Some of the writers were eminent masters of learning (*ollamh*) but often they were young apprentices, doing the dull chore of copying texts for their teachers,

---

[1] Because it is difficult to establish precise dates for many Irish historical sources, and because political and cultural processes proceeded at different rates of change, the chronological phases of Irish history are indicated in several ways. In this book **'early Irish'** means the entire period between the advent of Christianity and the rise of new dynasties in the fourth and fifth centuries, and the Norman invasion in the mid twelfth. **'Early medieval'** and **'pre-Viking'** indicate the period extending from the same threshold to the Viking attacks; these commenced at the beginning of the ninth century. **'Viking age'** is sometimes used to refer to the ninth and tenth centuries, and **'late pre-Norman'** to refer to the period of Norse-Irish symbiosis, and the emergence of a new group of dynasties, in the eleventh and early twelfth centuries. **'Late medieval'** refers to the period between the Norman invasion and the Tudor conquest in the second half of the sixteenth century; **'later Gaelic Ireland'** refers specifically to the indigenous community during this period. **'Early modern Ireland'** refers to the period of the Tudor conquest and the subsequent destruction of much of the indigenous culture.

whether of law, religion, or the native learning known as *filidecht*, which included poetry, narrative literature, genealogy and history. These obscure individuals wrote on the margins of the MSS, complaining of cold, hunger and the dying candle-light; or worse, of plague raging all around and the scribe's fear that humanity was about to be extinguished. Elsewhere they teased each other, played pedantic practical jokes, and made cynical comments on political developments (Plummer 1926). Though sometimes they gave their names and place of writing, on the whole their work is anonymous, dateless and unplaced — not by oversight, but because the learned class in Ireland (a marked segment of the élite) drew prestige from the antiquarian nature of their knowledge, and derived power from their monopolistic ability to interpret the obscure contents of the manuscripts.[1]

The most surprising feature of the Irish documentary record is the variety of genre, recently itemized by McCone: 'liturgy, homiletics, biblical exegesis and paraphrase, hymnody and eulogy, hagiography, Latin and Irish grammar, etymology, onomastics, topography, annals, genealogy, legal tracts concerning the church and lay society, gnomic literature, prophecy, vision and voyage narratives, saga and history' (McCone 1990: 1). Indeed, so compound are many Irish MSS, that the identification of genre — what piece of writing is 'history', what is 'story', what is 'law'? — is highly debatable. It is not at all uncommon, in fact, to find a legal text combining native prose writing with excerpts in translation from the Bible, Irish legal-poetic materials, and a narrative that makes some legal point. Even such dry works as the annals occasionally break into verse. This lively inter-genericity bespeaks a creativity on the part of a literary élite that was empowered, not constrained, by a traditionalism of which it alone was master.

The present study draws tangentially upon this broad range of writings, but is based primarily upon law-tracts. The existence of such varied non-legal materials, however, provides a way of checking whether the normative law-tracts reflected the values and social practices of other sectors of early Irish society. Some might argue, however, that since all the written MSS derived from the same sub-culture, the documentary legacy of the Irish learned class is a seamless web whose relationship to the world was all of a piece, with no part offering corroboration of another. Fortunately, recent archaeological work supports the credibility of some of the law-tracts' references to tangible aspects of early Irish culture. McCormick, for example, has shown that dairy cattle made up 71% of the typical herd at excavated early medieval Irish sites, which is the same proportion implied by the law tracts (McCormick 1983: 256, 259). Stout (1991) also shows that the dimensions for ringforts and for areas of farm land are consistent with models of farm use generated from a survey of ringforts in south-west Ireland. Even the dates provided by the Irish annals for prehistoric events have recently been argued to be unexpectedly accurate (Warner 1990). With the credibility of some items in the corpus of early Irish writings thus supported, the degree of consistency between different documentary sources as to social life provides a secondary-level check on the 'realism' of the whole. This is important in view of the absence of a substantial record of actual transactions — land-charters are few, for example, and wills and records of legal decisions mainly derive from the sixteenth century. On the whole, it may be said that the general depiction of early medieval society from all sources is quite full and consistent: the reader may notice how aptly passages from early sagas, cited in this book, complement the depiction of social relations in the law-tracts.

But while the Irish documentary record is thus extremely interesting, it also presents scholars with an array of interpretative problems. Of these the most severe are the formidable nature of the Old Irish language itself, the heightened obscurity of the language of the legal profession, the decimation of the manuscripts after the Tudor conquest of Ireland, and the highly politicized context in which serious scholarly work on the manuscripts began in the nineteenth century. As a result, sociological theory came to play a large role in the interpretation of sources, providing necessary working hypotheses which enabled scholars to make new inroads into the materials. The Irish law-tracts were interpreted in the light of nineteenth-century theories of social evolution, with the result that the social institutions represented in the law-tracts were analyzed in terms of the contrasts they offered to a conjectured model of ancient society. This model was itself based on stereotypes of the 'strict patriarchy' and/or 'strict patrilineality' of 'Indo-European society'.

Twentieth-century anthropological field work discredited such 'conjectural history' by showing how ambiguous as evidence for a social system are scraps of data, when isolated from a full, verified social context. Despite these changes, and despite a recent shift within Irish scholarship itself towards greater emphasis upon the connections between early Irish and other medieval European cultures (Ó Corráin *et al.*, 1984; Breatnach 1984; McCone 1990; Richter 1988) many of these evolutionary views on early Irish law and society have gained a degree of permanent acceptance, even without further corroboration or theoretical analysis of the concepts on which these propositions were based. Charles-Edwards' *Early Irish and Welsh Kinship* (1993) exemplifies this tendency to pile yet more date onto the framework of old hypotheses (in this case, the 'collapse of the *derbfhine*': see below) without critically reassessing their foundations.

With some exceptions, notably an overheated debate on the degree to which pagan culture influenced the Irish laws (see Ó Corráin *et al* 1984; McCone 1990), theoretical discussion has played little part in historians' reconstruction of early Irish society, reflecting a general trend towards 'a low level of concern with conceptual and theoretical issues generally among Irish historians' (Ruane 1992: 309). This contrasts with the lively and diverse theoretical approaches taken by archaeologists (e.g. Mytum 1992; Lynn 1983; 1992; 1993; Warner 1990); but even amongst archaeologists there is some reluctance to take issue with the frozen theories of documentary historians (see Patterson 1991b). This chapter therefore describes both the sources and the dominant theoretical paradigm within which they have been interpreted as evidence for social structure. It concludes with a brief description of my own theoretical stance towards the material.

General features of the Irish law-tracts

The major compilation of law-tracts is known as the *Senchas Már*, the 'great tradition' (Kelly 1988: 242). The tracts are also widely known as the brehon laws: 'brehon' is an anglicization of Irish *brithem*, meaning 'lawyer' or 'judge'. Most of the extant legal MSS are housed in the libraries of Trinity College, Dublin, the Royal Irish Academy, the British Library, and the Bodleian Library. These documents are all late copies of older manuscripts, dating mainly from the fifteenth and sixteenth centuries; few are undamaged or complete and most present severe editorial difficulties. The corpus of materials represents only a portion of the output of the law schools during the 'classical' period of textual composition (the seventh and eighth centuries), as is shown by the large number of references in the surviving MSS to texts that are now lost. Kelly's provisional itemization of the law-tracts indicates that of the more than seventy listed texts, about one third are lost, or survive only as fragmentary quotations to which late medieval commentaries were attached (*ibid*: 266-81).

A major cause of the loss of MSS was political; the colonization of Ireland during the sixteenth century led to the suppression of Irish institutions and the gradual loss of the Irish language. In this context, notwithstanding the early attempts of antiquarians such as Edward Lluid to find and purchase Irish MSS, many manuscripts were consigned to oblivion. Further major loss of historical documentation occurred in 1922, when the Four Courts were shelled during the struggle for independence from British rule. A secondary cause of the loss of texts may have stemmed from within the Irish tradition itself: Irish law was evolving in the later middle ages and differential attention may have been given to the preservation of the materials.[2] It is quite striking, for instance, that several complete tracts on the privileges of the various ranks of society have survived, whereas a whole group of texts that we may suppose interested the humbler members of rural communities is missing, namely texts that classified and evaluated types of dogs, cats, cows, and injuries done to and by them, and texts relating to hunting, trapping and beach-combing.[3] While this loss may have been accidental it is just as likely that the MSS that recorded the details of peasant social regulation were not kept as close at hand and as safely by the heads of legal families, as those that bore on relations in the upper strata of society.

The extant law-tracts are composed of three elements: the basic text (usually prose, but sometimes in verse), interlinear gloss, and commentary. The linguistically oldest stratum of basic text was dated to the seventh century by two of the leading earlier scholars of Old Irish history and language, Eóin Mac Néill and Rudolf Thurneysen. Their views have been confirmed by subsequent researchers (Kelly 1988: 1). These early texts form the canonical stratum of the laws, which was held to be immutable:

This is Patrick's Law. No human jurist of the Irish is
competent to abrogate anything that is found in the
Senchas Már.[4]

Some of the canonical texts (such as *Críth Gablach* and the pseudo-historical introduction to the *Senchas Már*) have been handed down with little in the way of glosses and commentaries, but many others were extensively supplemented by later scribes. The glosses typically employ the technique of etymological analysis in order to 'explain' the substance of the cryptic text. As Mac Néill pointed out, this technique was in fact another sort of mnemonic device, linking a series of references to the text and fixing them in the memory of the student by means of the etymological connection (1967: 112-3). Much work remains to be done on the medieval commentaries, which, although they sometimes mislead by attaching speculative interpretations to obscure old texts, often cut through to the basic sense of materials, as well as showing how jurists of later periods interpreted old textual elements.

The *Senchas Már* probably originated in the north-eastern midlands, but eventually gained national pre-eminence. It was already organized as a compendium of tracts, arranged in a fixed sequence, during the Old Irish period (Kelly 1988: 242-6). The majority of the tracts of the *Senchas Már* that are referred to in this book are found in the first third of the compilation:

1. *Introduction*: a mythical account of the conversion to Christianity of the likewise mythical high-king, Lóegaire, at Tara; Patrick's blessing of the laws; and an outline of the general provisions of the 'revised' law.
2. *Di Chetharshlicht Athgabála*: a tract on the procedures of distraint (removal of property) to obtain justice from an offender.
3. *Di Gnímaig Gíall*: a tract on the taking and handling of hostages. (Only fragments of the text survive.)
4. *Cáin Íarraith*: on the giving of children in fosterage; their care, cost, liabilities, etc.
5. *Cáin Sóerraith*: on the contract of free-clientship. (Only the first section of the tract survives.)
6. *Cáin Aicillne*: on the contract of base-clientship.
7. *Cáin Lánamna*: on marriage and divorce.
8. *Córus Béscnai*: on customary rules of general contracts, with special attention to the property relations of clerics.

Of the twenty-one surviving texts that comprise the remaining two-thirds of the *Senchas Már*, the most important for this study is *Bretha Comaithchesa* (a tract on relationships between neighbors in an agrarian community) and *Fodlai Fine (AL* title: *D'fodlaib Cineoil Tuaithi)*, a description of kinship relations and classes of dependents that made up the *cenél*, or clan, of the chieftain of a *tuath* (a petty kingdom; the minimal polity).

Another major school (or group of schools) of law flourished in early medieval Ireland; it is associated with the south-western region of Ireland, Munster, particularly the eastern areas extending from Cashel through Emly to Cork (Kelly 1988: 246). For the present study, the most important source emanating from this school is a tract on status, *Uraicecht Becc* (Mac Néill 1923: 272-81). Distinct from both these groups of texts were some important individual tracts. One of these, *Críth Gablach*, is of paramount importance for any attempt to understand early medieval Irish clan structure. It is therefore discussed in some detail in Ch. 2, as are the somewhat contrasting social backgrounds implied by differences between these regional jural cultures.

Extant editions and translations

The only comprehensive English translation of the laws is still the severely flawed, nineteenth-century, official British Government edition, *The Ancient Laws of Ireland* (Hancock 1865-1901). The faults of this edition are partly attributable to the deaths of the translators, O'Donovan and O'Curry, before the translation was revised for publication. Some examples of the difficulties facing the reader are the editors' failure to distinguish consistently between text and commentary, and the incorrect expansion of certain contracted word forms (Binchy 1943: 9-10). Within a short time of the completion of the edition, specialists in Old Irish demolished its authority. Plummer, for example, published a series of articles retranslating whole passages (1916, 1921, 1936). How misleading *AL* can be to the unwary reader is shown by such imprecise translations as 'legacy' for *díbad*, whereas *díbad* was a special type of legacy — property that passed into collective inheritance amongst kinsmen on the extinction of a descent line within the *fine* (Mac Néill 1921: 175; Charles-Edwards 1993: 494-5); 'tribe' for *fine*, whereas *fine* meant defined patrilineal circles of kin, embedded in larger, socially composite groups, sometimes termed the *cenél* (comparable to the Scots clan); 'adulteress' for *adaltrach*, whereas *adaltrach* means a secondary wife in a polygynous marriage, or a temporary wife in an informal union.

To make matters worse, the translation is often virtually unintelligible. For example, the opening paragraph of *Bechbretha*, an Old Irish tract on the distribution of claims to the produce of a bee-hive amongst members of the local community, includes such gems of obscurity as the *'tairsce*-trespass, crimes, and produce' of bees, 'in the four lands that are nearest to them' (*AL* iv 163). No footnotes clarify the nature of these concepts, but the reader who turns to the preface finds no guidance there either, for the editor of this volume, Richey, offered only a general exposition of the meaning of the text, and that entirely dependent on O'Donovan's short notes (*AL* iv 164, n.2; 165, n.3). But while the Irish text is left unanalyzed, the reader is treated to a long citation in untranslated Norman French from the Assize of Jerusalem, of another — ostensibly better — medieval law-tract on bee-hives (*AL* iv cliv - clv). In contrast, the editors of the recent edition of *Bechbretha* showed how the Irish jurists employed the concept of trespass to legitimize and organize the distribution between neighbors of shares in a hive's honey and swarms (*BB:* 30-38; 50-53: 90-96); an intelligible scheme is visible, which used a formula found in several other law-tracts that dealt with distributive justice. The scheme was well understood and employed by the draftsman of the tract (Patterson 1985), whom Richey condemned as the author of 'a most unfavorable specimen of the manner in which the Brehon lawyers ... discussed legal questions' (*AL* iv clv).

As if such technical problems were not enough, *AL* appeared in the hey-day of evolutionary social enquiry and was almost at once taken up as ammunition in their controversies by some of the leading contemporary theorists of legal evolution — Maine, Maitland, Vinogradoff and Seebohm. Many of the arguments put forward on the basis of *AL* were highly offensive to Irish scholars. Maine, for example, after pondering the use of numbers in the Irish representation of kinship relations (see Ch. 9), concluded that the family group was restricted to five adult males. This, he speculated, was the result of a natural inability, commonly found amongst primitive people, to count beyond the number of digits on the hand.[5]

The specter of Irish 'tribalism' and 'primitivism' re-emerged now, and helped to promote confusion and reticence on the subject of early Irish kinship, confusion that has clung to the subject ever since. Mac

Néill, for example, scoffed at references to early Irish society as 'tribal', a term no more precise, in his view, than the ballad by T. D. Sullivan: 'Chiefs and clans in all directions, with their far and near connections' (Mac Néill 1935: 1). Mac Néill claimed that the basic unit of early Irish society was the petty kingdom, or *tuath*; as to the medieval dynasties, they were, he stated, no more tribal than the Plantaganets or the Bourbons (*ibid*: 31). The core of his argument consisted of a contention that most of the ruling families of Ireland by the later middle ages were comparative newcomers to social dominance, and moreover, that they were not blood relatives to the mass of the tenants on their lands (*ibid*: 32). 'Tribe', in his view, was a term that should be confined to the population groups of prehistoric Ireland (Mac Néill 1911: 88).

In reacting to the pejorative views of early Irish society based on *AL*, however, Mac Néill confused the subsequent discussion of Irish kinship by de-emphasizing a number of important issues. One is the distinction between the actual existence of extensive kinship ties (such that everyone is related to almost everyone in his/her social universe through kinship) and the salience of kinship as a principle of social organization, determining the allocation of roles, rights and duties. Mac Néill attached importance to the limited set of inter-personal links established through kinship in medieval Ireland, because social-evolutionary theory maintained that kinship 'shrank' as societies developed. (Practically every nineteenth-century theory of social evolution began with the premise that the base-line from which human societies developed was a form of society consisting of undifferentiated aggregates of 'kin' [Harris 1968: 180-99]). But if, as was the case in Ireland, the kinship-group could restrict a member's economic actions, and was held liable for his delicts and debts, and if the individual had little access to other economically productive social relations (such as membership in urban manufacturing guilds), then kinship was very important indeed — even if much social interaction normally took place between non-kin. In this respect, Ireland in the late middle ages was far more of a kinship-based society than England had been for centuries.

Secondly, though the relationship between Irish lord and peasant tenant may not have been that of kinship, it is likely that the 'noble' segment of Irish society was relatively large, so that many relationships between people of high and middling social standing actually originated in kinship and were governed by norms of loyalty and obligations between kin. Ireland seems to have been one of the areas of Europe with a relatively numerous aristocracy (as were the Polish Commonwealth and eighteenth-century Spain), a condition resulting from the reproductive vigor of the well-fed upper class, untrammelled by rules stemming from a strong monarchy, which limited the succession rights of offspring (Bush 1988: 11-21). (Just how effective the laws of primogeniture and legitimacy were in snuffing out noble descent lines has been demonstrated by Perroy for France, McFarlane for England and recently by Grant, for Scotland, while Bush shows that there was a general tendency for the European noble classes to contract under the influence of descent rules.[6]) In Ireland, by the later middle ages, the result of uncontrolled upper class reproduction was, in Byrne's memorable paraphrase of Elizabethan views, that 'most Irishmen were bastards and claimed to be gentlemen' (Byrne 1987 [1983]: 1). Mac Néill noted that Irish upper-class families were large, but did not emphasize the social significance of the vertical spread of kinship ties from the chiefly families into the middle ranks of the farming population.

D.A. Binchy, who succeeded Mac Néill and Thurneysen as the leading modern translator and interpreter of the Irish law-tracts, rehabilitated the term 'tribal' in his study, 'Celtic and Anglo-Saxon Kingship'. Referring to the *tuath*, he wrote: 'for want of something better we are compelled to translate it tribe.'(Binchy 1970: 5). Binchy went on, however, to agree with Mac Néill that the *tuath* was not a group whose members were all kin to one another; once again, then, the question of the role of kinship in social organization was evaded on the basis of the misconception that kinship is not important to social organization unless the entire community is composed of kin. Binchy elected to call the *tuath* a tribe not in order to emphasize the role of kinship in *tuath* social structure, but in order to complement his view, which differed sharply from Mac Néill's, that the *tuath* was originally, 'not a petty state or principality' (*ibid*: 8) but rather a ritual community, centering on the king as a magical force for social and moral order. As to kinship, Binchy argued that 'the inner kindred' became smaller over the course of time. This argument, which assumed great authority in Celtic studies, is reviewed below.

Rigorous new editions of the Old Irish legal tracts began to appear in the 1920s, mainly as a result of the researches of the Swiss scholar, Rudolf Thurneysen. Since Thurneysen's invaluable translations are available only in highly technical German, however, it remains necessary to have some grasp of Old Irish in order to understand them. Stacey, for example, has made an important contribution by updating and translating Thurneysen's tract on suretyship, *Berrad Airechta* (1986). In 1978, Binchy's comprehensive edition of the entire collection of Irish legal MSS, the *Corpus Iuris Hibernici*, appeared. This will undoubtedly facilitate the eventual translation of the tracts into comprehensible English, but in its present diplomatic edition it is utilizable only by those with some knowledge of Old Irish.

Reliable English-language translations of a number of important tracts are available, however, such as Binchy's translation of an archaic section of *Di Cetharschlicht Athgabála* (Distraint), *Bretha Déin Chécht* (a tract on medicine and the medical profession), *Coibnes Uisce Thairidne* (a tract on water-mills), and two Old Irish penitentials; Mac Néill's translation of *Uraicecht Becc* and *Críth Gablach* (which students of Old Irish may use in conjunction with Binchy's untranslated edition), and Dillon's translation of two law tracts on inheritance, that appear in *Studies in Early Irish Law*. Most of the preceding appear, however, only in specialized periodicals and are in varying degrees difficult for use by non-Celticists, or even by students of Irish literature who lack a background in the legal tradition.

There has recently appeared a small number of new editions of primary sources, of which *Bechbretha*, mentioned above, and Breatnach's *Uraicecht na Ríar* are major examples. It is anticipated that further volumes in the Dublin Institute of Advanced Studies' Early Irish Law Series, as well as editions of short tracts in Celtic journals will amplify the body of reliable modern editions and translations. For scholars outside the field, however, it is probably of more significance that new secondary works of broad scope have appeared which provide the framework within which particular problems may be considered. Of these, the landmark study regarding social institutions is undoubtedly Fergus Kelly's *A Guide to Early Irish Law*. Other valuable surveys are Katharine Simms' study of later medieval political culture (1987) and Kim McCone's survey of the balance of pagan and Christian elements in the formation of early medieval Irish literary culture (1990). Older, but still indispensable are studies by Mac Néill (1921) and Hughes (1966). The general historical framework is described in Byrne's *Irish Kings and High-Kings*, in the volumes of the first and second *Gill History of Ireland* series (first series, ed. James Lydon & Margaret Mac Curtain) and in the *New History of Ireland* series (ed. T. W. Moody, F.

X. Martin & F. J. Byrne). On the whole, however, it must be said that a great deal of work remains to be done on basic aspects of the Irish law-tracts, after which a considerably more detailed understanding of early culture and society will become available than is possible now.

The law tracts as evidence for social history: theoretical approaches.

Ironically, though the critics of the *Ancient Laws* fulminated at its philological defects, they tended to share its editors' low opinion of the scribes of the medieval Irish legal MSS. Thurneysen, for example, described the work of the later scribes as '... an amalgam in which contact with the world of fact is abandoned in favor of elaborate calculations, minute casuistry, and strange constructions which often led to quite impossible results and can never have had any significance for the practical administration of the law ... the dreams of bookworms, of peddlers of antiquarianism' (1935 [1973]: 63). Similar views were expressed by Binchy, who went so far as to say that the commentaries are of value mainly in that the depth of their misunderstanding reveals the extent of social change between the Old Irish phase of composition and the post-Norman age (1967: 113; 1975 b: 21).

But although the canonical texts were held in higher regard than the post-Norman commentaries, even such major compositions as *Crίth Gablach* were viewed with considerable disdain as evidence for social structure. Of *CG*, Binchy wrote: 'More even than the average law-tract, *CG* is characterized by an extreme, and at time ludicrous, schematism: in order to preserve the uniformity of his picture the compiler does not hesitate to universalize rules which are of strictly limited application. For example, we know from the *Senchas Már* tract on base clientship (*gίallnae*) that only members of the freeman grades (*grád fhéne*) became clients of this kind; yet *CG* makes detailed provisions for nobles and even kings as base clients .... Again, although property was certainly an important factor in determining one's status, the property qualifications listed in *CG* for each grade (extending even to the size of an outhouse) are far too minute to have had any practical significance.... *CG* should therefore be regarded as a theoretical construction, which, although built of genuine material, bears only a very limited relation to the realities of legal life in ancient Ireland' (Binchy: *CG* xix).

The assumption behind such criticism is that the extant jural tradition was (in Thurneysen's words) 'a ruin' — the remains of an earlier tradition that made more sense, as law, than the texts do. The later scribes are regarded as 'fossilizers' of the pre-Christian oral legal tradition that had become moribund and barely understood (Binchy 1975b: 31-2). The supposed incompetence of Irish legal draftsmen, and the decay of jural standards, is widely remarked: McLeod, for instance, commenting on the use of analogy in an Old Irish tract on status, writes that 'although the author of *Uraicecht Becc* attempts to make his material comply with this illusion, when he goes into details he is not able for the task' (1986: 47); in *Bechbretha* it is said that the author of *BB* is 'insufficiently alive to the inconsistencies of his approach' (Charles-Edwards and Kelly 1983: 35). The propagandist composition, *The Book of Rights*, which describes what the King of Cashel would have *liked* to receive as his 'rights' from various alleged vassals is described by Binchy as 'that extraordinary fabrication' (Binchy 1970: 44), and by its most recent editor, Dillon, as 'another example of the work of the learned imagination' (1962: xv).

Modern scholarship has thus tended to put forward interpretations of early legal writers' intentions, and then indicted them for not achieving these supposed objectives; there is little willingness to believe that a different aesthetic, marked by a tendency to shift frames of reference without placing a signpost in the text, lies at the root of the supposed 'inabilities' of the early writers. The judgmental stance adopted by leading scholars towards the texts resulted in the authoritative dismissal of certain aspects of the sources as 'unreal', as in Binchy's comments on *CG*, cited above. Though Binchy softened his criticisms of the laws in his later writings (1975b: 36), many of his strictures not only remained in place but continue to be repeated, as for example where Charles-Edwards declares that 'there was much truth in (Binchy's) verdict' that *CG* was an example of 'extreme and at times ludicrous schematism' (Charles-Edwards 1993: 343).

The result is that the laws are avoided as sources of information by scholars who might otherwise find in them valuable evidence for comparative social analysis — for example, as regards the close parallels that exist between early medieval Irish and Icelandic institutions (Sawyer 1982 b: 345-6) and even as background material for the analysis of data on the material culture of medieval Ireland (Edwards 1990; Lucas 1989; Bradley 1988).[7] In fact, many aspects of the law-tracts are either corroborated by other evidence, or may be reinterpreted in ways which render them comprehensible and consistent with other institutions whose main features are not in doubt. *Bretha Comaithchesa*, for example, contains good descriptions of legally acceptable fencing on lands put to different agricultural uses. Ó Corráin shows that the consistency between the basic text and the later commentary points to 'thorough familiarity with the types of fence in question' on the part of scribes of several periods (1983: 247). Similarly, in a recent archaeological study of ringforts by Stout it was shown that the dimensions for residential buildings listed in *CG* could readily be modelled in conjunction with archaeological data (Stout 1991: 229-39).

In any case, Binchy's criticism of the detailed specifications of property-qualifications assumes that the purpose of the tract is descriptive. It is far more likely, however, to have served as a *prescription*, not description, of the social order of a political unit. That is, if someone wanted to claim a certain number of cows as compensation for dishonor or injury, or if he wished to swear an oath as to some quarrel, settlement of which would incur a fine of so many cows — then, the tract implies, he had better have a farm of a certain standard of productivity, and a matching fief from a lord (or if he was a lord, he should control the appropriate number of clients), so that he could back his oath in the event that he incurred a legal liability on account of his words. It was within just such a prescriptive frame of reference that *Cáin Aicillne*, the tract on base-clientship, was written; in this it was shown that if a lord wanted a client to take so many cattle from him as fief, then he and the client had to be sure that the client had the right to depasture that many cows on his family's common pasture, or the latter could lawfully return the fief.

Also in doubt is Binchy's sweeping assertion that base-clientship (which is described in Ch. 6) could not possibly have pertained between nobles and kings. Gerriets, basing her remarks on an analysis of several political tracts, states '... in the eighth and ninth centuries relations between over-kings and subordinate kings could be represented as forms of clientship, very often as forms of base clientship. The saga literature also uses the terminology of base clientship to describe royal exchange ... both base and free clientship were models for exchange between kings' (1987: 71).

Finally, it should be pointed out that at the theoretical level there are no grounds for maintaining that the fine distinctions of rank found in *CG* and other law-tracts on status 'could not' have practical legal significance. On the contrary, comparative evidence shows exactly this kind of social differentiation occurring in societies where competition was becoming severe, but where there were no conditions operating to produce a clear-cut, consolidated class system (Fried 1967: 109 ff). Further defense of the utility of *CG* and other law-tracts for the modelling of early Irish social structure will not be offered here; the use that will subsequently be made of them will, it is hoped, be sufficient to show that from them an outline can be constructed of the pattern of social relations in the kin-groups and petty kingdoms of early medieval Ireland.

Outsiders to the field of early Celtic literature may well wonder why there was such willingness on the part of scholars to employ elements of *style* as criteria for the negative evaluation of the law-tracts as sources for social history. From an anthropological perspective it is surprising that sources should be viewed as decadent survivals of pristine prior tradition, when there is no example of the latter against which comparisons may be constructed, and when so many of the stylistic criteria of evaluation (inconsistency, terminological obscurity, non-linear composition, extended etymologies and other 'digressions') are simply aspects of a non-expository, 'poetic' system of intellectual reflection and representation (Patterson 1989).

The assumption of hyper-skepticism towards the law-tracts was in large part due to the fact that some of the most influential scholars of the early twentieth century were interested in the documentary record of early Irish society as evidence not for the milieu which generated the first written texts, but more as evidence for the survival in Ireland of 'Indo-European' culture. Some quite striking parallels were found between Irish culture and the society depicted in Sanskrit texts — such as the practice of sick-maintenance, and fasting against social superiors.[8] (The former entailed the removal of an injured person to another house, where he or she would be nursed back to health at the expense of the injurer in a clean and quiet setting. Fasting was a legal procedure undertaken by someone with a legitimate grievance against an obstinate social superior, whom he could not bring to legal arbitration by normal means on account of the latter's high status).

But while some parallels were discovered, great discrepancies were overlooked or attributed to later social changes — for example, differences as to social mobility and divorce. What really gave life to the rather forced idea that ancient Ireland resembled the India of the Rig-Veda was the convergence in the late nineteenth and early twentieth century of several strands of international scholarship and nationalist political ideology, all of which had a strong theoretical and comparative interest in the ancient Aryan culture of India.

In the mid-nineteenth century, a flourishing new science, historical linguistics, had come into being, which was based on the premise that a relationship of common descent existed between a geographically widespread group of languages, which came to be labelled Aryan and eventually Indo-European. In the first half and middle of the last century there appeared a number of path-breaking studies of the grammar of the Celtic languages; thereafter historical linguists took a sharp interest in early Irish philology as an example of a distinct and barely surviving branch of the Indo-European languages (D. Evans 1981: 256-60). This not only stimulated new efforts at translation, but nationalistic Irish scholars such as Mac Néill, who rejected the denigration of Irish historical culture that was implicit in much of the introduction to *AL*, found in the model of ancient Indo-European society a comparative framework within which Old Irish institutions could be viewed as intelligible, dignified, and at the same time, distinctly un-English. Finally, a third field of scholarship, comparative jurisprudence, entered the picture to show that there were also similarities between Aryan Indian and early Irish institutions (Mac Néill 1921: 162 ff.)

The convergence of historical linguistics, legal history, and Irish historical scholarship, took place in the context of the upsurge of nationalist ideologies that swept Europe during the latter part of the nineteenth century.[9] In France, the anti-German Celtic chauvinism of the pioneering French Celtic scholars, Henri D'Arbois de Jubainville and Camille Jullian, gave way to a more sophisticated search for pan-European cultural origins which culminated in the school of Georges Dumèzil. This still flourishes as a comparative framework for the study of Indo-European myth and religion (Littleton 1966) even though this aspect of historical linguistics has drawn criticism from other branches of linguistics and from archaeologists (Renfrew 1987). Interesting findings have resulted from research of this kind, suggesting that aspects of the ideology of prehistoric priestly and technical groups were distributed over a huge area of the Old World, but the mechanism of distribution is in doubt, for common descent from an Indo-European parent-culture seems no more plausible or proven than repeated diffusion, resulting from the wanderings of craftsmen, magicians, shamans and entertainers in search of patrons. In other words, what seems like a deep inherited structure of ideology that evolved into different local traditions may be a web of words and notions cast over vast regions that comprised numerous local cultures with individual histories and 'origins'.[10]

In Irish scholarship, the Indo-European frame of reference was retained without challenge until very recently. The theory was developed and extended until it became a paradigm not only for the study of religious symbolism but practically every aspect of early Irish culture. It led to the imposition of an elaborate theory of social evolution onto the law-tracts, which in nearly every particular coincides with the ideas of Henry Sumner Maine (1861; 1875; 1887), who believed that 'original' Indo-European society consisted of groups of patrilineally related males, wives whom they acquired from other groups of the same nature, and leaders who dominated the group by virtue of their age and headship of extended families.[11] Although there was much that retained its value in Maine's history of legal concepts, holistic and unilineal theories of social evolution have long been discarded by social anthropologists in favor of other approaches to the question of social change, such as observation of the methods whereby societies retain identity while undergoing transformation. Moreover, the evolutionary interpretation of early Irish law is neither well-founded on textual evidence, nor helpful to understanding early medieval Irish society — indeed, as was shown, it is associated with exaggerated criticism of the brehon writers.

Of all the evolutionary theories, that which was applied to kinship has been especially enduring. This requires us to believe in the historical decline in the importance of kinship organization during the early middle ages, and 'the progressive recognition of the claims of natural kinship' (Binchy 1936: 186) notwithstanding the existence of vigorous and large-scale kinship formations throughout medieval Irish history. The persistence of this theory attests to the general avoidance of the subject of kinship by historians, and the associated tendency to treat kinship as a topic best left to highly specialized analysis — as if kinship may be meaningfully analyzed apart from political relations or indeed from social organization in general. A critique of these evolutionary theories follows below.

Evolutionary theories of Irish law and society

i. *Kingship and legal institutions.* Binchy argued that in pre-Viking, early Christian Ireland (the sixth to the late eighth centuries) the king was primarily a ritual and military leader, who played no part in the internal regulation of the society (1970: 8-21). (The theoretical debt is here to Frazer's *Golden Bough.*) He further argued that the law was exclusively in the hands of the lawyers, who acted rather like Roman jurisconsults, in that they arbitrated disputes between conflicting parties. The lawyers, being thus removed from the flow of events in political society, were also relatively unaffected professionally by the conversion to Christianity. This theory buttressed Binchy's assertion that the lawyers were extremely conservative, which in turn explained why they would trouble to preserve Indo-European legal 'fossils', even after the social developments of the early middle ages rendered the old legal customs obsolete. As to the collapse of the 'old order', Binchy maintained, on the one hand, that the 'old' kinship system had changed significantly during the conversion period, but that the final ending of the legal and political system, as he envisaged it, resulted from the Viking invasions of the ninth century (1962).

Several objections may be raised to these propositions. As to kingship, while there is abundant evidence of royal rituals, there is no reason to dichotomize the evidence on this matter into chronological 'strata'. Irish kingship was *at all times* highly ritualized, with a strong surge of re-emphasis upon earlier rituals accompanying the revival of the power of Gaelic lords against the Normans in the thirteenth century (K. Simms 1987: 21-40). Moreover, ritualization of authority obviously does not preclude the exercise of other forms of power. Direct evidence has recently been accumulating that pre-Viking-Age Irish kings were deeply involved with the jural process (Gerriets 1988) and that some disputes would end up before quite formal and elaborate courts (Kelly 1986: 77-82). What is more, the lawyers are no longer regarded as isolated from Christian culture, but as deeply affected by and participating in Christian literacy and learning (Ó Corráin *et al.*, 1984; Breatnach 1984; McCone 1990). Though some of this recent work seems almost to under-emphasize the continuity of pre-Christian culture after the conversion, in regard to the law-tracts its overall thrust is to reject the idea that early Irish law was a collection of Indo-European 'fossils', in favor of research into how it functioned as a vigorous new synthesis of different strands of culture, native and foreign.

Finally, the view that the ninth-century Viking attacks and wars caused radical social collapse has been challenged on several grounds — notably, that pre-Viking Ireland's peacefulness and Christian piety have been greatly exaggerated (Lucas 1966, 1967; Ó Corráin 1972: 82-9, 104-10; Doherty 1980: 70-2). In short, the political institutions of pre-Viking Ireland are now regarded as highly continuous throughout the pre-Norman period. By implication, it follows that the general features of the canonical law tracts are better understood in the light of whatever can be learned of the entire pre-Norman period in Ireland, than by comparison with Sanskrit literature. In particular, statements in the law-tracts should not be swept aside as 'unreal' because they depict a state of society not fully in accord with expectations based on models of 'Indo-European society'— or other expectations, for that matter.

ii. The evolution of marriage, and the status of women. The Irish law-tracts reveal a culture in which women, though socially diminished as compared to men of the same rank by birth, nevertheless held property, had honor, and could take limited autonomous steps to protect or enhance their social position. Like men, they were under the restraint of superiors — senior kinsmen — and the mutual restraints of each spouse on the other with regard to decisions that impinged upon the inherited fund of assets from which they had been endowed at marriage for the purpose of establishing a family. Such interference often extended into personal matters such as the choice of a sexual partner, but while it may be no surprise that women's marriages were arranged, it should be realized that men too were subject to restraints in these matters.

The only absolute distinction between men and women applied in the jural sphere: women took legal action through male relatives, whereas men could instigate action for themselves (*SEIL*: 88). In Iceland, a comparable requirement that women's interests be represented by a man at a *thing* meeting was connected to the fact that at assemblies opponents faced each other down surrounded by gangs of armed supporters[12]; this may well have been the case in Ireland too. The late seventh-century clerical law-tract, *Cáin Adomnáin*, for example, sought to exclude women from battle and vengeance (*SEIL*: 269-74) but at the same time insisted that their legal rights to engage in contracts were unaffected by non-combatant status (*ibid* 226), as if it would follow that when one could not violently assert one's rights, then one required another's permission to act at all, like a child or slave. During the turmoil of the fifth and sixth centuries, women may have become widely involved in combat — certainly, early sagas and later annals reveal upper class women in this role (*SEIL*: 271-2). Such heroines notwithstanding, a condition of society in which social privileges were tied to prominence in personal combat would have led to a temporary phase of general social degradation for women.

But aside from such a conjectured possibility, were women in Irish society generally in a social position comparable in terms of dependence upon adult men to that of a child or slave? The evolutionary model maintains this position. It holds that within local groups, power was in the hands of senior males who headed 'strictly patriarchal or patrilineal' descent groups. Women, it has been speculated, were once exchanged between these groups for brideprice (Thurneysen, *SEIL*: 113) and had no personal legal capacity; thus they controlled no property, could make no contracts, and conveyed no aspect of social identity to their children. This situation supposedly gave way during the seventh or eighth centuries to marriage with dowry, greater legal capacity, and concern with the status a wife could impart to her children (Binchy, *SEIL*: 180-6, 207-34).

The evidence for this reconstruction is ambiguous, at best. As to the payment of 'bride-price', Thurneysen's contention was based on a story in *The Book of Invasions* which recounts that when the ancestral heroes, the Sons of Míl, arrived in Ireland they lacked female companions, but eventually met some whom they invited to accompany them in their explorations. These refused unless chattels were paid on account of their leaving home. The story concludes:

> therefore in Ireland men always buy their women, though
>
> in the rest of the world couples buy each other. (*SEIL*: 113).

But the writer of this story was inspired less by distant memories of Irish tradition than by the Old Testament, for he described the women as 'Hebrew maidens'. In fact, Irish law-tracts show that the main economic payment before marriage was a gift (usually called *coibche*) which was supposed to be equal to the woman's honor-price and was to be shared between the bride and her father or nearest kinsman. This gift was, in any case, less important than the property each spouse brought to the marriage (see Ch. 11).

What of the assertion that after marriage, women 'originally' had no separate legal identity, and no capacity to transact legal business of their own? The evidence marshalled to make this case consists of passages in the law tracts, some of which prescribe categorical limitations on social action by women, such as:

> 'Thou shalt not buy from one who is 'senseless' according
> to Irish law, namely from a woman, from a captive, from a
> slave ...' (*SEIL*: 211 [1]).

These passages were collected by Binchy, and grouped together as type A, which he contrasts to other passages (type B), which offer substantial qualifications to the exclusion of women from legal activity as expressed in 'group A'. Binchy interpreted these differences as evidence for radical social change as regards the status of women, but he had to concede that the evidence did not lie in the texts, but in social theory: 'It is impossible to prove definitely, on linguistic grounds for example, that the passages in A are older than those in B: all one can say is that there is certainly no linguistic reason for believing them to be later. Here we are compelled to rely on the comparative method of legal study, and in so far as it is an accurate guide it testifies that the *rules of law* contained in A — quite apart from the period of their formulation in writing — are older than those in B. This assumption — and it is hardly a rash one — is necessary to my thesis.' (*SEIL*: 208).

At the outset of his argument, furthermore, Binchy had written: 'Scholars are now universally agreed that the family organization of the Indo-European nations was strictly patriarchal. In a society of this kind women have at first no independent legal capacity' (*ibid*: 207). Binchy thus called on theory as 'evidence' for the theory of 'original total female legal incapacity'; but in fact scholars were not 'universally agreed' on this theory. One of the foundations of this model is the argument (cited by Binchy: *SEIL* 180) that women lacked legal capacity because as daughters they were destined to be severed from their natal group, while as wives they were in-coming strangers.[13] But attempts to reconstruct aspects of social systems like post-marital residence on the basis of such ambiguous data as scraps of a reconstructed prehistoric or historic terminological system, were abandoned by British social anthropologists during the 1920s.[14]

At this time, however, the study of prehistoric Europe became the specialty of archaeologists and philologists. Amongst the latter, many scholars persistently clung to the outmoded sociological construct of Indo-European patriarchy, just as they retained 'the archaeological orthodoxy of nearly a century ago' (Renfrew 1987: 287). As late as 1969, Goody found it necessary to point out that the evidence used to prop up the theory that women were 'transferred' between Indo-European patriarchal and patrilineal groups, 'can be used to reach quite the opposite conclusions' (Goody 1969: 235). This warning too was ignored and in such recent publications as *The Welsh Law of Women* (Cardiff, 1980) one may still read that any evidence of a married woman's rights over property in Welsh or Irish law 'represent innovations over an otherwise obtaining incapacity' (McAll 1983: 19).

Recently, further objections have been mustered against Binchy's classification of the passages on Irish women's legal capacity into 'older' and 'later' groups (McLeod 1992: 78-80). These include the fact that archaic noun forms appear in two supposedly 'later' passages, while several of the 'older' passages have sources in the *Senchas Már* and thus are no older than 700 A.D. Since there is no force, then, to the idea that the variations in statements about women's legal capacity can be grouped together as earlier and later texts, other interpretations should be considered. One possibility is that the 'total incapacity' passages are gnomic statements from aphoristic texts, for several of the sources of the 'type A' passages are of this nature, such as the *Triads of Ireland*, *Tecosca Cormaic*, and the legal *Heptads*.[15] These presented only the crudest formulation of some rule of thumb, exceptions to which the jurist had to learn in discussion at school. A thirteenth-century poem, framed as advice to a law-student, makes it clear the abridgements of the law were in use then, but that students were also supposed to revert to the full legal MSS to understand the application of maxims to the case at hand (Ní Donnchadha 1988: 168 #5-6). Similarly, in the Old Irish tract, 'The false judgements of Caratnia' (Thurneysen 1925b) the jurist, Caratnia, explains in private to the king what exceptions should be made to crude legal rules — the king himself had been taught only the basics.

Alternatively, the two groups of passages may represent divergent influences, the 'total incapacity' statements drawing upon patristic and Old Testament sources, which promoted the marginalization of women in church and society (Bitel 1986: 27 ff), while the other passages may represent the native tradition, common to other north European societies.

As to the latter, it is particularly baffling that the theory of women's legal non-entity should have been applied to early Irish society since there is a glaring theoretical contradiction in the argument: cultures in which women have genuinely little social power (as compared with men of the same social background) do not countenance divorce initiated by a wife, especially when this may involve withdrawal of her marital contribution from the joint property so as to enable her to remarry or live unmarried (Goody 1990: 184-5). Even widow-remarriage may be opposed; as is well known, high-status Hindu marriage customs included (as an ideal), *satī*, ritual widow suicide. To defend an argument that 'originally' Irish women were subject to an extreme form of 'legal incapacity', it would be necessary to depict the tract on divorce, *Cáin Lánamna*, as innovative in every respect — introducing an entirely new status-package for women, including the freedom to initiate divorce and retrieve their property. This would imply that in the Christian eighth century, divorce laws were imposed upon a traditionally non-divorcing, erstwhile pagan society! Binchy's argument fails at the level of basic cultural history.

Comparative Celtic evidence from antiquity, moreover, would make an extremely patriarchal late pre-Christian Ireland a cultural oddity for its time. Caesar's description of Gaulish marriage accords, as regards the economic aspects, with Irish practices depicted in *Cáin Lánamna*:

> When a Gaul marries, he adds to the dowry that his wife
> brings with her a portion of his own property estimated to be
> of equal value. A joint account is kept of the whole amount,
> and the profits which it earns are put aside ... (Handsford
> 1951: 34).

The matching of the spouses' assets was a key feature of both Gaulish and Irish marriage, and was connected to the dispositional rights of women as regards property, as is implied by the reference to the Gauls' sharp-eyed domestic accountancy. As to ancient Britain, no credible accounts of marriage customs are available, but the well-attested power of two queens, Boudica of Kent, and Cartimandua of the midland Brigantes, casts further doubt on the notion of 'archaic incapacity'.

Irish tradition itself from all periods gives evidence of the participation of women of the élite in politics and warfare. These considerations can be squared with theories of the 'original' social inconsequence of women only by taking evidence that pertains to women as relating to 'goddesses'. Mac Néill, for example, when faced with evidence that the eponyms of numerous pre-Christian social groups were female, unhesitatingly assumed these were all goddesses, not leaders (1911: 64). This is reminiscent of Maine's stubborn disbelief in the existence of the matrilineal clans and female war-counsellors of the League of the Iroquois (Harris 1968: 191). Patriarchal, sometimes even misogynist, attitudes are found in Celtic studies itself,[16] and one can only conclude that such a determined effort to show that 'originally' Irish women had no legal autonomy has more to do with the attitudes of twentieth-century scholars than those of the fifth.

Matters were not improved by the seemingly limited use made of comparative studies in the construction of models of early Irish kinship and society. Cross-cultural references in the secondary literature are mainly to structural-functionalist studies by British social anthropologists of African segmentary unilineal descent groups.[17] Central to these social systems (whether patri- or matrilineal) were 'the joint-interests of brothers', whose mutual relationship is egalitarian. Combinations of fraternal clusters present a solidary front to other like combinations, with whom they may fight, and with whom they exchange brides, if there is sufficient genealogical distance between them (Mair 1965: 72).

In profound contrast, Irish and other early European descent structures were not egalitarian but *normatively* ranked, intensely competitive within the fraternal circle, and were structured not only on the principles of genealogical closeness but also on the basis of patron-client relations between kinsmen of unequal wealth and influence. Such structures are often described as 'conical clans' (Kirchoff 1959; 375: Goody 1983: 237). There were no rules of clan-exogamy, and thus no regular exchange of brides, but rather a tendency to in-marriage in order to curtail the outflow of property through bridal dowry. Thus, while Irish, Welsh, Scottish and Dietmarschen clans recruited heirs patrilineally, like African segmentary lineages, the rules of recruitment to the kinship-group — 'patrilineal descent' in this case — tell us little about social structure, since these very different societies all used the same rules of inclusion/exclusion to kinship groups.

iii. The theory of the collapse of the 'derbfhine'. Along with the view that women's status changed and society became less 'strictly patriarchal', this was the other important plank in Binchy's argument that a pre-Christian 'tribal' kinship system disappeared, leaving in its wake in the law-tracts an incoherent representation of kinship and an inconsistent pattern of kinship terminology. The *'derbfhine'* was thought to have been a prehistoric social formation consisting of agnatic second cousins, grouped together as a legal corporation under the leadership of its senior male. The idea originated with Mac Néill, who likened Irish *derbfhine* groups to Indian village-communes (1921: 164 ff.) but Binchy took this argument much further, making the evolutionary claim that the *derbfhine* was replaced by a narrower group of kin, agnatic first cousins (*gelfhine*), in the early historic period. This theory was prompted in part by the fact that later legal scribes preferred to describe groups of heirs as *gelfhine*, and often glossed older references to *derbfhine* with, 'i.e. *gelfhine*'. But the theory was also inspired by the false theoretical assumption, mentioned above, that a reduction in the scale of kinship organization is a sign of advancing modernity. In fact, Ireland swarmed with kinship corporations of all sizes until the Tudor Conquest, while agnatic Scottish clans persisted for at least another century.

I have elsewhere surveyed the textual evidence for the greater antiquity of references to *derbfhine*, and found that on the one hand, very early references of *gelfhine* are not hard to find, but were assigned to a 'later period' by Binchy on *a priori* grounds, and on the other hand that *'derbfhine'* does not always have a purely genealogical diacritical meaning, but in some contexts just meant consanguineal (blood) kin, as opposed to adopted, affinal or spiritual kin. Despite these grounds for seriously re-examining the reasoning behind the theory of the 'collapse of the *derbfhine*', it has been repeated by Charles-Edwards (1993) with little or no modification of his previously published statements on the subject (1972b). But variety in kinship terminology, I would suggest, may have resulted from other processes than a breakdown in kinship organization — for example, from the influence of canon law on the models of kinship used in Irish law at various periods. Such a source of outside influence, though hard to prove definitively, is suggested by a number of parallels between Irish jural models of kinship and those employed in canon law (Patterson 1990).

So entrenched is the theory of the 'collapse of the *derbfhine*' that Mytum (1992), in his study of the processes whereby Ireland re-entered the mainstream of European civilization after the fall of Rome, bases a complex argument about social change on the assumption that these postulated kinship changes occurred. He argues that the vector of social change was the population of Christianized Irish immigrants in late *Britannia*, who 'were quickly absorbed into the British social and economic system and must have recognized its effectiveness. This may then have been transferred back to Ireland ... (producing) a change in tenurial patterns away from sharing among a large kin-group to individual claims. The later documentary sources suggest a continual weakening of the communal control over land. The idea of individual landholding came from Britain...and was reinforced by the ethos of the individual ...' (Mytum 1992: 47).

It is unfortunate that Mytum attaches his potentially productive hypotheses to the empirically doubtful theory of the collapse of the *derbfhine* and Binchy's further speculations about the growth of individualism. The evidence points neither to contraction in effective kinship groups nor to the displacement of communal rights by individual ones during the pre-Norman Irish period (see Chs. 9 and 10). Throughout the middle ages, Irish land-tenure was a balance of contingent rights of individual disposition with those of immediate heirs, distant potential heirs, and the clan aristocracy. Thus whatever changes occurred in the early medieval period, they cannot be adequately described as 'increasing individualism', let alone Christian individualism. If anything, the influence of the Church may have been in the opposite direction, for one of the most clerically-inspired law-tracts to deal with general social obligations, *Córus Béscnai,* emphasizes that members of a kin group could validly assert kinship rights (e.g. to restrain alienation of land from the kin-group's control) only when they also fulfilled social obligations towards burdensome kin, such as orphans and the feeble elderly. As to transplantation of Roman property law into Irish law, to my knowledge, no one has found evidence of significant influence of this sort.

If one must speculate on the changes in Irish *mentalité* during the period of re-entry into European history, it would be best to abandon the hypothesis of change from communitarianism to individualism, for want of both evidence and theoretical plausibility. More probable, given the evidence of overseas raiding, incorporation of slaves, and the rise of new dynasties during the early middle ages, is that what preceded the clan-based medieval Irish social system — the system described in this book — was a period of social breakdown and *anomie*, a period of ugly individualism and violent anarchy that required all the energies of the proselytizing new religion and a gradually coalescing élite, to restore some degree of lawfulness and discipline (See Ch. 2). Whatever 'collapsed' in Ireland towards the end of the Roman Iron Age was probably more like an over-arching pattern of social and religious authority than shallow lineages, and the cause of change was more probably social disintegration and rebirth as the European geo-political situation convulsed, rather than ideological reorientation. But as long as the theory of the collapse of the *derbfhine* retains its sacred place in Irish historiography, scholars will no doubt continue to posit changes in kinship as the main act in the drama of this chaotic period.

Further discussion of the structure of early Irish kin-groups is reserved till Ch. 9, but here a word should be said on the confusing terminology used not just by Old Irish jurists but by modern commentators on their work. Charles-Edwards has recently rejected the applicability of the term 'clan' to Irish kin-groups, on the grounds that 'the later existence of Scottish clans makes the word almost unusable in a Celtic context' (1993: xvi). Why should this be so? Established anthropological usage defines the clan as 'a system of lineages and a lineage is a genealogical segment of a clan' (Evans-Pritchard 1940: 192). Subsequent usage stresses the ideological element in clan structures: they are groups that consist of a number of distinct descent groups, linked together by *the belief* that they are 'branches' of a founding ancestor's progeny (Goody 1983: 224).

Now Charles-Edwards shows that the *fine* groups of the Irish law-tracts were shallow lineages within large entities such as the *Ciarraige*, to whose ruling kin-group most other members would have been *dubfhine*, 'obscure kin' (1993: 133). The *Ciarraige* would thus be called a clan, or possibly the clans of a tribe, by anthropologists. Moreover, the kin-group called the *cenél* of a petty chief of a *tuath* included, in addition to the core agnatic group of fourth-cousins, all sorts of grafted-on branches (*CIH* 430.21-431.32 = *AL* iv 283 ff) — what in Scotland would have been called 'adherents'. A *cenél* could thus be either a small clan, or a segment of another clan if relationship with a broader group were stressed (a situational option). For example, the main branches of the Northern *Uí Néill* were generally designated *cenél*, while *Clann Cholmáin*, though it was recognized as a branch of the *Uí Néill* was called a clan (Charles-Edwards 1993: 140).

Irish clans certainly differed from those of sub-Saharan Africa, to which early anthropological concepts of descent groups referred. But as noted above, their internal division by rank and the inter-dependence of unequals in both Scottish and Irish kin-groups offer striking parallels to the 'conical clans' of Central Asia (Kirchoff 1959). Thus few anthropologists would support Charles-Edwards' exclusion of the Romano-Celtic word *clan* from general discussion of Irish kinship, for this implies a degree of uniqueness that would preclude comparison between the Irish social system and others.

There are several other aspects to the general theory of the social evolution of early medieval Ireland, but these will be noted, mainly in passing, in later chapters. I have, however, given special attention to the force that has been envisaged as causing the alleged 'collapse' of the archaic form of society. Proponents of the theory of kinship collapse, argued that the Irish jurists were not deeply affected by the advent of Christianity; they could not, then, attribute the 'collapse' of the 'older' kinship system to the conversion; nor could they accuse the Vikings (despite Binchy's rather contradictory assertion that these brought the 'old order' to its *finale*) because pre-Viking tracts such as *CG* were held to show that the 'old order' was already crumbling. A *deus ex machina* was thus required, and was found in the form of the hypothesis that major population growth occurred in the early middle ages, on a scale sufficient to change the social system profoundly. As this argument is widely accepted, but does not appear to me to be substantiated, I have examined its basis in an Appendix to this book.

Conclusion

Having criticized the evolutionary theoretical approach to early Irish history I must explain my own analytical stance, which is that of historical sociology. This approach attaches importance to the fact that some elements of coherence are always retained from the past in a changing social universe: the analyst always cuts into the on-going fabric of changing society at some point, and has to decide where to start the analysis so as to produce a meaningful result, rather than adopting the fiction (common to functionalist studies) that one can analyze a given set of social conditions 'as if' they were timeless. In historical sociology the object of analysis is a social process, not a state of affairs.

This analytical emphasis is linked to another theoretical position, namely that there is an ongoing dialogue between individual and collective (social) representations of social reality, and that there is mutual influence between these visions of human realities and the legal and other normative codes (especially religion), that constrain social action by individuals and by groups. This dialogue is seen as conducted both verbally and by means of other symbolic behavior, and through political and other struggles to re-define the terms of social relations. Hence, historical sociologists are interested in the expressive aspects of culture. To use a metaphor, institutional change is seen as the product of a never-ending social conversation, for the conditions that a society must grapple with, as an adaptive mechanism that enables human beings to produce, survive and reproduce, are constantly changing in unpredictable ways. People negotiate their responses to these changes amongst themselves in such a way that they can remain in co-operation with each other at least at minimal levels. When they fail, established societies fall apart and changes of all sorts follow.

This approach differs dramatically from one that views institutions as having gravid lives of their own with a capacity to determine how societies develop and how people will act. Historical-sociology sees institutions as the *outcome* of social experience and struggle, conducted in specific times and places and in the presence of the legacy of the past. The approach differs from both evolutionary and functionalist theories (the latter of which tends to personify societies as 'acting' like great unconscious ants-nests to meet their systemic 'needs'), both as to assumptions regarding the nature of the connections between the individual and the society, and in practical research interests. Historical-sociologists seek to establish models of recurrent social patterns and dominant normative structures both within the context of one society, so that one may then generalize effectively about 'the social system' of that society over time, and within groups of societies, so that one may discuss types of society.

These models are instrumental: they are analytical descriptions intended to facilitate the formation of causal hypotheses. The search for causation obliges historical sociologists to work at two levels: one is the conceptualization of the social forces at work in the society in question; the other focuses on the details of historical contingencies which affect the operation of the social forces. Therefore historical sociologists greatly appreciate the labor of historians in straightening out, as far as is possible, the record of what actually happened in history.

In conclusion, a concrete example may best illustrate the theoretical underpinnings of this book. One of the main institutions of medieval Irish society was the patrilineal descent group, the *fine*, mentioned above: how would the *fine* be analyzed by the approaches described above? A functionalist would ignore the question of its history as a social institution and treat it simply as a given in the social system which could best be understood by looking at all the social 'jobs' done by the group (Ch. 10 shows there were many). An evolutionist would be interested in the historical background, but here the focus would be on the descent of the *fine* from a prior culture-complex, in this case Indo-European patriarchy and patrilineality. This would be regarded as sufficient explanation for the existence of the institution, for the question 'why is a specific institution *retained*?' does not arise in evolutionism, which tends to assume that tradition carries such sacral weight that the persistence of institutions needs no explanation. The only question posed by an evolutionist would be: where can we see signs of what we assume happened, namely that kinship gradually evolved from being of great functional importance in society to being much less significant?

In contrast, a historical sociologist would examine the *fine* as one of several types of social group in the cultural repertoire, asking what other bases for social group formation co-existed with the *fine*, and whether these alternatives carried greater social significance at some periods than at others. Since some evidence suggests that patrilineal clans became more important and better organized as time went by, one then asks why did this happen? The answer is found by looking at the ideological representation of the well-developed clan — what was it supposed to be doing in society? — and then searching for evidence of conditions that made it vital to powerful groups in the society that these functions be performed.

In the actual analysis presented in this book, overwhelming emphasis is placed on the primary task of describing the main social institutions of Irish society, and assembling the findings into a model of the society as it persisted (with some changes) over time. Only in Chs. 2 and 11 is there some attempt to hypothesize as to causal stimuli that brought the system into being. Nevertheless, an open-minded curiosity about causation was a constant backdrop to the work that produced this book; it is hoped that others may find in it material for the framing of further hypotheses, unimagined by this writer, as to why medieval Ireland developed into the sort of society it was in pre-Norman times.

Notes

1. There is an extensive secondary literature on the Irish learned class. Two surveys represent older and more recent views on the relative influence of the prehistoric pagan heritage and the contemporaneous Christian milieu; see respectively, Ó Cuív 1961, and McCone 1990. Detailed discussion of the historical development of literary culture is found in several studies by Mac Cana (see especially 1970, 1971, 1974, 1980). Aspects of native history-writing are discussed by Byrne 1973, Kelleher 1971, and Ó Corráin, 1985, 1986. Secondary sources on the legal MSS are discussed below.

2. On the participation of brehons in the 'modernizing' sector of Irish society, see Patterson (1991).

3. For the tracts on status, see Ch. 2. The lost tracts on animals, and hunting and gathering are *Conshlechta, Catshlechta, Bóshlechta, Osbretha, Bretha Forma, Muirbretha.* See Kelly 1988: 275-6.

4. *ISi-so tra an cain patraic; iss ed nad cumaic nach breithem daenna do gaedelaib do taithbiuch nach ni fogeba i senchus mor. (CIH 342.19-20 = AL i 19.1-3)*

5. Maine (1875): 216-18. Maine's remarks were inspired, however, by a prominent Celticist, Whitley Stokes. The theories of Maine, McLennan and others were summarized by Richey in Part III of his Introduction (*AL* iv xlix-xciii). Mac Néill repudiated most of these ideas in Ch. 1 of *Early Irish Laws and Institutions* (1935).

6. Édouard Perroy, 'Social mobility among French *noblesse* in the later Middle Ages', *Past and Present* XXI (1962: 25-38); K. B. McFarlane, *The Nobility of Later Medieval England* (Oxford, 1973: 141-70); Grant (1985: 210-31); Bush 1988: 23-9).

7. Discussed in Patterson 1991b.

8. Binchy (1975 b: 23-27), summarizes the earlier research which identified similarities between Irish *troscad* and Indian 'sitting *dharma*'.

9. A survey of the relationship between nationalist ideology, racial myths, and English historiography appears in MacDougal 1982: 89-116; R. R. Davies (1979) examines the historical context in which the Celtic cultures of Britain came to be viewed as primitive; Chapman (1978; 82) discusses the relationship between the Romantic movement and the myth of the 'Celtic twilight'.

10. Ellis Evans writes, 'As for Indo-European groupings...We have all the while to consider areal influences, the reflection of substrata or adstrata; and I commend the view once put forward by Leo Weisgerber in a standard survey of Continental Celtic, that in attempting to establish the common basis of a linguistic branch or family all that we can hope to attain or establish is a strong blend of originally different or already strongly differentiated languages' (1981: 133, citing Leo Weisgerber, *Rhenania Germano-Celtica*. Bonn, 1969: 31) These remarks apply even more forcefully to attempts to model a proto-Indo-European social system.

11. It was not Maine, however, but the German legal historians who were cited by Binchy (*SEIL*: 186 n.2, 3; 208 n.2; 209 n.2), perhaps because Maine's comments on *AL* had not endeared him to Irish scholars. See Mac Néill 1921: 146.

12. Byock writes of medieval Iceland, 'at that time a woman could inherit a *godord*, although she had to empower a man to act on her behalf' (Byock 1988: 210), i.e. to act at the *thing*. A *godord* was a temple, with associated taxation privileges and social duties.

13. See Goody (1969: 235-9) for references to this model and its authors.

14. Radcliffe-Brown showed in 'The mother's brother in South Africa' (1924) that the exceptionally close relationship between mother's brother and sister's son complemented certain aspects of a patrilineal kinship system, and was thus not to be explained as a fragmentary survival of a former matrilineal system.

15. A similar argument has now been made by McLeod (1992: 78-80).

16. Mac Néill, for example, described Sir Walter Scott's novels as evidence for Scottish history on a par with what 'a woman told me that a woman told her' (Mac Néill 1935: 13). Father John Ryan, referring to St. Patrick's many female converts, wondered 'what services such virgins rendered to St. Patrick and his colleagues', and answered: 'To provide vestments for the clergy, cloths for the altars, decorative hangings for the walls, and to see to the general cleanliness and beauty of church interiors would doubtless be their chief work...'. (1931: 134) Nevertheless, the oldest hagiographical images of Brigid, Moninne, and Ita are of women of great influence, mobility and courage.

17. Comparison of Irish with African lineages is found in Charles-Edwards (1972 b: 16 n.25) and Byrne (1971: 139). Nicholls merges 'clan- or lineage-based societies, whether in Medieval Ireland, in Asia or Africa' into one social type (1972: 8). McCone explicitly likens Irish *fían* to Masai age-sets (1990: 210) on the basis of similarities which are universal amongst segregated bands of young males, but not specific to the quite distinctive features of age-sets.

CHAPTER TWO

The Development of Early Irish Law and Society

By the early medieval period, Irish population groups that were recognized in Roman times had been widely displaced. Ptolemy's map, which is dated to the second century, gives (in Greek) the names of several Irish groups, some of which had a bi-coastal distribution, indicating the importance of contacts between Ireland, Britain and Gaul prior to this time.[1] Yet only about a quarter of the named groups are identifiable as political units in the oldest stratum of the annals and genealogies, following the long period in which Britain and Gaul had not been freely accessible to Irish traders and potentates. Massacres are not necessarily denoted by these findings, but loss of identity, or change of political status are implied.

Mac Néill added further evidence, based on internal sources, which also showed that major changes occurred in Irish society during the fifth and sixth centuries (1911: 87); group names formed on the basis of collective nouns (such as the 'deer-people', *Osraige*, or 'smith-folk', *Cerdraige*), were succeeded by names that indicate direct patrilineal descent from important individuals, as in formations based on 'grandsons of' (*uí*, e.g. Uí Néill). Mac Néill identified these as 'sept names' (i.e. names of dynastic families). Some of the 'collective' names may be traced to prehistoric populations; by the early historical period, the majority of such names were those of conquered people, in vassalage to dynastic lineages bearing the names beginning with *uí*. To the latter denominations were added (at a sightly later date, according to Mac Néill), names based on *cenél* (e.g. *Cenél nAengusa*, the descendants of Angus) and *cland* (e.g. *Clann Cholmáin*, the children of Colmán). These suggest a broader type of group, with vaguer or more attenuated links between members and the founding ancestor, and between each other, than is suggested by the *uí* names. Mac Néill's

36

views have been largely accepted as valid by such scholars as Byrne (1971: 151-2), and Mac Niocaill (1971: 4).

Later, there also appeared names based on *síl* (seed). An example is *Síl Muiredaig*, the 'seed' of Muiredach Muillethan, who died in 702, but whose progeny were a distinct and dominant branch of the Uí Briúin Ai, a segment of the ruling dynasty of Connacht, the Uí Briúin, who were themselves probably collaterals of the Uí Néill (Ó Corráin 1972: 9). As the generations succeeded each other and successful dynasties branched into ruling local groups, those groups composed of recent descendants of a leader who had captured the paramountcy of the whole clan political structure would obviously have wished to differentiate themselves from their less distinguished relatives, but without forfeiting the prestige of identification with the founder of the clan by assuming a new name based on *uí*; hence the adoption of *síl*.

Evidently then, the period between the late fourth and early sixth century was one of social upheaval in Ireland. The emergence of conquering groups coincided with the conversion to Christianity, the collapse of Roman power in Britain, and frequent raids by Irishmen upon western Britain for slaves and loot (Mytum 1992). Irish sources offer no reliable accounts of the turmoil of this period; apparently, then, the real roots of the new dynasties were nothing they could boast of. Kelleher memorably describes the Uí Néill emerging into history 'like a school of cuttle-fish from a large ink-cloud of their own manufacture; and clouds and ink continued to be manufactured by them or for them throughout their long career. Only one thing seems consistent, their claim of sole right to the kingship of Tara. In the early historical period that claim was as new as it was vast. To support it history had to be rewritten.' (Kelleher 1963: 125).

Change, however, was heavily disguised in most types of early Irish texts as a continuation of tradition. This fiction was especially important in legal writing, for Irish legal mythology was preoccupied with the legitimation of the continuation of pre-Christian law, and the status of those who were experts in it, after the conversion. This was accomplished by means of a doctrine which held that the pagan Irish had been bound by the covenant between Noah and God, Christians were bound by the Gospel 'preached to all nations', while 'the laws of the Irish' (specifically, the *Senchas Már*) harmonized the two moral systems (Carey 1990: 18). The ideology of the laws is set forth in an Old Irish tract, known to scholars as the 'Pseudo-historical Prologue to the Introduction to the *Senchas Már*',[2] in which is described a fictional meeting between St. Patrick, Lóegaire, the high-king of Tara, and representatives of the legal profession, the poets and the druid priests.

In the context of such theological and legitimative preoccupations, the lawyers had no interest in discoursing on the varieties of legal systems maintained by Noah's Irish associates before the advent of the Gospels, although the Introduction to the *Senchas Már* reels off a tantalizing list of different compilations of law attributed to various personages, some divine, some quasi-historical. In contrast to the lawyers' emphasis on the national jural synthesis, literary tradition always recognized two basic culture-areas in Ireland, *Leth Cuinn* ('Conn's half', the north), and *Leth Moga* ('Mug's half', the south). It is, then, no more likely that pre-Christian Irish law was a uniform system than that the summit-conference at Tara actually took place. Internal evidence from the law-tracts shows that the *Senchas Már* was a grand synthesis based on the *senchas* of a number of regional jural cultures (Binchy 1975b: 34), whose features we shall now examine.

It has long been recognized, in fact, that there were two, and probably more, early foci of legal scholarship and literacy: one center, associated with a group of texts labelled the *nemed* group, was in the south-west, in Munster; the other, associated with the *Senchas Már*, was in the north-east midlands (Kelly 1988: 247 [map]). Geographically, these two centers coincide with the heartland of the new dynasties, respectively with the Eóganacht at Cashel, and the southern Uí Néill in the hinterlands of Dublin Bay. In addition, tracts exist which were recognized as coming from neither of these 'schools', notably *Críth Gablach*, the tract which offers the most detailed information on early Irish social structure. *CG*, however, though recognized as a distinct piece of work by the compilers of the *Senchas Már*, derived from roughly the same area as *SM*, and depicts the kind of system of social stratification and social control assumed by *SM*. This contrasts with the major Munster tract on status, *Uraicecht Becc* (Mac Néill 1923: 272-81). Although these sources were written during the height of the process of legal homogenization (the seventh and eighth centuries), and thus bear considerable affinities to each other, some aspects of *CG* and *UB* remain strikingly different. By comparing these it is possible to get a sense of the social changes that led up to the establishment of a more or less unified legal and social system, based on the claims of clans to control their members, after the new political order had become widespread.

CG described social rank in terms of the distribution of status amongst the membership of land-holding clans. These were male individuals whose rank depended, basically, upon the fact that they stood to inherit shares of a clan estate, in land and chattels. Largely excluded from the description in *CG* were the landless (itinerant and tied serfs, and slaves), and craftsmen, druids, poets and priests, although the presence of such social categories (excepting druids) was acknowledged by the tract. Moreover, in *CG* adult women were also excluded from separate discussion, and were subsumed instead under the status-categories of males, as their wives, despite the evidence from one of the *Senchas Már* tracts, *Cáin Lánamna*, that the legal situation was more complex than that (for example, a woman's honor-price was based on her own property, as heiress, if she had no brothers. See Ch. 11). Likewise out of focus are the ranks of military specialists, on which *Míadshlechta*, an early eighth-century tract on status, which was also not part of the *Senchas Már*, offers considerable detail (Binchy 1962a: 63 n.166).

CG's compiler was quite single-minded, in fact — he was only concerned with the relationship between individuals' holdings of land and chattels within a clan structure, and the bearing of this wealth upon their participation in social control through the jural process. All the ranks listed in *CG* had oath-value, witness-value, fiefs in clientship, rights to act as sureties, claims to damages, rights to hospitality and to provide protection, based on their honor-price. This in turn was based on the individual's position as an heir to land and chattels in a clan, not upon craft skills, learning or martial power. Qualifications in terms of skill or learning were confined to special segments of society, whose members had honor-price on the basis of degrees of skills and learning. Amongst the socially entitled members of the population (i.e. excluding slaves and foreigners), society was divided into two main divisions (i) the *óes cerdd / óes dána* (people of art, poetry, learning and crafts) and (ii) the ranks of *aire* (lords and freemen, members of landowning and farming clans). These were such distinct social segments that it was not possible, for example, to hold rank as the owner of a middling size farm and at the same time practice a craft well enough to have rank on that basis too: it follows that the crafts were hereditary professions. *CG* constructed its description of *aire* society lineally, working up from the youngest members of a farming family, to its seniors, then through ranks of social superiority within a lineage of farmers, culminating with a description of the legal representative of a *fine* (an agnatic kin-group) of farmers. These various ranks of the farmers were collectively known as *grád fhéne* (Binchy 1941: 98). After this, it moved on to depict the ranks of the lords (*grád fhlatha*), where status depended on the ability to enfeoff farmers as clients. Here too, assumptions of kinship relations between some of these ranks are discernable in the text.

Whereas *CG*'s social hierarchy was based on the political, jural and economic distinctions between king (*rí*), lord (*flaith*), and cattle-farmer (*bóaire*), the Munster tract, *Uraicecht Becc*, described a more variegated and complex social order, based on the distinction between *nemed* (privileged) and non-*nemed*; and between *sóer* and *dóer* (free and bond), (Binchy 1955a: 4-6; 1958b: 44-54). The free-*nemed* consisted of poets, churchmen, lords and *féni*,[3] while the unfree-*nemed* consisted of a wide variety of craftsmen and people of learning, including lawyers and druids. The *dóer-nemed* were those who were tied to the paid service of a king (*ibid*, and 277 # 37), or other free-*nemed*. Craftsmen who were masters of their skill, however, might have independent status if they were not tied to the service of a king. In that case, they had the franchise of the lower grades of the lords, in terms of honor-price and in terms of being free (*sóer*) to exercise judicature regarding their profession and apprentices (*CIH* 1612.4-22; 1613.9-16, 22-37. See Mac Néill 1923: 277 #37-280 #55). The status of these individuals was protected from the particularism of early Irish society, for whereas most people only had status on their home turf, master-craftsmen retained their status when working outside their local *tuath*, or on monastic grounds (*CIH* 1616.37-1617.4. See Mac Néill 1923: 280 #53). Like *CG*, which recognized that landless workers existed, but did not discuss them (another source, the *Fuidir* tract, does this in great detail), so *UB* ignores the non-*nemed*, who were presumably non-natives, slaves, and degraded persons in general.

UB, then, attempted to describe a composite society, with parallel but distinct rank systems for its segments. This difference, however, might only suggest that the tract had a wider frame of reference than *CG*, but as we shall shortly see, there are reasons for thinking that it actually described a rather different social system from that which lay behind the other tract. Two other features of *UB* also contrast to materials of north-eastern background, whether *CG* or *SM*. One is the inclusion of '*féni*' as free and privileged/*nemed* (see n.3). This is at odds with its understood meaning of 'commoner, land-holding farmers' in the *Senchas Már* tradition, where *féni* are distinguished from the nobility, who alone amongst the 'unlearned' were regarded as *nemed*: to this point I shall return later. Secondly, the tract shows that in Munster, aspects of the druid priesthood, though eclipsed by the Christian clergy and somewhat Christianized *filid* (poets), retained a degree of prestige into the eighth century, for in *UB* #37 the druid is included in the same group as wrights, blacksmiths, braziers, whitesmiths, leeches and lawyers (*CIH* 1612.8 = Mac Néill 1923: 277 #37). Most of these held the rank of the lowest lord, the *aire déso* (#39). In the *Senchas Már*, the druid is either absent, or downgraded, as in the tract on sick-maintenance, *Bretha Crólige*, where he was consigned to the status of a commoner (*bóaire*), and was classed with other social types that had strong pagan associations — *díbergach* (a brigand, associated with pagan war-cults), and *cáinte* (a satirist, associated with pagan word-magic), (Binchy 1938 a: 41 #51).

The contrast between these two law-tracts as regards the druid's status, complements others peculiarities of the Munster region that have been pointed out by several scholars. As to literature, some have emphasized the 'subtly different character' and 'otherworldly atmosphere' of the region (Byrne 1988 (1973): 165; Rees & Rees 1961: 131-37). Likewise, the prominence of women in Munster mythology (*ibid*) stands in contrast to the status of women in the *Senchas Már*, in which, though accorded a fair degree of autonomy, their exclusion as heirs from patrilineal descent groups necessarily marginalized them and curtailed their claims to legitimate positions of power and leadership. The early medieval political structure of Munster also differed from that of the midlands and north, the areas dominated by the Uí Néill. The latter maintained dominance through a branching dynastic clan structure, which precluded participation in the highest levels of political activity by allies who were not descendants of the dynasty. In contrast, the Munster élite (eventually known generically as the Eóganacht) was not a dynastic clan, but a confederacy in which the over-kingship was shared by many separate groups (Ó Corráin 1972: 111-3). The special character of the south-west was also reflected in the mythic geography of early Irish culture, which attributed to the people of that region skills in music and magic, but servile status, while ascribing to the north, skills at warfare and high-status, and to the east, agricultural and domestic skills (Rees & Rees 1961: 118-45).

These cultural differences are, I believe, the manifestation of productive systems that differed as to the way in which the social domination of the producers of wealth was achieved. Society in the north-east was stratified on the basis of control of farmers through clientship, and the diversion of their produce and services to support the jural/military functioning of the clan corporation, its élite and its patrons. There too, of course, as throughout late iron-age Britain, potentates, kings and lords commanded the services of the skilled (Warner 1988: 66-7). Archaeological evidence strongly suggests that at widely distributed sites, such as Garranes and Garryduff in Co. Cork, Ballinderry in Co. Offaly, and Lagore in Co. Meath, craftsmen were concentrated at defended sites — but in what relationship to the political order of society (independent guild-castes, or under royal control?) is not indicated by the material remains.[4] Possibly craftsmen throughout early medieval Ireland had their own social organization, perhaps along the lines indicated in *UB*, but there is no evidence to suggest that after the rise of the Uí Néill, kingship in the north was strongly associated with the produce of skilled groups, or that control of such groups was an objective of kingship. On the contrary, control of territory was what drove the Uí Néill political economy, and drove them all over Ireland in its pursuit. In Munster, however, control of artisans was a serious political objective, as we shall now see. For convenience, I shall refer to this political-economy as the 'agro-artisanal system' of the south-west, in contrast to the 'agro-pastoral clan system' of the north that was eventually to dominate Irish society and law.

The vassalage of communities of skilled crafts-people in Munster was legitimized in an early (probably eighth-century) political tract, *Frithfholaid ríg Caisil fria thuatha*, which stipulated the reciprocal obligations pertaining between the King of Cashel and the east-Munster peoples (*tuatha*) that were in vassalage to him.[5] Byrne summarizes: 'the *ollam* or chief poet of the king of Cashel must always come from the Múscraige. Similarly, the brehon of the king of Cashel must be of the Déisi. Other subject tribes send officials or craftsmen appropriate to their tribal names or origin legends; physicians from the Dál Mugaide, harpers from the Corco Ochae, bronze-smiths from the Cerdraige, dairy-stewards ... from the Bóindrige, charioteers and horsemen from the Arada Cliach, champions from the Uaithni, Orbraige and Corco Athrach

... fools and door-keepers from the Corcomruad.' (Byrne 1987 (1973): 198).

One need not take all these stipulations literally (onomastic speculations may have fleshed out the picture offered by the text), in order to note that skilled labor was a major object of political control. In contrast, other 'political texts' make no such specifications (Gerriets 1987), while the eleventh- or twelfth-century list found in the *Book of Rights* (Dillon 1962), which is also ostensibly a list of the claims of the King of Cashel, likewise makes no reference to control of skilled labor. The demands for skilled personnel set forth in the *frithfholad* tract are generally interpreted as demands for services (with raw materials and maintenance of the personnel perhaps adding to the burden of the tribute; Gerriets 1987: 51-2), but the implied centralization of such diverse functions, the small numbers of personnel involved, and the fact that some of the people summoned to Cashel simply served as household attendants do not suggest that production for consumption was the only goal of these demands.

An alternative interpretation is that some of the people who were brought to Cashel under the political obligations of *frithfholad* were representatives of subordinated indigenous people, representatives who would ensure that producers at distant copper mines, for example, would be answerable to Cashel, not to their own chiefs and priests. Local control of skilled labor was strongly developed and must have required some such political pressure if the Cashel-based élite was to dominate the circulation of wealth in the south-west. This is shown by the fact that the rank of master-craftsman in metallurgy (master of 'test', master-blacksmith, master-whitesmith and master-brazier) was conferred on an artisan by his own people, *tuath (CIH* 1618.34-40 = Mac Néill 1923: 281 #60). Moreover, the indigenous legal profession was closely tied to the organization of the arts and crafts, for the lowest rank of lawyer is described in *UB* as one who was able to give decisions in cases involving craftsmen, the value of their work, and their remuneration (*CIH* 1613.38-1614.8 = Mac Néill 1923: 278 #43).

Other very early tracts connected to the *nemed* school also place great emphasis upon social relationships based on the exchange of skilled services, with the jurist and the king both being expected to play a role in mediating the social standing of individuals by correctly evaluating the worth of manufactured objects, as well as raw materials. This is a prominent feature of the advice to a king, compiled in *Audacht*

Morainn (Kelly 1976). The involvement of the king as ultimate evaluator of the worth of things recalls other signs that the Cashel kingship, even well after the conversion, tended to conjoin techno-religious and military power to a greater degree than is found elsewhere. Byrne notes that in *UB* the king was dignified with the same label, *ollam*, as the arch-poet, and formerly the arch-druid, (1971: 175); the acceptability within southern Irish culture (*Leth Moga*) of this convergence of functions is manifested later in the emergence, unique to Munster at such a late stage in the development of medieval Irish society, of formidable bishop-kings, such as Feidlimid mac Crimthainn (d. 847), and Cormac mac Cuillenáin (d. 908), (*ibid*: 214).

Also probably connected to the *nemed* school of Munster are lost tracts attributed to pre-Christian 'craft-gods': the judgments of Goibniu the blacksmith, Luchta the wright, Crédne the metal-worker, and (the extant) judgments of Dían Cécht, the healer (Binchy 1966a: 2-3). The greater political and social significance in the south-west of the wealth produced by artisans, may also lie behind the peculiarities of an Old Irish law-tract on distraint. As is shown in Ch. 7, commoners (the *féni*) were normally compelled to yield to processes of law by means of distraint — the forcible seizure of some of their cattle. Lords, ordained clerics, and poets, in contrast, when sued by commoners were first subject to a ritual attempt to shame them into lawfulness, by means of a fast undertaken by the plaintiff. The complicated rules on the distraint of commoners' cows are given in a long tract that forms part of the *Senchas Már*. But another tract on distraint, that is not part of the *Senchas Már*, applies ritual sanctions instead of seizure of cattle to a broad spectrum of society; here the operative mechanism was the tabooing of actions or implements that were essential to the performance of a craft or profession. For example:

> 'to distrain a smith, tie a withe[6] about his anvil and give notice that he is not to work any material on it until he shall have done right by you...' (Binchy 1973b: 78-9 #5).

As Binchy points out, some of those subject to taboo were 'relatively humble persons', such as base-clients on church-land (*ibid*: 83), and 'all persons who use an anvil' (*ibid*: 78-9 #5). The provenance of this tract is not firmly established, but Binchy notes that one of the craftsmen, the *tuathait* (perhaps a shield-maker: *ibid* 82 #5), appears also in *UB*. The tract is also linked to *Gúbretha Caratniad*, but of that tract's provenance it is only known that it did not belong to the *Senchas Már* (Kelly 1988:

248).[7] While the direct evidence that this source stemmed from the south-west is thus slight, it represents a system of social control that differs from that which appears in *SM*, and seems much closer to the society that lay behind *UB*.

Taking this tract on distraint as a further clue to the kind of social order that prevailed in early medieval Munster, it seems likely that the more prolonged survival of druidism in the south-west was due to the greater importance of traditional rituals to the maintenance of social order in this region. In the north-east, sanctions depended upon exclusion from the privileges of clan-membership; the main instrument of social control was not ritual prohibition from doing one's work, but fines (mainly in cows), which reduced honor-price, and likewise reduced a person's capacity to take action at law (oath-value, etc.). This is the system that dominates the *Senchas Már* tradition, and it is therefore the system analyzed in this book. Under such a jural regime, ritual aspects of social sanctions were less essential to the credibility of the threat of punishment for social deviance; the role of the druid as a protector of the social order was accordingly more dispensable, and ritual could be handed over to the new religion. In the south-west the converse was true, and the druid retained a positive role in society for much longer after the conversion than in the north. Both systems of social control nevertheless had much in common, especially the fact that social position was highly hereditized (whole *tuatha* were assigned certain skilled tasks in the south-western polity), and that crafts, because they entail degrees of skill and authority, are easy to adapt to a more stratified system of social rank. Thus it was not difficult to blend them after the period of dynastic expansion had carried the Eóganacht and Uí Néill to the limits of their capacities to subordinate local populations.

As to the origins of these somewhat different social systems, it would seem likely, on account of its druidic associations, and the prehistoric lineages of some of the peoples bearing collective names linked to crafts, that the 'agro-artisanal' political-economy of the south-west was established during one of the great prehistoric periods of metallurgic manufacture and trade, the last of which was the resplendent 'Dowris phase', which flourished c. 700 B.C. for an uncertain period (O'Kelly 1989: 149-55). Its provenance in Munster need not indicate that it had always been confined to that area, for the wide distribution of druidry, and of centers of skilled metallurgic production, would argue against this.

The features of the 'agro-artisanal system' could have arisen from the fact that the geographically fixed nature of extractive metallurgy and the requirement for the manufacture of bronze that tin be imported to copper-bearing regions in Munster from outside the region (O'Kelly 1989: 259-60), made metallurgy vulnerable to the imposition of élite political controls from an early prehistoric period, even without the presence of a developed military system. Technological specialization, magic, and the ascendancy of a priesthood, would seem to have laid the prehistoric groundwork for a class system in the south-west — a class system that was basically theocratic (in the broadest sense), but which was taken over by an in-coming military élite which superimposed its political organization upon the area. This, it appears, was not interested in (or capable of) wiping out the native social order, so much as appropriating it. Perhaps it is for this reason that the Eóganacht did not develop into formidable, expansionist military rulers until after the advent of the Vikings.

In addition to the probable differences in political economy between the south-west and the north-eastern and central regions of early medieval Ireland, it is likely that regional social differences were accentuated by the fact that during the formative period of the rise of the new dynasties, the south-west and north-east were exposed to different external influences. The political élite of Munster had ties with Gaul during the earliest phase of their ascent to power (Byrne 1987 [1973]: 181-2; Binchy 1958b: 44-54). The midlands and north-east, in contrast, were influenced by the Patrician mission and therefore by aspects of late Romano-British culture.

The legendary founder-saints of the south (including Leinster) were predominantly natives, and generally associated with skills and learning, which suggests that Christianity percolated into these areas and was adapted to local society without the aid of a major campaign to proselytize the ruling class. The premier female saint (ultimately second only to St. Patrick), Brigid of Kildare, was formerly the high-goddess *Brig*, patron of food-production, war, and knowledge — including leechcraft, metalwork and poetry (McCone 1990: 162-3). In her Christian *persona*, she was a healer, food-provider, and protector of the poor and outcast. Ciarán of Clonmacnoise was a carpenter, and the abbots of that leading monastery were regularly drawn from the *aithech-tuatha*, the vassal-peoples, from all over Ireland (Byrne 1973: 171); Brendan of Clonfert was a navigator, who bore the distinctly unaristocratic, 'tribal' name, *Bréndán moccu Altai* (*ibid*). In contrast, Patrick came to Ireland on a well-funded, well-planned mission to subject kings to spiritual discipline. While Brigid, too, reviled the sons of kings as vipers, Patrick wrote threatening letters to the soldiers of kings. The north-east, then, received a Christian mission that had much to say about war, politics, law and order.

In contrast to the 'agro-artisanal' political economy, the clan system focussed upon the production of wealth through control of the distribution of cattle and the diversion of agricultural produce and services to the support of élite military activities — specifically, to raiding, which generated the wealth with which a lord could enfeoff clients and sustain his political standing. This system depended on the élite's ability to coerce dependents into staying in social groups that contributed to their activities. Without a geographically extensive military apparatus, the élite could not have prevented low-status clansmen from running away from their obligations — with their cows and families — and undermining the system. For this reason, it is not likely that the clan system existed in the form that we see it in the law-tracts before the rise of the new dynasties, for these excelled above all else in maintaining political control over broad regions. The maps provided by Ó Corráin of the political geography of pre-Norman Munster and the southern Uí Néill lands in Meath (1972: 4, 18), show that in both areas the élite criss-crossed the region, especially in the vicinity of the political foci at Cashel and Tara, with branches of their own organization and their allies, thus keeping indigenous peoples in disarray and simultaneously making defection from the system difficult for those who wanted to escape and establish autonomous communities. The only true alternative was the *fían* — forest-based groups who lived by hunting and mercenary activity. Their immense popularity as the subject of folktales attests to the powerful appeal of a life that entailed less hard work, routine, and sexual restraint than was customary. For most, this alternative life-style could only be contemplated in escapist fantasy, for in reality, *fían* groups had relations with kings, for whom they seem to have worked as enforcers (McCone 1990: 211).

But although Munster, too, was under the political control of a military élite that had worked out a system of territorial control, the region had a peaceable (not to say obscure and remote) aspect until the Viking Age, whereas the Uí Néill continually sought conquest of new territories (Byrne 1971: 199-201). Indeed, the main political foundation-legend of the Eóganacht depicted their founder, 'Eógan of the stores', as a distributor of food, who was consensually elevated to the regional kingship. He was contrasted to the founder of the Uí Néill, 'the second Míl Espáne', who simply invaded. This propagandist (probably tenth-century) text comments on the Uí Néill:

'That is how they seized sovereignty at first, and it will
always be so: by force they take lordship' (*ibid*: 200).[8]

It is probable, then, that the 'agro-artisanal' system supported the élite through a more genuinely productive economic system, and one which also required less investment in military domination of the productive population.

In contrast, the background of *CG*, and therefore of the social system described in this book, was a region far more riven by warfare than the south-west. The compiler of *CG* refers respectfully to the Law of Adomnán, which indicates that its writer was working within the sphere of influence of the *familia* of St. Columba, namely the axes of Iona, Kells and Derry (Herbert 1988: [maps] 312-5).[9] Adomnán's promulgation (697 A.D.), was aimed at the pacification of society, for as noted in Ch. 1, it specifically forbade the involvement of women and clerics in hostilities. His predecessor at Iona, Columba, had himself been a great peace-maker, though more as a diplomat than legislator, for Columba helped facilitate the peaceful separation of the Scottish Dál Riata from its Irish parent society, an arrangement that was negotiated at the Convention of Drumceat in 575 A.D. (Smyth 1984: 116).

Stemming from Scottish Dál Riata, from perhaps a hundred years after the important concordance at Drumceat, is another tract that depicts a society that in some ways closely resembles the one depicted in *CG*. This tract, the *Senchas fer nAlban*, enumerates the branches of the ruling clans of Scottish Dál Riata, the number of houses in clientship to them, the expeditionary forces that they could muster for naval operations, and the contribution of groups of clients to these musters. It is dated by Bannerman to the late seventh century (1974: 39), and is thus roughly contemporary with Adomnán's law. Its depiction of society, as well as the history of Scottish Dál Riata after the Convention of Drumceat, explains why the Abbot of Iona should have felt that social pacification was an urgent matter for the attention of bishops and kings. Fighting between the Dál Riatans, the Ulster Cruithin, and the Uí Néill high king had ruined the fortunes of Dál Riata for much of the mid-seventh century, while Iona itself was eclipsed by the rising Church of English Northumbria at the Synod of Whitby in 664. Bannerman shows the connection between the warlike world of Dál Riata, as depicted in *Senchus fer nAlban* and the political system of *CG*, pointing out that according to both sources, clients were attached to their lords in groups of five, and that the lords themselves were ranked into five levels of leadership (1974: 134 ff.).

Following the calamities of the seventh century, and in the wake of Adomnán's peace-movement, those who were responsible for the thinking behind *CG* seem to have concluded that the best hope for peace and order was that the military élite should be legitimized in their power by being honored with prestige and legal status if they used their wealth to stabilize society through processes of law. This is a far cry from a society in which booty only served to buy retainers, flattering poets, and unreliable allies. Whereas the earlier Dál Riatan tract, the *Senchus fer nAlban*, described an actual extant power structure, the author of *CG* spelled out the precise and theoretical relationship between status, property, honor-price, and jural function; both this emphasis on law and order, and the likely date of *CG* (early eighth century) place it in the context of a more sophisticated cultural climate than the earlier Dal Riatan tract, a climate characterized by legal compilations and compositions, many of which, such as *Cáin Adamnáin* itself, were drafted by prominent clerics. These *cána*, which are listed by Kelly (1988: 281.73-282.77), attempted to impose universalistic agreements on the population, reaching out beyond the peoples, the *tuatha*, to deal with problems beyond the regulatory capacities of small and weak local populations — problems such as indiscriminate slaughter during war, cattle-raiding, and the enforcement of the Christian prohibition of work on Sunday, a taboo which facilitated Church attendance by the laboring population. If viewed as related in general intent to these *cána*, *CG* must be regarded as the most sophisticated document of this sort, for it went beyond the *ad hoc* generalizations of the *cána* (which, in any case, were tinged with the sectarian interests of the clergy), and attempted to establish the foundations of a rationalized, generalizable legal-political order for secular society.

Nevertheless, *CG*'s roots in a warring, clan-based society, which eighth-century clerics (and presumably, kings and their advisers from the secular learned orders) were trying to tame and civilize, are exposed by its affinities with the Dál Riatan tract. The single strand that ties both tracts together — internally, and to each other — is that status depended on the ability to mobilize resources, human and material, for aggression. The vehicle was the clan, the instrument was clientship, but the product of the system of social relations was warfare — either opportunistic war, or war moderated by law as *CG* intended.

In the period of time between Columba's attendance at Drumceat, and the writing of *CG*, however, some group had developed an approach to the violence of the military élite which accepted the fundamental features of its social existence, but turned its very greed for wealth and status into a method of social control that applied to all. Although the sources of this reformist jural effort are lost to view, it is not likely that the basic premise of *CG* — that wealth should be systematically deployed to support social order — would have been congenial to the founders of the new dynasties. A pre-existing ideology — stemming from the indigenous theocratic social order, and possibly carried forward both by the *filid* and the clergy — may thus have been grafted onto, civilizing somewhat, the polities spawned by the Uí Néill. As Binchy pointed out (1961: 17), it cannot be insignificant that as a young man Adomnán spent some time studying with a prominent poet, whose caste at this time was still a repository of pre-Christian legal knowledge. Howbeit as to origins, the militarism of the social order that inspired, in their different ways, *CG*, the *Senchus fer nAlban*, and *Cáin Adamnáin*, offers a considerable contrast to the magico-religious powers which in the *nemed* law-tracts of Munster were presumed to play an important role in holding society together.

A similarly militaristic milieu may be detected behind the *Senchas Már*. A major stream in the legal tradition of *SM* was *fénechas*, the customary native secular law, as opposed to canon law or the laws of the poets. In the law-tracts, this term denoted the customs of the *féni*, namely the ranks of those farmers who were land-holding members of clans (Binchy 1941: 88-9). But *féni* also had an ethnic connotation, being contrasted with the people of Ulster and those of Leinster (Meyer 1910: viii). Thurneysen suggested that the word originally connoted 'warrior, member of the army' ([1935] 1975: 69), and O'Brien emphasized the connection of the *féni* with Tara (D. O'Brien 1932: 183), a connection which was put forward in the Old Irish glosses to the Introduction to the *Senchas Már*.[10] Since Tara and the northern midlands were the geo-political focal area of early medieval Ireland, changing hands between Leinstermen, Ulstermen and finally being seized by the Uí Néill, the dominance of *fénechas* as *the* traditional law of Irish farmers and warriors is probably connected to the rise of the Uí Néill as the major paramountcy in early medieval Ireland. The emphasis that *fénechas*-law placed upon wealth as the main determinant of status becomes intelligible against this background, for the rise of the Uí Néill involved not only successful dynastic expansion at a rapid rate throughout the midlands and the north-west, but also put pressure on all neighboring people to respond by becoming vassals or allies.

By the time the laws were being written, then, much political change and cultural diffusion had occurred throughout Ireland, and all the law-tracts show signs of homogenization of jural traditions from other parts of the island (Binchy 1966 b: 89); but in this process, one ingredient in the blend — *fénechas* — had come to the fore. At this point, we may recall that in *UB* the *féni* had been included amongst the highest stratum of society, the free-*nemed*, suggesting the presence of an overlay of rather poorly 'harmonized', *Senchas Már* traditions in this south-western tract. A context in which such diffusion could have taken place is the movement of Munster clerics beyond the borders of their province into the midlands, where they founded numerous monastic communities in the sixth and seventh centuries (Byrne 1971: 170-1), and where their exposure to the *Senchas Már* and Patrician doctrines would perhaps have been refreshing to energetic Christians seeking to break away from what seems to have been a rather cozy alliance between the heirs of the pagan tradition and the Christian elite in Munster.

But whatever the causes, diffusion of *Senchas Már* influence into the south-west did occur, as the Munster law-tract *Cáin Fhuithirbe* shows (Breatnach 1986: 51). *Cáin Fhuithirbe* contained a passage on martial-law that seems only too likely to have been learned in the north; it was 'concerned with the right of the lord to use violence in certain circumstances, whether in the case of non-fulfillment of duties, or in the case of attacks upon him or his honour' (*ibid*: 39). Breatnach has dated the composition of the tract to within a few years of 680, close in date therefore to *CG*, the *Hibernensis* (a collection of Irish canons), and the *Senchas Már* itself. Indeed a fragment that refers to a lost Munster tract, but that appears to have been modelled on the later 'introduction' to the E text of *Cáin Fhuithirbe*, makes the following claim:

...the reason for its composition was that Cumain was unable to decide on a point of law in Aine Cliach[11] after studying ecclesiastical learning, and he had not studied Irish law

(*fénechas*) previously, so that he went to the North to learn it'
(Breatnach 1986: 37).

The idea of one synthetic law for diverse regional populations seems to
have struck the locals as absurd, for an 'introduction' to *CF*, which is
found in MS T.C.D., H.3.18, apparently satirizes the whole idea. In this
it is said that 'the men of Munster' would not agree to meet to ratify
Cáin Fhuithirbe, unless they could all be assembled on one plain, with
one lake large enough to supply them all with fish and water, one wood
supplying enough firewood for all, and one hill from which all could
obtain timber and thatch — only then would they submit to one law![12]

But submit they seem to have done, for *Senchas Már* influence in
the south-west thereafter progressed rapidly. Very soon after the
composition of *Cáin Fhuithirbe*, the leading clerics from Munster went
to Birr in Co. Offaly for the great meeting which ratified *Cáin
Adomnáin* (Ní Dhonnchadha 1982: 186-8). Still later than either *Cáin
Fhuithirbe* or *Caín Adomnáin* was the (now lost) *Cáin Phátraic* (736
A.D.), which apparently imitated (and rivalled) *Cáin Adomnáin* in
attempting to protect clerics from violence by imposing sanctions —
fines payable to the Patrician monasteries — upon violators (Picard
1982: 163). It too was received in Munster in A.D. 842 (*Annals of
Inisfallen*). The outcome of the superimposition of Patrician and *SM*
influence is demonstrated by the treatment in *UB* of the status of the
indigenous jurist who specialized in evaluating the work of artisans; his
rank was slightly lower than that of a blacksmith. In contrast, a jurist
who knew *berla féni*, the technical language of the *fénechas* — *féni* law,
as well as *filidecht* and how to judge the merits of a poet — had a
considerably higher rank (*CIH* 1614.20 = Mac Néill 1923: 278: #43-4).
It seems most likely that before the northern influence prevailed the
status system of the south knew neither *féni* nor *fénechas*, and that
judges either were assessors of the crafts, or *filid*, who regulated general
social relationships, rituals, poetry, and the organization of knowledge.
The latter probably always had higher status than the craft-regulators
because they controlled social relations in general, but they did so, I
believe, through ritual and taboo (as explained above), rather than
through the system of fines that lies at the heart of *fénechas*.

Although the present state of research permits only a working
hypothesis in this regard, the considerations reviewed above suggest that
the large-scale, stratified, patrilineal clans described in this book were
a social formation that spread out of centers of military expansion,

notably Dál Riata and the southern Uí Néill bastion that extending from Dublin Bay through the midlands, and that both the Columban and Patrician monasteries had a hand in aligning the social demands of this military élite to the aspirations of Christian communities. In contrast, a less aggressive, less materialistic, but nevertheless probably more productive social system prevailed in the south-west until approximately the late seventh century.

The difference, of course, is one of degree, on a continuum of social relationships, at one end of which stands a political economy in which power and status depended upon the dominance of pasture and farm labor as a means of securing a clientele. This in turn depended upon the continuous exercise of coercive power against rivals and against producers who would defect from the system under some circumstances. At the other end, stands a more complex system based on the division of specialized labor, the restricted flow of arcane knowledge, and the exchange of produce on the basis of free contract. Here, gradations of status depending mainly on degrees of expertise in a special skill. Expressed in terms of fundamental social dyads, the status systems of the two political-economies were typified by the relationship between a military lord and his client, on the one hand, and on the other by the relationship between craftsman and consumer, and craftsman and apprentice. It is unlikely that the ideal type (in the Weberian sense) of purely contractual exchange between craftpersons and 'customers' actually ever existed in the south-west, but nevertheless, it is clear that social stratification increased in the south, when a new political regime rose to power in Munster at the beginning of the middle ages. This, despite the long leash on which it kept the master craftsmen of the region, ultimately had the capacity to demand tribute from them. Moreover, the social, political and cultural differences of the regions were progressively effaced as unrestrained and unpredictable warfare again swamped Ireland in the ninth century, when the Vikings arrived.

The broad theory of social change which I have attempted in the foregoing pages, though tentative, may be further supported by references within the body of the *Senchas Már* to legal and social changes; these also point towards a society that was becoming more tightly structured within the framework of patrilineal clans. One of the most striking signs of this is the fact that reparations (*díre*), which were paid to relatives when an individual was injured, were not confined to patrilineal relatives, but were distributed bilaterally (to relatives through both mother and father, including the mother's sister's son). Curiously removed from this frame of reference was the payment of wergeld (*cró*); this was paid only to patrilineal kin, and was a fixed amount, regardless of rank. The provisions regarding *díre* are found in linguistically early sources, whereas *cró* was a relatively late addition to the array of social sanctions. The *cró* texts are in post-classical Irish and one lists as its most recent authority Cormac mac Cuillenáin, an early tenth-century bishop-king of Cashel.[13] In general, *cró* has features which suggest an alignment of Irish, Viking and Anglo-Saxon wergelds in the late pre-Norman period (Patterson 1990; see Ch. 9). *Cró*, then, supplemented the older bilateral payment of honor-price and intensified the importance of agnatic relationships to social order.

Another legal innovation that strengthened agnatic corporations as instruments of social control was the restriction of an individual's jural capacity to issues that involved no more than the value of his own honor-price. Prior to this regulation, according to the tract on suretyship, *Berrad Airechta*, the most ordinary farmer could make oaths on matters where the amounts of restitution or fine far exceeded his capacity to pay (Stacey 1986: 216 #41). The myths of origin of the *Senchas Már* tell the same story within the general framework of explaining how Irish law was brought into harmony with Christianity. In the Introduction it is said that before the legal convention at Tara, mentioned above, equal honor-price was given to military strongmen, legitimate kings, *filid*, and the hostel-keepers of the *tuath* (the brewies), but that subsequently each was ranked according to his property.[14] It is only too easy to dismiss such stories as fabrications and to infer that they are therefore meaningless; but I would suggest that they are fabrications with a lot of meaning, recalling different methods of securing compliance to laws and norms. Again, what comes to mind is a magico-religious system in which oaths and taboos carried so much weight that differential economic penalities (the honor-price standard) were not required to bind people to the social order.

The integration of the *comaithches* into the legal framework of the clan system also suggests the advance of social control by a war-oriented élite. A *comaithches* was a small group of contiguous people who might cooperate in agriculture. Although the tract states that such a community originated in the existence of many heirs and the division of patrimony,[15] it does not follow that the *comaithches* consisted of next of kin, but rather that heirs who were squeezed out of the family holding were regrouped with other such unfortunates on clan lands under the aegis of the clan chief; the law states that by 'new custom' such people could now establish contracts amongst themselves without sureties,[16] as if they were close kin. At the same time, like kin, they had certain liabilities imposed upon them. Where they were base-clients, it is not too much to suppose that they were answerable to one lord, who imposed the normal restraints of kinship on them in order to ensure their performance as clients. The 'new rule' attests to the systematization of social control through the application of the norms of corporate kinship solidarity to social groups who need not actually have been recruited on the basis of closeness of kinship.

Finally, there is evidence regarding kinship itself which undermines ideas that kinship was universally patrilineal at the dawn of early medieval Irish society, but was basically bilateral until agnatic land-holding clans acquired the controls described in Chapters 9 and 10. Most of the evidence is given in these later chapters, but we have already noted one point, namely the bilateral structure of honor-price payments, described above. Against a background of bilateral kinship, early Irish clerics' references to kin as *cognationes* (not *agnates* [Bieler 1975: 271 V 2]) become intelligible as more than a mere misapplication of Latin terms. It is striking, for example, that in the poems of Bláthmac (mid-eighth to early tenth century?[17]), Christ's crucifixion was treated as a horrifying *fingal* — kin-slaying — because of the implication of Mary's people, the Jews, his *maithre*. Here *fine* (normally understood as a six-generation patrilineage) included the *maithre*, to whom Christ was *fírbráthair*, a true kinsman.[18]

Early Irish kinship had as its context an old north European pattern of bilateralism with agnatic emphasis, found in Wales, England and most of the Germanic and Scandinavian areas. Bilaterality was noted by Tacitus amongst the Germans in the first century A.D., while the linguistic evidence, as far as that goes, shows that early northern Europe was in general 'an area of endemic bilaterality, combined with agnatic structures of various sorts' (Friedrich 1966: 21). The strongly agnatic, strongly corporate, land-owning and fighting clans of medieval Ireland, Scotland and Wales, are thus exceptional historical regional formations, which cannot be assumed to be 'survivals' of an 'original' patrilineal culture, uniformly blanketing ancient 'Indo-Europe'. Moreover, the process of agnatic clan emergence was not confined to the early medieval British Isles, but was repeated in late medieval Ditmarschen. Whereas the people of the whole north-Frisian and Danish area were otherwise bilateral in kinship, in Ditmarschen the special value of the lands retrieved from the sea, and the intense labor demands of the dikes, stimulated the emergence of solidary, male-retaining, land-owning corporate kinship groups, which, however, retained bilateral group organization for the payment of wergeld (Phillpotts 1913: 127; 131). In this respect, these patrilineages closely resemble the Irish and Welsh legal systems, which confined control of land to agnatic groups, but obligated a bilateral circle of kin to contribute movables to wergeld-payments, so as to ward off vendetta. (In feuds men sought out emotionally important kin, not only legally significant ones, as targets: an enemy's sister's son would do well, though not an agnate.)

Having developed as a means to defend the land on which the clientele of the dynastic élite survived, agnatic clans acquired legal forms and a normative force that were tantamount to a 'way of life'. I have suggested that a crucial step in the development of the normative order of clan society occurred in the late seventh or early eighth centuries, just before and during the time when *Críth Gablach* was written. Clans, as institutional social groups, became so firmly embedded in society at this time, that notwithstanding the impact of the Vikings and the Normans, no revolutionary changes subsequently took place in Irish social structure — indeed the Normans developed Gaelic-style clans of their own (Curtis 1910; Lydon 1973: 50-1). Not until the Tudor conquest were the clans uprooted from much of Ireland, and the clan system, as a form of social organization, destroyed.

Stasis, change and history

For all its theoretical deficiencies, the evolutionary approach was an attempt to grapple with the difficulty of establishing a chronological framework for the Irish law-tracts. If this approach is abandoned, along with the assumption that the law-tracts are the detritus of a collapsed pagan culture which was preserved merely as a collection of 'fossils' by a backward-looking learned 'caste', then a position must be taken regarding the relationship of the laws to Irish medieval society as it changed and developed.

In the first place, stasis in cultural expression must be distinguished from stasis in social relations. As regards the former there is no doubt that Irish high culture was a-historical; the 'men of learning' fetishized history and at the same time denied the reality of the flow of events. Once the grand harmonization of different regional law-tracts had taken place between the seventh and eighth centuries, new phenomena were interpreted by means of ancient symbols and stories, the present being thus represented as continuous with the past, and in some ways *becoming* more continuous as a result (Patterson 1985; 1989; 1991). The ironing-out of time and difference was undertaken with deliberation and skill by lawyers whose intention it was to depict the law as immutable, and at the same time to obscure the principles of the law so as to enhance their professional powers. In this respect, Irish law perpetuated a stylistic feature of Druidic learning, namely the construction of an impenetrable body of sectarian knowledge. Caesar's account of the Gaulish Druids could well describe those of Ireland:

'The Druids believe that their religion forbids them to commit their teachings to writing, although for most other purposes, such as public and private accounts, the Gauls use the Greek alphabet. But I imagine that this rule was originally established for other reasons — because they did not want their doctrine to become public property...' (Handford 1951: 32).

The lawyers, then, make it hard for us to judge where they had tampered with tradition; 'before' and 'after' contrasts are very difficult to establish. However, some sense of the probable relationship between the tracts and social 'actualities' may be derived from aspects of the situation that pertained in sixteenth-century Ireland. Social practices that are referred to in the canonical texts of the law-tracts are attested in English descriptions as flourishing at the end of Gaelic society — a fact underscored by the continuation of work on Irish legal MSS, even as war raged around the scribes in the 1560s and 1570s (Patterson 1991). These long-lasting native institutions included: distraint, competitive succession, polygynous marriage and temporary marriage, affiliation of children of concubines, collective kin-liability, payment of wergeld instead of capital punishment, clientship contracts, including a type of free clientship, and payments of renders in kind and in services (Nicholls 1972: 3-87).

Behind these customs lay a social landscape of lords, 'horsemen', 'foot-kerne' (retainers), and cattle-raids, an economy still scarcely monetarized, and a landscape still heavily wooded (Jäger 1983). Clan structures, too, persisted long enough for the lineage chief, *cenn fine*, to be recorded as 'canfinny' in English sources. For example, in the sixteenth-century Ó Doyne (*Ó Duinn*) manuscript, which documents the internal relationships of members of the ruling lineage of Iregan (Co. Leix), heads of minor Ó Doyne families bore the title of canfinny. They were responsible for forwarding rents and services to 'The Ó Doyne' (O'Hanlon and O'Leary, vol. 1 [1907]: 775). These sub-chieftains in the Ó Doyne clan structure received the Irish equivalent of 'heriot' (death-duties) from their own junior kin, while their own heriot went to the Ó Doyne. There was at least one *ceannfine* in each quarter-land. It was complained of the ruling branch of the clan that the current chieftain usurped the heriots due to these sub-chiefs from their own dependents (Nicholls [1983]: 67.24).

This complaint points to what was the main drift of social change; the enlargement of the powers of the high aristocracy, and their interest in seizing tangible assets in an economic situation where wealth could readily be translated into political power by hiring mercenaries, and where the importance of the loyalty of dependents was accordingly diminished. But changes that had gradually occurred in Irish society since the Viking age, and which the law tracts could not assimilate, they simply ignored or accommodated by stretching old law to meet new conditions. It is noticeable, for example, that they offer little information on land-holding and transfer. This is an area in which the power of the lords had probably advanced greatly since the early medieval period (Nicholls 1978: 4-5; 1983: xii). Noticeable, too, is that they treat legal issues within the framework of the *tuath*, though the boundaries of these units had long ceased to contain political structures. (Scott argues, however, that the brehons's fixation upon the minimal polity as the unit of legal relations makes sense in that hegemony over several of these was a very unstable phenomenon [1970-73: 202]; this is a view I share.) It is probable, then, that in some areas, clans, though still corporate in respect to legal protection (*sláinte*), were quite different structures from the old, multi-functional groups in which men were tied to each other through propinquity and shares in the common heritage. In general, a far more polarized class structure must be envisaged during the later middle ages, and also, as Katharine Simms has argued, an even more violent, war-driven, upper class.

Not surprisingly, then, elements of continuity and change jostle side by side in all the sources of evidence for the social history of Gaelic Ireland. In this situation there are two dangers facing the scholar who approaches the law-tracts; one is to take everything literally as a straight-faced empirical description, the other is to react against literalism by denying that the law-tracts depict anything real at all — and then to select some bits of the data as credible and deny others as 'impossible'. These sources, however, do depict — albeit shorn of historically verifiable details — basic aspects of a structure of social relations, many of whose principle institutions survived with modifications from the eighth to the sixteenth centuries. They permit, therefore, the assembly of a model — a critical interpretation of the jurists' own model, in the light of a general understanding of principles of social relations. To uncover the pattern one would ideally survey the *corpus iuris* as a whole. This, of course, I have not done, but I have interpreted data from several of the major texts in relation to each other. While most of the materials used in this book may be regarded as depicting a state of affairs that pertained in pre-Norman Ireland, I have not hesitated to draw on late, even very late evidence, that derives from aspects of culture that had some extremely conservative aspects to them. Historical-geographical studies based on early modern data, for example, reveal aspects of the rural social landscape that were continuous with the early medieval, and indeed the late prehistoric, terrain. Superb studies of folk-culture by Máire Mac Néill, Kevin Danaher, and Estyn Evans, also offer information on rural practices, some of which may reasonably be viewed as both indigenous and very old. I could not, however, offer a theoretical defense of every single reference as chronologically appropriate; it will be up to the reader to decide where I have in this respect overstepped the boundaries of common sense and historical sensitivity.

Notes

1. Warner (1976). Earlier writers were skeptical of the authenticity of Ptolemy: see O'Rahilly 1946: 1-42; Pokorny 1954: 94-120. The modern consensus rejects the arguments put forward by these scholars. See Mallory 1984: 65.

2. The major discussions of the Prologue are found in Binchy 1975-6 a; Ó Corráin *et al.* 1984; Kim McCone 1986b; Carey 1990.

3. *IT E SAERNEMEAD .... FILEAD AND .... ECALSI .... FLATHA .... FILIDH
.... FEINE.* The interspersed glosses interpret the references to lords (*flatha*) and
commoners (*féni*) as subdivisions of the poets (*filid*) (*CIH* 1593.4-6), but
obviously one must view the text either as meaning that only poets and priests
were *nemed*, or that the landowning warrior clans were included, both lords and
commoners. Mac Néill took the latter position (1923: 273 #6). Another text of
UB, in T.C.D., MS H.3.18 (*CIH* 634 ff.), is decisive in listing '*flaith*' and '*féni*'
amongst the privileged, but the glossator was uneasy about the inclusion of the
latter and tried to explain the existence of privileged *féni* as restricted to
commoners with high-status on account of their offices as stewards of
hospitality for the *tuath* or the king's household, the 'brewy' (*brugaid* = Old
Irish *briugu*) and the king's steward (*rígrechtaire*). (*CIH* 636.30-2).

4. Cramp has identified defended or enclosed late iron-age sites where a high
level of superior craftwork took place, as distinct 'craftsmen's sites' (1986: 185-
201). M. Ryan has objected that the fact of enclosure is ambiguous as to the
relationship between craftsmen and society, since ringforts and crannogs were
not distinctively 'royal' sites (1988: 37-8). Further discussion of data pertaining
to this topic will undoubtedly be profitable.

5. The text is printed in J. Fraser *et al.* 1931 i: 19-21. Discussion is found in
O'Buachalla 1952: 81-6; Byrne 1973: 197-8; Binchy 1976: 21-31: Gerriets
1987: 40-52.

6. Withes are flexible twigs. They had strong supernatural associations in early
Irish culture. See Binchy 1973b: 82 # 3.

7. The opening lines of the tract describe Caratnia as being of Dál Cuinn (*CIH*
2192 ff), i.e., the north, but as evidence of provenance this attribution is
ambiguous, since Caratnia, though wise, was politically inept: he was a bad
judge in public situations and had had to take refuge from his angry people at
Tara.

8. Like all propagandists, the author seems to have taken a basic truth,
enshrined it in a good story (apparently of Biblical origin) and then drawn a
message from the new legend. See Ó Corráin 1985.

9. For secondary literature on this tract see Ní Dhonnchadha 1982: 2.

10. *7 feni temrach. (CIH* 356.15).

11. A seat of the Eóganacht kings of Munster, near Limerick.

12. See Ó Coileáin (1989); the view that there is a satirical overtone to this passage, however, is my own.

13. See Binchy's notes in *CG* to *díre* (p. 84), *enech* (pp 84-5), and *eraic* (pp 86-7).

14. *IS AND ROAIRLED DIRE CAICH FO MIAD AS ROBUI IN BITH I CUTRUMA CONID TAINIC SENCHAS MAR. (CIH 348.10-1 = AL i 43).*

15. *CAIR CAN FORBEIR COIMAITHCHES. A ILCOMARBUS... (CIH 64.18 = AL iv 69.22 ff).*

16. *IMDINGAIB NAIDM NAESAIB (CIH 64.29 = AL iv 71.7)*

17. Ó Cathasaigh (1986: 128 n.2), points out that Carney gives the earlier date, but Binchy believed 900 to have been the earliest date of composition.

18. *Poems of Bláthmac*: 16 #47; 36 #103. See the comments of Ó Cathasaigh 1986: 128-33, and Kelly 1988: 127 n.17.

CHAPTER THREE

The Material Context of Social Relations

Whatever the regional differences in the political economy of ancient Ireland, by the time the laws were synthesized early Irish society was generally supported by a mixed-farming system in which livestock production predominated. The integration of the two sectors of agricultural production, tillage and livestock farming, is a key to understanding the political nexus between lords and clients, and will therefore be examined in detail in this chapter, against the background of the society's general economic interests.

The economy seems in some ways to have been backward compared with Romanized northern Europe, though crafts, such as fine metal-working and manuscript illumination, were practiced at a high level of sophistication during the classical Old Irish period, and woodwork, though poorly attested, is also thought to have been a well-developed skill (Laing 1975: 260-66; 339-73; Earwood 1989/90). The great age of gold-production, however, was long over by the early middle ages, and Ireland, like the rest of Europe, had little gold. Iron production, on the other hand, seems to have occurred on nearly all excavated occupation sites (Edwards 1990: 86), probably in conjunction with such rough metalwork as horse-shoeing, which was a farmer's skill elsewhere, as in the Viking Shetlands.[1] Silver was readily available, though whether from native or external sources is uncertain (M. Ryan 1981: 45-8; Mallory 1986: 31 ff).

There is only slight evidence of overseas trade during the early middle ages, mainly the export of textiles and leather goods, and the importation of wine (Doherty 1980: 76-9; C. Thomas 1976: 245-55). Such trade is unlikely to have stimulated the economy in a general way, for it was probably under royal control. Gallic wine merchants are known to have visited some early medieval royal sites, while the Old Irish text on kingship, *Audacht Morainn*, refers to maritime trade as one of the benefits that a good ruler brought to his people (Doherty 1980: 76-9; R. Warner 1988: 61-5). Political protection was essential to trade in early Ireland, for mechanisms of social control normally operated only between members of localized economic and political units. There is evidence of some legal development to accommodate foreigners: Old Irish sources mention that kings made *cána* (the supra-local regulations mentioned in the last chapter) which governed the legal standing of visitors from over the territorial boundary (Doherty 1980:79). The Introduction to the *Senchas Már* also asserts the legal entitlement of foreigners to choose a jurist from outside the local area for arbitration.[2]

The small surplus generated by domestic production was diverted to members of the nobility, who used it to support their households and retainers, reward craftsmen and the *literati*, and entertain their own overlords and allies. The agrarian taxes levied on the farming population were consumed directly, principally at feasts. Market exchange was undeveloped, for although there were opportunities for economic exchange at the local level at seasonal 'tribal' gatherings (*óenach*), trade was hampered by the absence of such commercial institutions as money and urban market centers (*ibid*: 82-5). As a result, access to specialized manufactured goods was largely restricted to the upper stratum of society, which entertained and protected craftsmen (Gibson 1988: 54). Under these circumstances, farm and domestic craft production had to be adequate for subsistence, if not at the household level, at least within a rather small local community. *CG* depicts all the ranks of the farmers as maintaining balanced and diversified resources, symbolized by equal numbers of cattle, sheep and pigs on the farmer's land, with the actual amount depending on the rank of the farmer and the size of his land-holding. Farmers are also depicted as sharing in the collective ownership of the major agrarian fixtures — plows, mills, and kilns.

Farmers were not entirely self-sufficient, however. Although the undeveloped economy of early medieval Ireland offered only limited possibilities for the economic subordination of social classes, a system of social stratification based on cattle-loans and clientship emerged. This remained for many centuries the nexus between lords and dependents, forming the backbone of relationships within and between clans. Even if, as I have argued, a historically specific social development catalyzed the emergence of clans and cattle-clientship as a complex of political relations, the persistence and formal elaboration of this pattern of social domination can only be understood against an enduring background of ecological and infrastructural constraints; these will now be described.

The natural environment and farming practice

Despite the generally low elevations of land in Ireland, the island is considered to fall within a distinct ecological zone, often termed the highland or pluvial zone of Britain, on account of the high rate of precipitation which characterizes the whole area (Fox 1932; J. Evans 1975:147-50; Megaw & Simpson 1988: 20-22.)[3] The environment presented very similar conditions to early farmers in Ireland, Scotland, Wales, and Cornwall, the areas in which the languages of prehistoric Britain survived longest. Abundant rainfall, extensive areas of rough hilly country, poor drainage which tends towards the center of the island, and strong Atlantic winds, all worked to produce in Ireland a landscape of heavy forest, natural grassland in some coastal areas, and (partly as a result of cultivation), extensive interior bog-lands. The biggest areas of cultivable land were scattered around the perimeter of the island, and along the better drained river valleys, with the greatest concentrations of good soils being found east of the Shannon.

This verdant landscape was deceptively promising. In his *Topographia Hiberniae* (1185-8 A.D.), the Norman-Welsh cleric, Giraldus Cambrensis, wrote:

> The island is, however, richer in pastures than crops, and in grass than in grain. The crops give great promise in the blade, even more in the straw, but less in the ear. For here the grains of wheat are shrivelled and small, and can scarcely be separated from the chaff by any winnowing fan. The plains are well-clothed with grass, and the haggards are bursting with straw. Only the granaries are without their wealth. What is born and comes forth in the spring and is nourished in the summer and advanced, can scarcely be reaped in the harvest because of unceasing rain. (O'Meara 1982: 34).

Irish tradition itself associates strong rain-storms and flooding with Lugnasad, the festival which opened the harvest season in early August (M. Macneill 1982: 61-2). But while wheat cultivation tended to languish, stock production was stimulated by the virtually perennial growth of forest browse and natural grass (Caulfield 1983: 202). The typically wet and cool weather which governed this floral pattern set in during the first half of the first millennium B.C.; from this time, then,

Map 2. Aricultural potential: lighter shading indicates greater capacity. (after The Irish Committee for Geography 1979)

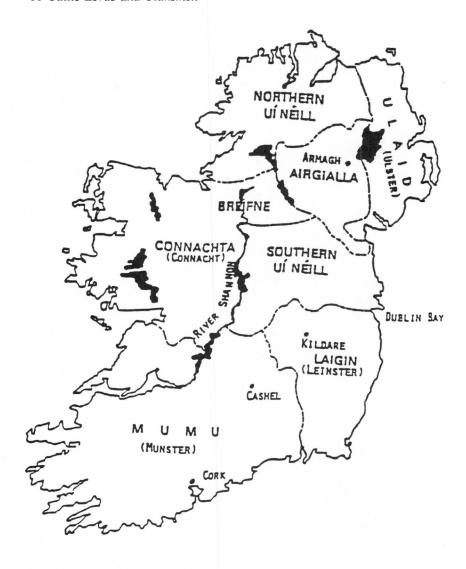

Ireland in the ninth century: major political divisions, and locations mentioned in the text.

the natural constraints upon the balance of the tillage and pastoral sectors of farming were in place and remained relatively constant, though periodic episodes of warmer and drier weather occurred (Barker 1985: 211-18). Within this framework local agricultural variations may have been quite marked: fishing was important in the numerous coastal, riverine and lacustrine communities (O'Loan 1965: 152-3), while crop production was greater in areas such as the lower Bann valley in Ulster, the Golden Vale of North Munster, the hinterlands of Wexford and Waterford, and the Eastern Triangle (extending inward from the Dublin Bay area). In the stony northern Drumlin belt and the wetlands of the interior, however, bovine stock must have completely outweighed any other element of farming.

Taking Ireland as a whole, the diet included oats, barley, wheat and rye (in that order of importance), prepared as bread, porridge and alcohol; dairy produce from the cow and sheep, prepared as cheese, butter, curds or liquid; meat products from cattle, pigs, sheep and wild game; fish, shellfish and seaweed; vegetables, especially watercress, garlic and leeks; fruit, nuts and berries (Lucas 1960-2). As the middle ages advanced, peas and beans were added to the diet (Monk 1985-6: 31-6). Some commonplace modern vegetables, though available in the early middle ages, seem to have been rare; carrots, for example, are said to make 'a queen's mash' in the twelfth-century gastronomic satire, *Aislinge Meic Conglinne* (Meyer 1892: 98 1.21). In addition to native brews, imported wine was also consumed by the wealthier members of the nobility and monasteries (C. Thomas 1976: 245-5). As elsewhere in medieval western Europe, honey and bees-wax were valued; hence the survival and extensive glossing of the Old Irish law-tract on 'bee-judgments', *Bechbretha*. Goats' milk was much used in Viking Dublin (Bradley 1988: 52), and was accorded medicinal value in more recent peasant communities (Lucas 1960-2: 29), but goats were not prominent in the early medieval Irish economy (McCormick 1983: 260).

Of the domesticates, the generic dog was present from the beginning. Special breeds, however, can only be detected from c. 500 A.D. Their emergence is connected with the greater sophistication of farming at this time and with direct contact with the Roman world. Aristocratic women were associated with lap-dogs, which may have served as living hot water bottles to relieve abdominal cramps. Legend had it that the first lap-dog in Ireland was stolen from Britain, then a Roman province. Another special breed were killer-dogs, which according to Symmachus, were exported to Rome for use in the games (McCormick 1991: 7-9). Two other mainstays of the later peasant farmyard, domesticated fowl and cats may also have arrived in Ireland only during the later Roman period (Van Wijngaarden-Bakker 1974: 348; Proudfoot 1961: 111). Recent archaeological data shows that *felix felix* was large, well cared for, and probably bred to specifications, one of which would have been good fur, for the cat may have been raised to harvest its pelt as much as for its mousing abilities (McCormick 1988). Chicken and eggs are not listed amongst the early medieval renders, nor in the basic text of *Cáin Lánamna*, the tract on marriage and divorce (dated to the eight century). They were sufficiently rare that in the early medieval 'Irish Canons', twelve hens were equated with one female slave and one fowl with just under one Anglo-Saxon *siculus*, or two silver pennies (Bieler 1975: 160 I.9).

In addition to producing foodstuffs, Irish farming families grew and prepared flax to make linen, gathered wool and manufactured woollen cloth and several dyes and colorants for fabric and leather, prepared leather and other meat by-products such as tallow for candles, and made a variety of implements and building materials from wood, reeds and grass. They also slaughtered their own stock and preserved the meat. These activities were carried out with very limited sources of energy, including a small human labor-force. Oxen and horses were available for traction, but a rudimentary road system made long-distance haulage uneconomical. Most wasteful of human energy, however, was the use of female labor to grind grain by hand. Mills spread only very slowly between the fifth and tenth centuries in northern Europe (Dockès 1982: 167-8) and archaeology does not suggest that Ireland was an exception to this trend. Despite the prominence of the Old Irish law text on water-mills,[4] only a few are known to date from the early middle ages, and the earliest of these is dated to c. 630 A.D. (Edwards 1990: 64). Thus, while the productive activities of the working population were varied and complex, the low level of division of labor and investment in infrastructure resulted in a style of life that was both simple and vulnerable to environmental upsets.

Like other non-market farmers living close to the margins of survival (Barker 1985: 257-8), Irish farmers were technologically conservative; improvements that were adopted in other medieval European areas diffused only slowly in Ireland — indeed a large number of 'iron-age' implements, such as the scythe, entered Ireland only during the late Roman period (Laing 1985: Mytum 1992). Elements of very primitive agricultural techniques, which yielded low returns to the worker's own manual efforts but demanded little capital investment, remained quite common until a relatively recent period, alongside more advanced methods, operated in richer communities. Some examples are; hand-cultivation by spade or hoe on cultivation ridges (E. Evans 1939: 36), hand-grinding of grain by means of the stone quern (Proudfoot 1961: 106, Table I), burning grain from the standing crop in the field, instead of reaping (Butlin 1976: 152), and winter grazing of stock instead of harvesting hay for stall fodder (O'Meara 1982: 53). Horses went unsaddled and consequently military horsemen did without stirrups, usually dismounting to engage in combat (Kavanagh 1988: 93; Simms 1975/6: 105-6). Surveying the archaeological evidence as to the technology of farm-production, Harbison concludes: 'In many respects, the basic style of life in prehistoric Ireland was not too far different from the folk-life we know to have survived down to the last century and even into this' (1988: 195).

This is not to say, of course, that there had been no big changes in Irish farming and society during earlier prehistoric phases. Climatic deterioration alone would indicate strong pressures to change, at least by the mid first millennium B.C. (Champion *et al* 1984: 322). Signs of contrast between the Bronze Age and later Iron Age economies include discontinuity in the making of burnt mounds and associated pits, and discontinuity in the use of hillforts. Burnt mounds consist of heaps of cracked and discarded stones that had been used to heat water diverted into large excavated pits. These sites were long thought to be of late Iron Age or early medieval provenance, but were, in fact, Bronze age structures used by settled communities for many purposes including (possibly) the washing of animals and of cloth. Though popularly known as *fulachta fíadh* ('the cooking places of deer') and associated with the *fían*, the hunter-warriors of medieval legend, few were used and none actually built during the Iron Age. Their builders are thought to have been 'a thriving and possibly large population living in enclosed and unenclosed settlements of round-houses .... practicing unknown rituals within their stone circles' (Brindley *et al* 1989/90: 32). Many of their settlements were on open terraces beneath large hilltop enclosures, which were themselves often clustered together in groups (Condit 1992). The functions of these 'hillforts', even where they are impressive, may not have been mainly military (Rinne 1992). This way of life obviously differed from that which prevailed during the period covered in this book, when the main field monument was the ringfort (see Ch. 4).

We should, then, while giving due note to the technological simplicity of early medieval Irish farming, be careful not to underestimate the advances made in agriculture during the late Iron Age in Ireland. The shift to integrated mixed farming in the later Iron Age, with its characteristic resort to heavy plowing, preserved fields of winter grass for stock, and garden patches near settlements, implies 'substantial yet invisible investment' in new techniques, even though new artefacts of the period may not have survived in large numbers (Jones 1991: 87). Such technical investment involved, at least on the rich clay soils, more intensive use of animal power in larger ox-teams for the heavy plow; more intensive use of fertilizers to create deeper soils; and more intensive use of human and animal power to weed and drain the richer soils.

Moreover, those ancient techniques that persisted through the Iron Age were retained not out of mere inertia but because they were highly cost-effective in terms of labor input: some, such as the skin-covered boat (the coracle), could scarcely be improved upon in terms of their suitability to local conditions (Johnstone 1980: 127-32). Peasant housing was likewise flimsy and rapidly constructed, but had a sturdiness difficult to appreciate without experimental reproduction; at Butser Hill, for example, wattle and daub houses have been shown to last up to six years without repair (Reynolds 1979: 47). Indeed, more importance was attached to the warmth and impermeability of woollen cloaks, which were of such quality that they constituted one of the standard items included in lists of tribute in documents ranging from the eleventh to the sixteenth centuries (Dillon 1962: 679-681; 730-3). Simple housing may have been preferred because dispersed land-holdings and seasonal transhumance (see Ch. 4) did not foster attachment on the part of the farmer to the house-spot. In later medieval Tipperary, settlement sites were sometimes moved to permit cultivation of the manure-enriched soils around the byres and milking yards (Leister 1976: 13-4). (It has also been shown that medieval Danish farms were moved periodically within the neighborhood, so as to better exploit the area's resources.[5]) The most permanent fixtures on the landscape were the ringforts, but these only show that there was a need for solid enclosures, not that fixed and permanent residence was the norm (see Ch. 4). Their embankments were in fact one of the few labor-intensive investments for which physical evidence survives from early medieval Ireland; so serious were their relative labor costs that clients, even high-status ones, were obliged to help raise them for their lords (see Ch. 6).

Low levels of investment in agricultural production persisted in many parts of Ireland until the end of Gaelic independence in the late sixteenth century, providing continuity in material culture which helps to explain the endurance of basic institutional forms throughout the middle ages. In sixteenth-century western Ulster, for example, there were no water-powered mills, and grain was still ground by hand; there were no tanneries, iron-works or tucking mills for cloth, and production seems to have been geared entirely towards local consumption (Robinson 1976: 68). It is sometimes argued that continuous warfare depressed economic growth during the late medieval and early modern period, but it must also be acknowledged that clan society was geared towards warfare from the early middle ages, and that the lands seized by the Normans in the twelfth century were, from their point of view, quite undeveloped (Lydon 1973: 3-21).

The economy offered little buffer against agricultural deficits, the direct consequence of which was likely to be hunger, increased morbidity and depressed fertility. The human labor force was apparently too small to facilitate significant in-take of wild land for cultivation, with the result that large swathes of Ireland remained thickly forested until the Tudor period (Jäger 1983: 56-63). A homeostatic pattern of production and reproduction may be envisaged, for the pastoral economy neither required an increase of labor, nor offered the basis for increased food-production, while the political economy of pastoralism, with its endemic cattle-raiding and clan warfare, discouraged clearance of the protective forest cover. The large-scale slaving of the fourth and fifth centuries, and the later Viking period (Morris 1973: 159-63; Holm 1986) suggest that the early Irish élite wanted access to more labor than their productive system permitted through normal reproduction, but that the value of this labor was not sufficiently salient to political power to stimulate the élite to make efforts towards agricultural growth through forest-clearance, drainage, and intensified demesne farming. It has been widely believed, nevertheless, that early Christian Ireland was the scene of socially significant population growth, on a scale sufficient to have caused plagues, changed the class structure, and brought about the collapse of the prehistoric kinship system. Since I maintain that political factors stimulated the emergence of the clan system, as analyzed in this book, and that no such historically decisive population increase actually occurred during this period, I have surveyed the relevant evidence and arguments separately (see Appendix I). With this background of static and low-energy production in mind, we may now examine the two sectors of agricultural production, and their interdependence.

Mixed-farming in early Ireland

Cattle: The Old Irish law tracts on status show that the farmer kept a mixture of animals — cows, bulls and oxen, pigs and boars, sheep and horses. According to *CG*, his herd should be balanced, so that for each cow there should be one sheep and one pig, which may be the compiler's way of describing — or advocating — general balance in the livestock of the farm. The rank of *ócaire* in *CG*, for example, was supposed to own seven cows, seven sheep and seven pigs, while the next rank up had ten of the same. This ideal balance is to be found also in Scandinavian sources; the ninth-century Norse chieftain Ottar, who was wealthy in tribute from clients, kept only a small livestock complement for farming, namely 'twenty cattle, twenty sheep, and twenty pigs'.[6] Since these animals did not have the same worth (one cow far outweighing one pig or sheep), the rule of balance in *CG* actually amounts to no more than a prescription that a farmer should invest more in his cattle than in small stock, but keep some of the latter to balance his resources for domestic consumption.

   Within this mixed stock there was a definite prestige-hierarchy — an 'animal farm' that reflected the social significance of the different types of beasts. So persistent were Irish farmers' attitudes that, regardless of major social upheavals, the prestige-hierarchy on the farms of Donegal in this century corresponded, roughly speaking, to that which prevailed in early medieval Ireland: 'Pigs...are regarded with disfavor...Goats are rarely kept...The donkey is in fact regarded with suspicion and contempt, and the possession of one lessens the chances of marriage for the daughters of its owner...On the other hand, the horse is held in high regard, and ownership carries prestige, so that a horse is sometimes kept even if it does little or no work...The cow is universally kept and carefully treated, and was housed in the kitchen-byre a generation ago. Hens are important. Sheep contribute to the family income..' (but got no prestige on that account). (E. Evans 1939: 32-3).

   Attitudes towards most of these animals had deep roots in native culture, as this legal proverb shows:

> 'The hound is more beastly than the pig, the pig more
> beastly than the cow.'[7]

The pig and dog in fact shared a quality of magical impurity in relation to agriculture that was opposed by the converse, ritually purifying, quality of the cow. If a pig rooted up the earth of a field with its feet and snout, the hole was to be filled with corn or butter.[8] If a dog defecated on someone's land, its owner was obliged to dress the 'wound' to the earth, by cleaning the contaminated area, covering it with a clod of earth and with cow-manure for a month[9]; in addition he or she had to give the owner lumps of butter, dough and curds, each the size of the offending feces.[10] The curative power of milk is also manifest in the poultice of smooth clay, cow dung and new milk recommended as dressing for a valuable tree (literally, a 'chieftain tree', such as ash, oak and holly), when someone had barked it to tan leather.[11] The taboos on pigs and dogs seem intended to reinforce the norms of farm practice — plowing with ox-traction and manuring with cow-manure — for pigs tear up the soil like a plow and have sometimes been substituted for the plow (in Hungary), while dog manure might similarly tempt the farmer to substitute another animal for the cow.

The cow was undoubtedly the most ubiquitous animal in early Irish farming, its bones constituting over 70% of the animal remains at the majority of major excavated settlement sites, and in some cases, as at Cahercommaun in Co. Clare, constituting virtually all such remains (Proudfoot 1961: 109-10). Next to the riding horse, the cow was also the most prized animal, on average worth between six to eight sheep. The high status of bovine stock is reflected in the use of cows as units of value in social transactions, especially to pay honor-price to compensate for damage to someone's status, or to effect a legal change of status, such as marriage. Of course, though cows served as a standard unit of value, they were too big to serve as 'money' in direct economic exchange, however. This was effected by barter, or less commonly by payment in silver. A common equivalence was one milch cow (*lulgach* or *bó mlicht*), with her calf = 24 'scruples' (*screpall*) = 1 ounce (*unga*) of silver. (The *scripul* was the Latin *scripulus*.) Sometimes 3 cows or 3 ounces of silver = 1 *cumal* (originally a female slave). Another unit was the *sét* (chattel), which was typically equated with 'half a cow' (a virgin heifer); 6-8 *séoit* thus gave 1 *cumal*. But another type of *cumal* existed which was equated with 20 *séoit*, or about 7 cows (Kelly 1988:

112-6). Female slaves seem to have ceased to function as exchangeables during the period when the law texts were written, and silver too seems to have been in limited circulation as currency until the Viking period. After this, however, there was ample opportunity for both silver and slaves to circulate again. Cattle remained, however, the most common unit of value in Ireland until the late middle ages.

The cultural elaboration of bovine worth was triggered by the role of cattle-loans in relations of political dependence. In other words, cattle-as-money in the Irish context is not to be thought of as comparable to Trobriand kula tokens or other pre-monetary standard exchangeables which lacked instrumental productive significance. Had early Irish farmers been able to extricate themselves from cattle-loans (becoming shepherds instead, for example), they would have ceased to use cattle, as they ceased to use slave-women, as the unit in which the claims of honor and duty were satisfied, adopting instead some other more convenient moveable item as the standard unit of exchange, such as the bolts of cloth (*wadmal*) widely used in early Scandinavian trade. The political manipulation of cattle-loans enhanced the social importance of the cow, but was only possible because this beast, of all the domesticates, was pivotal in primitive mixed farming. It is well established that pastoralists are in some measure always dependant upon cultivators, but in mixed-farming that has advanced beyond slash-and-burn clearance and hoe cultivation, a like dependence exists between the cultivator and the pastoral sector. The need here is for productive inputs — manure and traction. It is perhaps insufficiently realized how interlocked these activities were in iron-age and medieval northern Europe, and how distinctive and defining of the culture of this area was the social integration of tillage and pastoralism. In none of the other major zones of human occupation was pre-modern cultivation entirely dependant for sustaining an established standard of living upon the successful supply of animal resources to the arable producer, in terms of manure and traction, and from the latter back to the pastoral sector, in terms of pasture withheld from cultivation and the grass preserved for animals who were wintered at the farmsteads.

Of these animal inputs the most critical was manure. In primitive communities where the landscape was still open to human settlement, the easiest method of clearing surface vegetation was simply to burn it, then break up the sod and roots with some implement — in ancient Europe a stone axe was the main tool (O'Loan 1964: 246). This method obviated the need for artificial soil enrichment, as the ash produced nitrogen and phosphates, while uprooting the burned plants turned the ash into the ground. Burning was employed in Ireland until recently amongst upland farmers practicing infield/outfield cultivation, but only on the patches of inferior land used as 'outfield'. Where more intensive cultivation was undertaken, however, ways had to be found to better enrich the mineral content of the soil.

Before the discovery of the benefits of crop-alternation, farmers throughout northern Europe depended on minerals derived from other sources. Seaweed was an important source of fertilizer in Ireland, for the coast was a major zone of human occupation, being indented and therefore extensive. Fertilization with sand and shells is also described (E. Evans 1957: 218-32; Lucas: 1969). In the mountainous region of Mourne in the early part of this century seaweed was so important that some inland townlands had rights to a proportion of the wrack harvest. The value of land increased according to closeness to the shore, for example by 25% if within a mile. Wrack served also as winter fuel and fodder (E. Evans 1940: 172-80). The rights of inland townlands mentioned by Evans must have persisted from earlier forms of community cooperation as described in the law tracts, for Mourne was not an area that had been subjected to plantation and agrarian upheaval. Kelly points out that the Old Irish law text on land values states that land which gave access to a 'productive rock' — bearing seaweed and shellfish — was valued at three cows over and above its basic worth.[12] Generally, however, access to shore was not privatized, though harvested heaps of kelp and adjacent pastures were. These details indicate how sketchy any reconstruction of the material life of early medieval Irish communities must remain, for there is only passing reference in the early sources to the exploitation of the sea shore.

Lime was also used as fertilizer, but like seashore resources, was uneconomical to transport far from its source (Clancy & Ford 1980: 119-20). Obviously, the most available fertilizer was animal dung. Therefore, during the period after the crops had been saved and the animals were back near the community, they were housed as close to the fields as possible. As these were located around the settlements, the animals were generally brought within the enclosures for the night (Lucas 1989: 25-33), this being the time when ruminants drop most of their manure. Within the enclosure it was possible for farmers to ensure that cattle manure fell on straw, (which was necessary to absorb its moisture) and received an admixture of ash, a supplement necessitated by the paucity of nutrients in cattle manure (Mercer 1981: 211). (Sheep manure seems not have been favored in Ireland, and sheep were not generally brought into enclosures during the winter. Probably for this reason, early Irish sheep dogs were wolf-hounds [Lucas 1989: 22-3], though not as large as the classic wolf-hound [McCormick 1991: 9]). Manure was thus readily available during the period between the harvest and spring plowing, the time when the vitality of the soil had to be restored.

Dependence on manure meant that the more a community sought to cultivate, or the poorer the soil it had at its disposal, the more animals it would have to maintain nearby. For a society biased towards pastoralism, this requirement posed no systemic problem, but it must nevertheless have placed a limitation on the geographical extension of cultivation by local communities. Self-sufficiency as regards manure would have obligated a community to keep as many as three cows per acre of wheat.[13] Winter manuring, however, depended on cows' consumption of the sparse vegetation of that season, implying a fairly extensive grazing ground per animal. These grounds had to be traversable between dawn and dusk, so that the cattle could be folded at night for protection and dung collection; early Irish custom regarded the cow's pasture as having a radius of a mile (*BB*: 101). Attempts to increase tillage could only have been accommodated by acquisition of manure from outside; this was an incident of the clientship contract (though how organized is not clear), so that groups headed by higher-status individuals were probably able to sustain larger arable sectors within their demesne farmlands. Most communities, however, appear to have been small and scattered, indicating that farmers opted for extensive land use which allowed the soil to rest without frequent manuring (see the discussion of field systems, below). Growth and an increase in demand for tillage would then have led to fission and new settlement, producing the kind of even spread of small settlements found on the historical landscape.

The other role of cattle in cultivation was to supply traction. Plowing was not the only method of opening the earth, for the farmer also had recourse to cultivation by spade (O'Loan 1964: 245-58). 'Ridge cultivation', a method whereby the soil is heaped up in ridges and the seed planted on the crest, had a number of advantages; the crop was virtually weed-free and therefore easier to harvest with the sickle; it was suitable to heavy wet soils as well as lighter ones; and it was cheap. Nevertheless, the productivity of a group of men or women using the plow, especially the heavy plow drawn by a team of several beasts, far exceeded that of a group of diggers. Thus, where plow-beasts could be obtained, and higher levels of production were required of the farmer, animal traction for the plow was necessary. This was nearly always provided by oxen because of the limitations of early harnessing techniques. Until the latter part of the first millennium, when modifications in harnessing were introduced from the orient, the horse was half-strangled by the attachment of the yoke around its throat — a problem that did not arise with the ox because the yoke could be attached to its horns or on a bony hump on the back of its neck (Langdon 1986: 4-21). Cows were not much used for this purpose, because they might abort the calf and lose their milk. In the Welsh laws it was well recognized that damage would result if any beast but the ox were used:

> Neither horses nor mares nor a cow ought to be placed in a plow, and if they are so placed, though mares or cattle should miscarry, there is no compensation. (Owen 1841: I, 320).

The size of the early Irish ox-team varied. *CG* assumes the presence of teams of four and six oxen, since the low-ranking farmer, the *ócaire*, was supposed to maintain one ox, and a quarter share of a plow (*CG* 95), while the higher-status *mruigfher* maintained a whole plow and six oxen (*CG* 194-5, 181-2). Lucas cites several examples from non-legal sources that imply teams of two, six or eight animals (1972: 53-5). But whatever the size of the team, the requirement that individuals of the farming strata maintain oxen in order to qualify for the privileges of their rank in society put pressures on the farmers' management of the pastoral sector of farm production, pressures that are examined below.

In addition to contributing to cultivation, cattle constituted a 'walking larder' of milk, blood, veal and eventually beef (Clutton-Brock 1989), so that when crops failed or enemies burned the fields, the more powerful members of society, at least, had a mobile subsistence-base that could be driven off into the wilderness, there to be enjoyed in peace until nature or society seemed benign again. Cattle had another advantage: they were fairly easy to herd and, as long as the calf was nearby, easy to milk. The cow was safe in most environments in Ireland and thus imposed none of the irksome demands of the pig or sheep (see below) for regular custodial care in remote and dangerous places. Its only real imposition upon the life of the farming population concerned adjustments to the seasons, reflected in the practice of transhumance (Further discussion of seasonal transhumance is found in Ch. 5.)

Transhumance entailed the removal of livestock and part of the farming population for the duration of the summer, to upland or rough land at some distance from the area of cultivation. The practice was once commonplace in Europe, surviving longest in areas in or adjacent to uplands (E. Evans 1940). A description of the move, with the characteristic emphasis on light, moveable, accommodation, and the primary involvement of women and children, is given in a Life of St. Senán:

> At Magh Lacha (i.e. in Co. Clare[14]), then, at first were the dwelling and farm of Senán's parents before Senán was born. They had another farm at Trach Termainn. Now there is a long space between these two farms; so when Senán's parents desired to make a removal, Senán would go a day or two days before them to make a house and sheds and farmyard and every needment besides, which they required to be ready for them. Now Senán used to do this for love of helping everyone who needed it...Once upon a time his mother was angry with him about the matter (i.e. his helping everyone)...'verily it will arise,' saith Senán (referring to his mother's booley house, which he had neglected in his altruistic excesses). When they were saying these words, they beheld coming towards them in the air the sheds and the farmyards, the ties and all the needments which they required, and which they had left in the place from whence they came. (Stokes 1890: 204).

The main task performed at the summer dairies was the preservation of milk in the form of butter and cheese, which played an important role in meeting general food requirements (Lucas 1958: 81-2). But despite the importance of dairy produce, recent research suggests that early medieval Irish cattle-farming was an unspecialized business that attempted to supply dairy produce, meat, manure and traction from the same pool. McCormick has shown that at the three sites that provide most of the data relevant to determining kill-off patterns and production goals, the majority of slaughtered juvenile stock had been carried until their second year, showing that meat-production was an important secondary goal (McCormick 1983: 255). Rather different evidence from the remains of cattle supplied to Viking Fishamble also points to unspecialized stock-raising, with decisions regarding slaughter being perhaps made opportunistically rather than according to a policy of specialization (*ibid*: 261).

Another indication of the dual objectives of stock production comes from the description of an acceptable cow in the law-tract, *Cáin Aicillne*. It was to measure twenty fists in girth and be one third fat in composition, a ratio that indicates interest in the palatability of the meat, which is maximized at these proportions (O'Loan 1965: 171). O'Loan calculated that the measurement in *CA* shows that a good beast (not an exceptional one) in early medieval Ireland was of the same size as 'a biggish animal in any of our modern breeds'. The persistence of ancient large stock from the neolithic until the early historic period also indicates interest in beef-potential within a basic dairying pattern, for a smaller cow is a more efficient unit for the dairy farmer (Van Wijngaarden-Bakker 1974: 335-6; O'Loan 1965: 142).

Large cattle are especially associated with the royal sites at Lagore and Knowth (McCormick 1983: 264), a finding that confirms the high status of beef in the law-tracts' references to the clients' renders to their lords (Gerriets 1983: 51). Upper-class individuals' insistence on provisions of beef in their diet would have overshadowed efficiency considerations that might otherwise have impelled the ordinary farmer to kill off all young except replacement stock when the cows began to run dry in autumn. Dairy production is generally much more efficient than beef as a use for pasture; Legge estimates that the protein yield of beef cattle is only 27 kg per hectare as against 115 kg/ha for dairy cattle (1981: 89). Caulfield argues that the disparity may be less unfavorable to beef producers where cattle were bigger (1983: 200-1), but presumably dairying was still considerably more advantageous to the poorer ranks of the farmers. The demand for meat meant that the farmer restricted both his own consumption and his absolute calorie production, thus enhancing the reproduction of the upper class at the expense of his own family and social stratum, and indeed, at the expense of overall population growth. This condition, combined with upper class polygyny contributed to the tendency of upper class lineages to grow rapidly and spread downwards into the status of farming clients.

When livestock was healthy and abundant, however, the Irish farmer was better supplied with protein than many a medieval plowman; even in the desolation of the seventeenth century, Petty noted that amidst the squalor of their 'miserable cabins', Irish peasants enjoyed good food and clothing (1719: 79). English commentators in the early modern period frequently noted that milk was the ordinary person's food (Lucas 1958: 82-3). O'Loan calculates that a prime milker in early medieval Ireland yielded nine quarts at a milking (presumably in summer), which compared favorably with early twentieth-century standards (O'Loan 1965: 171), and greatly exceeded the late nineteenth-century rates for Dexters, the small cows on which prehistoric cattle farming is modelled. But although milk was the peasant's staff of life in Ireland, the small-scale farmer had little ability to secure control of his supply. This vulnerability was partly endemic to the life of a cattle-man, for disease can strike rapidly, but was also generated by those to whom the small-farmer would turn for help during a period of cattle murrain — lords who maintained large numbers of stock in scattered herds.

The small-farmer's dependence upon the large-scale cattle-keeper's resources was institutionalized in Ireland, through law, through the implicit coercive power of a lord, and through the economic pressures which the demands of lords constantly maintained upon the resources of the small farmer. By the time the law-tracts were written, there existed a class-structure in which the small-scale producer was locked into a relationship with one or more lords which generated ties of obligation and loyalty that required little coercion or managerial supervision by the aristocracy, and in which the lord's role had been mystified so that he was viewed as a gift-giver rather than an exploiter (see Ch. 6). Lords intensified the inherent vulnerability of the small-scale cattle-keeper's food supply by granting loans of cattle on terms that not only made it hard for the farmer to repay the loan, but that also threatened the farmer's herd balance. The structure of the contract is described in Ch. 6.

As to herd balance, field studies of pastoralists in undeveloped contemporary rural areas show that herds normally contain a substantial number of non-productive animals, such as un-bulled cows, from which replacements are drawn for the stock-in-use (Dahl & Hjort 1974: 73-4). Farmers have to sustain a careful balance in their total stock-holdings, for too high a proportion of these animals reduces the milk supply available to the farmer, but too few threatens long-term replacement. In Ireland, balance was most difficult for the small-scale farmer because his individual herd was very small; seven milch cows for the *ócaire*, 12 for the *bóaire*, and 20 for the *mruigfher* (*CG* 93, 157-8, 194). The demands on his pasture made by the lord's requirements of beef and grain added to this problem, for the ox and the calf raised for beef consumed the grass that could have fed reserve cows. The ox's fodder needs were especially onerous in the spring, when all the wintered stock were weak from malnourishment. So serious was this problem that after the introduction of the horse-collar, Irish farmers universally abandoned ox-traction in favor of the *afer*, 'rascally small horses' which 'shift all the year round...without housing or fodder'.[15] But for the obligations of the cattle-contract, many small-farmers would have preferred to keep more cows and revert to digging their arable lands. Such options were closed off, however, when a farmer turned to a lord for the loan of an animal, for he could not simply ask for a specific number or type of animal to meet his need, but had to bargain with the lord as to the terms of the clientship contract. The latter seems typically to have sought to impose as many cows in the contract as he could, so as to receive a higher render (see Ch. 6). Many a client would have had to trade political protection, which was one of the main social benefits of clientship to the farmer, for economic utility, taking more cows than he perhaps wanted, and being tied thereafter to servicing this debt by supplying grain and alcohol to the lord and being obliged to keep the oxen that jacked up the supply of grain.

The Irish military aristocracy, cattle-raiders *par excellence*, were obviously in a position to dominate the farming population by exploiting the sensitivity of the latter to fluctuations in their herds. Essentially the same agrarian economic situation existed in England, but English society had evolved politically so much by the twelfth century, that cattle-loans within the framework of clientship are not found. Instead, cattle were either bought from long-distance drovers coming from highland areas such as the Welsh borders, or in some areas tenants-in-chief set aside one manor in the county for herds of breeding cows intended to supply oxen to be trained for plowing. The peasants themselves maintained only the work oxen and obtained what dairy produce they consumed from sheep (Trow-Smith 1957: 68-98).

In Ireland, where arable encroachment onto pasture was far less advanced, the peasants still kept their own dairy herds, and wilderness preserves were still adequate to support the great herds (*creaghts*) of the aristocracy. These had to be large, not only because it took a lot of cattle to secure the services of a lord's requisite number of clients, but because the breeding rates of medieval cattle could not guarantee a steady increase of stock. Indeed, Hilton argues that a general theme of medieval English history was a shortage of livestock, in part because of the expansion of the arable sector, but also on account of the unpredictability of long-term herd demography (Hilton 1954: 166). An illuminating example of the problem is the stock-breeding experiment of Henry de Lacy, a Norman baron with family connections in Ireland. Henry leased out units of between 75-80 cows, along with moorland and forest parcels of land in the Lancashire hills.[16] Each herd was composed of 37-40 cows, 1 bull, 5-6 steers, 5-6 heifers, 13 yearlings, and 14-16 calves. In twenty five years the project was a complete failure and the vaccaries had been let out as normal mixed farms. Part of the reason was that only 2 of every 5 cows raised a calf in each year, either because one bull was insufficient for inseminating the number of cows, or because winter malnourishment took its toll on weaning calves.

The only real insurance against low breeding rates, periodic disease, famine, brigands, wolves and poor herding was the maintenance of very large herds, scattered in many different areas. In medieval Ireland, where the human diet depended much more heavily than in England on dairy produce, the group that could achieve this stood to dominate a large number of people over a broad region.

Swine: Other livestock complemented the herds, but were usually secondary in importance. Swine fattened easily on a versatile diet that could include household scrap, and yielded meat that is the easiest to preserve by salting or smoking. Medieval Irish food included *tinne*, bacon, and *maróc*, sausage (Lucas 1960-2: 17). In their forest habitat, swine fattened rapidly during the autumn, supplying the winter larder without competing with cattle and sheep for pasture. (Cattle like leaf fodder, but may sicken on acorns, a favorite swine food. Sheep are vulnerable to blowfly and liver-fluke attacks in damp environments and dislike woodlands [Higham 1967: 101].) Pigs were also easy to manage; or to put it more accurately, their intelligence is such that the swineherd's role was more to track them than to move them around or rescue them from danger. Left to themselves swine establish a routine pattern of movement which further permitted the swineherd to relax his vigilance. They offered relief from the anxiety of cattle care, for the large number of young born to a breeding sow during the year meant that in times of hunger, herds of pigs could be extensively culled, and still regenerate rapidly. They could also be left untended in the woods during winter (the medieval pig could fend off wolves), and gradually culled as winter advanced and food dwindled (Higham 1967: 94).

Swine could not be maintained entirely in the forest, however (Trow-Smith 1957: 53) and necessitated some social organization of their management. Grown pigs were difficult to handle in the setting of a village or hamlet, being potentially aggressive towards people and devastating to crops, which they ate, and to seeded arable, which they churned up with their snouts and feet (Reynolds 1979: 53). Piglets, being small and alert, were viewed suspiciously as likely to 'show the way to the herd' through fencing and into the crops. The commentary to *BC* shows that even after centuries of domestication, swine were viewed as in need of segregation when they were brought in from their range; ideally they were to be housed in a sty at a cross-roads — where they would be equally destructive to all the neighbor's gardens if they got out.

Pigs were evidently deemed worth this modest effort, however, for pork was the most frequently consumed meat of the general population in traditional Ireland, as in medieval England (Lucas 1960-2: 15; Trow-Smith 1957: 80). *Cáin Lánamna* shows that brood sows with their litters were commonplace on early medieval farms, and that piglets might be fattened on milk and corn for slaughter.[17] Early monasteries also kept herds of pigs (Lucas 1960-2: 17). But pork, though relished by all social classes, lacked prestige because swine had none of the elaborate social connotations of cattle. If anything, a certain social ambiguity attached to swine, for roast wild boar was the quintessential feast meat of the *fían*, the military groups that lurked in the forests (McCone 1986: 5; Nagy 1987: 56-7, 145, 220, 250). Swineherds themselves, like the *fían*, had a pronounced association with Druidic magic, in part because the herds kept in forest deaneries were so close to the wild state that their keepers too were viewed as not quite normal. (For further discussion see Ch. 5). The collection of legal proverbs called 'Succession', states flatly that a chief should not keep swine, but should receive salted pork from his clients.[18] *CG* indicates that pigs were the typical stock of the ranks of the farmers, and implicitly confirms the proverb referred to above, for the lowest grade of lord, the *aire déso*, is called 'lord of a pig's side', highlighting the fact that although he did not keep swine he received their flesh from clients.[19] Higher grades of lord were entitled to beef.

Sheep: If cattle were noble and pigs plebeian, sheep were feminine in their cultural associations. Their main value lay in their milk and their wool, which was the most important textile produced in Ireland because of the damp-repelling qualities of lanolin. Sheep's milk was prized as 'the treasure that is smoothest and sweetest of all food' (Meyer 1892: 32.35, 98.29-30). Mutton was also eaten, but neither sheep's meat nor manure were valued highly in Ireland.

Disparagement of sheep may be partly explained by their frustrating qualities. Individuals have their special spots on the pasture from which they are difficult to dislodge, while flocks that are forcibly moved to a new pasture are literally deranged unless the farmer has left one or two sheep (a bell-wether) from a flock long used to the pasture to 'haunt' it (Tani 1989). The domestication of sheep imposed a number of demands on mankind, including, as noted previously, transhumance. Communal grazing of the uplands, for instance, was a necessity because traditional fences could not control sheep movements (Clancy & Ford 1980: 106). Sheep also posed conflicts regarding farmers' goals, since they were highly inclined to eat the flowers on which the production of honey depended (E. Evans 1967: 74).

Dislike of the sheep in early Ireland is evident. Even that luxury by-product of the flocks, vellum, was eschewed by the Irish, who invented a calf-skin substitute which remained in use until the seventeenth century (O'Sullivan 1985: 353). In the heroic tales of cattle-raiding, there is no celebration of the sheep that were probably swept up along with the cows. Anthropomorphic imagery also reflects the difference. *Lóeg*, calf, was a term of endearment, like 'darling', while in the story, *'The exile of the sons of Uisneach'*, Noisiu compared his lover, Deirdriu, to a 'fair young heifer', which she took as a complement and reciprocated by comparing him to a young bull. At the end of the story, however, when her vengeful husband promised her to Noisiu's slayer for a year, he likened her to an ewe between two rams. At this insult, she leaned out of the moving chariot and smashed her head on a boulder (Tymozko 1985-6: 153).

In general the early sources tend to ignore sheep. There are strong traces of the pre-Christian cult of the mare, the wild boar, and the bull, but little sign of the cult of the sheep or ram in the classical Old Irish sources (Ross 1968: 343). Moreover, though *CG* indicates that every farmer owned some sheep, the ram is omitted. To this day in Donegal, livestock are regarded as 'lowly sheep and exalted cows' (Shanklin

1976). There, and presumably in the earliest times, the sheep-farmer was viewed as something of an exile from responsible, diligent, dairying society. Shepherds were out in the remotest areas of the community's grazing lands during the day, as was the lot during his captivity of St. Patrick, who wrote: 'every day I had to tend sheep', sometimes 'staying in the woods and on the mountains' (Bieler 1953: 25.16). St. Kevin, too, as part of his regime of self-mortification, herded his own sheep (Plummer 1922: II, 157.xii).

The cultural marginality of the sheep got its fullest expression in their identification as the livestock property of women. One of the 'leading cases' of early Irish law is cast in the form of a dispute between two women over damage done to crops by livestock; the plaintiff was a queen whose woad garden had been eaten up by a flock, and the accused was a woman-hosteller whose sheep had done the damage (O'Grady 1892: 288). Another legal example is the ritual procedure for legal possession of unoccupied land (*tellach*); male claimants were required to drive horses onto the pasture while a woman claimant made her claim by driving ewes onto the land (Kelly 1988: 186-8). A well-known passage from a Life of Kevin of Glendalough describes the association that sheep had for the saint:

> Where there is a sheep, there is a woman, where there is a
> woman, there is sin, where indeed there is sin, there is the
> devil, and where the devil is, there is hell.[20]

St. Kevin probably had more than sex on his mind, however. There are signs that a feminine, pre-Christian cult of the folks existed that was virtually obliterated, rather than transformed by the church; this is further discussed in Ch. 5. in connection with seasonal rituals.

Horses: At the opposite end of the prestige spectrum from the sheep, the horse, though of only modest utility, was at one time worshipped. The Gaulish equine divinity, Epona, left traces in the Welsh goddess-queen of the Mabinogion, Rhiannon (Ford 1977: 4-12). In Ireland, Giraldus imputed ritual consumption of mare's flesh to the kings of Cenél Conaill during the inaugural ceremonies (O'Meara 1982: 109-10). Horses were, of course, the principal animal used in warfare and games, where their appearance contributed to the prestige of the owner. Fighting from horseback was never very popular in Ireland, however, so the utility of the horse resided in the speed with which its rider (or driver) could get to and from conflicts and other public meetings

(Piggott 1986). In particular, horses were necessary for cattle-raids, in which a speedy round-up and getaway was essential to success. Horse races seem to have been popular and there are signs that they were included in the seasonal assemblies during which, in pre-Christian times, funerary games were held in honor of deceased ancestors and/or deities (Ettlinger 1952).

It is, then, the association of the horse with speed and scope of social connection, with warfare and public life, that imparted prestige to this animal, but its main productive utility lay in its manure (Mercer 1981 a: 211). Useless at the plow, the horse was also forbidden flesh; even mare's milk was associated with pagan war-cult activities, not only in early literature but archaeologically: horses were consumed at the Ballinderry crannogs (Proudfoot 1961: 111 n.58) and apparently in Viking Dublin (Kavanagh 1988: 105), while dogs — also beasts of the war cults (McCone 1986 a: 16; 1985: 175-6) — were consumed at Newgrange (Van Wijngaarden-Bakker 1974: 348). The only direct use for a horse in early medieval farming communities was as a pack animal: it was faster and more sure-footed than the ox, and less likely to get bogged down. It was, in fact, the small sturdy work horse that *CG* specified as part of the livestock of all the ranks of the farmers in early Ireland (*CG* 91, 158). The ranks below the *bóaire* possessed no other kind of horse, but the *bóaire* and higher grades were also required to keep riding horses as attributes of their rank (*CG* 158, 196, 345). The lowest grade of true lord was to have five riding horses, one with a silver bridle and four with blue bridles (*CG* 345-6).

We have now surveyed the chief material resources of early Irish society. The horse-riding cattle-lords, and the farmers who supported them, pursued their interests in these resources, no doubt literally, within the framework of local and regional territorial organization. This was the theater of social relations; in the next chapter we shall examine its structure.

Notes

1. Kavanagh (1988: 116), citing J. R. C. Hamilton, 'Excavations at Jarlshof in Shetland'. Edinburgh, 1956: 110-1.

2. *obus tar muir ticfa d'acra a dala, a roga breithemon i neirinn do, 7 obus tar crich .u.id ticfa, a roga .b. isin .u.ed do.* 'if a person comes over the sea to prosecute a cause, his choice of the judges of Ireland, and when he has come over a provincial boundary, his choice of the judges of the province.' *(CIH 340.12-3 = AL i 7).*

3. Megaw and Simpson (1979: 346-7) warn, however, against too sharp a dichotomy.

4. *CIH* 457.11 ff; Binchy 1955b.

5. Sawyer (1982: 68), citing T. Grongaard Jeppesen (1981), *Middelalderlandsbyens Opstaen* (Fynske Studier 11), Odense.

6. Sawyer (1982: 71), citing A. S. C. Ross, 'The Terfinnas and Beormas of Ohthere (Leeds School of English Language Texts and Monographs, no. 7, 1940): 21.

7. *uair piastamla cu ina muc 7 piastamla muc ina bo. (CIH 278.32 = 944.18 = AL iii 245.1-2).*

8. *Cia robai i seinbrethaib gach clas roclaideadh do línadh do arbaim, alaill do imbim... (CIH 191.3-5 = 576.20-3 = AL iv 87. n.2).*

9. *... buaine in conluain-sin i talam 7 fod ind dara eise 7 bochor fair co ceann mis. (CIH 197.10-1 = 579.1 ff = AL iv 123.6-8.)*

10. *... TEORA HOIMEITE CHACHA INA DIRE AIMEITT DO IM... (CIH 74.27-8 = AL iv 121).*

11. '*... uir minn 7 boco 7 lemlacht...*' *(CIH 202.21 = AL iv 149.25-30).*

12. Kelly 1980: 107. See *CIH* 676.9 = *Ériu* 22 (1971) 82.36.

13. This is a proximate figure, based on McConnell's recommendation of 5 tonnes manure per acre and Mercer's statement that Dexters on unimproved grassland drop just over 3 tonnes solid and liquid waste per acre over the six months of summer grazing. See Mercer (1981): 235.

14. The remarks in parentheses are my own.

15. Sir William Temple (1697), *Miscellanea*; cited by Lucas 1973: 70.

16. C. H. Tupling, *The Economic History of Rossendale* (Chatham Society, 1927, lxxxvi). Cited by Trow-Smith 1955: 72.

17. *CIH* 509.2; 509.14-5. Petty confirms that pigs were regularly given the whey after milk had been processed for cheese (*Political Anatomy*: 52).

18. *Ni dlegar muca la flaith, 7 dligid saill chean. (CIH 1291.16-7 = AL IV 382.6-7, 383.8-9). (CIH* corrects *AL*, which breaks up the text at '*flaith*'.)

19. '*is sí flaith mucleithe*', *CG* 350; see also note to line 350, p. 34.

20. See Bitel (1986: 31) for discussion and sources.

CHAPTER FOUR

The Spatial Organization of Society

Introduction

The territorial units of society cohered around upland areas that served as summer grazing grounds, areas without which lowland-based settlements could not have supported the large numbers of cattle upon which the farming system depended. To a great extent, the basic prehistoric and early medieval Irish political community, the *tuath*, corresponded with large, composite ecological units. Since the political community was identified in terms of descent groups, however (which would expand, contract or move beyond natural boundary-lines), its territorial aspect must be seen as its ideal package of physical resources and not as the strongest determining element in the shape of human groups. In this respect Irish society was probably similar to Germanic societies during the migration period, both on the continent and in England. As Davies and Vierck state, 'It is groups and associations of people that form the raw material of early political development, not the carving up of territory.' (Davies and Vierck 1974: 224).

Human populations moved between ecological units, as circumstances dictated, but those in power attempted to exact payments from the occupants of a given area of land, according to expectations of the land's productivity if it were adequately stocked with animals and people, and if the latter did their proper work. Circumstances varied, of course; in some instances migrant groups entered weakly controlled territory under the leadership of their own head, while in other cases immigrants had to seek protection and submit to the overlordship of an adjacent polity. Examples of relatively autonomous migration are found from the late middle ages,[1] while legends of early medieval migrations suggest 'sponsored migrations' into areas already under political control, as was alleged of the ancestors of the Déisi of Munster.[2]

In this fluid social landscape, political organization cannot be

89

viewed in terms of the evolution of 'tribal chieftaincy' to 'territorial lordship'. There seems not to have been a clear-cut absolute trend in this regard: what was stable was knowledge of the land, vested in the *literati*.[3] Where effective over-arching political structures existed, the élite imposed demands on subordinates in the light of what they thought they could get. Where the élite was weak, farmers would have been able to exercise greater freedom of choice as to the terms of clientship, though such freedom might rapidly yield to outside aggression and new, stronger, lordship. In order to visualize the organization of early Irish society it is thus important to understand the ecological units which Irish lords tried to keep populated and productive.

Since cattle were so central to the economy, control of pasture was a major political focus. Two aspects of animal husbandry influenced territorial organization. One was 'booleying', the commoning of herds at the local level during summer transhumance, mentioned in Ch. 3; the other was the use of wilderness to maintain large herds which served as reserve stock, on which lords drew to enfeoff clients and sue for peace from stronger competitors. Both these facets of territorial organization seem to have been relatively inflexible, whereas settlement patterns and field systems (discussed in the second part of this chapter) seem to have been morphologically fluid, as changes took place at the micro-levels of demography and political control.

Pastoral territories

Local booleys. A summer pasture was known as *airge* ('high place') and latterly as *buaile* (a 'cow-fold'), the sheep again being ignored (E. Evans 1940: 134). Many Irish hills still bear traces of small stone beehive huts that sheltered earlier dairy-workers (Ó Moghráin: 1944). In Mourne the huts consisted of one or two-room dwellings, usually situated beside running water. Dating has proved very difficult because of the virtual absence of artifacts, but Evans suggests continuity of use over many centuries (E. Evans 1940: 134).

The Irish landscape was so variegated that most communities were near some higher land, forest, or bog (*ibid* 1940: 52-3). Graham records that in the early nineteenth century, young girls from Achill Island were sent with the cattle to summer pastures a few miles away from the farms. They stayed up all summer between May 1 and November 1, returning occasionally to take down some of the butter (Graham 1953: 74-5). Transhumance does not inevitably depend on the presence of uplands, however, though the custom survived longest there. Hill, in fact, stated that the peasants of early nineteenth-century Gweedore used different types of land, 'flitting' between upland, shoreline, and island farms (Hill 1887: 24). Graham showed that place-names based on *buaile* are distributed in areas that now have no traditions of transhumance, having been brought under cultivation during the seventeenth century (Graham 1953: 76). Her map shows a virtually island-wide distribution, thinning out only in the interior boglands.[4]

While each family and residential group had its own habitual spot in the booleys, the openness of the terrain and the need to move the animals around the pasture necessitated some social relationship between the cowherds. This need was especially strong where, as was often the case, the booleys were on hills that formed the upland boundaries between lowland hamlets whose denizens did not otherwise interact daily. A scene in the *Táin* depicts the same kind of tensions witnessed by anthropologists in contemporary Iranian summer pastures. When the herds of two enemy groups began to mingle, the young cowherds threw stones at each other's cows, and eventually at each other. The adult men then woke up and battle ensued (O'Rahilly 1967: 4609-33). The importance of political integration for areas with common booley grounds was further intensified by the fact that women, children and stock were lodged in the hills, probably without a substantial male presence, during the season favored for cattle-raiding.

The main method of securing equitable use of the pastures was to divide the mountain ranges, not physically, but in terms of rights to depasture a specified number of animals. The basic units of measure for pasture was the amount of land that would support a standard animal, usually the four year old cow. A given share in the community's arable entitled individuals to put a specific number of animals on the pasture. Different animals were estimated in comparison with each other, for example, in some areas during the present century, one cow = 3/4 of a horse = 4 sheep = 6 goats = 18 geese (Danaher 1964b: 124-5). These rates varied, of course, according to the fortunes of the species in question, but the principle was the same. The later medieval commentary to the Old Irish tract on *comingaire* (joint-pasturing by co-tenants) equated one ox = a cow plus a heifer; one cow = two heifers = four yearlings = eight sheep = sixteen geese (*CIH* 192.9-17 = *AL* iv

101). Each group of animals, composed whichever way, was generally known as a 'sum' in the north, and a 'collop' in the south (Mac Aodha 1956: 19-21; E. Evans 1940: 179; Graham 1953: 74; Granlund 1976: 80-4).

The matching of pasture rights to arable holdings was found in medieval England, where it was known as stinting (Homans 1941: 60 ff) and in medieval Scandinavia (Granlund 1976: 81). Supervision of this system to prevent abuses was a matter for manorial officials in England (Homans 1941: 79 ff). In Ireland the social pressure was different, for here it was the community and kindred that supervised access to the pasture. As is shown in Ch. 10, these guarded the common waste jealously from encroachment by individual members of their community, who might take excessive cattle-loans from lords and overcrowd their pasture. Even in recent times, the ratio of animals to the size of the farmer's holding was carefully scrutinized by local communities, who dealt with the problems arising from substitutions, such as individual exchanges of pasture rights for arable usufruct, by appointing an authority from within the local community who had powers to uphold community norms. Significantly, the man chosen to play this role was known by traditional titles recalling the native social order, such as *rí* (king), or brehon (Morris 1939: 289). The lowest rank of these, in Gaelic law, had been the *rí* or brehon of the *tuath*.

Not surprisingly, then, the basic political units of early Irish society, the *tuatha*, were largely shaped by the distribution of common waste. Graham showed that in south-west Clare, the boundaries of several large English political units (baronies) meet in the middle of the central uplands, the heart of the booleying country (Graham 1953: 77). The Normans recognized the physical and social integrity of these territories, for their political and administrative units, the cantred or barony, largely preserve the boundaries of one or more pre-Norman *tuath*.[5]

The king of a *tuath* had as his chief function the organization of peaceful interaction between different groups, both within his *tuath*, and with other *tuatha*; he met with the groups of his own polity at the *tuath* assembly and took sureties from them as to the maintenance of lawful behavior. He also made treaties with outsiders (*cairde*), and promulgations regarding the protection of visitors. The various lords who ranked beneath him in status (who would often have been his kinsmen), buttressed his power by offering material security for the legal agreements reached between the *tuath* and outsiders (see Ch. 12). The interaction of different groups in the booleying zones necessitated such mediation and insurance against violence, whether at the level of the local *tuath*, or aggregates of these, the *mór-tuath* (great *tuath*). At this level, or perhaps beyond it, lay the major unit of military levy, the *trícha cét*, about which more will be said in Ch. 6.

It seems as if the principle of balanced, multi-resource, territorial structure was applied not only to large political units headed by kings, but to all levels of agricultural organization, down to the *mruigfher* farmer (who owned a complete plow). Working with cartographical data, McEarlen (1983) showed that the medieval sub-divisions of the *trícha cét*, the *ballybetagh* (which are discussed in Ch.6), were similarly composed of different types of land, and resembled the Welsh 'multiple estate' (Jones 1972: 281-382; 1976: 15-40). In a study of south-west Donegal, Graham found that lesser land units also typically had their own complement of all types of land (Graham 1972: 139); this unit was named the *ballybo* (equated with English 'townland'), and was a sub-unit of the *ballybetagh*.

Both large and small geo-political units possessed a physical integrity which often outlasted the vagaries of political dominance. Anngret Simms maintains that continuity was especially strong at the level of internal manorial organization (A. Simms [1988]: 34). But larger units also persisted: the *tuath* was taken as the basis of Norman knights' fees and parishes, as well as manors. For example, the Norman knight's fee and parish of Slieveardagh in Co. Tipperary, was known as the *tuath* of Kenel Rathonere, while the manor of Drom was originally the *tuath* of *Kenelfenelgille* (Hennesey 1985: 63). Generally the Norman royal administrative unit, the *cantred*, was also based on native territorial units. In the case of the Tipperary fief granted by John in 1185 to Theobald Walter, the land had been newly divided into five and a half cantreds, but Theobald reorganized it into four manors based on the Irish divisions of Arra, Owney, Ely O'Carroll, and Eliogarty (Empey 1985: 78).

In this respect, the Irish landscape resembled that of other early medieval north European regions. In England, for example, 'parish boundaries may perpetuate estate divisions which go back into the Roman period or even into the pre-Roman Iron Age.' (Hoskins 1979: 151). As in Ireland, a good number of cemeteries were placed on early English inter-territorial boundaries which later evolved into parish boundaries (Bonney 1972: 168 ff). This practice recalls aspects of the spatial organization of the pre-migration Angles in Angeln (Jutland and Upper Schleswig Holstein), whose settlements were surrounded with unpopulated waste in which were extensive bog-burials of sacrificed or executed persons (Davies and Vierck 1974). Jones' analysis of early medieval political organization in Wales (1972), has also shown that large political units, based on the integration of lowland tillage and upland pasture, persisted into the later middle ages. In the areas of England settled by Scandinavians, the latter took over similar large units, and kept them going as if familiar with this pattern of farming (Sawyer 1982: 105), which was probably the case, for early Scandinavian administrative units also had clearly defined natural boundaries, and had in many cases been at one time autonomous lordships, or even petty kingdoms on about the same scale as an Irish *tuath* (*ibid*: 56).

The organization of land into such 'multiple estates' implies a social system in which those in power sought to promote agro-pastoral integration, and specifically the productivity of a spectrum of resources, for 'multiple estates' ensured that all types of land were worked by all ranks of local landholders. The system stemmed from a political economy that not only maximized land use, however, but also minimized productive specialization within small groups, which itself meant that men of roughly the same social status were in no position to take advantage of each other's needs through disadvantageous exchange. Only the élite could do this, through cattle clientship. Not only did the élite pacify the common wastes, making it possible for small farmers to use them in peace, but nobles also made direct use of wilderness as reservations for the large-scale herds which enabled them to supply clients with cattle loans. This was a key to their ascendancy, and it too had implications for territorial organization, for legal and military control of the waste first empowered élite groups locally, and then enabled them to bring separate and largely self-sufficient local groups into political association through clientship with lords of the same élite group. Hence the rise of dynasties that dominated the populations of many *tuatha*, most of which had little identity as population groups and were merely local areas possessed of strong geo-political boundary features. The linch-pin of the political economy was therefor the control of wilderness.

Wilderness. By the fourteenth century, there existed large areas of wilderness reserved for the support of huge herds (*creaght*) belonging to ruling members of royal lineages (K. Simms 1986: 386-91; Lucas 1989: 68-124). The twelfth- century recension of the *Táin* describes how the quarrelling and competitive royal pair, Ailill and Medb, had their chattels brought to their abode for assessment, driven in from the woods and waste places of the entire province.[6] The animals are described as 'their herds of cows, their cattle and their droves'.[7] The latter imply herds on the hoof, and may have thus been the precursors of the *creaghts*. These herds were probably kept as a breeding reserve from which to make cattle loans and pay indemnities to enemies. This is illustrated by the Lord Deputy's comment on the wealth of the Earl of Tyrone in 1593, that 'there must be three times more of barren kine besides other cattle.' (Lucas 1958: 78-9). Simms suggests that the *creaghts* of the late middle ages represent an intensification of an older and less specialized form of wilderness exploitation, the practice of *imirce*, going on 'expedition'. A *creaght* was a permanent mobile social and economic unit, headed by a captain, whereas groups on *imirce* seem to have been *ad hoc* formations, in Simms' words, 'exchanging one place for another, moving with some definite goal in mind, and the context of the word in the annals is that of landowners displaced from their homes for one reason or another.' (K. Simms 1986: 389).

Although the word *'creaght'* gained a much greater currency from the mid-fourteenth century, there are signs that the practice of wilderness exploitation by the élite was very old. *CG*, for example, alludes to the storage of dry-cattle on waste land near the borders of a *tuath*, though it does not comment on the scale of such herds. According to the tract, one of the privileges of a king was to appropriate dry-cattle on waste-land when he was returning from an expedition or meeting across the *tuath* border; he was obliged to repay the owner, but incurred no fines.[8] Scattered and admittedly cryptic allusions also crop up elsewhere in the law-tracts, as for example, 'barren cattle not (kept) in a *buaile*'[9]; 'the borderland wilderness of a *tuath*'[10]; 'deer and dry cows kept in a wood or plain.'[11] (The presence of the hair of either deer or dry cows served as a legally recognized marker of a territorial boundary.) Since there must have been regular routes across borders, it is possible that storage of dry-cattle where they might be needed by the king in an emergency was a regular feature of political organization. One direct allusion to wilderness herding appears in a late commentary to *Bretha Comaithchesa*, which states that the owners of cows were not to be fined when the animals trespassed in three types of land, namely, a wood, a moor, and a *'foach'* of the *tuath*, since all cattle were free to roam in wild places.[12]

Slightly stronger indications that big herds did exist are found in early references to farmers who 'farm in hundreds'. This was often an allusion to the *briugu*, a wealthy peasant who played the role of inn-keeper for itinerants who were benighted beyond reach of kith and kin. (See Chs. 6 and 12). The Life of St. Kevin depicts the discovery of the Saint in the wooded fastness of Glendalough by a cattle-rich hosteller (*brughaidh bóicheadach*, literally a hundred-cow man), who along with his sons, servants and slaves was moving his herds through the forest browse, on a 'circuit of grazing' (Plummer 1922: I, 57). More certainly Old Irish than these literary texts is the reference in the Book of Armagh to the grant by Endé to Patrick's community of 'grazing for a hundred cows with their calves and twenty oxen'.[13] These references cannot be dismissed as conventional phrases, for as Mac Niocaill has argued, the whole economic structure of lordship as depicted in *CG* implies that lords maintained large herds in order to be able to enfeoff the number of clients on which their status was based. He estimates that this would require almost a hundred cattle on the part of the *aire désa*, the lowest rank of lord, apart from whatever personal stock he kept as a reserve for direct utility, for restocking clients who fell into difficulties, and paying reparations as these might arise (1981: 8).

Other uses of wilderness were for hunting (see Ch. 5), and for the practice of 'expedition', *imirce*, mentioned above. *Imirce* was undertaken because pasture, no less than arable, can become exhausted, dehydrated, swamped, or tainted by cattle disease, leaving early cattle-farmers in need of alternative pastures. Since it is unlikely that people would pick themselves up and depart permanently to land 'without a chief or kin-liability, with only fierce and lawless (people)',[14] *imirce* probably involved only migration to other areas within the same polity, though whether to a wilderness area, or an area left to regenerate under the regime of shifting agriculture, it is impossible to say. One legal passage depicts *imirce* as a normal occasional practice, for it maintains that no one could be subject to distraint of cattle at this time; 'for it is customary that *imirce* be a protection against distraint'. This can hardly mean that a liable person could cart himself off with impunity, and indeed the text lists several circumstances under which a plaintiff could unyoke the carts of a would-be 'migrant', such as where the latter was turning vagrant in order to escape the demands of *tuath* law, or absconding from obligations to his kin-group (*fine*), or to his chief. In other words, *imirce* is here viewed as occurring within the *crích*, the territorial boundary, and as compatible with future response to legal claims.[15]

'Migration' of this sort depended on institutions of social security such as the formal protection and rights to hospitality described in Ch. 7. But though guaranteed to some extent, trekking out of their usual haunts must have been a daunting proposition for most people, and something of a test of courage. In the tract on the relationship of status to personal qualities (*Míadshlechta*), one of the categories of disgraced men who had lost legal and political standing (in most cases on account of cowardice) was termed the 'cow-grazer of a green' (*faithche*), a man who never went beyond the *crích* (local boundary), or attended a king's court, but confined himself to the safety of the local *faithche* (*CIH* 585.14-6 = *AL* iv 353.23 ff.).

To some extent, early polities attempted to diminish people's feelings of danger and make mobility less unattractive by patrolling frontier areas, for the Old Irish text on *athgabál*, legal distraint of property, refers to the crime of 'stealing past watchmen'. The late gloss views this as the crime of the watchmen, 'the people (soldiers) of the border', who let the property of the territory get past them.[16] The danger to herds on the move, or at pasture in wilderness, increased the further away they moved from areas of effective political and legal defense against outlaws and *fían*. The latter had strong association with hunting, and with liminal geographical zones such as the sea, and the Slieve Bloom mountains that rise in what was a vast central area of bog and marsh (Nagy 1985: 111-5). This suggests that while there was wilderness that was politically secured, there were also no-man's-lands that were not. Smyth points out that it was one of the five taboos of the King of Leinster to march through the Fortuatha and the Wicklow hills, in other words, to undertake any expedition into that wilderness. When Richard II did so, his army almost starved to death (Smyth 1982: 110). Uncontrolled wilderness was concentrated in the central bogland, where 'so many ancient kingdoms met in a labyrinth of passes and roads' (*ibid*: 104). Through this central area there passed from time to time great armies intent on the depredation of a whole province. Little wonder then, that in folktale it remained the home of the magical warrior Finn, and his *fían* band, magical because though they had military might, these warriors had no social identity. That was obtainable only within the bounded territories within which kings, lords, judges, poets and bishops exercised control and jurisdiction.

Settlements and field systems

Within the framework of the big pastoral units, settlement forms were fluid, and people were mobile. For a long time, the evidence has been typologized, dichotomized and subjected to evolutionary theory, but modern researchers tend to view variations in the morphology of field systems and settlements as phenomena manifested at different points in community development within the same agrarian regime, or as alternatives dictated by environmental circumstances, rather than as the outcome of radically different social systems or ethnic patterns.

Settlement types. The basic pattern of population distribution was one of dispersal, with a trend towards slightly greater nucleation in the major ecclesiastical centers towards the end of the first millennium A.D. The biggest enclosures are the hillforts, but these are not very numerous in Ireland, where only sixty hill-top and six promontory forts have been noted (Raftery 1976: 534).[17] The Irish hill-forts are curiously lacking in signs of military function, such as the elaborate entrances and close-set multivallate defenses typical of British late La Tène hill-forts. Many indeed seem to date far back into the bronze age and to have retained some focal interest for local populations, without any necessary military importance. Most archaeologists agree that they do not suggest that substantial invasions of Ireland occurred in prehistory (Raftery 1972: 43-8). Few were in use by the sixth century A.D. (Barry 1987: 20). One can, perhaps, envisage periodic head-counts of cattle, musters of armed men, and community rituals at some such sites, but certainly not population settlements comparable to the virtually urban 'tribal capitals' (*oppida*) found in Gaul and Germany on the eve of Roman conquest.

By far the most ubiquitous settlement remains are the raths, or ringforts.[18] These are enclosures, normally circular, within a ditch and embankment, or a stone wall (depending on terrain); in the stony west, the ringfort is called a cashel (from the Latin, *castellum*), while many ringforts are also named *dun*, *cathair* or *lís*, followed by the name of a person. Some show the remains of solid wooden houses, while many contain traces of lightly built internal structures which sheltered the occupants. There are between 30,000 and 50,000 discernable on the first edition (1840s) of the six inch ordinance survey maps, but only about 120 have been excavated, and these may have been the most unusual (Barry 1987: 14). More or less on the same scale as substantial ringforts, in terms of the effort required for construction, were crannogs, artificial islands in lakes and marshlands, where the occupants's wattle and daub buildings were often surrounded by a defensive palisade. These have an overwhelmingly northern distribution, however, whereas ringforts and other settlement forms appear throughout the island (O'Loan 1965: 150; Wood-Martin 1886).

The social and historical significance of the ringforts has been much debated (Barrett and Graham 1975: 33-45; O'Flanagan 1981: 321-26).[19] Dating, for one thing, is in doubt. Many scholars believe that ringforts generally date to the first millennium and were the defended farmsteads of single family groups (Barry 1987: 16; Proudfoot 1970; Laing 1975: 147-9; O'Kelly 1990: 306-8). Others think that ringforts existed as far back as the Bronze Age (Raftery 1972: 2). Caulfield points out that ringforts have often been dated to the Early Christian period without positive chronological evidence, on the assumption that the absence of La Tène style artifacts indicates a post-La Tène date. But, he argues, it is unlikely that the La Tène style had spread throughout Ireland, so that its absence cannot signify the later dating of a site (1981: 206-7, 211).

Lynn, however, emphasizes that there is no positive evidence in favor of earlier dating either, and that there is no reason to assume that ringforts were indigenous and ancient settlement types. He points out that similar structures begin to appear in adjacent areas of Britain during the period of Roman occupation and withdrawal, and emphasizes the defensive aspects of ringforts, and especially of crannogs, many of which were fortified with strong palisades at this time. The implication, in his view, is that ringforts reflect a more militarized society, stimulated by renewed interaction with mainland Britain (1983: 54-7). Given the upsurge in Irish raiding on Britain in the fourth and fifth centuries (Mac Néill 1919: 133-60), and the appearance of new dynasties in the sixth, this view has much to recommend it, though we should probably not envisage in Ireland wide-scale warfare — against which the ringforts would seem to have been feeble defenses — but rather increased demands from a newly empowered élite for tribute and other military 'contributions' from the farming population. Since status and social protection depended on ability to honor these obligations to the lord, even quite small-scale farmers would have needed protection from cattle-rustling. Ringforts would have prevented rustlers from making a quick surprise get-away with the stock enclosed inside them. The same would also hold true against slave-raiders, another menace of the early middle ages, especially the Viking age.

The agricultural interests of the ringfort-dwellers are as archaeologically enigmatic as the dating of the structures. On the whole, they chose median elevations near streams, and avoided both uplands and heavy lowland clays, preferring sandy or gravelly soils where pasture and arable that would yield to the light plow could be found (Norman and St. Joseph 1969: 41). Ringforts display no clear pattern of aggregation: some were isolated, others in clusters, while many appear in pairs or loose groups, beyond earshot but within sight of each other (Norman and St. Joseph 1969: 38-41). However, near some important royal sites, such as Clogher, a dense massing of ringforts is found (Warner 1988). There was great variation in the internal dimensions of the ringforts, though those with excavated early medieval houses within their banks averaged about one hundred to one hundred and thirty feet in diameter (Norman & St. Joseph: 41).

In addition to ringforts, there were monastic enclosures, some on a considerable scale, and in many ways resembling the ringforts of the secular population (Hamlin 1985: 279-85; Swan 1983: 269). There also existed enclosed settlements which, though not identified as monastic sites, had a non-royal ritual aspect, including combinations of the following features: a church, holy well, burial ground (sometimes a children's or infant's burial ground), and a liminal position on the boundary of two or more townlands. These sites appear to have gone out of use after the Viking period, and are interpreted as a modification of pre-Christian plebeian ritual and/or settlement sites (Swan 1983: 274-8). Monasteries are often located close to important early royal sites. At a number of these there is found a complex of constructions, including a royal ringfort, a nearby prehistoric ritual center, and a monastic enclosure (Warner 1988: 57-65). Such dispersal of different social functions (feasting, royal rituals, political assemblies, and Christian religious services) amongst separate locations in the same area offers a parallel to the tendency of the Irish élite to disperse its livestock and its children amongst various allies — a policy expressed in the macabre saying, 'better a mountain of bones than a mountain of stones'.

Recent research, however, suggests that in some areas ecclesiastical sites were substantially larger on average than secular ones and are interpreted as 'central places' of the *tuath* community (Swan 1988:5, Gibson, 1990: 301). Swan has also shown for Westmeath that early ecclesiastic sites were distributed in relationship to territorial units that are still recognized as parishes, with only one site found per parish (allowing from documented changes in boundaries), (*ibid*: 28). This finding complements what literary sources show: that the power of the Church was vested in territorially localized, fixed resources: burial grounds, relics, depositories of the valuables of the community, an altar on which to swear oaths, and the Church itself. Spiritually protected, these assets could remain static and concentrated. (Prehistoric ritual sites likewise retained prestige, despite their lack of physical protection [Warner 1988: 52].) In contrast, the power of the secular élite was vested in mobility and dispersed assets. The contrast should not be overdrawn, of course; churches too took their relics on circuit to collect tribute and held scattered estates. They also acquired bands of retainers to protect them (Hughes 1966: 167-72). Nevertheless, it was clerical, not secular, settlements that grew into small 'proto-towns' in the middle ages (Butlin 1977).

Stout's recent survey of ringforts in the south-west midlands has added new ideas on the typology of ringforts in that area, some of which may apply in other areas of Ireland. Amongst the most important of his observations are the fact that only 19% of the ringforts had outer, secondary encircling banks ('the ramparts of base-clientship'), which implies that the vast majority of ringfort dwellers belonged to the non-noble ranks of clan land-holders (Stout 1991: 207). Statistically average ringforts (measured on several parameters) conformed well with law-tracts' references to the dwelling of a *bóaire*, a farmer of middling status amongst the non-noble grades (*ibid*: 218). Cluster analysis showed that these 'typical' ringforts were rarely located in townlands where there were high-status forts (*ibid*: 217), nor did they cluster in relation either to townland boundaries or centers (*ibid*: 240).

In contrast, high-status ringforts were often associated with small groups of small ringforts, which Stout suggests may be the residences of *ócaire* farmers (men of low rank amongst clan landholders), possibly under the leadership of the occupant of the imposing ringfort (*ibid*: 235). Big, probably multifunctional, ringforts tended to be located near townland boundaries, where they were also close to communication routes (*ibid*: 235). Stout's main sociological finding is that the archaeological data generated by this survey is consistent with the view that 'the townland framework may have evolved from a society that was stratified both vertically and horizontally' (*ibid*: 218). In other words, there was a relationship between a household's social status and its geographical location, with higher-status units tending towards the edges of the townland, lower-status units adhering to these, and middle-rank units scattered in the interior.

Unenclosed settlements also existed, though the archaeological evidence for their early existence is as yet slight.[20] These are known as clachans, where built of stone. McCourt has shown that in remote parts of northern and western Ireland, where native social patterns were still firmly entrenched in the nineteenth century, clachans tended to form spontaneously when the local population grew. Moreover, wherever estate maps reveal the pattern of settlement back to the seventeenth century this is shown to have been at all times a mixture of settlements ranging from the *Einzelhof*, the isolated single-dwelling type of unit, through to clachans of substantial size (*ibid*: 134). In other words, no dichotomy can be postulated between single farmsteads (of which a ringfort might be one form) and clustered communities, but rather these must be seen as stages in the waxing and waning of farming communities.

Many commentators have suggested that unenclosed communities were occupied by low-status members of society, while ringforts sheltered the higher ranks (Ó Riordain 1979: 33; Mitchell 1976: 168; Proudfoot 1961: 119; Barry 1987: 21). Proudfoot found an interesting relationship between types of place name in Co. Down. The names were in two groups, those beginning with ringfort, or its equivalents, *cathair* or *lios* (*lís*), and those beginning with *baile*, a word which means 'place', rather than a construction (like *rath*), and which often appears as part of the names of *clachan* communities. Proudfoot showed that *baile*-named townlands were complementary to ringforts (1977: 93), and he suggested, therefore, that the ringfort was the settlement of a nobleman or 'strong-farmer', while his dependents lived in the various 'places' of the townland.

Some documentary support was derived for this theory from an entry for A.D. 1010 in the Annals of Ireland, which recorded the burning of Duneight 'with its baile'. The linkage between ringforts and *baile* also appears clearly in the use of 'the people of one *lís* and of one *baile*' as a legal definition of a territory in which notice had to be given of the use of certain hunting hounds, for example, or the finding of lost property.[21] This commentary is certainly of post-classical date, suggesting that *baile* acquired a firmer association with the farming dependents of the *lís*-occupiers as society became more thoroughly militarized from the tenth century onwards. Against Proudfoot's theory, however, Barrett showed that the relationship between the place-names does not hold in other areas except for the Dingle peninsula.[22] *Baile*, it seems, did not have such a clearly-defined meaning[23] that the relationship found by Proudfoot could be expected to occur everywhere. A looser usage meaning 'estate', for example, appears in a land-grant to the Church mentioned in the Life of Mochua of Balla.[24]

Other evidence suggests, however, that those ringforts that housed humans were likely to shelter members of the clan who held the surrounding lands. That is, there was probably no sharp distinction regularly pertaining between ringfort occupants and people dwelling in the vicinity of the ringfort, but a gradation of status, depending on status within the clan that held the land. Although the law-tracts offer few clues as to the territorial arrangements of kinship groups, some references are found which link the *fine* kin-group to the local ringfort. In a section of the law-tract on distraint, *Athgabál*, that deals with the common obligations and the common property of the agnatic kin-group, two references are made to lost legal materials on 'the regulations of a *dun*' (i.e. a ringfort). Glosses indicate that this material concerned an individual's 'share in the common *dun* of the *fine*'.[25] Further evidence is found in the inclusion of the obligation to help build a *dun* amongst a group of legal actions that concerned relations between kin or immediate neighbors.[26] An Old Irish tract on estray (lost and found property) also depicts a *cathair* (i.e a ringfort) at the center of a complete land-unit, which the commentary interprets as the possession of one group of close agnatic kin (see below).

It is therefore reasonable to assume that the head of a local land-holding community, generally a patrilineal kin-group, was 'seated' in a ringfort. As Stout's data (above) shows, such a head was in most cases merely a well-to-do farmer, not a nobleman. Several tracts on status imply that unmarried junior clansmen might live in small huts of their own (see Ch. 8), probably outside the ringforts. This kind of distribution would best serve the defensive needs of communities, obliging would-be cattle-thieves to penetrate a network of huts where the group's prime fighters dwelled, before reaching the cattle-pound. Where ringforts were grouped together, their occupants could have held different rank within the same land-holding clan (social stratification is described in Chs. 7, 8 and 12).

Field systems

In varying degrees, depending on local agricultural potential and traditions, all early Irish communities, whether ringfort-dwellers or not, participated in the chores of tillage (Proudfoot 1961: 109). As with settlement forms, both the archaeological and post-Norman documentary evidence suggest that patterns of cultivation were diverse and flexible, with no one type of field system emerging as an identifiable, 'typical', native Irish form. Earlier interpretations, however, sought to dichotomize the evidence, and attach social significance to the 'types' produced by this procedure.

Perhaps the most influential theory was Meitzen's (1895), which distinguished between 'Germanic' agriculture, supposedly based on the village commune (*markgenossenschaft*), and Celtic agriculture, which was identified with the individual family homestead (*Einzelhof*). The latter, of course, was thought to be associated in Ireland with the ringfort. 'Germanic' social forms were deduced from the remains of large, sub-divided open fields, while 'Celtic' agriculture was deduced from the remains of small, enclosed fields. A legacy of this theory is that the distinctive, small, square fields found in various parts of Ireland and Britain are still known as 'Celtic' fields, even though recent archaeology shows that some 'Celtic fields' are too ancient to be 'Celtic' (as in Wessex), while some open fields derive from a late prehistoric or Romano-British 'Celtic' context, and are too early to be 'Germanic'. Moreover, evidence for types of communal farming is found in medieval Welsh, Scottish and more recent Irish sources. The distinction and its ethnic association are thus blurred both in the case of Ireland and regarding early Germanic agriculture itself (Latouche 1961: 33). It also follows that the assumption that early Irish agriculture was typically based on individual family farms is open to doubt (Dodgshon 1980: 64).

The overall pattern of field distribution in the landscape of early medieval Ireland has been described as 'patchy, and essentially nodular', without any sign of extensive regular field layout (Aalen 1983: 367). While some ringforts stood at the center of fields that radiated out from their embankments, others stood in open land, on which small, irregularly shaped patches of land had been enclosed. Cultivated fields were in some cases bounded by dry-stone walls or embanked ditches, whose antecedents may be seen on neolithic sites. While not as neat as English open-fields, these enclosed arable lands were bigger than so-called 'Celtic fields' and generally lie close to adjacent ringforts.[27] Where ringforts are clustered together, their fields, though looking like *ad hoc* intake, were quite numerous, and may have been intermingled as to ownership (Norman and St. Joseph 1969: 55-66).

Unenclosed areas of cultivation were, perhaps, even more widespread than enclosed fields, and as is shown below, were an aspect of traditional, early Irish farming. From the eighteenth century on, unenclosed fields have been associated with communal farming systems known as rundale in Ireland, runrig in Scotland and open-fields in England (the term subdivided fields is currently preferred). The essence of rundale was that members of a community (about four or five households) equalized their access to the different *types* of resources in their neighborhood; all members of the community held some land in each block of cultivable land, as well as sharing access to waste on a proportional basis, as described previously. In many cases, the arable land was a permanent feature on the landscape, continuously in production and intensively manured. This 'infield' was divided into blocks of land in each of which each household held one strip. Thus the household that held the first strip (going in a clockwise or 'sun-shift' direction) in the first block, held the first strip in the second and subsequent block.[28] In this way everyone received shares of the better and worse lands within the infield, and had his strips plowed and harvested as soon as his neighbors. (Evans' map of Glentornan in Donegal offers an excellent illustration of lands laid out in this kind of way [E. Evans 1939: 35]).

Another method of equalizing access to arable of different quality was to rotate ownership of whole blocks of land, a regime sometimes termed change-dale. It was suitable to areas where good tillage was scattered in small patches, in a stony or waterlogged environment. Dispersed fields are common in such terrain; they are demarcated by walls built of the stones cleared from the land when it was prepared for plowing. As was noted above, these used to be interpreted as evidence of *Einzelhof*, but McCourt cites examples from the west of Ireland, especially South Connemara, of individual holdings consisting of several small, oval-shaped wall-enclosed patches that were held as dispersed individual plots in a rundale system, and rotated between members of the community (1971: 131). Archaeological evidence of early medieval field enclosure does not, then, provide evidence against the practice of rundale in early historical Ireland. 'Change-dale', under the aegis of the local chief, is well documented for many parts of late medieval Ireland (Nicholls 1972: 60-4).

Intermediate in physical type between subdivided open fields, and rotated enclosed fields, was the field-grass system. Under this regime, the plowed parcels of land were changed every so often, the arable moving on in a fixed cycle around the settlement, with every cultivator getting a share in the plowed land, while the rest of the land was left under grass. In Europe, field-grass systems are widespread in areas with high precipitation (Ühlig 1971: 103-4). They constitute an extensive use of cleared land as arable, which would be compatible with low demand for arable and low levels of labor for manuring (necessary to fixed infield); they thus represent a simpler form of agriculture and may well have been employed in Ireland alongside the shifting cultivation of patches of marginal land by means of slash-and-burn clearance (E. Evans 1956: 229). The Hebridean term for the arable parcel in the field-grass system (*machair*, big field) is found in Old Irish also (*machaire*). Where population levels rose, such field-grass systems might develop into permanent infields (Ühlig 1971: 104); the reverse process might presumably occur also.

What forces may account for the communitarianism of rundale systems? Thirsk (1964: 16) and recently Dodghson (1980: 18-20) suggest that transhumance may have played a formative role in this development. Early communities, living (we suppose) in an uncongested environment, might have been free to hold their cultivation plots as privately owned discrete blocks, scattered about on the arable, but for the problem of synchronizing the timing of the movements of the animals between the winter settlement and the summer pasture. The possibilities and dangers of individual advantage were enormous; a man who kept his cattle too long near the fields in late spring might be responsible for ruining someone's crops, while fattening his own cows. Similarly, a man who brought his cattle down first would have them grazing the stubble before anyone else's herds got the chance. Perfect fencing and policing of individual arable plot and herds was one solution, but far easier was for all members to share the risks and benefits by holding the arable in an open field, sub-divided by temporary demarcations into individual strips, onto which everyone's animals were turned lose at the same time, November 1 (see Ch. 5). The closer farms were to each other the more pressing would this problem be; clustering would have been unavoidable where good arable was in short supply, as was often the case in highland-zone Atlantic Europe. Competition for good arable, and mutual suspicion of privately owned herds would together have impelled the formation of communal, open-field systems. These would thus seem to be integral to transhumant mixed farming across a large area of Europe.

But notwithstanding such explanations of open-field communal farming and Gray's early identification of rundale as common throughout highland Britain (Gray 1915: 189-98), the assumption that *Einzelhof* settlement, with 'individual' land-holding was typically 'Celtic' became entrenched in Celtic scholarship (Proudfoot 1961: 94; Buchanan 1970: 148). Evans, who pioneered the study of clustered settlement with communal fields, complained that 'some Irish historians still regard it (communal farming) as a unique aberration arising in response to population pressure in the eighteenth century.'[29] Smyth attributes the dogmatic retention of the *Einzelhof* model by Irish historians to declining interest on their part in historical geography, and a 'heavy and stultifying emphasis on philology' (Smyth 1982: 2). Other reasons also exist: the charge that Irishmen had no 'definite' rights in land, but merely notional ones (lacking both title and aerial concreteness) carries dire historical associations with land confiscations during the colonial period and charges of primitiveness by Victorian scholars. It is, furthermore, not easy to reconstruct in any detail how Irish inheritance customs, which combined individual tenure with methods of redistribution and shared usufruct, actually worked during the early medieval period. Nevertheless, the Irish law-tracts do hint that multi-household, agrarian co-operative groups were a normal type of social organization in early and later medieval Ireland, alongside more nucleated farms operated by co-residential extended families. We shall now look at this evidence.

Comaithches : textual evidence for agrarian communities

As Kelly points out, early Irish farming was cooperative, but not
collective, for produce was not pooled and divided up on a *per capita*
basis (1988: 102). The major source on agrarian communities, *Bretha
Comaithchesa*, implies the existence of varying degrees of cooperation
during different phases in community development. *BC* shows that after
'many heirs' had been born on land, community fission occurred and
'the heirs' would fence off their separate holdings.[30] The emphasis of
the tract was upon the validity of rules of cooperation and mutual
liability, even *after* such fencing went up. It is therefore implied that
many a little community existed that had no such divisions, where
initial colonization took the form of a single farmstead, followed by a
rundale system in which the successors held strips in the open fields,
until such time as re-division into smaller units was necessitated by the
growth of the community. The tract also makes no reference to
subsequent divisions amongst the heirs, leaving us to assume that the
initial division would give rise to small co-operatives, consisting of the
descendants of those who divided the land. In other words, the tract is
compatible with the kind of settlement expansion and contraction
observed by McCourt in late historical sources. Moreover, though the
community was legally divided after partition, a rule of *comaithches*
cited in a different Old Irish legal source, *Bretha Nemed,* shows that the
community preserved much of the integrity of an undivided unit, and in
this resembled known rundale systems:

> This is a rule of *comaithches*, any holding that does not
> include a portion of uncultivated land and mountain is
> entitled to such a portion and to access to it.[31]

BC envisaged the households as clustered together on the best
grain-growing land, as this Old Irish passage on the right of 'easement'
shows:

> A co-tenant who is between two lands is entitled to full
> passage; six persons are to be about them (the cattle), three
> from the owner of the land and three from the man of
> passage.'[32]

This rule is another instance of the tendency of social regulation in early
'multiple estate' agrarian systems to inhibit competition and exploitation
of unequal resources by farmers of roughly similar social standing. The
idea behind the above rule was to prevent people from imposing a fee

on neighbors whose passage-way was blocked. The route in question was probably not a track in daily use but a route that lead out of the area, for the tract refers to people moving on *imirce*, 'expedition' (see above). An example of a tax for passage-way survived in Warwickshire, England, until the last century. Here peasants had to pay the Duke of Buccleuch his 'wroth silver' on Nov. 11 for passage between the villages and Dunsmore Heath, where the peasants' presumably had summer grazing grounds, turbary, and so forth. Fines were high and archaic in form — a pound for every penny unpaid, or a white bull with red ears (Hole 1976: 217-8). The latter is a well-known Celtic specification (Mac Cana 1970a: 34), so the 'wroth silver' custom, which is dated to pre-Norman times, may be reasonably regarded as pre-Anglo-Saxon also, dating back to Romano-British multiple estate organization. In this English example, charging a fee for passage-way was the privilege of a lord. The Irish rule cited above was designed to prevent the social distance that ensued from the fission of a farming community turning into pseudo-lordship on the part of some members through their mere ability to dominate a route. Again, one sees that lordship depended on control of the social organization that could dominate large areas of waste, not merely local access to resources.

The clustering of residences does not imply that houses lay side by side in compact villages, but only that residences, be they unclosed houses or ringforts, were near enough for people to interact together regularly. At the nucleus of some settlements there would have been a patch of open land, the green, *mag*. This was a protected area of cleared but uncultivated land, adjacent to the residence of some person who had legal authority to forbid unlawful behavior there. No one of lower status than a middle-rank farmer (*bóaire*) could claim fines for violation of his 'precinct', however, so that where there existed a green that had any social utility as a meeting place we can assume the presence of some legally competent person and, close to the green, his house.[33] Where higher-status individuals resided, there would also be a pound for the confinement of trespassing or distrained animals, situated on the *mag* or *faithche* (Kelly 1988: 178).

Faithche is another term for cleared land at the center of the community, but this was typically cultivated land. *BC*, for example, discusses fines imposed when someone's pet piglet escaped from within the *lís* (i.e. ringfort) or *faithche* (from a pen on the *faithche*, presumably) and got into the garden or arable (*gort*) on the *faithche*

(*CIH* 72.18 = *AL* iv 109). A commentary to the same text classifies the 'crimes' of hens in a way that sheds light on the farming arrangements of a community centering on a ringfort. Three degrees of nuisance were recognized: (i) if hens broke out of their spancels (flexible hoops, tying the legs), and got into someone's house, where they were likely to steal, spill or waste grain (griddle-cakes and porridge would be made on the domestic fire); (ii) if they got into the enclosure of the ringfort, where they were thought likely to swallow bees, and damage leeks, the red-dye plant, *roid*, and herbs; (iii) if they got out of the ringfort, then they were likely to cause damage (i.e. to grain) in the kiln, mill, stacks of corn, barn, fields or vegetable garden (*CIH* 74.7-14 = *AL* iv 119). In this jural model, the interior of the ringfort (during the summer) is depicted not as a cattle enclosure, but a place where all the ingredients for cooking, health-care and textile manufacture - the domestic arts *par excellence* - were close at hand. (The picture is, of course, schematic and localized; mills cannot be assumed to have stood outside every enclosure.)

Beyond the green and the settlement, the community's cleared lands stretched out. Several tracts depict this as divided into four quarters. The distribution of the honey from a swarm of wild bees was organized on the basis of division amongst neighbors who held 'the four nearest farms' (*BB* #2; #6). An old gloss on the text implies that as individual's lands were interspersed with those of others; otherwise the system of assessment would have depended on the bee-keeper's lands being in a central location, which would have made the distributive rules inapplicable in many cases.[34] Under rundale, however, a person who had his bee-hive on the edge of the arable would have owned as much land in the center as anyone else. Groups of four tenants were also assumed by the section of *BC* that dealt with confiscation of the lands and property of a member who was neglecting his social duties. The discussion of the procedure (described in Ch. 12) assumed the presence of four parties; the 'evader of duties' himself, his next of kin in the coparcenary, and two 'solvent landholders' who were the aggrieved parties. The commentary on the tract on estray (lost and found property) defines the *faithche* as the four cultivated fields (*gort*) nearest the settlement (*baile*).[35]

Members owned individual shares of these lands, typically described as ridges, which were either lazy-beds (spade tillage) or furrows in plowed fields. One of the major aspects of *comaithches* organization was the protection of neighbors' lands from each other's straying animals. *BC* recognized three grades of land; cornfields, pasture land, and mountain pasture. The Old Irish law-tract, *Tír Cumáile,* offers a much fuller itemization of different types of land and their utility, including the evaluation of different kinds of rough land (Mac Niocaill 1971). It was on such knowledge and memorization of traditional assessments that the brehons were able to assess the potential stocking ratio and renders to a lord from every farming unit.

In the canonical text of the source on estray, mentioned above, there appears a classification of social space in terms of the likely frequency with which the settlement's inhabitants would venture there. The old classification begins with the house, then proceeds to the *cathair* (enclosure) and on to the *faithche* (fields), the *raite* (common pastures), the *rofida* (great forest, i.e. not coppice) and *slíab* (moor or mountain). In the commentary, the pasture is referred to as *sechter faithche* (outer *faithche*); these lands were depicted as extending as far as the limits of the cow's grazing before it turned home for milking, or as far as the sound of a bell could be heard (on monastic lands? *CIH* 57.16-18 = *AL* v 329.14), or the crowing of a cock (*BB* #46). Lands that lay beyond, i.e. the forest, moor or mountain, were viewed as unsafe areas, into which livestock or implements should not be taken, and where the animals were unlikely to be found if they strayed.

This conceptual organization of the local community's social space was profoundly entrenched in Irish culture, for Glassie obtained from a twentieth-century farm-owner in Ballymenone, Ulster, a description of her farm, in which she depicted her lands as radiating out from her kitchen, just as the commentator to *BC* started the itemization of the hen's mischief with the damage it might do to food as it was being prepared in the house. The modern farmer envisaged her lands extending out from there, by concentric circles, through an inner rim of work and storage areas, to an outer ring of tillage, then a circle of moss, and finally bog (Glassie 1982a: 352). This description applied to one farm, of course, whereas the multi-resource land-unit described in the source on estray was assumed, in the commentary, to have been the shared lands of several closely related families, a *gelfhine* (normally understood to be a group of adult agnatic first cousins and their households).[36]

Land-assessment and 'taxation'

The early medieval populations of the western regions of the British Isles tended to cluster together in small groups consisting of more than one, but less than ten, nuclear families. The Old Irish law tracts symbolize the closest circle of kin (*gelfhine*), and the agrarian cooperative community (*comaithches*) as, respectively, a group of five or four households. Although a rich lore of number symbolism lies behind such designation (Patterson 1985), it is probable that the number five was acceptable because it had an air of realism to it. Five households were commonly found in early modern Irish and Scottish hamlets under the runrig field system, prior to the eighteenth- century population explosion, and were noted by Buchanan in Lecale, and by McCourt in a number of areas (Handley 1953; Buchanan 1973: 600; McCourt 1971: 135). Leister also found groups of four to five Irish peasant tenants (*betagh*) to be typical in the thirteenth-century Lisronagh (Tipperary) manorial rental (1976: 10, 45). Romano-British upland villages (Hanley 1987: 16-7), and the pre-Roman settlement at Glastonbury were also characterized by domestic hut-groups ranging in numbers from four to five households. In Glastonbury the fifth site was a 'mega-unit' of greater size and complexity than the others, and emerging during the latest phase of the community's development. (Clarke 1972: 808, 830-35).

But even with a trend towards hamlet-clustering, much variation must have existed. The four-fold division of the lands of a *comaithches* could not possibly reflect a universal physical norm for community layout (as the commentator on estray observed). Many *Einzelhöfe* must have existed, alongside bigger and lesser aggregates of cooperating households. The four-fold model is an abstract jural one, suggesting that the quadripartite division was made for the administrative convenience of jural authorities. Anticipating the discussion of military organization in the next chapter, I shall here point out that the Irish law tracts' assertion that military obligations were assessed against one of the subdivisions of the kin-group (*gelfhine*), which was itself linked to the agricultural cooperative group, the *comaithches* (see below), suggests that the latter unit was one on which charges were laid by the élite. Also pointing to this conclusion is the fact that the *comaithches*, though associated with the *gelfhine* in the eyes of early brehons, and originating in the fission of a growing lineage, according to *BC*, might include non-kin; the term *comaith* had nothing to do with kinship, but referred only to joint-liability for taxes (Kelly 1988: 233 n.23). The existence of a system of assessment implies some degree of social planning. For instance, the various privileges of social ranks discussed in later chapters of this book were graduated according to individuals' shares of land and capacity, in order to put pressure on the farmer to maintain commensurate stock and arable. Planning can also be inferred from the ideal of balanced ecological composition in the different levels of social territory, described previously. The purpose of such self-sufficiency was, basically, to maintain productivity and population levels, and to ward off debt and its political dangers.

Conclusion

It seems that the basic political entity, the *tuath*, was an agglomeration of communities that shared the problems of inescapable social interaction with each other, on account of shared pastoral use of waste. Similarly, the bigger kingdoms were identified by physical boundaries which largely confined the interaction of the component parts to internal relations. Viewing the social process in terms of successful social aggression, it seems likely that political units formed when dominant groups succeeded in wresting control of critical areas of pasture, and from this basis succeeded in compelling those who needed to cultivate adjacent regions to enter into relations of debt and obligation. Once such a structure of social relationships was in place the élite enforced a degree of egalitarianism as to exploitation of natural resources upon the farmers, within a land-use system characterized by G. R. J. Jones as a 'multiple estate'. The productivity and cooperation of the agrarian producers was crucial to the élite's survival, but even more basic to its power was domination of the large ecological unit, centering on the politically vulnerable waste, which could only be policed by a horse-borne military élite. The latter waxed, waned, and sometimes migrated altogether, as fortune would have it.

Middle-level mixed-farmers who belonged to land-owning clans may often have lived within ringforts; the aristocracy certainly occupied the bigger and more elaborately constructed ringforts. Some cultivators may have operated farms with the labor of only a single-family or extended family, but many, especially those under clientship obligations, grouped together in *comaithches* organizations. The cultivators, being dependant, retained a more fixed relationship to the landscape, though they too moved around within their more confined space. They interacted and cooperated within the smaller ecological units, which lay around or in the midst of the wastes and wildernesses. In the law-tracts, cultivators are depicted as occupying settlements laid out on a quadripartite field plan, within a concentric area of land-use focusing on the ringfort or groups of houses. But on the ground there was much variety in physical lay-out and also in the structure of groups, as social processes worked out in various ways, for rundale-type cooperative farming and single-household farming appear to have represented different phases in community development.

Much of the later chapters of this book will be taken up with an examination of the social relations of these groups of close kin and neighbors, and their integration into the wider community. Before examining these aspects of social structure, however, we should complete our picture of the physical setting of Irish society by gaining a sense of how human beings organized their use of resources and of space over time, for all the social action that followed from the structure of social relations was choreographed on the two dimensions of place and time, in rhythmic and regular sequences. This is the subject of the next chapter.

Notes

1. See the example of the wanderings of Clann Mhuircheartaigh Uí Conchobhair in the fourteenth century. See Simms 1986: 382.

2. Byrne 1971: 182-4. There are several 'expulsion' stories, which served to rationalize the low status of the group, or some of the group, in question. Actual migrations, however, are likely to have happened during the rise of the new dynasties, though the details cannot be recovered directly from the legends.

3. Sixteenth-century English officials, attempting to transform the indigenous system of renders into a fixed taxation system, acquired much of their knowledge of local conditions from the brehons. See Patterson 1991a.

4. Since *buaile* only means a milking place it does not necessarily imply a summer pasture. Graham's study was therefore based on names that appear only in areas not permanently settled until the nineteenth century.

5. Binchy 1941: 109; Dillon and Chadwick 1967: 92-5; Nolan 1979: 7-8; A. Simms 1988: 34; Hennessey 1985: 63; Empey 1985: 78-9.

6. *'a fedaib 7 fásaigib in chúicid'*. O'Rahilly 1967: lines 69-70; transl. p. 139.

7. *a mbothainte bó 7 a n-alma 7 a n-immirge.* O'Rahilly, *ibid.*

8. *e(i)rrech di she(i)scshlabrai i ndíthrub íar tuidecht tar crích.* CG 561-2. See Binchy's note on *errech*, *CG* p.87.

9. *Athgabail sescaich nad biat i mbuaili (CIH 897.32 = AL ii 119 = Binchy 1972b: 78-9: #2.1)*

10. *BES AON I NAONMETHUS (CIH 1464.1 ff, 1752.22, 1954.31 ff = AL ii 107.1).* For *methus tuaithe* see *DIL.*

11. *noise 7 sesca i fid 7 i muigh (CIH 581.23 = AL iv 143 31-2).* ('deer or dry cows in a wood or plain').

12. *Atait teora sealba na beiread ba donahib caithaib-seo .i. rudh 7 roilbe 7 foach tuaithi... uair is a nirind do cach ceathra olceana. (CIH 198.4-6 = 579.6 ff. = AL iv 125, 35-8).* DIL has no definitive translation for *foach*.

13. Bieler 1979: 140-1 # 22, cited by Doherty 1982: 304.

14. *TIR CEN CONN CIN COIBNE ...cin coibnesta s tetnuis 7 burba. CIH 1863.1-2)*

15. *TAIT .UII. NATHGABALA GABAR LA CID FOR IMIRGI NOCH SCUIRID A CARRU NOCHIS GNATH IS TURRTUGUD DO ATHGABAIL IMIRGI. ATHGABAIL FOENLEDAIG FONINDLI TUATHA. ATHGABAIL ELODUIG ASLUI ARA FINE. ATHGABAIL FUIDIR ASLAI ARA FLAITH. (CIH 38.29-32 = AL v 61 [xlii]).*

16. *FOXAL AR AES FORAIRE...(21) in smacht fuil ar lucht na norcrich da ructha .s. na crichi... (CIH 390.8, 33-4 = AL i 189.42-4).*

17. Edwards (1990: 41) points out, however, that at the beginning of the century, Westropp recorded large numbers of promontory forts. Of these only eight have yet been investigated.

18. The reference to 'fort' is not very helpful, but the Irish word, *rath*, is easily confused with the same term meaning a fief from a lord.

19. For a recent survey of archaeological findings and disputes regarding ring-forts, see Edwards 1990: 6-33.

20. Desmond McCourt 1971: 151-3. McCourt cites Proudfoot 1961: 119, and E. Watson, 'Prehistoric sites in south Antrim', *Ulster J. Archaeol.* 19 (1956): 87-91.

21. ... *luch aenlis 7 aenbaili. (CIH 285.15, 19 = AL iii 273.14-5, 23).*

22. G. F. Barrett, 'The ring-fort: a study in settlement geography with special reference to southern County Donegal and the Dingle area, county Kerry', unpublished Ph.D. thesis Queens University, Belfast. Cited in Barry 1987: 21-2.

23. Price has argued that its original meaning was simply a piece of land, and not a hamlet or group of houses. Price 1963.

24. Stokes, *Lismore Lives*: 142.4759. Cited by Doherty 1982: 309.

25. *IM CORUS DUIN, i. a cuit isin dun coitcend na fine. (CIH 369.35-6 = AL i 131.38-9). FINEBRETHA...im corus duine, im corus treibe. (CIH 388.18, 20 = CIH 1692. 38, 40 = AL i 183.1 ff).* (*corus treibe* could here be translated as 'rules of a tribe', since *DIL* notes that *treb* (b). 'household, tribe', is probably influenced by Latin *tribus*.)

26. *ATHGABAIL DENMA DUIN. (CIH 399.3 = AL i 215.34-5)*

27. Norman and St. Joseph 1969: 48 n.1. See plates 29,30,32,34,35 for examples of fields that abut the embankment of the ring-fort.

28. Details of how this method worked in medieval English villages are found in Homans 1941: 92-101.

29. Evans, 'Introduction' to Hill's *'Facts from Gweedore'*: x-xi.

30. *CAIR CAN FORBEIR COIMAITHCES. A ILCOMARBUS.* Whence does co-tenancy arise? From many heirs. *(CIH 64.18 = AL iv 69.22-3).*

31. Gwynn 1940: 18-26. Translation from *DIL.*

32. *COMICHEACH DO BIS ITER DA TIR DLIGID LANIMIRCHE BID SEISEAR UMPU TRIAR O FIR TIRE 7 ARAILI O FIR IMIRCHE. CIH 205.1, 11 = AL iv 156-7.*

33. The *bóaire's* 'inviolable precinct', *maigen*, extended from his house to wherever he could cast a spear of specified size from his threshold while sitting down. The *maigen* of an *aire désa* (the lowest rank of lord) was twice this distance. *(CIH 1431.37-1432.2 = AL iv 227).*

34. *Bechbretha* #2 b; shares in honey and swarms went 'to the people of the land which is next to them on every side, on the two sides and the two headlands of the land.'

35. *(CIH 57.15-6 = AL v 329.9-12).* The writer added that as far as the rules of estray were concerned, even if the settlement were right next to a mountain, the latter would count as *faithche* in terms of being a place where a person might readily lose or find something. Clearly this spacial scheme was used quite consciously as a model.

36. *(CIH 55.28 ff = AL v 323.25 ff).* AL describes the kinsmen as occupying the four nearest townlands, and the four adjacent ones, but the commentary to the tract only mentions the four 'points' of the community *(cetharard: CIH 55: 28-9)*, whose members shared the common pasture as far as its limits (theoretically, the mountain boundary).

CHAPTER FIVE

The Seasonal Rhythms of Social Life

As the last chapter suggested, people were more physically mobile in early Ireland than stereotypes of the parish-bound medieval peasant would imply. Their movements were not entirely free, however, but structured by the demands of agriculture, particularly the cycles of animal life, which had a strong seasonal basis. This chapter reconstructs the relationship between animal and human behavioral rhythms, looking at how the former helped pattern such major social activities as work, war, sexual relations and festivals.

Unfortunately, social rhythms were not matters that our sources found worth emphasizing: Irish literature produced many descriptions of monstrous pigs and mythic bulls, but no Hesiod, Columella or Thomas Tusser. One must rely, then, on scattered references from the following types of sources to supplement what may be gleaned from the early Irish sources:

(1) Agricultural histories of other parts of the British Isles. These have been used while bearing in mind such regional differences as the absence of winter-sown crops and hay harvesting in early Ireland.

(2) Later accounts of Irish and Scottish Highland folk practices. Again the comparability of these sources with those from early Ireland is limited, for later Celtic folklore derived from peasant societies stripped of indigenous aristocratic culture.

(3) Another anachronistic source used in this chapter is *Beatha Aodha Ruaidh Uí Dhomhnaill* (Walsh 1948), an Irish biography of Red Hugh O'Donnell, a sixteenth-century northern Irish chieftain. It is used to model the seasonality of warfare because it offers a level of detail unobtainable elsewhere. Despite the changes that had occurred by the sixteenth century, many conditions relevant to warfare persisted from the early middle ages, notably the dense forest cover (Nicholls 1972). The English found that sophisticated weaponry was less important than adequate food supplies, and money to pay informers and guides. When

these failed they adopted a scorched earth policy to starve the Irish chieftains into submission (Lydon 1972: 68-70, 128 ff; Mac Curtain 1972: 39-112). This implies that Irish lords depended on fresh farm produce to sustain their military efforts. Since farming still followed ancient rhythms, warfare too remained seasonal.

An outline of the seasonal pattern

The Irish divided the year into a warm summer period, *sam*, and a cold winter period, *gam*.[1] These were respectively associated with light and dark, work and rest, male and female. These paired qualities were also linked with south and north, sacred and profane (Mytum 1992: 88). In contrast to the Julian and Gregorian calendars, the Celtic year began on November 1, *Samain* (later Halloween) — the commencement of the winter period of rest and darkness, just as the Celtic day was reckoned from dusk to dusk (Rees & Rees 1961: 85-89). Although the 'dark' period was strongly associated with death, it was also depicted as generative (*ibid*: 84; 88), for all the social arrangements of the coming year were planned in the dead of winter.

This primary division was based, in Ireland at least, on the movement of livestock in transhumance: winter began when the last animal was brought down from the summer pastures and the crops were all in, while summer began on May 1, when livestock was moved away from the growing crops to the hills or other rough pastures. The pastoral basis of the two halves of the year shows up in terms for food; meat was called 'winter food' and dairy produce was called 'white meat' as well as 'summer food'.

With its strong links to pastoral rhythms, the Celtic year did not emphasize the solar cycle (Rees and Rees 1961: 83-94), as may be seen by comparing the dates of equinoxes and solstices with those of the Irish 'quarter day' festivals. The spring equinox is March 21, but the Irish spring began with the festival of *Imbolc* on February 1; the summer solstice is June 22, but the Irish summer festival was *Beltene* on May 1; the autumn equinox is Sept. 23, but the Irish autumn festival of *Lugnasad* was on Aug. 1; the winter solstice is Dec. 22, but the Irish winter began with the festival of *Samain*, on Nov. 1. Irish seasonal festivals thus fell mid-way between the solar dates, showing that the phases of the annual cycle of the sun were not themselves the object of celebration.

In the nineteenth century some antiquarians theorized that the Old Irish year was the product of Christian influence, which had suppressed ancient solar customs and moved the traditional festivals away from the solstices and equinoxes. Modern scholarship rejects this view and shows that the Old Irish quarter days celebrated pre-Christian festivals. What is more, though the Church suppressed pagan rituals it did not attempt to appropriate the quarter days. Most of the major Christian feasts were positioned at points on the calendar where they did not compete with the pagan holidays of northern Europe. Thus Lent and Easter fell between *Imbolc* and *Beltene*, and Christmas between *Samain* and *Imbolc*. Only minor religious feasts were superimposed on the pagan ones, and at a relatively late date. These were the Purification of our Lady (Candlemas) on Feb. 2, the day after *Imbolc*; the first Sunday after Pentecost (usually May 1, *Beltene*), which became the Feast of the Commemoration of All Martyrs; and the feasts of All Saints and All Souls, which were placed at Nov. 1 and 2, at *Samain* (James 1961: 199-238).

The Church could not totally efface the indigenous social calendar because this was linked to important agricultural practices. Traditions of the 'quarter days' therefore survived for centuries after the demise of Druidry, with an aura of magic and danger clinging to them. Their relation to the turning points in the seasonal rhythms of the main domestic animals has been observed by some scholars (Lehmacher 1950: 146-7; Sjoesdted 1982: 68), but without any comment on the social complexity of these connections. Whitlock also comments on the existence of 'two rural calendars, an agricultural one and a pastoral one', but deals mainly with recent British seasonal folk customs (1978: 9-10). This chapter thus attempts a new synthesis of scholarship regarding the social organization of time in early Ireland. It should be noted that the discussion concerns only mundane time: the vast subject of time in the otherworld, a subject which fascinated the Irish imagination, is best left to students of Irish literature.

The year's round of human activities followed the overlapping cycles of growth in several living resources — grain, vegetables, fruit, flax, nuts, cattle, sheep, pigs, game and bees, to name only the most important. Like other northern people, the early Irish plowed and sowed grain in the spring and hoped to reap in August and September. They busied themselves with the birth of livestock from late January to April, with moving the stock up-hill in early May, and milking them all summer. At mid-summer, sheep were sheared and lambs separated from their mothers in preparation for breeding. So busy was the upland pastoral season throughout highland Britain that the Welsh noun, *hafod* (summer residence) supplied a verb, *hafota*, 'to work hard', while *hendref* (permanent residence) supplied *hendrefa*, 'to rest'. By the end of October the latest crop, oats, had been harvested, supplies were known, and surplus livestock slaughtered. A period of rest from outdoor work followed, during which, however, much labor was expended on preserving food and making feasts.

This is the broad pattern of seasonal rhythms. It meant that people shifted continuously from one type of work to another, and to a lesser extent, from one type of social group to another. There was only one decisive break in routine, namely *Samain*, after which neither land nor animals required major efforts, but people stayed indoors, not idling it is true, but at least working with a preponderance of their own species for a change. Following the native model, our discussion begins with the Celtic new year's day and the arrival of winter.

The festival of *Samain* and the winter season

An Old Irish poem conveys the security of life in winter when the turbulent elements kept sea-raiders away:

> The bitter wind is high tonight
> It lifts the white locks of the sea;
> In such wild winter storm no fright
> Of savage Viking troubles me. (Flower 1979: 38)

During this period of domestic coziness, people busied themselves with the work of forming all the social bonds that produced kinship organization, patron-client relationships, and war. The agricultural profile of the winter season is dominated by the unproductiveness of the earth and people's dependence on stores of preserved foods. The grain harvest, even in bad weather, was supposed to be in by November 1; in the Welsh laws no one might claim compensation for crop damage by cattle after this date (Owen 1841: 157). Cattle too should now be down from the hills where snow was generally expected thereafter. The young animals had long since been weaned from their mothers so as to facilitate breeding, and most sheep and cows were carrying next spring's young. Only the occasional cow was allowed to stay in milk over the winter with its *gamuin*, winter calf, keeping lactation going beyond October.[2] With fresh milk no longer abundant, people turned to the reserves of cheese gained from the summer's milking and churning. Even the fruits of orchard and hillside were now regarded as rotten, the spirits having fouled them, and were not to be eaten even if they looked fit (Rees and Rees 1961: 92). Such taboos ensured compliance to a set routine of consumption and production despite the great variations that occurred in natural conditions over short spans of time.

Though some outdoor work was always required, the season's emphasis was on domestic labor, principally meat production (slaughtering, butchering, preserving, cooking and presenting meat as food), activities that all took place in and around the farm settlements. *Crith Gablach* describes the standard farm equipment of a low-ranking freeman, the *ócaire*, as including an outhouse big enough for him to divide his food in it and put aside the *bés*, the customary render due to his lord (*CG* 104). Similarly, the farm of the higher-ranking *mruigfer* was supposed to have salt and equipment for butchering and preserving meat (*CG 190-1*). Although agricultural historians now believe that the Martinmas slaughter (November 10) has been greatly exaggerated, this was nevertheless the time to cull whatever older animals seemed unlikely to survive the rigors of winter, and those young males calculated to be surplus to farming needs by the next spring (Ryder 1981: 340-45).

The domestic focus of *Samain* was all the more intense because people who had dispersed during the summer now returned to their home bases. These included whatever women and children had remained with the livestock on the summer pastures from May 1 until the end of the transhumant season. There was some regional variation regarding the timing of the return to the winter farmsteads, but *Samain* was the traditional outer limit of the use of upland pastures.[3] Lowland communities were also swollen by other arrivals: from *Samain* on, nobles and kings required their dependents to 'quarter' their servants, animals and mercenaries. Keating describes the seasonal movements of the warrior bands known as *fían:*

> The men of Ireland would house and feed the *Fían*
> from *Samain* to *Beltaine (sic)*, and in turn the *Fían*
> would preserve order and prevent wrong-doing for the
> kings of Ireland; also they protected and guarded the
> coast of the kingdom against the invasion of

> foreigners; from *Beltaine* to *Samain* the *Fían* would
> hunt and perform any other service which the king of
> Ireland requested of them .... However from *Beltaine*
> until *Samain* the *Fían* were obliged to depend on the
> products of their hunting and of the chase as
> maintenance and wages from the kings of Ireland ...
> the flesh for food and the skins of the wild animals
> for pay. (Dinneen II: 326-9)

Historians are skeptical of Keating's observations on Irish history, but
Le Roux points out that in this instance there is corroboration, for a
poem by Tadhg Dall O'hUiginn mentions the distribution of warriors
'from house to house, with their horses and dogs' (1961: 484, 487).

The quartering of the *fían* closed the season of true warfare,
and opened what may be called the season of plotting. Not that violence
ceased: as we see below, the annals are peppered with references to
assassinations at this time. (House parties made it easy to trap and burn
enemies.) In contrast, there are hardly any references to large battles.
Instead, the nobility took advantage of the period when the *fían* were
grounded to meet each other at rounds of feasts where relationships
were tested, marriages arranged, and the resources of allies assessed.
'Guesting and feasting', *cóe*, extended from the 'calends of January to
Shrovetide' according to several law tracts (*UB* 297 #10, 298 #111; *CG*
334, 384, 400).

Feasting is further examined below, but first we must ask why
the *fían* were demobilized at *Samain*, for the Irish climate was not so
severe that war had to end then. I suggest that Keating's description of
the *fían* bands points to the underlying reason, namely the existence of
customary closed seasons for the hunting of deer and wild boar.
Throughout northern Europe from ancient times until the late middle
ages, hunting was an essential complement of the military life, serving
both as an important food source and as a form of practice for warfare
(Gilbert 1979: 72). We need not doubt, then, that a closed season for
hunting would greatly affect mobile military groups.

The surviving Irish law-tracts provide no information on closed
game seasons, however, compelling us to look at the better data on
hunting in Scotland. An early fifteenth-century poem in the Scottish
Book of the Dean of Lismore (Gilbert 1979: 67) described Scottish
hunting as confined in practice to the period from *Beltene* to *Samain*.
According to Gilbert 'the hind and doe could be hunted in the closed

season during the winter', but in fact they were largely protected by prohibitions against hunting during snow falls, when they were forced to come down the mountains in search of food. This protection stemmed ultimately from ancient conservation practices which sought to ensure that hunters would kill game animals during their peak condition but leave them alone to breed (Gilbert 1979: 69). The open season for stags appears to have run from March to late September, but the most popular months were July, August and September (Gilbert 1979: 67). Given the common cultural origins of Scottish and Irish medieval society and comparable economic and ecological conditions, it is reasonable to assume a similar *de facto* winter closed season for deer-hunting in Ireland.

More important than the deer, however, and central to the mythography of *Samain* was the wild boar, the most ferocious and intelligent of game animals and the one most frequently depicted as a cult object in Celtic art (Ross 1974: 39 ff). *Samain* coincides with the onset of the breeding season of the wild pig, which lasts from November to January (Ryder 1981: 391), whereas that of the red deer commences in August (Johnson 1848: 'August'). *Samain* therefore marked the close of another period of human 'work' with animals, that is, pig-hunting. But because large-scale hunting was the 'work' of the warrior nobility, and was in fact this group's only direct connection with the production of food, the termination of pig-hunting received great attention in mythic and ritual aspects of the holiday.

Fían rituals gave special attention to the boar-hunt. In *The Instructions of Cormac*, Cormac relates that as a *gilla*, a young man in military apprenticeship, his first significant deed was to kill a pig by himself (Meyer 1909: #7, #8). This may have been a *rite de passage* of a *gilla*, for an elaborately tabooed, single-handed, slaying of a boar is also associated with Finn, the heroic *fían* leader. In the story called *The Feast of Conan's House*, Finn relates that one of his 'deaths' (a positive taboo which he must perform to preserve his life) was to kill a wild boar without rousing it and to carry it without help, to cook it himself, and to distribute it himself to all of his company at the house where they were (Joynt 1936: 1497-1520). The requirement that the animal be killed before it rose or screeched indicates that it had to be a mature male, for the adult boar is the only game animal to die silently (Johnson 1848: 73). Another requirement was that 'there should be no north wind blowing', suggesting that the feast should be held before the onset of winter, probably at *Samain*, then.

Not only was the wild boar formidable, but medieval domestic pigs were also a challenge to manage. They were half-wild, more like those of the ancient Celts described by Strabo (Tierney 1960: 268) than modern porkers. Cormac glosses *muc* (pig) thus:

truculent her nature, for she takes no teaching from
anyone *nisi carnis*! (Stokes 1869: 115).

In early Irish literature and law, pigs were depicted as agile, bold, willful, carnivorous and on terms of sexual intimacy with their feral kin. Hence, rounding up even domesticated pigs in their forest deaneries was more like a hunt than most dealings with farm animals. The continuum between wild and domestic pigs probably helped sustain the seasonal focus of *Samain* on the boar hunt, for even peasants killing a large sow in autumn faced a test of their killing skills.

The pig, wild or domestic, was thus the 'sacrificial animal' of *Samain* (Le Roux 1961: 494-5), but where culinary values prevailed, the domestic kind was preferred. By *Samain* it was at its best, having been fattened all autumn on the acorns of the oak forests and finished to perfection on the stubble of the crops. *O'Davoren's Glossary* associates the pig with tribute from clients to lords:

Fuirec...the name of the food that is carried to the
lord before Christmas...that is to say, the *Samain* pig.
(Stokes and Meyer 1898-1907. II: 373).

The Church added its own explanation, depicting St. Patrick as giving the original *Samain* pig to St. Martin, in gratitude for his tonsure (Mulchrone 1939: 232). The tract on lords' fiefs and renders, *Dliged Raith & Somaíne la Flaith*, stipulates that a *molt* (a wether) was the render due at *Samain* itself, while the *fuirec* (defined as the *Samain* piglet, and 'the tested young pig of the Feast of St. Martin') was due at 'the feast of entertaining' between 'the two Christmases', i.e., Christmas and Epiphany.[4] Pork was again served during this period at the 'feast of waiting', this time in the form of sausages and sides of bacon.[5]

Boars were also major items of tribute claimed by regional kings from their vassals. In *The Book of Rights*, the king of Connacht, for example, claimed from the Luigne one hundred and fifty boars to be delivered at *Samain*; the Cashel 2 list shows that two groups owed the king of Cashel one thousand boars, and one group owed two thousand; the King of Tara, whose allegedly 'national' feast was held at *Samain*, was owed by his various vassals 1,050 boars; and the king of the Laigin was due 1,600 boars (Dillon 1962: 50-1, 179, 186). These gifts were the makings of great feasts and stores of bacon rather than huge stud farms, and the large numbers of animals, even allowing for hyperbole, were just what would be produced by a characteristically Gaelic type of hunt, the drive. This was a sweep of animals by beaters and dogs towards an ambush, where the nobility killed the stumbling game *en masse* (Gilbert 1979: 67).

Samain was the most mysterious period of the year, and the pig shared its awesomeness. The *Metrical Dindshenchas* names several magic boar hunts and the Irish boar was as liable as the Welsh *Twrch Trwyth* to come and go between this world and the otherworld, and to shift his form between human and animal guise (Gwyn 1913: 151, 370, 386, 393, 552; Stokes 1894: 370, 373). The wild pig may have acquired its supernatural associations from its habit of eating acorns — a nut that is poisonous to other domestic animals, but which seems to have been used both as food by pigs and as a hallucinogen by early peoples. There are several instances in early Irish literature of swineherds who possess magical powers (Ní Chatháin 1978-9: 200-11), while men of the *fían* were also depicted as able to penetrate the otherworld, and they too were forest-dwellers (Nagy 1985: 39). *Samain*'s intensely sacral character may thus have stemmed from the convergence of cultural traditions that derived from neolithic forest-based farmers, practicing mixed farming on the basis of a leaf-fodder economy, and also from later Bronze/Iron Age peoples who practiced the more intensive farming associated with upland pastoralism and lowland plowing.

Less enjoyable, perhaps, than 'going nuts', but also emotionally intense, was the social stress that built up at this time of the year under the conditions of Iron Age mixed farming. Until the present century, *Samain* was the time when creditors and debtors (the lords and clients of early times) settled their accounts (Danaher 1972: 206). Lords expected their winter tribute now and partly consumed it in lavish feasts as they made 'circuits' around the homes of their clientele (Binchy 1940: Simms 1978). The political tension at these feasts is shown by the number of banquet brawls that are described in the Old Irish narratives. Though this was drunken violence, it was also, as Philip O'Leary shows (1986), structured, competitive and socially purposive violence, serving in the end to establish the rank order of prestige between peers and to demarcate relationships that had deteriorated to the point of open enmity.

Men gauged the respect in which they were held by their peers and their clients according to the quality of the feast laid on by the latter. There was great pressure, therefore, on the farming population at this time, not only to produce the goods, but to deliver them in perfect condition. Moreover, clients were expected to comport themselves with special sensitivity to the decorum of their noble visitors. According to *DRS*, a client could be fined, for example, for absent-mindedly lighting a candle after his lord had retired, which might cause the latter to think he was about to be assassinated, or it might disclose him 'overtaken at his coupling'. Either way, the lord would be upset and the client liable for reparations (Crigger 1991: 357.14 gloss 1). Timeliness and seemliness were thus demanded of clients' households under conditions that would make it easy to have a fateful mishap.

DRS mentions four separate feasts with different foods, held between *Samain* and Easter:

i. At *Samain* a wether was served to the lord at a feast to which he could bring a retinue of eight men: there was a fine of three *séts*, plus double the worth of the item, if the client failed to provide adequately. The fine was not trivial: it was the equivalent of the honor-price of an *ócaire*, a low-ranking land-holding clansman (in this tract the *sét* was probably worth one milch cow and one heifer).

ii. Between Christmas and Epiphany (Jan. 6), the *fuirec* pig (see above) was served to a retinue of four: the fine for failure was two *séts*, plus double the food's worth.

iii. In the same period, a feast of sausage, bacon and other preserved meat was given to a retinue of five men: failure incurred the same fine as above.

iv. Between Shrovetide and Spy Wednesday (*Cétain*: the Wednesday before Easter) the feast of 'butchering between two flames' was given to a retinue of six, incurring a fine of three *séts* plus double restitution for failure (Crigger 1991: 356.12).

The political sensitivity of the winter season is echoed in mythic conflicts set at this time of the year, conflicts that were recounted at story-telling sessions throughout the season. In Old Irish literature, *Samain* is a time of confusion, the setting for voyages to the otherworld, sexual relations between mortals and others, and gender-blurring customs of cross-dressing (Rees and Rees 1961: 90). It was the occasion of the Feast of Tara,[6] the symbol of supreme political authority, and also, as Mac Cana shows, the setting for attacks on the assembly hall at Tara and the person of the king himself. It was a time so dangerous that a passage from a law tract states:

> It is the poet's duty to be with the king at *Samain* and
> protect him from enchantment. (Mac Cana 1979: 456;
> *CIH* 668.12)

One of Finn's heroic deeds, for example, is to save the royal court at Tara from its annual burning at *Samain* by a hypnotic singing monster (Nagy 1985: 186-8). Legends of class conflict are also encountered: *Lebor Breatnach*, for example, states that the British arose against the Romans at this season on account of their excessive demands for grain tribute (Van Hamel 1931). The great battle between Ireland's legendary prehistoric inhabitants, the *Fomoir* and the *Tuatha Dé Danann*, is also set at *Samain*, when the *Tuatha Dé* rose in revolt against the tribute of grain which their half-Fomorian king, Bres, had imposed on them (Gray 1981-3; 1982). These traditions cannot be linked to verifiable events, but they do reflect an assumption that if clients were to defect, this would be the time to do it.

Samain did not mean that all lords suffered a necessary political decline, of course, but only that there was a natural pause in the flow of political interaction now, and that it might be necessary to renegotiate with some clients. It was not until the beginning of the spring season that actual military campaigns recommenced (see below); the holiday season was a period of latent rather than actualized alliances and enmities. It was perhaps the shadowy and foreboding nature of winter fears and hopes that gave rise to the expression of danger as monstrous and other-worldly, for it was the dreamed-of enemy and ally, to be known in his true colors only in future action, who dominated thought at this time.

During this season, as kings planned the military economy and dynastic marriages, lesser men planned their domestic economies and tried to arrange marriages with neighbors. Later folk tradition suggests that informal courtship often started during customary visits to mountain-tops in early August (MacNeill 1962: 424), which set the scene for familial marriage negotiations during the winter. If all went well, the couple would be married before Shrove Tuesday (Danaher 1964b: 158). There is almost no direct Old Irish evidence on the existence of a marriage season, but Cormac glosses *gam*, which can mean both winter and November, with 'wedding', and in gloss B appears to allude to the Attic *gamelion*, the season 'when the ancients were wont to wed' (Stokes 1869: 82). *Gamelion* extended from the second half of January to the beginning of February; in medieval terms, from Twelfth Night to Shrove Tuesday. This gloss may have been an interpretation of literature in terms of actual Irish social practice, for it would have made sense to celebrate marriages after the end of the season of feasting on Twelfth Night, so as to make full use of the preceding period to settle all the details of the match. It would also have been good to marry before Shrovetide, so as to avoid throwing a party during Lent and 'hungry spring'. The connection between marriage and the post-Christmas season may be assumed to have been stronger than the evidence, for the rhythms of work would have made marriage in the summer even less convenient in early medieval times than in the nineteenth century.

The festival of *Imbolc* and the spring season, *Errech*.

Spring extended from *Imbolc* on February 1, to *Beltene* on May 1. During this quarter, guesting and feasting largely ended, Lent began, and work with the land and with farm animals resumed. Sowing, however, did not take place until March; it was the return of animal vitality, with the birth of the year's first lambs and kids, that initiated the new season. With the Christian conversion, the rituals that opened spring on *Imbolc* were changed to celebrate the feast of Ireland's second saint, Brigid, whose traditions reveal a Christian expression of some of the attributes of the pagan arch-goddess, *Brig* (McCone 1990: 162-3). There are many hints that before the conversion the ritual focus of the season was on motherhood, both human and animal. The new moon at the winter solstice had been the date of major pre-Christian north European festivals of female fertility, such as Old English 'mothers' night', *Módranicht*, and the Norse 'offerings to the goddess', *Dísablot*, (Lehmacher 1950: 145). In Rome, the *Lupercalia* had also had pronounced fertility aspects (Hamp 1979/80: 111 ff). Only in the eleventh century was Candlemas, the penitential rite of the purification of the virgin after the birth of Christ, superimposed by the Church on the complex of women's rituals of this season (James 1961: 230 ff).

There are strong associations between St. Brigid and the protection of women, infants and sheep. The Old Irish Life of Brigid shows the saint rebuking her lazy sisters as she headed out into a winter storm saying, 'I love very much to pasture sheep' (Ó hAodha 1978: 32-3 #46). This was a saintly statement that suggests that mortal women felt quite otherwise about being a shepherdess in February. Several scholars believe that the name for Brigid's feast day, *Imbolc/Oimelc*, may preserve traces of the older religious associations of the festival, for the 'false etymology' of this word in Cormac's glossary is:

that is sheep's milk, that is the time when it comes to
the sheep, milk... (Stokes 1869: 127)

Vendryes (1924) proposed an etymology that would have connected *Imbolc* to the verb *folcaim* (I wash) and went on to suggest that anciently *Imbolc* was a purification festival celebrated with lustration rituals and similar to the Roman *Lupercalia*. His argument was attacked, but other scholars have revived it on new grounds. Guynovarc'h (1961: 471), for example, noted this passage in the *Hibernica Minora*:

Tasting of each food according to order, this is what
is proper at *Imbolc*: washing the hands, the feet, the
head... (Meyer 1894: 49)

Stronger than these traces of lustration rituals, however, is the ritual emphasis on women's interests and on milk at this time of year. Cormac's association of *imbolc* with the arrival of lambs and of sheep's milk probably reflected farming practices that ensured that lambing would precede calving. This would be due to the sheep's ability to crop lower for grass and survive better than the cow on the meager vegetation of late winter. Thus farmers anxious to resume milking as soon as possible in the year on account of their dwindling store, would naturally choose the sheep for early breeding rather than the cow. The dangers of early calving were known in highland Scotland: 'If the cows calve before the first week of March it will be sometimes a month or six weeks before they have milk sufficient to feed the calves' (Robertson 1813: 249). Old Irish tradition suggests that early calving in February was also avoided then, for the most mature calves of the spring were called *dartaid inite*, a Shrovetide male calf (*CG* 109), i.e. born in late February/early March. A similar pattern appears to the present day in Crete, where milking of ewes runs from January to July, after which the flock is washed, sheared, weaned and allowed to run with the rams. (Outerbridge 1979: 112 ff). Shearing and washing break the bond between dam and lamb and bring about weaning. This in turn causes ovulation soon after the summer solstice, since ovulation in the sheep is triggered by the lengthening of night-time after mid-summer (Ryder 1981: 378). Given a gestation period of five months, the first lambs would drop in late January or early February.

The importance of the return of fresh milk at this time can hardly be exaggerated. For one thing, ewe's milk was greatly enjoyed: one of the delectables mentioned in the vision of Mac Conglinne is 'fair white porridge, made with sheep's milk' (Meyer 1892: line 35). It is also higher in fat content than cows' milk (Ryder 1981: 314-5) and all the more valuable therefore in the context of the cold weather and typical food shortage of early February. According to Petty (1719: 51) cows' milk had long since petered out. The Irish viewed the annual milking cycle as 90 days of full milk in May, June and July (3 gallons); 90 days of one third of that (1 gallon); 90 days of about one quart daily; and ninety days of no milk, starting in January. Stored foods had been largely consumed during the preceding period of 'guesting and feasting'. On this socially induced hunger, Fynes Morrison, the sixteenth-century English observer, wrote: 'the wild Irish in time of greatest peace impute covetousness and base birth to him that hath any corn after Christmas, as it were a point of nobility to consume all within those festival days' (Myers 1983: 189).

The onset of 'hungry spring' is depicted in an Old Irish story that describes how a woman saved her father, Gulide, from dishonoring his lord, who had come a-feasting in the dead of winter. Her eloquence appeased him:

> You have come at a bad time. The wind is piercing....
> Our old food is gone, our new food has not come.
> You have come at a bad time, the time when the old
> hag shares her cakelet with the girl. The raven's tail
> stands high with us, the hound's low. The noses of
> our women are strained. There is water in our milch
> cows after our heifers have run dry. Our women are
> pregnant, our kine barren. There is great dryness in
> our kilns, drought in our mills, dearth in our hounds,
> our cats are keen and greedy. (Meyer 1894: 68 #6).

Gulide's daughter was not the only woman to be put in this situation. Throughout the narrative literature, women are shown to have been in charge of the administration of hospitality to guests — a function that went far beyond modern 'housework' in that it involved supervising the use of the domestic assets for private and social consumption. In later Irish folk tradition February 1 was the day for opening up all the cupboards to take stock of what supplies remained to last out the cold weather (Danaher 1972: 14). It is likely that the Old Irish ritual of 'tasting all the food', mentioned above, was connected with a similar assessment of the supplies. Women as managers, then, had good reason to rejoice when lambing began.

Lambing may also have been important in connection with the seasons of human sexuality. In traditional rural Ireland there was a tendency for young men and women to separate on May 1 (*Beltene*: see discussion below), when the transhumant migration took place. With marriages concentrated between Twelfth Night and Shrovetide, and post-nuptial co-residence of new spouses being interrupted after May 1, many first-born babies would have been born between mid-October and February 1. Thus *Imbolc* marked the end of the period of first child-birth and the beginning of breast-feeding by inexperienced new mothers, which in turn meant that the mothers' need for good nutrition coincided with 'hungry spring'. Just at the beginning of this dangerous period, however, the sheep came into milk. It seems likely, then, that a pre-Christian, feminine, celebration of the flocks took place at *Imbolc* in Ireland, but was largely suppressed after the conversion.

Women's child-bed was complemented by men's combat, for a second distinctive feature of spring was raiding. Appropriately, St. Brigid had as one of her secondary manifestations the *persona* of *Brig ambue*, Brigid of the 'cowless' warrior, a particularly desperate type of hired swordsman (McCone 1990: 162-3). Warfare is generally thought of as a summer activity in early northern Europe, but the medieval Irish genealogical tract, *The Tribes and Customs of Hy Many*, records the obligation of clients to provide military service in 'the hostings of spring and autumn' (O'Donovan 1843: 66.3). There was only one time in spring when the local clientele could be raised in a tribal 'hosting', namely between the end of the main part of the guesting season (Twelfth Night) and the beginning of plowing, i.e. between mid-January and early March.

A seasonal pattern of raiding at this time appears in the Life of Aodh Ruadh. His career got off to a shaky start for he was captured in 1587, failed to make good an escape on Twelfth Night 1591, and got out only a year later, at about the same time of year (##8-10: 13-19).

After a year of vigorous military activity, Aodh spent the winter in his 'princely residence' at Lifford, until January 24 when he launched an attack on Turlogh O'Neill (#29: 58-9). The year 1593 saw various successes that culminated in an encounter with the English army on October 6. This resulted in stalemate and the biography records that fighting now gave way to a winter season of negotiation: 'the English and the Irish after that were parleying without either attacking the other, for three months of winter up to February ('*Imbolc*') of the next year' (#32: 66-7), at which time hostilities were resumed when the Deputy seized the castle of Aodh's ally, Maguire. Not till June did Aodh help Maguire, which was unexpectedly late in the year, and Aodh was 'ashamed at being so long' without assisting his ally (#33: 68-9).

The year 1594 proved to be one of Aodh's great ones (defeating the English army at the Battle of the Ford of the Biscuits) and the winter that closed the year was one of intense political organization. This culminated in a foray in which Aodh led various regional clan leaders over his borders and into those of their enemies. This occurred quite late in spring, on March 3, and the biography notes that after the foray Aodh and his allies returned to their homes and rested 'until the end of spring' (#42: 84-5).

The following winter was quite anomalous, but helps us to understand the distribution of military activities over the year. In the winter of 1595/6, instead of quartering himself at home from November to mid-January, Aodh assembled his forces and entered Meath in December to settle the contested succession to the chieftaincy of MacWilliam. Aodh named the MacWilliam, stayed to celebrate Christmas, then returned to his home base on January 15 where he 'rested' until June 1 without any of the usual springtime forays (#65 122-3). What had happened this year was that regional internecine strife had come to a head earlier than usual, in connection with the MacWilliam chieftaincy, and had been settled early, so that none of the usual acts of regional pacification remained to be carried out at *Beltene*. The various attacks that Aodh and others usually made in early spring were aimed at aligning *regional* forces and eliminating local rivals. When we look at summer warfare (below), we see that it was then that the *nationally* dominant military leaders faced each other, after covering the Achilles heel of provincial rivalry.

Springtime warfare was secondary to summer campaigns because it was far less profitable. In the rather late spring raids of 1595, for example, Aodh's men expressed unhappiness with their livestock plunder because they were far from home and because of 'the weakness and feebleness of all kinds of cattle then' (#50: 92-3). Cattle seized at this time of the year would die in numbers if they had to be driven any great distance to the raiders' homes. Summer plunder, on the other hand, included livestock in prime condition, worth driving long distances.

To sum up: in most of the years covered by the biography the spring campaigns were preceded by three months of 'rest' in a secure home base during which lords and their retinues were fed by clients. This winter season was the time when new alliances were forged and plans for the year drawn up. The spring campaigns served to clear away any trouble that was fomenting at the regional base of the alliances of that year, and were often followed by inaugurations of O'Donnell's vassals as lords of their territories. Later in the summer major military confrontations occurred between national-level leaders, which in the sixteenth century included the English governor as well as O'Donnell and O'Neill. Several hundred years earlier equally island-wide struggles and confrontations took place between the ruling heads of nationally paramount dynasties. The probability is that they too attempted to make an early springtime settlement of internecine disputes and rivalry amongst their allies and vassals before they confronted each other in the summer and autumn.

The other main activity of the spring season was the opening of the earth for the crops. This traditionally occurred in March (Danaher 1972: 14), after which the pace of agricultural work quickened. In the low-manpower economy of Old Ireland it was necessary to make sure that the burdens of clientship did not interfere with the demands of cultivation. A potential conflict existed since the Church definition of the season of guesting tied it to a moveable Church feast (Shrovetide) which might fall any time from mid-February to mid-March. A late Shrovetide and Easter would leave the season of guesting open through half the month when plowing was supposed to take place. To counteract the inadequacy of calendar customs at this point secular law maintained that kings should disband their entourages for the whole month:

> There is a month when a king does not go
> accompanied but by three (lit. does not go but four.)
> What are the four? King and judge and two in
> servitorship. What month does he go in this wise?

The month of sowing.' (*CG* 535-8, trans. Mac Néill
1923: 304 #127)

This restriction would have eliminated both feasting and warfare.
Normal legal procedure was also temporarily suspended, for the law
tract, 'On the confirmation of right and law', states that it was a right
of the farming population that no distraint might be made of their
property (usually livestock) 'at an unseasonable time, that is, in spring',
on account of failure to supply the proper food render to their lords
(*CIH* 229.13-14; gloss 14 = *AL* v 443.24-6). The contrast between this
feature of mid-spring and the preceding period (winter and early spring)
is thus very great: on the one hand, men's labor began again, but on the
other hand, the male focus on politics, law and social organization was
temporarily dissolved in favor of material production. What Georges
Dumézil (1968) calls the first and second social functions (rule and
force) competed at this time with the third function (production), with
each function following the other sequentially on the calendar.

The festival of *Beltene* and the summer season

May 1 was celebrated by the rituals of *Beltene,* the fire of the god Bel,
the 'Apollo' of the Gauls (Mac Cana 1970a). At this time important
assemblies and inaugurations of new chiefs occurred. Simultaneously,
the farming communities were split up as the animals and their new-
born young were moved away from the settlements to the summer
pastures. Major rituals accompanied the transition from one half of the
year to the other on May 1 and November 1 (Rees and Rees 1961:
83-92), and some evidence as to their nature has survived, especially
from the Scottish Highlands. But as the symbolism of these rituals can
only be understood in terms of the social forces of the season, it is first
necessary to look at these, beginning with the transhumant shift which
cleared the way for summer military activity.

European transhumance is a very old practice, possibly going
back to the mesolithic (Hicks 1972-3; Fleming 1972). The earliest
documentation is Homer's description of Polyphemus, the Cyclopaedian,
who made cheese of ewes' milk in a remote cave and was probably
engaged in island transhumance comparable to modern Hebridean
practice (*The Odyssey*, ix). Farmers in Spain still follow pre-Roman
trackways to the summer pastures (Outerbridge 1979: 18).

Transhumance probably originated in communities that emphasized sheep-farming, for sheep naturally move uphill in the early spring; they are so difficult to restrain that farmers who wanted their milk and wool had to follow and stay with them on the uplands (Hilzheimer 1936: 195-206).

It must have been uncomfortable to move uphill as early as May 1, but several agricultural pressures dictated movement at this date. One was the fact that the vegetation on the upland pastures was more acceptable to stock at the start of the growing season: by nibbling down unpalatable plants like heather and blaeberry, the flocks and herds conditioned the pastures for summer-long use (Franklin 1953: 32-3). Secondly, there was a shortage of fodder by late winter in the lowland settlements. Cattle were not slaughtered in large numbers before winter (Ryder 1981: 340-41), as was once believed, but were grazed first on the stubble of the harvest and on the lands nearest the settlement, and then on 'preserved fields of winter grass'. Trespass on these fields was punished with heavier fines than trespass on most other kinds of field (*CIH* 69.19-29 = *AL* iv 79.1-17). In the Welsh laws it was a fineable offense in the serfs' hamlets to let beasts stray into the lowland settlement and its adjacent fields (the *tref*) after 'the calends of May until the time of reaping' (Jones 1972: 356). Hungry as they were, the cattle would not make good neighbors to the crops that began to emerge in late spring. Their hunger was such that even getting them from the winter homestead up to the summer pastures without their looting the cornfields was envisaged as difficult.[7] In Ireland, then, as in many other parts of Europe where marginal land was abundant (Ühlig 1971: 102), the community tended to divide on May 1, as some members departed to the 'booleys' with the flocks and herds and all the necessary equipment for cooking, dairying and spinning. The departure was simultaneous because everyone wanted to be sure that no one else's cattle remained near the corn.

In Ireland and Scotland it was women and children who stayed with the animals, while some men returned to the hamlets to weed and protect the crops, and others prepared for warfare. This division of labor by gender was facilitated by the growing season of one of the most valuable crops, flax, which was also an object of women's work. Flax was planted in late April and not pulled until mid-August, when many women would be able to return from the summer pastures and help with the wheat harvest, since at this time both ewes' and cows' milk declined. Doubtless some women also remained at the lowland settlements throughout the summer, to garden, milk, and cook for the remaining community, including working men, the sick and the elderly.

Like *Samain*, *Beltene* was a period of acute social anxiety, for at this time, 'commonly, the Irish captains and lords use to bargain and compound with their tenants' (Sir Philip Sydney, *State Papers, Ireland, 1576*. See Danaher 1972: 6). Deals were cut at other levels of society too, for a law tract refers to the pact between a landless cattle-owner and a land-owner without stock, as running from one *Beltene* to the next.[8] As mentioned above, over-lords got part of their tribute now, and peasants at this time would have to decide whether to enter new clientship relations, according to their stock needs and local politics. In recent folk tradition social anxiety was displaced onto the envious neighbor and the fairies (MacNéill 1962: 69). In Ireland and Scotland it was feared that milk could be stolen on May Day by a witch in the form of an old women, the hag of spring, or a hare that could suckle the cows (Davidson 1958-9: 22-37; Danaher 109-119). But it is not hard to see in these anxieties a suppressed fear of food-taking lords, who required food renders of butter, curds and milk for the 'summer feast', and also cheese and milk at the *craumfes*, the 'feast of garlic' (Crigger 1991: 356 12.6,7). The latter was probably not held at *Lugnasad*, though this is widely known as 'Garlic Sunday', but on the last day of June (*DIL: crem*). Like the main winter dues, both these payments incurred fines of three *séts* for failure to supply, plus double the value of the defective item, and were thus not trivial prestations. It is probable that for the farmers, renders of cheese and milk at the beginning of 'hungry July' were especially onerous.

Supernatural protection from these pressures was sought, often from St. Brigid. She is depicted in her Old Irish Life performing numerous miracles at Easter that protected cattle (Ó hAodha 1978: #22-5). Nearly all the miracles were aimed at averting danger to the social relationships mediated by the gift of cows or milk, not danger to the animals, *per se*. To take one example, #22 relates how a cow and its calf became separated while being driven through a forest by two women. A prayer to St. Brigid brought the cow to the saint, who sent it on as a gift to Bishop Mel. Brigid then miraculously also sent the calf to Mel, since a cow without its calf would soon lose its milk. The point of the miracle, then, was not the safety of the animals, which would have survived on their own, but the delivery of the gift of a cow in milk to an appropriate recipient.

Similarly the magic of this season was directed at social relationships rather than nature. Most of the charms were supposed to protect proprietorial interests, ensuring that only the owners got the 'first fruits' of *Beltene*, such as the first water from the well, the first milk from the dairy, and so on. The focus on 'first things' obviously stems from the status of May 1 as the beginning of the new crop season, but the unstated question was not 'will fertility prevail?', but 'will *I* get what I need out of the common resources of the land in the face of all this competition?'

Some threats to human physical well-being were also envisaged at *Beltene,* as at *Samain.* Spirits were abroad again, this time intent on stealing human children (Danaher 1972: 122-3). This anxiety may have been connected to the end of the season of female ritual potency, and with the weaning of toddlers from breast-milk to gruel made with cereals and animal milk now that dairy produce was available again. Under pre-modern conditions the weaning period is highly dangerous for children, having a death-rate second only to the neo-natal period.

May 1 was also the end of the marriage season, with May Day itself being viewed in later Irish folk tradition as a singularly unlucky date for a wedding (Danaher 1964b: 158). This belief may date back to the practice recorded in Old Irish sources of ending temporary marriages on this day. In *Cáin Lánamna* it is said that a temporary wife received a sack of wheat for each month the couple lived together, up to a year. The gloss adds: 'that is, until next *Beltene*, which is when those who would divorce separate' (*CL* #28, *SEIL* 56). This passage does not imply that *Beltene* was the traditional day for *contracting* such marriages (*pace* Binchy 1958a); if anything it implies that a temporary marriage could be set up at any time, and the woman rewarded on the basis of the number of months of labor she contributed to her husband's farm. Latter-day tradition links temporary marriages with the fair of Taltiu at *Lugnasad*, the August festival described below. Features of the human cycle of labor strongly suggest that temporary marriages would have been desirable in August, before the harvest and the heavy domestic work of the winter season, and least needed at *Beltene*, after which men and women could work independently of each other for the summer, and were in many cases parted by transhumance.

Little is known of the religious rites of *Beltene* in pagan

Ireland. Keating associated spring ceremonies with the hill of Uisneach, a site in the east central lowlands which was traditionally regarded as the center of Ireland. Here, he claimed, a bonfire (bone-fire) was lit amidst a large assembly on whose behalf sacrifices were made (Dinneen 1908: ii. 246). But Christianity suppressed *Beltene* traditions, and there is no other evidence to confirm Keating's remarks (Binchy 1958a: 113-5). Archaeological excavation on the summit of Uisneach, however, revealed a large area of scorched earth containing the charred bones of many animals (MacAlister 1931: 166). Two Old Irish sources also hint that pagan *Beltene* rituals were concerned with protecting livestock at this time. In the tale of 'The wooing of Étaín' it is said:

> the young of every kind of cattle (livestock) used to
> be assigned then to the possession of Bel.[9]

Cormac glosses *Beltene* thus:

> lucky fire, that is, two fires the Druids used to make
> with great incantations and they used to bring the
> cattle (as a safeguard) against the diseases of each
> year to those fires. (Stokes 1869: 19)

In *The Silver Bough*, Marian MacNeill recounts Scottish Highland *Beltene* traditions as recorded by early modern travellers. These emphasized symbolic sacrificial rituals on May 1, performed exclusively by men. Pennant described Hebridean *Beltene* rituals in which herdsmen lit a fire and cooked a mixture to which each one contributed ingredients, the ceremony ending in sacrifices of cooked food to propitiate potential enemies of the animals in the summer pastures (Pennant 1772). Similarly, in Moray and Ayreshire, the ceremony of lighting the fire was performed by men only (Shaw 1882; Carmichael 1928-71). In Perthshire a similar ceremony was performed by 'all the boys in a township or hamlet', but here, one boy who had drawn a specially blackened cake out of the bonnet was 'devoted' to the god, *Bel* (Sinclair 1791-9). Both the gender and age of the boy were subverted, for he was called the 'carline', the hag of *Beltene*.

Customs where one man played the role of victim are reported from several other Highland localities, and MacNeill sees in these survivals of Druidic human sacrifice (1957: 55-62). It is more likely, though, that the 'victim' served as a representative of the community's male family heads who attended the ceremonies; men who had liabilities to lords, tithes to pay to their church, and debts to settle with neighbors.

Traditions of sanctions at this time against those who defaulted on their dues come from two localities described in early modern accounts. Martin Martin, writing in the late seventeenth century, stated that all fires were extinguished in the community on the eve of *Beltene*, and that the *Beltene* fire was ritually kindled by nine groups of nine men. A firebrand from this was carried to each hearth of the community to re-light the domestic fire, but was withheld from those who had failed to pay their tithes or other obligations (Martin 1695). Similar sanctions were described for early nineteenth-century Rannoch and the uplands of Lochaber.

These traditions impart meaning to the powerful May 1 taboo on fire, widespread in recent rural Ireland and Highland Scotland. It was traditional to delay lighting the domestic fire until as late as possible on May Day, or even on the next day, for fear of theft of the fire or its smoke by witches (Danaher 1972: 112; MacNeill 1957: 60). It was believed that anyone asking for a coal or brand on this day must be a witch, for in earlier times only social deviants, excluded from the community's *Beltene* fire would have needed to beseech their neighbors. Faint traces of *Beltene* fires and male-only ceremonies survived in Irish folk tradition, enough to show that the customs that flourished in the Highlands had once been widespread in Ireland too. Danaher cites May bonfires in Dublin, Limerick and Belfast, and in rural districts of Waterford, and southern Kilkenny and Tipperary. In the latter area, as in Highland Scotland, the cattle were driven around the fire to protect them from evil (1972: 96).

In Ireland there are few vestiges of male-only ceremonies, but the trans-sexual quality of the Scots *Beltene* hag is found in numerous customs. A description of a Mummers' May Day parade in Wexford in 1897 noted that the part of the fool and his wife were both played by men and that 'for once the admiration of the crowd was given to the men and their ornaments' (Danaher 1972: 100-1). Sir William Wilde noted in *Popular Irish Superstitions* that there was no May Queen in Irish spring parades, but that the leading female figure was always played by a man (Danaher 1972: 103). These cross-dressed male figures may be linked to the transition on May 1 from the old, hag-like, female, winter half of the year, whose ritual potency was now over, to the new, young, male, summer half.

The festival of *Lugnasad* and the autumn season.

After the changes of May 1 the summer half of the year stretched ahead. Even more dramatically than the winter, it was divided into distinct sections by the quarter day of August 1, *Lugnasad.* This was the festival of Lug, the Celtic god of social contracts. Although no *Lugnasad* ceremonies survived the Christian conversion, traces of an agricultural myth are found in *The Second Battle of Mag Tuired.*[10] This centered on the conflict, referred to above, between the legendary prehistoric peoples of Ireland, the *Tuatha Dé Danaan* and the *Fomoir,* a struggle in which the *Tuatha Dé* prevailed thanks to the intervention of Lug, who appears as a superhero possessing all the special skills of the other gods. At the climax of the story, when the villain, Bres, was cornered by Lug, he offered in return for his life an unnatural abundance of crops and milk. The *Tuatha Dé* refused the offer, saying that all they wanted was to know the correct days to start to plow, sow, and reap (Banks 1938: 131-43). Lug, then, was a polyvalent deity who possessed all the technical skills except those of cultivation; these he wrested by force from those who had this knowledge, freeing his own people from dependence on others, be they gods, divinatory priests, aboriginal peoples, or the laboring classes. His season of triumph is summertime and *Lugnasad* seems to have been a harvest festival, for the first crops (wheat and barley) were reaped in August in early Christian Ireland.

The pagan importance of *Lugnasad* was so pronounced that it was utterly transformed under Christian influence. The shining, victorious god of the festival was forgotten and replaced by Crom Dubh, the Dark Crooked One, defeated by St. Patrick, or in the Dingle peninsula, by St. Brendan (Duignan 1940: 296-306). The early Irish Church may also have attempted to introduce a Christian festival at *Lugnasad* for Columcille is said to have let his monks have a feast to celebrate the harvest. However, the surviving traditions of *Lugnasad* are secular and largely of folk provenance. The only hint that these customs derived from an old religious context is found in Cormac's Glossary, which explained the word *'Lugnasad'* as:

> a commemorating game or fair ... *nasad* ... of Lug son
> of Ethne, or Ethlenn (Stokes 1869: 99).

Scholars have been unable to determine the meaning of *nasad* but the link between old commemorative (funeral?) rituals and the later games and fairs of the season is strong. These customary celebrations were analyzed by Máire MacNeill in *The Festival of Lughnasa* (1962/1982). This began on the first Sunday in August with the head of the family cutting a few sheafs of corn, or digging some new potatoes, which formed the basis of the day's main meal.

More prominent and much stranger than first fruit ceremonies, however, are the traditions of customary gatherings on this day on the summits of local hills, at sites rich in wild fruit and flowers. The day was accordingly known as 'Garland Sunday', 'Bilberry Sunday', 'Heatherberry Sunday', etc. The meeting places were always distant from settlement sites, involved a strenuous hike that precluded children and old people, and drew together young people from areas as large as the whole parish. MacNeill found evidence of this tradition in many parts of the British Isles, as well as throughout Ireland. One of the features of the expedition was that organized 'faction fighting' took place on the hilltop sites between young men from different localities. Though some injuries were sustained, no serious damage was deliberately inflicted. Where the *Lugnasad* gathering was at a river-bank it was also customary to have a swim-race of horses (MacNeill 1962: 244). Horse racing was, in general, an important custom of the season in early medieval Ireland, as shown by the infliction of a full fine for failure to restore a pledged horse in time for the owner to go to the races.[11]

In late folk tradition, July was regarded as a period of scarcity, known as 'famine July' and 'the staggering month' (MacNeill 1962: 44). It was also called 'the month of shaking out the bags', a custom resembling the *imbolc* custom of opening up all the cupboards to show everyone exactly what was left to eat. Tradition held that farmers at this time were down to their last oats, turf and potatoes; in early Ireland, where there were no potatoes, oats may have been the sole fare. MacNeill thought it odd that large groups should gather on distant hills to carry out rituals of conflict during this time of want (MacNeill 1962: 63). A plausible explanation, however, may be found in the routines of sheep farming. The Old Irish tractate on joint-pasturing, *comingaire*, states that 'farrow pigs and lambs do not come into the common pasture until lammas-day'.[12] This must refer to the separation of the lambs from the dams and their removal to lower common pasture, for historically, throughout the British Isles, sheep were rounded up at this time, and the young separated from their mothers. This practice has been described for the Sperrin mountains of central Ulster (Mac Aodhe 1962), where all farmers removed lambs in August until recently. The reason for doing so is a timeless corollary of the use of upland grazing: 'The older sheep can forage for themselves during the winter on the farmlands below the 'crossline' (i.e. below the line where the mountain begins)... But there is not enough grazing there for all the flock, nor can enough hay be saved during the summer for all of them. The previous spring's lambs, being not yet hardened to winter conditions on the mountain, are the obvious choice, while the fact that they are less troublesome to handle and that they are more easily 'haunted' (i.e. grow used to new ground more quickly) clinches the matter' (Mac Aodhe 1962: 245).

Only a few references to lammas-day as lamb-weaning-day survive in modern Irish folk customs and MacNeill's example of *'Domhnach Chrom Dubh'* (*Chrom Dubh*'s Sunday) hints that lamb-weaning rituals were suppressed on account of their pagan associations (MacNeill 1962: 33, 64). It is probable, nevertheless, that early Irish farmers followed a pattern found, for example, in nineteenth-century England, where the sheep were sheared and lambs weaned at midsummer. In the west of England there were great sheep fairs, called Lammas fairs (derived from Anglo-Saxon *hlaf-mass*, loaf-mass), some of which were three day affairs like Old Irish festival assemblies. In Welsh tradition, August 1 was known as *dydd degwm wyn*, lamb-tithing day (Máire MacNeill 1962: 64), which also involved rounding up the lambs in order to select the tithe beasts. MacNeill noted many parallels between English August customs and those of *Lugnasad*, such as the payments of some rents at this time (MacNeill 1962: 374), ceremonial cutting of a first sheaf (*ibid:* 375), and hilltop assemblies 'held entirely for enjoyment' (*ibid*: 376).

The central fact of this season, then, was the weaning of the lambs. Shearing was an antecedent of weaning because removal of the fleece, followed by a dip in a stream, causes the lambs to lose their mothers' scent in the water. In the bedlam that ensued, weaning occurred abruptly which brought on ovulation quickly in the ewes. This not only resulted in the early onset of sheep's milk, as explained above, but would also produce numbers of January-born ewe lambs, some of whom would reach puberty between June and November and would enter the breeding season with the rest of the flock in late August (MacGraw Hill 1982: 12. 341). It is interesting that while *Imbolc*, the day associated with ewe's milk, was a woman's festival, *Lugnasad*, the day that ended ewes' lactation, is in some places called 'Men's Sunday' (MacNeill 1962: 39; 40; 172). In recent folk custom it was linked to the importance of male labor to the grain crop, but it may also have had phallic connotations since this day saw the end of the maternal phase of the flocks and the resumption of mating.

While the life-cycle of the sheep dominated *Lugnasad*, as it did *Imbolc*, other creatures also went through transitions at this point in the seasons. It is likely, for example, that when the boys went up to the booleys to help with shearing, they also took up some of the bee-hives, for the Old Irish law-tract on bee-keeping, *Bechbretha*, makes reference to the moving of bees (#27), and to bees being kept beyond the settlement area (*sechtar faithche*: # 53). 'Bee-transhumance' was a common practice throughout the British Isles, enabling the bees to make heather honey after August, when the white clover and other summer flowers were over (Graham 1893: 159).

The survival of customs of swimming horses and racing them, and the record of the sale of unbroken Kerry ponies at Puck Fair, suggests that foals were also weaned at this time and that their dams were raced to help establish the value of the foals. In early Ireland, the typical major event of the season was a regional fair, *oenach*. This word was glossed by Cormac as 'a contention of horses', i.e., horse-races (Stokes 1869: 127).

Little is known, however, of the *Lugnasad* fairs, which fell into such desuetude that the site of the most prominent Leinster gathering, the *oenach* at Carmun, is not even known with certainty. According to the poem on the *oenach* of Carmun in *The Metrical Dindshenchas*, this assembly was held by the provincial king and had a judicial aspect. Binchy argued that this could not have been a 'national' assembly, but there is little reason to be skeptical of this *oenach*'s jural function or that it was under royal aegis. Significantly, the Old Irish life of Brigid describes her meeting St. Patrick at the assembly at Tailtiu, another of the *Lugnasad* assemblies, where she performed a miracle in the context of a legal dispute concerning a false paternity charge levelled at one of Patrick's priests. The episode is presented with realistic social detail; Brigid, for example, did not go before the assembly, which as a woman she had no right to address directly, but instead the case was brought to her.

It seems reasonable to regard all the quarter-day assemblies as multifunctional, though each had also its peculiar seasonal focus.

Trading, entertainment and the resolution of disputes would have occurred at each, simply to take advantage of the concentration of the normally dispersed population. If the early *Lugnasad* assemblies had a strong legal aspect, as tradition maintained, an important focus must have been on marital contracts, for a feature of the human life cycle that comes to the fore at *Lugnasad* is sex and marriage. As noted previously, there are strong traditions that at the *oenach* at Tailtiu people could contract temporary marriages which could be dissolved at will by the next May Day, with payment of wages to the woman, and without the mulct of honor-price or the need to give grounds for divorce. Cormac, for instance, glossed *coibche* (the usual word for the pre-nuptial gift to the bride and her kin), by referring to 'the hill of *coibche* at the *oenach* of Tailtiu' (Stokes 1869: 48). He also glossed *coibche* with *cendach*, purchase, suggesting that the marriages transacted at the fair were temporary and that the bridal gift in this case was far closer in meaning to 'wages' than it was in more conventional marriage contracts (see Ch. 11).

The tradition of temporary marriages at this time is complemented by the injunction to keep the peace at the *Lugnasad* fair of Carmun, where men were forbidden to brawl or to think about acquiring second wives: many likely candidates were no doubt at hand seeking a domicile for the winter season, but, the *Metrical Dindshenchas* poem maintains, men who already had wives should not stir up trouble by making their polygynous arrangements at the fair. Enmity could only result when such plans were carried out in full view of wives, the latter's kin, and all the poorer, wifeless men at the assembly. Traditions of fornication clung to the assembly of Tailtiu, nevertheless. St. Ciaran, for example, heard a case there in which a married man was successfully accused by his wife of adultery (O'Grady 1892: I, 416, II 453). In *Lebor na Huidre* it is said that the two queens of Diarmait quarrelled at Tailtiu while he presided over it, when one bribed a woman-jester to pull off the other's headdress to reveal her bald head. These stories clearly take Tailtiu as the setting for sexual competitiveness on the part of women.

The other great activity of the summer was warfare. No thorough analysis of the data on the seasonality of warfare has been undertaken, but a survey of the *Annals of Connaught* suggests the following pattern. During winter, from *Samain* to *Beltene* there were many assassinations but few battles.[13] April offered an almost complete respite from fighting, perhaps on account of Easter, then the main Christian festival. But after May 1, the number of entries concerning conflicts increased, with assassinations still outnumbering battles until June, after which battles begin to be noticed more often.

By July the picture changes: the entries record fewer assassinations and more battles, some famous enough to bear names. There were also 'great expeditions' and 'major hostings'. A major battle was fought on July 3, 1247 (#7 p.91); a 'large expedition' from Offaly and Meath invaded Connaught on July 10, 1406 (#4 p.397); the Feast of St. John in late June, 1407 was the date of the Battle of Cell Aidhe (#8 p.401); July 1, 1411 saw the Battle of Bel na Muilled (#28 p.413). Big battles were less frequent during the harvest month, August, though the Fir Cell and Clann Colman battled on St. Colmcille's Day in 1463 (#17 p.515), and the Battle of Athenry occurred on Aug. 10, 1316 (#5 p.247). During September major plundering expeditions were common, as lords enforced their claims on recalcitrant tributaries who now had their grain harvests in. Lords invaded tributaries in 1249 (#9 p. 99); 'burning of the corn' occurred in 1260 and 1266 (#3, p.133, #11 p.147); in Carbury in 1307 (#20 p.215); in Tír Conáill in 1309 (#17 p.377); in 1405 (#15 p.395); in Tirhugh in 1419 (#3 p.443); in 1503 (#12 p.675); and in 1542 (#14 p.727).

Patchy as is this data-set from one source, it does support the impression that warfare followed the pattern outlined previously: that there was plotting and assassination during the winter; small-scale raiding to subdue local rivals and replenish stores during 'hungry spring'; more conflict during 'famine July'; and large-scale confrontations, sometimes at the inter-regional level during August, followed by punitive attacks on rivals and dissident allies after the harvest was secured.

Conclusion.

During all the seasons, there were parallels between social phases of human sexual behavior and those of warfare. Winter (from November 1 to February 1) was a season of match-making as well as plotting. In February, marriages were consummated and there was also a spate of raids. Summertime was likewise a period of synchronized military aggression and sexual competition. As we have seen, unimpeded courtship (which preceded the social formalities of match-making) was easiest during the summer period of mild weather and relative freedom from supervision on the part of unmarried women in the booleys, where they were visited by young men. Warfare too built up from May 1 to a climax in July.

These parallel phases in the expenditure of military and sexual energy were both tied to the demands of labor and the supplies of food. Rituals, many half-obliterated by Christianity, still highlighted and celebrated the turning points in the cycle, but underlying the social organization of time lay the cyclical rhythms of the animals that sustained human life. Of these the sheep seems to have played the leading role because of the narrow time-frame and inflexibility of two of its basic biorhythms, namely upland migration in spring and ovulation shortly after midsummer.

Charting and celebrating the recurrence of the seasons and their long-term constancy must have offered a kind of existential security for early peoples in the face of the terrible uncertainties of harvests, health and human nature. This order in nature was not something for which humans had to assume responsibility and so, unlike the Christian concern with personal damnation and salvation, it was not a cause of anxiety. There was a solid otherness to natural seasonal rhythms which must have imparted a feeling that social life had grown organically out of its framework and that it too was reliable and meaningful, notwithstanding abundant evidence to the contrary in the form of plagues, Vikings and diverse other disasters of the times. When one wonders at the endurance of population groups through the seemingly endless progression of catastrophes in the early middle ages, their connection to unchanging seasonal rhythms must surely be thought of as a major source of encouragement to persist at the routines of production and reproduction.

Notes

1. '...*SMACHTA CACHA RAITHE. NI CUMA DO SMACH SAMFUACHTA 7 GAIMFUACHTA...* 'the fine of each quarter. Not equal is the fine for summer season and the winter season' (CIII 69.29 = ALI iv 89.23-5).

2. Cormac glossed *gamuin* with 'a milking cow with its *gamuin*, milk in November' (Stokes 1869: 85).

3. *IM TELGUD MBROGA .i. im telguin in broga feoir don senbaili im samain.* 'For removing to the houses, that is, for removing to the hay-loft of the old winter residence at *Samain*' (*CIH* 370.15-16 = *ALI* i: 133.14-19).

4. *Dliged Raith & Somaíne la Flaith* H.3.17 Additional.12. Crigger (ed. and transl.) 1991: 356. I am very grateful to Dr. Crigger for making available the text and translation of *DRS* from the unpublished MS of her doctoral dissertation.

5. *Ibid.* It is O'Davoren (983: cited in *DIL*), who glosses *furnaide* as sausages and bacon.

6. Modern scholars reject Keating's picture of the Feast of Tara as an annual ceremony of the High King of Ireland (Byrne 1973:48-69; Binchy 1958: 172), holding that it was a local feast, held intermittently whenever a ruler felt it appropriate to publicly celebrate his reign. The ceremony is thought to have been a *'banais rig'* (king's wedding feast), which affirmed the legitimacy of the king through his symbolic mating with the local goddess of the earth, as for example, in the ceremony as described by Giraldus Cambrensis for the *Cenél Conáill* in the twelfth century (Binchy 1958a: 134-5; O'Meara 1982: #102). Simms has shown that the motif of the sexual union between king and goddess persisted until the later middle ages in literature and possibly in ritual (Simms 1980: 132 ff). Binchy also suggested that the Feast of Tara was not held at *Samain*, but in spring, 'seed-time' (Binchy 1958: 134-5), because it was 'the supreme fertility rite, designed to secure that man and beast and earth shall be fruitful throughout the king's dominions' (*ibid*: 134). However, the ceremony of *banais ríg* seems to have been intended to enhance the king's power, through the goddess' affirmation of his suitability as her consort. *Samain*, the time of greatest political crisis, would therefore seem appropriate as the setting for the Feast of Tara.

7. *IM DINGBAIL FAITHCHE. .i. don faithche feoir 7 arba .i. dona gortaib imach i mbelltaine, no dul o faithchi in senlis for airge.* 'For taking care of the green, that is, the field of grass or corn, that is, (keeping cattle) from the fields when (going) out at *Beltene*, or going from the green of the winter homestead to the *airge* (summer pastures). *CIH 370.11-3 = AL i: 133.14-19.*

8. *NO DIA I NAENTALLAIND FOR TIR NAENFIR .i. IN foltach fuithrime 7 in carpat ar imram; is e a naichi-side: tir .iiii.ri .uii acin dara de 7 ceithri ba xx.it ar araile, 7 comaentu doniat o belltaini co belltaini.* 'or two men with one holding on the land of one, that is, the '*foltach fuithrime*' and the '*carpat ar imram*' are in this condition: one has land of four seven-*cumals* and the other has twenty-four cows, and they covenant from *Beltine* to *Beltine* (*CIH 260.13-15 = AL* iii. 142.19-20).

9. *Do... asselbhthea dine cecha cethrae for se[i]lib Be[i]l.* Meyer (ed. and trans). *Tochmarc Emire.* 1890: 442-3, line 1.

10. See the analysis of the symbolic structure of *Cath Maighe Tuired* by Gray (1981) xviii (pt. 2) 183--224; (1982) xix (pt. 1) 1-35; (1983) xix (pt. 2) 230-262.

11. *T[ECHTA] F[UILLEMA] G[ILL] ECH AIGE IS COMDIRE ... MANI TECCMAI LUGLASANAD* 'The lawful pledge-interest on a race-horse is equal-honor-price ... unless there should be Lamas-day ... *(CIH 471.22-4 = AL v. 407).*

12. *ni tiaghad oirc na huain a comingaire co lunasadh.* (*CIH* 192.2-3 = *AL* iv 101.6-7).

13. The *Annals of Connaught* indicate assassinations or small fatal skirmishes, for example, during December in: 1337 (#8 p.279); 1407 (#4 p.399); 1452 (#3 p.495); 1472 (#3 p.385); a 'house-burning' on Jan. 8, 1415 (#12 p.427); assassinations between Feb. 1 and March 1 in 1401 (#9 p.379); 1403 (#3 p.385); 1417 (#15 p.435): 1420 (#2 p.451): 1462 (#3 p.509); 1468 (#2 p.547); between March and April 1 assassinations occurred in 1402 (#3 p.383); 'in spring', 1411 (#26 p.413).

CHAPTER SIX

The Political Economy: Clientship

An outline of clientship

The political relationships which formed in the territories discussed in previous chapters focussed on local leaders and kings. As these controlled fluctuating groups of clients according to their own political fortunes, it is futile to try to conceptualize a political unit in terms of fixed territorial boundaries (Byrne 1971: 159-60: Ó Corráin 1978: 11). But though neither population groups nor ecological units coincided permanently with the structures of political control, the polity (*tuath*) was a moral community, in which social relationships were governed by law, not merely by politics. The basis of this social unity was the propinquity of the productive population, itself reinforced by the boundedness of the ecological units with which *tuath*s were associated. One of the complexities of early Irish culture was that the enforcement of law was dependent to a considerable extent upon the will of powerful lords whose interests had no direct relationship to justice — and yet without justice, social stability and the maintenance of the élite itself would founder. The fact that, despite the absence of a state, the lords were harnessed to the law (except in the matter of succession), was a major achievement of early Irish intellectuals — the poets, jurists and clerics — for this made social order and cultural growth possible in the face of political turbulence.

    Tuath society was internally divided into different social ranks based on control of productive property, and on social standing; each of these influenced the other, but social standing was also affected by the community's perceptions of the morality, lawfulness, prestige, and even the stylishness of an individual's behavior, and that of his/her kin. Clientship — contractual personal relationships of dependence/protection — linked people of different rank. These ties permeated the entire social and political hierarchy, giving formal expression to the factious relations between over-kings and under-kings, lords and independent farmers, and lords and dependent farmers. All clientship relationships shared a basic feature, that is, they were legitimated by the giving of a 'gift' (*rath*) by the superior to the inferior, which created an obligation on the part of the client to reciprocate in a stipulated fashion. The highest clientship entailed the giving of *túarasndal* (later *túarastal*) by an over-king, and its repayment in tribute by the under-king.

The *túarastal* described in the tenth- or eleventh-century *Lebar na Cert, The Book of Rights* (Dillon 1962) was paid almost entirely in honorific items symbolic of royal office — such things as bridles, horses, swords, hunting-dogs, ornamented horns, and slave women were prominent.[1] The tribute, on the other hand, was largely paid in livestock. At the lowest level of society, the base-client, *dóer chéile*, received a *rath* of cows and made a repayment in cooked foods and other manufactured items for his lord's table. Between free-client and lord, however, an exchange of cattle took place, with the lord getting back rather more than he gave out. In various combinations, then, all clientship dyads involved exchanges of goods as well as political allegiance.

The Irish lord's wealth had as its nucleus personal usufruct of demesne lands worked by landless laborers and slaves.[2] These provided the reliable core of farm produce that enabled the lord to feed an expanded household that included some retainers.[3] This element of potential force put the lord in a position to sanction the behavior of his local clients, and thus keep order in the local political hierarchy. The importance of control of good land in demesne farming is evident from the distribution of the most powerful dynastic groups on the most fertile arable and pasture areas in Ireland (Smyth 1981: 5). Beyond his demesne, a lord's patrimony consisted mainly of livestock, precious objects, and the rights to take the 'rents' of the clients in his ancestral domain. These 'rents' consisted of the food-renders of dependant farmers and their manual services, and the cow-payments and personal services of independent farmers who entered free-clientship. A lord's rights in these clients were contingent however; he had for ever to be looking over his shoulder at his competitive kinsmen, who were also entitled by birth to seize local leadership if they had the resources with which to supply clients with fiefs.

Even allowing for some home-field production, it is likely that much of the lord's crop was produced on dispersed lands that he granted to *fuidri*, a class of landless tenants-at-will, who depended entirely on the lord for access to land and social protection. Their provision of produce, however, while vital to the lord's economic base was not sufficient to guarantee his political status. Judging from the emphasis in the texts upon the obligations of base-clients, it was on his relationship with these farmers that the lord depended to maintain the network of dispersed power-nodes that protected his status. Since I shall not be considering landless laborers any further in this study, I shall briefly describe their social position here.

Servility

Although not great estate builders, Irish lords kept enough lands for their direct personal use that they were able to support *fuidri*, men who had lost their share of patrimonial land through having incurred serious debts or committed serious crimes. Another similar status category was the *bothach*, a term which suggests that this man was a 'hutted' dependent, granted both usufruct of land and a hut (*both*) by the lord (Kelly 1988: 35, n.128). Perhaps, then, this group was typically recruited from outside the territory, possibly originating as enslaved captives that were subsequently settled on the land. Slaves, though not generally available on a large scale, were important (Ó Corráin 1972: 45-8), and probably supplied a lot of the domestic labor in the homes of the élite, as well as being a source of revenue through the international slave-trade of the Norse ports during the Viking period (Holm 1985). They were probably especially important, politically and economically, during the period of the rise of the new dynasties; this is a subject that has not yet been systematically examined.

Fuidri constituted a tied agrarian labor force (Kelly 1988: 35-6), but their social position differed in a number of ways from that of a medieval English serf. In the first place, *fuidir* status was essentially transitional. *Fuidir*-ship was not thought of as a positive status category but as a social aberration, resulting from the loss of the basic patrimonial resource of all free men, a share of clanlands, *fintiu*. In legal theory, there were two main kinds of *fuidir*. A 'free *fuidir*' could terminate his relationship with his lord and depart if he cleared his debts and surrendered two-thirds of his produce (*CIH* 428.12-5 = *IR* I: 66 #8), whereas the unfree *fuidir* was under a number of restrictions that made legal departure very difficult. The 'freedom' of any *fuidir*, however, may have been of little significance to him, but may only imply that the lord had no right to detain him, as against another lord who wanted to pay off the *fuidir*'s dues and induce him to leave. Competition between lords for clients was keen; competition for *fuidri* may also be inferred, or else the rules governing their social position would have hardened into caste-like hereditary servitude. But on the contrary, various 'degrees' of *fuidir*ship were recognized, according to how long the *fuidir*'s ancestors had served those of the lord (Binchy 1984). In my view, these rules were not designed to protect the inconsequential *fuidri*, but to safeguard rising local lords from charges of illegality when they poached their kinsmen's labor-force. Such laissez-faire provisions protected the brehons from the consequences of having to rule against emerging local powers. Competition within the élite was a matter that the lawyers generally shied away from, as witness the absence of even a pretence at prescriptive rules governing the choice of successor to lordship.

According to *CG*, hereditary serfs, *senchléithe* (literally 'old house-posts'), were attached only to the actual ruling segment of the élite — specifically to the king's expected successor, *tánaise ríg*, as an attribute of his estate.[4] The tract on free-clientship that we discuss below actually refers to continued service from clients to external lords over three generations as a 'hill of lordship', *tulach tiagharnuis* (*CIH* 1774.31 = *AL* ii 207.32-3) — evidence, that is, of a lord's solid and great social standing. Prolonged *duration* of a lord's patronage of clients was in general a great source of honor and legal entitlement; in *CG* 316-7 it is said that one of the things that ennobled a lord was 'the long-standing submission of a *tuath*'. Conversely, an early source describes the situation in which *fuidri* gained their freedom as 'a time in which the lord's produce perishes so there is failure of corn and milk and fruit' (*CIH* 231.15-7 = *AL* v 451.18-9).

The unfree *fuidir* was recruited in a number of ways, for example by being rescued from death on the battlefield, or gallows. He was tied to his lord for life, but the status of his descendants was indeterminate. On the one hand, it was possible for the sons and grandchildren of a *fuidir* to return to the position of native freemen in the society if they fulfilled three conditions. One was that there had to be enough of them in existence to be able to constitute, numerically, a legally recognized minimal kin-group of five households. Secondly, at least five had to accept land-holdings, thus constituting something like a *comaithches* community. Thirdly, they had to accept the responsibility that came with free status - namely, that they were mutually liable for each other's debts to the lord and to society, whether these were incurred by failure to provide contracted renders to the lord or to pay fines that had been charged to them for other offenses.[5]

Such a *fuidir* (or perhaps just the head of the group) was said to be 'capable of paying for his offenses and feeding his lord', and to receive two-thirds of whatever honor-price was due to him, the remainder going to his lord (*IR* I: 63 #2). In other words, he then had the status of a base-client, as described below. Such upward mobility may have actually been possible, but it seems more probable that most of the people who were free *fuidri* were clansmen who had become impoverished without necessarily having committed any great offense, and who still had free kinsmen. These people had a chance of returning to normal society, in part because the rules of collective inheritance (described in Ch. 10) made it possible for individuals to acquire pieces of clan land from distant kin.

If a lord could keep a *fuidir* descent-group in this status beyond 'nine ages' (perhaps three generations; Binchy 1984), its members' status became irretrievably set as *senchléithe*, 'old retainers'. For many lords, however, such a feat would have been impossible, not only because of pressure from other lords, but because *fuidri* entailed social costs. *CG* refers to the *fuidir* and *bothach* as a burden:

> Double-edged is every uncertain service, it brings the
> clinging of *bothach*ship and *fuidir*ship onto the land,
> for the profits are greater than the remissions. (*CG* 45).

The 'double-edged' quality of *fuidir*ship lay in the mixed blessings it offered. The problem was that while the *fuidir* could be almost infinitely exploited, the lord was also obliged to make good whatever damage he and his progeny caused in the community, which might well exceed his profitability.

The impression given by the laws is that the Irish lord was not often able to function as a large-scale land- and serf-owning lord during the pre-Norman period. In part, this was the result of a manpower shortage, in part it was a function of intense competition within the branching dynasties; it was better for a lord to permit his potential clients to retain vested interests in their land and to enforce dependency on them in less openly coercive ways than by the threat of usurpation and expropriation. The Gaelic historian, Keating, firmly believed in the efficacy of farmers' landownership as the glue of political loyalty.

Explaining why Irish lords were not great estate holders, and why land was left in the hands of 'fraternal partnerships' — clans — Keating pointed out that in many lordships, the cost of mercenaries to defend a territory would normally exceed the revenues of the district (*cíos na críche*). On the other hand, he explained, if everyone had a share of land-ownership,

> 'the kinsman (*bráthair*) who had the least share of it
> would be as ready in its defense, to the best of his
> ability, as the tribal chief (*ceann-feadhna*) who was
> over them, would be'.[6]

Arable landownership, then, was normally the right of one farmer as against another, not against his lord. As we shall see, the small farmer was not totally secure in his land-tenure, but the threat of deprivation of land was used against him not as a means to coerce him to supply produce and services to his lord, but to get him to cooperate with his kin and neighbors. These were the people who could, under certain circumstances, dispossess him. As groups, of course, these served the lords, but as we see in later chapters of this book, they, not the lord or his functionaries, exercised direct social control over each other, leaving the lord unencumbered by this managerial problem and free to focus on a job that he would not wish to delegate because it was too empowering — warfare and the management of large-scale livestock holdings.

Free-clientship: *sóer chéilsine*

The main Old Irish source on this relationship, *Cáin Sóerraith*, does not survive in a complete version, so that only aspects of this category of relationship may be reconstructed for the early medieval period.[7] As Thurneysen pointed out, the commentary reveals (at two points) that its author viewed this type of free clientship as undertaken by a middle-rank farmer, a *bóaire* (*IR* II: 240 #2). The non-aristocratic nature of free-clientship is implied throughout the commentaries to *Cáin Sóerraith*. A gloss defines the contract as 'the free fief of the farmers', *saorrath bóairech* (*CIH* 1770.20 = *AL* 195.8), and there is no evidence that there was a *saorrath* of the lords. Further evidence, offered below supports the view that a free-clientship contract that involved only a small gift of stock typically involved men of such rank. The provisions in *Cáin Sóerraith* should therefore not be assumed to apply to contracts in which the free-client was a noble or king.

In *CS*, the free-client is depicted as taking three cows in fief from a lord. For the first three years, he paid back annually the equivalent of one-third of the fief — one cow in return for a fief of three cows — so that by the end of three years the equivalent of the fief had been restored. For the following three years, the equivalent in value of one cow was paid over in dairy produce, calves and (possibly) dung, or its value. In the sixth year no payments were due at all, but in the seventh year the original fief had to be returned to the lord. The seventh year was termed the *iubaile*, a Latin loan (*iubileus*) probably derived from Biblical sources.[8] No honor-price was paid by the lord to a free-client (in contrast to the base-client; see below), and therefore the lord had no claim to a share of any reparations received by the free-client. In real terms, this meant that the free-client was a man who had adequate social resources with which to defend his status in normal social confrontations. The free-client's social power is also manifest in the fact that both he and the lord were entitled to end the relationship and restore the fief, without penalties to either; in contrast, a base-client who returned his lord's fief was viewed as dishonoring the lord, and owed heavy fines. Translating these conventions into 'real terms' again, we can say that the free client was not so economically dependent on the fief as to be unable to surrender it at once on request.

In addition to caring for his lord's stock, the free-client owed his lord homage and manpower services; these are described as 'the worst' (aspects) of free-clientship. Homage, *aireirge*, meant that the client gave symbolic expression of his allegiance by rising to his feet in the presence of the lord (or, if already standing, raising his knee). This was an act of considerable importance in assemblies and other social gatherings where men of similar rank met and sized up each other's political strength. Like all other obligations arising from clientship, the duty to 'rise up' was limited, in this case to three gestures; further risings by the lord which would involve the clients in rising along with him were regarded by the law as dishonoring to the clients' rank, for all the bobbing up and down would be laughable, in the words of a gloss, making them look like 'assembly fleas'. (Crigger 1991: 352.#4)

The term for labor-service, *manchuine*, seems to have derived from clerical culture (like *iubaile*), for it referred originally to the labor-duties of monks and their tenants (Kelly 1988: 33). The extent of labor-services was specified only as *fer cacha samaisce* (a man for every heifer), once in three years (*CIH* 1770.23; 435.25; 436.13; Kelly 1988: 33). The three heifers given in a fief of free-clientship would thus obligate the client to go once a year on some customary labor service, such as construction, harvesting, or military service. These aspects of free-clientship have struck a number of scholars as incongruous with the expected high status of these clients. Since *CS* is poorly preserved it has been argued that the 'original' free-clientship was different. It would seem, however, that not all free-clients were necessarily of high status, but that many were commoners (such as the *bóaire* mentioned by the commentator to *CS*) who were able to enter 'free' clientship because they belonged to independent, but non-noble, or non-dynastic, clans.

The first question concerns the labor obligation. The glosses to *CS* specify 'a man for every heifer' every third year, to work on the lord's fort, help with reaping, and give military service (*CIH* 1770.24-6), but Kelly has suggested that probably *manchuine* only meant the duty of attendance on a lord, and that where later glosses specify actual labor, the client could have satisfied this by sending a servant (Kelly 1988: 33). While this is possible, later evidence suggests that free clientage was not so honorific a relationship as to eschew actual labor by the clients. For example, on the early fourteenth-century manor of Swords, which had retained many native Gaelic features of physical and social organization, the legally free, rent-paying burgesses, were obliged to perform menial, servile duties — to 'work for the lord in the autumn, helping with reaping, transporting of crops and turf and doing suit of the vill.'(A. Simms 1988: 37). This was a far cry from English burgage tenure, which suggests that native Irish customs were in operation. Of course, if this were our only evidence we might infer that *this* feature of tenure was neither Gaelic nor English, but some colonial exigency. But other evidence, offered below, also points to the non-aristocratic nature of some Irish free-clients. More probably, then, the English burger at Swords corresponded to an Irish *bóaire* who was a free client, in that neither were indebted to the lord, but both needed his physical protection; in return they had to pitch in with work on the lord's fortifications, roads and food supplies.

The 'economic aspect' of the payments made by free-clients have likewise been viewed with suspicion. Gerriets argues they were insignificant to the lord, in terms of 'net changes' in his holdings of stock and food supplies (Gerriets 1981: 173). Others have maintained that the terms were 'stiff' and 'burdensome' to the free-client (Kelly 1988: 32; Mac Niocaill 1972: 61). Nevertheless, there are many suggestions in the texts that free-clientship was not only more honorable than base-clientship, but that it was an acceptable relationship for the free-client. The Old Irish law-tract on the customs of clientship, *Di dligiud raith 7 somáine la flaith*, recently edited by Crigger (1991), contrasts the free fief with a *rath* of cows given in other relationships, where the *rath* could not readily be returned nor the relationship changed (the usual case with base clientship, discussed below):

'A free fief is the best fief, for each is capable of
returning it, or of stretching his hand to his grant.'
(Crigger 1991: 342, I. B. 2; *CIH* 433.1-2).

Cáin Sóerraith declares that 'the worst of free-clientship is manual labor' — not renders (*CIH* 1770.14, 23-5 = *IR* II: 240 #2). The laws in fact assumed that free-clientship did not disadvantage the client, but that base-clientship did, in that it benefitted the lord at the client's expense. Thus, if a lord pressed the free-client for the return of the fief, and the latter were unwilling or unable to comply, but offered instead to take more cattle and enter a contract of base-clientship, the lord should accept this offer because, according to a commentary on *CS*, 'it is a benefit for him'.[9] This statement can hardly be construed as encouragement to lords to throw good money after bad; it reflects rather a general sense that a productive base-client was more profitable to his lord than a failing free-client.

Fundamentally, free clientship was an exchange without profit or loss to either party. The client merely replaced the stock given him by the lord, paying first out of his own herd, and then with the offspring of the three cows he had taken. The client, of course, assumed the risk and the managerial costs, and it is true that if the three cows and their progeny did not breed at maximum capacity, the client would suffer a loss. But it was a small risk, for as we see below, the three cows taken as the text-book case by *CS* was a typical fief of free-clientship. Margins of profit were not the point for either party to free clientship, but rather the provision of political security. A vivid glimpse of the political utility of free-clientship comes from a late source. Graham writes: 'In parts of west Ulster (Irish lords) still followed an old practice known as 'commyns'. They distributed the large herds of cattle which comprised their wealth among their landholders, who grazed the cattle with their own stock. It is not clear what return these farmers had by the seventeenth century, but in earlier times they had gained protection. In 1613 several letters were written to Chichester by Irish lords imprisoned in the Tower of London, asking that he would cause some of their commyns to be recovered to provide for their families and to repay loans. For example, in order to repay his debt of 40 pounds to William Lusher, Sir Donnell O'Cahan listed the holders of 40 in-calf cows belonging to him.' (1972: 148-9).

Nearly all the holders belonged to the same clan (the O'Moilans), and holdings ranged from five cows (the most common amount) down to two cows held by a group. Graham continues: 'Néill Garve O'Donnell listed the distribution in commyns of 60 cows, which he asked to be recovered to repay a 60 pound loan. These cows were only part of the herds which were distributed among their people. It is apparent that each man took in only a few cows, and that in many cases these were the joint responsibility of several families, usually, but not always related. It is likely that the latter cases arose because the families held joint farms. The burden on any one man's grazing, whether commonage share or severalty land, was not great. Such a pattern does not suggest that these farmers were concerned only with cattle, but rather that a few extra cows could be incorporated into an established system of mixed farming without exhausting the winter pasturage of either individuals or communities.' (*ibid*: 149).

The loan of cattle is here referred to not as *rath*, but by another Old Irish word, *commain*, (mutual wealth), which implies reciprocal gifts or services. The relationship described above is nonetheless the functional equivalent of a free-clientship contract. Its advantage to the lord is evident; abruptly, under the pressure of need, he could withdraw this 'loan' without causing any hardship to the farmers and thus dishonoring himself. Another facet of the relationship is also revealed in these data; although the individual recipient only took between 1-5 cows, one clan held a herd of nearly forty interspersed with their own cattle. It suggests that fiefs of free-clientship, were given only to strong and numerous clan groups, who could physically and legally protect them against the day when they were urgently recalled. This interpretation of the Old Irish free-clients as members of a strong clan is borne out by the maxim : 'No one is independent (*sóer*) whose clan (*cenél*) is small, who (?) has not five 'raths' of a hundred'.[10] The precise sense of the last words is obscure (one gloss took it to mean that a free clan had at least five *raths* for its members, with a hundred animals in each), but the general implication is not in doubt — lots of kin, with lots of cattle, were prerequisites of the status of being *sóer*, and of course, only the *sóer* could undertake free clientship (*sóer chéilsine*).

Not only was it unnecessary for individuals to be of high status in order to become free-clients, but the contrary must have been true, for the object of the relationship was to disperse the cattle amongst a large number of clan members. Indeed, O'Donovan, whose translations provided most of what is valuable in *AL*, expressed misgivings about the translations of *sóer* and *dóer* as 'noble' and 'unfree' (*AL* ii xlviii). Duffy and Nicholls have subsequently shown that in the later middle-ages, the distinction had little to do with wealth and social status, but with the type of legal relationship between a patron and client (Duffy 1981: 8; Nicholls 1972: 69-70). On the one hand, many men who were 'free' were not wealthy, and were continuously threatened by debt and expropriation, while the converse also held true. For example, a 'bondman and servant' of Sir Thomas of Desmond in 1547 was described as 'a great gentleman of the said lands' — a description well in accord with *CG*'s statements that even kings could be in 'base-clientship' to other kings (*CG* 455, 467). *CG*, furthermore, shows that even the *lowest* lord had free-clients (*CG* 331), thereby implying that some free-clients, at least, came from the ranks of the farmers.

The importance of free-clientship to the security of the local polity is revealed by the legal entitlement of the local chief or king to demand the services of men in this relationship (*CIH* 1774.34-37 = *AL* ii 209.1-7). From the Ulster materials, cited above, it is evident that the system was designed to protect the lord's herds from cattle disease and raids (both threats to the herds concentrated in the wilderness), and also to conceal his wealth from overlords and fraternal competitors who might press demands on him. The clients, in turn, gained protection from the repercussions of a change in local lordship, which could lead to expropriation of their lands in favor of the followers of an intrusive lord. The social consequence of regional political slippage may be inferred from historical evidence such as the following: 'By about the middle of the ninth century there were some fifty distinct land-holding branches of the Dál Cais in east Clare. By the eleventh and twelfth centuries, excluding the ruling O'Briens, who were themselves highly prolific, there were some 200 Dál Cais families in the same area, each bearing an individual surname. We can take it that each surname represents at least ten individuals. This gives us a rude statistic of about 2,000 persons... given the nature of the Irish economy and the relative poverty of the area (this) must represent a large proportion of the total population of the area and a sizeable section of the better class of farmer.' (Ó Corráin 1972: 45).

Followers of lords, then, were implicitly competing with the followers and kinsmen of other lords, and had to make decisions about where to place their loyalties. The laws made provision for the possibility that men might indeed become free-clients for outside lords or kings, but no outsider could *demand* that anyone become his free-client. The terms used in these provisions ('his own king', *ríg budein*, and 'external king', *ríg nechtrann*) differentiate between a long-established local power, and one that was encroaching from outside. Changes in free-clients' allegiance were evidently a sensitive barometer of political change, and must often have been a prelude to the outbreak of warfare at the local level. The fundamental importance of their loyalties helps to explain why at least part of *Cáin Sóerraith,* the text on free clientage, survived. In contrast, there survived no legal sources on noble free-clientship — if such ever existed, other than the documents referred to as 'political tracts', such as the Book of Rights.

Base-clientship : *dóer chéilsine*

This was the most important political and economic nexus in early Irish lordship. Like free-clientship, it was initiated by the acceptance of a fief of cattle from the lord, but in this case the fief was substantially larger. It seems that several types of goods were legally acceptable as a binding fief: *DRS* mentions 'petty fiefs' of which the most substantial was a fief of pigs (Crigger 1991: 351. H.3.17 Add.2). Petty fiefs apparently included other small stock such as sheep, for another passage in this text states that clients had the right to stipulate what they wanted in the fief, whether cattle, horses, pigs or sheep (*ibid*: 354 #7.2). It also mentions fiefs for which only labor services, not food renders were due: these consisted of arms and equipment or clothing (*ibid*: 352. H.3.17 Add. 3). The reason given in the glosses for the reduction in the client's renders was that equipment was unlike livestock in that it would only depreciate not reproduce.

This text stated emphatically that 'oxen are the best of fiefs' because they could be used in legal conflicts as pledges to forestall retributive action by a party claiming damages. It also added that oxen made the best fiefs because they produced (through plowing) grain and malt for beer, 'which they produce that are wont to be lords' (*ibid*: 351. H.3.17 Add.2.2). The same passage also refers to land being given in fief, and elsewhere the text explains that the lord was then due not only his summer and winter food-rents, but also four supplementary food-renders (*ibid*: 356.comm.), i.e. the wether at *Samain*, the pig after Christmas, sausage and bacon after that, and the meat 'between two flames' before Easter (see Ch. 5). In this case, the lord was supposed to give the client 'a double-handed vat and a cauldron' to do all this cooking, because as a non-noble the client was not obliged to maintain this equipment himself. This implies that the other feasts were prepared on the premises either of a lord or of a hosteller, *briugu*, described in Ch.7. The client who took a fief of land is said to have owed the lord 'the service of a slave' (*mughsaine*), which may imply that at the other feasts the base-clients enjoyed some of the food themselves and did not do the actual cooking and serving, whereas feasts given for land-fiefs necessitated that the client's household personally serve the lord's party.

But while fiefs varied, the main tract on the obligations of base-clients, *Cáin Aicillne*, takes the cattle-fief as its prototype for the discussion of the rights and duties of lord and client, presumably because this was the most common and useful of fiefs. The main part of the fief, the *taurchrecc*, or pre-payment, secured the lord's claim to the renders that were due in return from the farmer. The other part of the fief was termed the *séoit taurchluideo*, the 'chattels of subjection', so called because it equalled the value of the recipient's honor-price (*CIH* 1780.9 = *IR* II: 361 #18-9). On account of its receipt the lord had a one-third interest in all payments due as reparations to the client. *CA* states that the *séoit taurchluideo* of the *ócaire* (the lowest rank of properly equipped, house-holding farmer) was three *séts* (*CIH* 1779.23-4 = *AL* ii 225.8-9), while *CG* 119-20 also gives this as the *ócaire*'s honor-price, stipulating cattle. Two cows and a calf would probably have made up the *séoit taurchluideo* of an *ócaire*, while higher grades received more (see Chart).[11]

The lord's honor was thenceforth involved with the client's welfare, and the latter's social security was increased to the extent that the lord was powerful and honorable. The *séoit taurchluideo*, however, served more than a symbolic role in the transaction, functioning in fact as a pledge from the lord (though not acknowledged as such, since it was beneath a lord's dignity to pledge to a base-client), for in the event that the lord removed his fief from the clients' possession, the client could keep half the *séoit taurchluideo*. For this reason some lords evidently delayed handing over this part of the cattle-loan, but if it failed to materialize during the chief's lifetime, the client was entitled to keep one third of what he had received in the fief proper, the *taurchrecc* (*CIH* 1786.4 ff = *AL* ii 265 1 ff). The ninth-century learned compilation, Cormac's Glossary, also shows that the *séoit taurchluideo* could be treated as a separate transaction by the client, who might seek to establish a relationship of mutual honor and legal interdependence with a lord (presumably one who had power), but borrow cows from someone else on more convenient terms, such as the upwardly mobile farmers discussed in the next chapter, whose commoner status deprived them of the right to demand payment other than grain from their clients. According to the Glossary, however, the laws upheld the class-interests of the lords by forbidding farmers from splitting up clientship into two deals, thus playing off hereditary lords against prospering farmers (Stokes 1869: 9 '*aicillne*').

The actual amount of the fief has caused scholars difficulty because the two main sources, *Críth Gablach* and *Cáin Aicillne*, although they stipulate roughly the same amount and kind of renders due from each rank of farmer, are unclear as to how much of the stock held by the farmer derived from his own family, and how much from the lord. To take one example, according to *CG*, the *ócaire* had a fief of eight cows, for which he annually owed the lord a *dartaid*, a yearling bullock. According to *CA* too, the *ócaire* owed a *dartaid*, in return for a fief of 'twelve *séoit*' (between 6 to 8 cows). *CG*, however, also itemizes the *tothacht*, or *folud* (resources, substance), of the *ócaire*, which roughly matched the amount given by the lord, whereas *CA* does not specify what personal property the clients had. The question therefore arises, whether *CA* omitted to list the client's own possessions, or whether the client in fact had no cattle of his own. On the latter reading, *CG*'s list of the client's chattels would have to be interpreted as nothing but a reiteration of the data on his fief, for it is very unlikely that two men — the clients envisaged in *CG* on the one hand, and in *CA*, on the other — would have the same rank when one had no chattels of his own and the other did.

It has recently been argued that *CG* did in fact repeat itself when it moved from describing the fief to listing the clients' own resources, and that the client should therefore be viewed as contributing only land and labor to the relationship with his lord (Charles-Edwards 1986: 67-71). Given the slipperiness of Old Irish legal 'definitions' — to say nothing of economic happenstance — it seems very likely that this was sometimes the case. On the other hand, it is doubtful that this is what either of the two law-tracts held to be the ideal state of affairs. For one thing, in *CG*'s list of the *ócaire*'s own resources, his *tothacht* (i.e not the fief, *taurchrecc*), there were seven pigs and a domestic boar, seven sheep, seven cows and a bull, an ox for plowing, and a work-horse (*CG* 90-1). None of this other stock was included in the fief (which was a plain 'eight cows'), so why should the cows in his *tothacht* not be his own also? Charles-Edwards dealt with this objection to the theory of cattle-less *bóaire* clients, by arguing that *CG*'s enumeration of equal ratios of pigs, sheep and cows on the clients' farms is 'demonstrably false', because archaeological evidence shows the overwhelming preponderance of cattle in the livestock sector of farming (Charles-Edwards 1986: 69, 71). The demonstration of falsity, however, consists only of references to excavated royal sites, not the middens of the *ócaire* class. New archaeological techniques, moreover, show more variety in consumption patterns at excavated sites; at Moynagh Lough crannog, Co. Meath, calculations show that cattle constituted 39%, pigs 36% and sheep 25%. At Rathmullen in Co. Down, pigs outnumbered cattle, with the ratio increasing in later historical phases (Edwards 1990: 57-8).

In any case, the mere mention of these other animals, not the question of how many were on the average farm, rules against the argument that *CG*'s two lists were actually only one list — i.e. the fief, repeated. *CA*, too, makes mention of the client's separate property, in a commentary which explains why the fief given to man who had neither property nor a kinsman to act as surety from him (an *oenchinnuid*), should be greater than that given to an adolescent, even though the latter had *tothacht* — resources.[12] The distinction between the *rath* (fief) and *tothacht* (resources) implies that the latter belonged to the client. Commentary is often viewed as suspect, but in this case it complements *CG*'s separate listing of *tothacht* and reinforces the view that clients brought their own stock to the relationship, stock that the lord may have required as collateral for his fief. As to *CA*, it should be assumed that this tract simply did not itemize the client's property, as it similarly failed to specify how much land he held, even though its author went to great lengths to stress that the fief be proportionate to the farmer's assets in pasture, or else his kin could cancel the clientship contract.[13]

All things considered, then, we should regard the base-client as having his own chattels as well as stock from his lord. In return for the fief, the client owed a broad range of services and renders; any default in these was sanctioned by heavy fines.[14] The renders paid by the client were of two kinds, the *bés*, or livestock payment, and the *fosair* or *timthach* (literally 'strewing' and 'wrapping'), which mainly consisted of cooked foods — bread, wheat, ale, honey, bacon, milk, butter, onions and candles. Gerriets showed that the value of the latter, according to the terms used in the tracts, was considerably greater than that of the livestock renders paid by the base-clients (Gerriets 1983: 51). Moreover, in both *CA* and *CG*, the livestock renders for nearly all clients consisted only of castrated and immature males, some of which would have been slaughtered for consumption, and some added to the store-cattle of the lord's herds, from which he could obtain bulls and plow oxen. It was only the *bóaire* (in *CA*) or *mruigfher* (in *CG*), who paid a *bés* of a mature milking cow that could be put into circulation by the lord in his system of cattle fiefs to other men (see Appendix).

The renders were handed over, fully prepared for consumption, in the form of cheese, bread, ale, bacon, and beeves. As explained in Ch. 5, the bulk of the renders were paid in winter, which was the season of *cóe*, the 'visitations' of lords and their companions to the base-clients. The numbers of guests that the lord could bring, and the quality of the food due from the client, were very precisely stipulated. A commentary to *CA* states the basic rule:

> ...and if the chief should bring too large a company,
> it would be 'feeding beyond honesty' on the part of
> the chief...and it is right for (the client) to separate
> from him in consequence of the indigence of the
> chief. (*CIH* 1781.15-20 = *AL* ii 233.7-11).

The protection of the client was balanced by careful specification of the condition of the renders when presented to the chief. If the animals or food were of poor quality — 'bitter or mawkish' — the chief could refuse them, and the client, though not necessarily guilty of dishonesty and liable to a fine, would nevertheless begin to run up debt (*CIH* 1782.3 ff = *AL* ii 235.36 ff = *IR* III: 345 #6).

The season of *cóe* lasted almost two months. Binchy points out that in *CG* the ratio was always 4 guests : 1 base-client (*CG* p. 81). Units of five base-clients, and multiples of these, are mentioned throughout this tract. The lowest lord, the *aire désa*, would thus bring twenty people to be fed by his five base-clients, while higher lords could bring 40 or 60. (*CG* rather piously stipulated ten married couples as the twenty people in the *aire désa*'s retinue, but gamblers, story-tellers and courtesans were certainly present at the sixteenth-century *cuid oidhe*, night's supper [Kelly 1988: 30, n.85]). Presumably, a lord who took ten men and their wives to eat his base-clients' produce needed comparable invitations to keep him fed and entertained during this time. Although no sources describe *cóe* in any detail, it seems most likely that the groups who went on *cóe* consisted of other lords, probably kinsmen within the same local ruling group, and that the whole band progressed through the local territory visiting each other's base-clients. (How they were accommodated, however, is a mystery not to be dispelled here.)

In saga literature, feasts were the occasion of great social tension, as insults were perceived in the order of seating, in the lavishness or otherwise of the client's 'housekeeping', and as guests took umbrage over who got the best pieces of meat (especially the 'hero's portion'). In ordinary life, too, a feast, or even ordinary hospitality, must have been stressful, for the treatment meted out to people was a measure of the host's respect for them. The combination of perceived insult and hunger was so explosive that elaborate provisions governed just how much each rank of society could expect when they went seeking entertainment. Failure by the base-clients to supply their lord with abundant good food impinged upon the lord's dignity in the most dramatic and dangerous of ways. Consequently, it was severely sanctioned with heavy fines and the possibility, if the client ran away, of confiscation of his land by his lord, his surety and his agnates.

Another tribute that is recorded as a major imposition on the farming class by the later middle ages was *congbáil* (in English sources of the sixteenth century, known as 'coine and livery'.) This involved the billeting of soldiers and functionaries on farmers' households when the local king had ordered a muster of soldiers for an attack, or when a meeting for ecclesiastical purposes (*senod*) had been arranged (*CIH* 890.1-5; Kelly 1988: 31). Tudor sources refer to these dues as 'uncertain services', because there was no limit on what the king could demand, unlike the orderly and specific arrangements of *cóe* and the payment of summer food rentals (K. Simms 1987: 130-31, 140-41). It is probable that, intermittently, this was by far the heaviest burden on the base-clients during all historical periods. The importance of the practice can hardly be underestimated, for it was the provision of guaranteed food, shelter and protection to those who were travelling on the business of the local political community, that made possible the degree of public and governmental activity that existed, notwithstanding the absence of state institutions (see Ch. 12). The clients' homesteads, under obligation to serve the lord's political apparatus at his will, constituted the dispersed power nodes referred to in Ch. 3. Of all the many lacunae in the data for early medieval Ireland, the paucity of source material on this subject is perhaps the most to be regretted.

In addition to these obligations, base-clients owed manual labor services to the lord, such as the 'reaping party of the base-clients' (*meithel gíallnae*), in which farmers banded together to reap the corn and bring it in. The lord got the pick of the clients' calves; presumably, then, he could demand the labor of his clients in his home-fields or his *fuidri*'s fields on the first day when the harvest was ready, and before the rains could ruin the crops. This was still a privilege of landlords until recent times, as Glassie heard from a small-farmer in Ulster: 'Do ye see; the land was all owned by landlords... They had big crops. And they'd come by and if you wanted to save your wee harvest, they could order you away to theirs, leavin your to rot.'(Glassie 1982b: 83). Base-clients were also obliged to raise the embankments of the lord's *ráth* or *dun*, as we noted in Ch. 4. A specially onerous and symbolic set of manual obligations arose at the time of the death of the base-clients' lord, according to the law-tract, *Di Dligiud Raith 7 Somaíne*. These included digging the lord's burial mound; a payment comparable to English *heriot* and Welsh *ebediw* (the commentary indicates that one cow was demanded of each client); and attendance at his commemorative feast (*CIH* 434.27-32. See Kelly 1988: 30). Since the base-clients kept the fief given by the lord when he died, they were now free to choose which of his heirs they would serve as base-clients, if any. Thus the death of the lord was also the death of a particular political link.

In the early medieval period an important service provided by the base-client was participation in his lord's troop whenever the latter needed to put on a show of force. The Old Irish tract, *Berrad Airechta*, compares the futility of an ignorant judge attempting a decision, or a poor person attempting a purchase, to the futility of a nobleman attempting a military expedition without base-clients (Stacey 1968: 220: #61). *CA* lists the clients' duties in this regard as aiding the chief in redeeming his pledges, backing him at the assembly (*dáil*), aiding him in vendetta (*dígal*), and going out on duties of offense and defense against enemies (*fuba* and *ruba*), (*IR* II: 364 #24). The same rule of thumb that applied to free-clients, also appears in reference to the base-clients' service: 'a man for every heifer on a hosting, every third year' (*CIH* 435.25). Since the fief to the base-clientry could range up to the value of thirty heifers for the highest grade (the *bóaire*), it seems that base-clients supplied more manpower than did free-clients. The evidence on this military duty is very limited, however.

From a later period comes evidence that armies recruited in this way were unreliable, and that the great lords of the later middle ages preferred mercenaries to dependence upon local musters (K. Simms 1987: 121). The virtual absence of evidence on the nature of the military service of clients in the law tracts may thus reflect the attrition of base-clients' military services, *slógad*, at an early point. Citizen-soldiers were never totally obsolete, but they may have become little more than local gangs facing down similar gangs in disputes between petty lords, or they may have served as a last resort, rather than a prime fighting force. The latter would have been hired fighters — Irish *flan* bands, Vikings, Normans, and eventually *galloglass*, large and fierce Scots from the Inner Hebrides.

One reason for the inefficiency of base-clients as retainers was that their loyalties were likely to be divided. *CA* gives considerable attention to the fact that a client might legally have up to three lords from whom he had accepted a fief and to whom he owed services. This condition was endemic to the competitive, branching, Irish élite families, in which each heir strove to establish his own clientele. Where family solidarity was weak, clients would presumably hedge their bets by aligning themselves to as many promising leaders as they could. If, in addition, population densities were low at a given time and place, clients could take short-term contracts and juggle their options and obligations, as described by an English commentator, Sir William

Weston in 1593: '...the tenants do often times change their dwellings, sometimes being tenant to one and within half a year after tenant to another of those chief men, and many times wandering into other Counties, often changing and not long continuing in one place...' (Nicholls 1978: 10).

The social conditions of the late sixteenth century were extremely unsettled, of course, due to the advance of the English conquest, but the canonical pre-Viking texts of *CA* and *DRS* also depict a loose and free-wheeling society in which individuals cut clientship deals of extremely varied nature according to the bargaining strength of the parties. In addition to the choice between free and base clientship, men could also take on loans from 'lords of second contract' and even 'lords of third contract' (Kelly 1988: 32). *DRS* shows other variations on clientship. For example, the fief given with a child in fosterage would seem, on the face of it, intended to offset the cost of feeding the child. But *DRS* suggests that in fact a child could be sent in fosterage as one of the conditions in what was primarily a clientship arrangement between the adult parties, an arrangement where the fief of fosterage was accompanied by a true fief. This is the implication of a passage that discusses contracts in which a kin-group collectively entered into base-clientship with a lord. Here it is said that the normal arrangement was for the lord to give the group 'the full of a farmland' of livestock, and to let the recipients sort out amongst themselves who got what number of beasts, but that a distinction would be made if one of the group undertook to foster the lord's child. The fosterer would receive an 'apportioned' fief (Crigger 1991: 342.I.B.4; 351. H 3.17 Add. 1). This may mean that he took in fief the numbers of cattle appropriate to his individual property holding (as well as the specific fosterage fee, presumably), while his kin took the remainder on an undivided basis in which there was no individual accountability to the lord for default.

The competitiveness of lords for clients is further revealed by reference to lords contracting with clients in anticipation of the death of the client's lord (*ibid*: 342.I.C). Where it was the client who approached a lord with this kind of deal it seems that his bargaining strategy was the one mentioned above, namely to split economic obligation and political loyalty into separate contracts. The new lord was not offered food-renders, but was promised the client's political support and labor services even while his old lord lived (*ibid*: 349. H 3.18. Add.1). This was a legally recognized contract — regulated because it could not be prevented. It could be undertaken by a man who found himself in command of a number of dependent adult males — sons, foster-sons, and slaves — who could perform the political and labor services of clientship on his behalf.

Beginning at some point in the pre-Norman period, attempts were made in some regions of Ireland — probably in the north-east — to rationalize military contributions in such a way that a given territory would yield a given measure of support for warfare, as opposed to the unpredictable outcome of arrangements based on clientship contracts. The native system of fiscal assessment — the *trícha cét* system mentioned in Ch. 4 — served as the framework within which farmers' produce was exacted in order to support military functions. As noted previously, the system of assessment has received little notice from historians after Hogan and Mac Néill, so that it is possible only to outline some of its basic features. Nevertheless it is important to do so, because the demands imposed through this framework contributed to the pressured state of the farming population, its vulnerability to debt, and the response of society to these pressures — which was to transform kinship groups into instruments of social control for the protection of property and the defense of status.

Most of the evidence on the *trícha cét* appears in late documentation, compiled by the English government as a prelude to the colonization of the native society (Duffy 1981: 4-7). The largest unit in the system, the *trícha cét* ('thirty hundreds') was subdivided into thirty 'feeding places' (ballybetach; *baile biattagh*); this is unlikely to have comprised a levy of 3,000 soldiers, but rather some other element within the unit of assessment. Cows naturally come to mind, but there is no means of resolving the question. The thirty *ballybetagh* were each internally divided into quarters, which themselves broke down into 4 *ballybo* (townlands), or 3 plowlands. The townland unit was again subdivided; in Ulster there were 4 household units, known as *tathes*, or *tates*, but a variety of terms appear elsewhere (Hogan 1929: 179; McErlean 1983).

It is very tempting to assume that the *comaithches*, because it was often depicted as divided into four quarters, was an early precursor of the townland; this may be, but the current state of information on the historical geography of Ireland does not permit certitude in this respect. On the basis of a study of late Gaelic land-units in Monaghan, Duffy describes the *ballybetagh* as: 'the collective property of the sept or lineage group, to be divided and periodically redistributed among separate families of the group. Inheritance was partible. The operation of the system shaped the territorial organization of the land. The *ballybetagh* was the fundamental property unit of the lineage group. It was the estate of Gaelic society, and the *tate* was the territorial mechanism by which property was allocated among the members of the sept.' (1981: 7-8).

Robinson has come to similar conclusions regarding Tyrone (Robinson 1976: 4). These studies are not only of late aspects of the system, however, but of local types of assessment. Variety should be stressed, both at the conceptual level and as to the application of any method of assessment to real landscape. Leister's study of medieval Gaelic land-units in Tipperary (1976), for example, reveals an extraordinary richness of organizational detail, only some of which corresponds to the Ulster system.

As to the origins and pervasiveness of the *trícha cét* system, however, there is only one historically reliable reference from the pre-Norman period, namely an entry in the Annals of Ulster for 1106, which records that tribute was taken in Munster from 'each area of a *trícha cét*' (Ó Corráin 1978: 11). Most allusions to the *trícha cét* appear in heroic literature, in manuscripts written during the eleventh and later centuries, and only show that the institution was accepted as traditional, without establishing its actual antiquity. But that there *was* a native system, which worked back from the assessed productivity of a given land-unit to demands for military supports from its inhabitants, a system that shaped the units that had to satisfy these demands, is proven by gross features of the social landscape, such as the fact that townland size, and barony size progressively increase from east to west, as the productivity of the land declines.

But above all, it is the existence of systems like the *trícha cét* in other areas of the medieval British Isles that suggests that though the Irish law-tracts make little reference to these units, they were nevertheless important to military organization and thus had an impact on the socio-economic condition of the farmers. As Hogan pointed out, the resemblance between the Irish system and the Welsh divisions of land into cantreds and their subdivisions is very close. There is also some resemblance between the Irish system and the groupings of assessed lands (hides) in the Anglo-Saxon tribal hidage. In this, multiples of 300 hides formed higher units of, for example, 2,000,

4,000, 5,000. In this context it may not be unimportant that *CG* is a very similar type of document to the late Anglo-Saxon *Rectitudines Singulorum Personarum*, which *CG* probably ante-dates.[15]

The strongest evidence for the antiquity of aspects of the *trícha cét* scheme, however, comes from the concordance between its internal subdivisions and the assessment schemes employed in medieval southwest Scotland. In the early middle ages, this area was the Irish kingdom of Dál Riata, whose system of military assessment was already noted in Ch. 2 as having been similar to the system used in *CG*. Here households were grouped into units of four or five, paying four 'ounces' (of silver), or five pennies each to their lords (MacQueen 1979: 72-3). Together they formed the quarter, as in the *trícha cét* scheme in Ulster. Four quarters combined to make the equivalent of a ballybetagh, termed in Scotland a *tirunga* ('ounce-land') or *dabhach* — a 'vat-land'. Jackson has suggested that this was 'the amount of land necessary to produce a fixed amount of grain, enough to fill a large vat of a fixed size.[16]

The *dabhach* does not appear as a land-unit in the Irish lawtracts, but as we have seen, *DRS* does mention that land given in fief incurred obligations to fill a vat and a cauldron with food for feasts. There is also a reference to 'the great cauldron of the season', which is associated with the house of the brewy.[17] Since base-clients provided the seasonal fare, it is probable that their renders ended up in this 'widemouthed cauldron'; the Scottish *dabhach*, then, may have signified a unit of land and people responsible for a night's feasting before the commutation of dues to payment in coin.

Students of Scottish history have disputed whether Norse influence led to the imposition of a monetary tax on these units, as well as a manpower levy (oarsmen for galleys), but no one has argued that the units themselves did not originate in Gaelic political culture. The parallels between *CG* and the *Senchus fer nAlban* (see Ch. 2), and the similarity of the schemes depicted in them to the taxation systems of later medieval Ulster and Scotland, suggest that the latter are an outgrowth of the former — probably dating to between the Viking age and the eleventh century. Ultimately there must be a connection between the various north European military assessment systems and the Roman system of 'centuriation' (Hogan 1929: 151-4; Mac Neill 1911: 103 ff; Bannerman 1974: 139-46) — not because Rome originated centuriation *per se*, but because Roman military expansion stimulated the militarization of adjacent peoples even before Caesar and Tacitus wrote their accounts of these (Thompson 1982; Cunliffe 1988).

As to the relationship between the *trícha cét* and the *tuath*, the evidence suggests different origins for these groupings (Ó Corráin 1978: 11). The *tuath* was an internally defined unit, based on concepts of group identity that probably dated back to pre-Christian times; the *trícha cét* had no necessary social basis, but was a unit of assessment, applied to population groups by superior and external powers that had the capacity and the need to coordinate military activities on a considerable scale. The connection between the two bases of social organization was that dynastic rulers made demands upon their clients that were ultimately met by contributions generated at the grass-roots level of the base-clients; the dynasts did not move in a world where the *tuath* had much significance, but the base-clients certainly did. In the obscure relationship between *tuath* and *trícha cét*, there probably survive faint traces of the accommodation reached between local rulers, with deep roots in their native areas, who became vassals of members of the trans-regional dynasties when these established their grip on less powerful groups during the early middle ages. Few branches of the early medieval new dynasties survived the Viking Age, which saw a second round of new dynasties emerge in Ireland, but the latter were heirs to the social pattern based on dynastic clans, their free-holding lesser kin, and *aithech-tuatha*, vassal peoples.

During the Viking crisis in England, the *Burghal Hidage* was drawn up in Wessex to facilitate revision of the system of assessment for military contributions (Blair 1962: 75-80). This suggests that there may have been a similar background to the rise of the *trícha cét* and comparable systems of territorial assessment in Ireland, as strong Irish war-leaders emerged in response to the threat (and later the opportunities) presented by the Vikings from the ninth to the eleventh centuries. The details of the *trícha cét* system, however, did not become a matter for the brehons, any more than did the regulation of internal dynastic competition. Their concern was with the regulation of normal social life; this is described in the Old Irish law-tracts in terms of relations within kin-groups, the *fine* or *cenél*, which themselves are treated as social components of the ecologically stabilized unit, the *tuath*. These groups had more permanent and far-reaching significance in day-to-day social interaction than did the functionally specialized units of the *trícha cét*.

The lord's power and farmers' dependency

Why did men become base-clients? The *taurchrecc* given to the base-client was ideologically disguised as something good to have — a 'gift', *rath*. In one sense it was, for the small farmer, whose problems of herd balance were always the most acute, was now somewhat relieved of that managerial problem. In the fief, he could obtain whatever was lacking in his herd's composition, whether heifers or milch cows, oxen, horses, pigs or sheep. There is some evidence that suggests that the lord's contribution to the base-client's herd was typically or ideally in heifers — young cows at the threshold of their milking careers. There is, for example, the maxim 'a man for every heifer', mentioned previously.

In contrast, milch cows and oxen are included in a list of seven types of fief whose 'restitution with double' (i.e. punitive forfeiture for offense against the lord), would be very difficult for the base-clients to provide because their forfeiture would cut too deeply into his working capital (*CIH* 26.29-30 = *AL* v 221.11-14). Fiefs of heifers are also suggested by the nature of the renders paid to the lord; free-clients paid renders in milch cows or their produce, while base-clients contributed only very young or castrated male animals, reserving the milch cows for themselves. On the whole, it seems fair to conclude that base-clients usually maintained their own plow-team, as *CG* implies, and that the lord balanced their requirements of lactating cows. This meant that the farmer was free to eliminate all store animals from his herd other than replacement stock, and concentrate his resources of fodder on the milch cows. It also meant that the base-client could not easily migrate from the area, for the milch-cows were not all his own.

When a successful lord reduced his clientele's needs for store animals to the minimum, he shifted the burden of raising the animals during their unproductive periods onto others. How important this was may be appreciated when it is realized that early medieval cows did not calve until they were four years old (Kelly 1988: 113, n.97; McLeod 1987: 93), while their fertility peaked at seven; by stealing someone else's grown cow a man could double the productivity of his pasture. We have already observed that Irish lords kept large herds in reserve, but the cattle-raid was just as integral as these 'cattle-banks' to the lord's role as distributor of herds to his clients. On coming of age, a youth of noble lineage was expected to test his manhood in a raid 'over the border.' A whole category of stories relate 'the first adventure of a young lord.' Upon inauguration, too, a king launched a *crech ríg*, a 'royal foray' against his enemies. His followers then received gifts, *tuarastal*, which initiated their political obligations towards him (K. Simms 1987: 100-4).

But although a lord who was a successful raider of outsiders benefitted his own base-clients, the adjective '*dóer*' that described base-clientship (*dóer-chéilsine*) had a general sense of 'disadvantageous', 'bound', 'restricted', and it is doubtful that anyone chose to enter the contract of *dóer chéilsine* if he could be a free-client. The disadvantage resided in the clientship contract's implications for land utilization. The basic patrimonial endowment of every free Irish man was his claim to a part of his clan's *fintiud*. According to *Críth Gablach*, the larger the size of his landholding, the larger the fief given to the farmer by his lord. When a chief gave a farmer a fief of cattle, the upshot of the arrangement, from the farmer's point of view, was that a certain proportion of his pasturage and labor supply had to be allocated for the support of the chief's cattle, for which renders were due. Without these, the farmer would have been able to expand his herd up to the carrying capacity of his land and labor supply, and maximize his calory production by raising only dairy animals.

Moreover, the seven-year duration of the term of base-clientship, only after which the base-client 'owned' the fief (in that no more renders were due) was almost certain to have made the original fief useless except for consumption as beef, since under natural conditions cows typically go into decline after the seventh year of life.[18] To terminate the relationship with his lord, the base-client had to return the original fief in its entirety (or, perhaps, its equivalent), no matter how much produce and service he had given the lord (*IR* III: 384). This requirement tended to entrap the client, whose ability to expand his own herd in order to deal with the shortfall occasioned by returning the fief was limited, both by the unpredictable nature of herd growth, and also by his restricted access to pasture, illustrated in the restrictions placed on the amount of his fief by his kin (see Ch. 10).

It was also disadvantageous to the base-client to assume the risk of caring for the lord's cattle: whatever losses occurred, the client was still liable to meet the renders due for the fief, and also to produce the cattle if the chief had grounds to terminate the relationship. Basically then, the contract between lord and base-client had a number of features which tended to entrap the client in the relationship. This type of arrangement is commonplace in societies where livestock constitutes significant wealth, and where other factors promote social stratification, so that loans of stock may be invested with features that promote the dependency of the recipient (Cassanelli 1982: 51-2; Karp 1960: 49-70).

Although it is not possible with the available data to model early Irish farming in any detail, it seems probable that farmers' lands were kept stocked at close to carrying capacity, and that the fief did not leave room for the client to expand his personal holding - unless, that is, the client found some way of shifting the care of his cattle onto someone else's land and labor. Evidently such situations did occur - *Cáin Sóerraith* referred to 'the loan of one *aithech* (a base-client) to another', and even a loan by a commoner to someone of noble stock (*CIH* 1777.3 ff = *IR* II: 251 ##7-8 = *AL* ii 215.16 ff) — but the nobles and the jurists were reluctant to grant the full 'profits' of clientship to such loans: client-taking was a social activity that the lords tried to monopolize. Pressure of stock on the land was envisaged in *CA*. Describing the fief given to the very lowest grade of farmer, the juvenile *fer domun*, the tract says he should only be given three heifers, and only have to pay a calf the value of one sack of grain along with the 'accompaniment':

> this is the food-render to which the *fer domun*
> submits, unless his father had incurred it before'. [19]

A similar warning that 'it is not lawful to impose more on him' was also made in *CA* about the fiefs given out to the next grades above the *fer domun*, namely the *oenchiniud* and *fer midboth* (*CIH* 484.33-4; 485.9-10 = *AL* ii 257.35-7; 259.20-24). What was at issue was that a larger fief would trespass on the pasture-rights of the client's kinsmen, who were entitled to return the lord's excessive fief (see Ch. 10).

In addition to the strain of meeting the obligations of the contract, the client faced the danger of becoming indebted to whoever had given securities to guarantee that he would make good what he owed on account of the fief. Suretyship for base-clientship contracts had some features that differed from suretyship in desultory, *ad hoc* transactions, as one would expect, in view of the political importance of the base-clients' obligations. For example, in *BA* #42 it is shown that the responsibility to make restitution when a client defaulted passed from the debtor to his first surety (*ráth*) and then to the ultimate surety (the *naidm*). In other situations, in contrast, the latter was only obliged to distrain the debtor or the *ráth*, not pay up himself. Often these sureties would be kin, so that default in clientship endangered not only the individual and his next of kin, but also higher status members of his kin group who played the role of *naidm*-surety. (Suretyship is explained in the next chapter.)

CG also makes a reference to the pressure brought to bear on base-clients, mentioning that on the outer perimeter of the king's household, next to his guards, sat 'the man who is the *gell* (hostage or pledge) for the base-clients'. Binchy interpreted his role as guaranteeing with his entire property, including his land, that his kinsmen in base-clientship would conform to the law — not only or especially regarding their clientship contracts, but in relation to the demands of the Church and social regulation (Binchy 1941: 38 n.587). Indeed the oldest and most general term for base-clientship was not *dóer-chéilsine*, but *gíallnae* — the condition of being pledged (*CG*: p.96). A cryptic passage in *CG* seems to suggest that the base-client's land served as the *gell* (security) for his fief.[20] Normally, fines were levied from an individual's chattels, but under some circumstances a defaulting client forfeited his land to his surety, to the lord, and the remnant to his kin (*CIH* 1780.29-36 = *AL* ii 229.23-36). It is true that references to seizure of land that was pledged are mainly found in late commentaries,[21] and it is well known that pledging was a widely used method of transferring land-ownership in late medieval Gaelic Ireland, but loss of land for debt seems to have been an inherent aspect of the structure of social sanctions in pre-Norman Ireland. There is no evidence that it was, *per se*, a late development, even though no early sources go into the question. Without land, the peasant had neither the material resources to feed himself, nor the social protection required to keep the world at bay.

Given the disadvantageousness of the fief, why did farmers enter into base-clientship? Clearly free-clientship was associated with membership in economically independent extended families and clans; base-clientship is conversely associated with the economic weakness of an individual family and its next of kin. Loans for productive functions and security in legal transactions were social services that men would try to obtain first amongst their closest kinsmen (see Ch. 10). Where these were few or impoverished it was difficult for families and individuals to defend their status. Voluntarily or under duress, men who lost their property or who lacked adequate support from close kin, entered base-clientship for economic and social protection. The influence of the threat of litigation, debt, and forfeiture of property on early Irish kinship will occupy most of the second half of this book. In the next chapter, where we survey the formal aspects of insurance and credit, we already begin to glimpse the outlines of the clan system.

Notes

1. Dillon (ed.) *Lebar na cert*: 179-89. See also Binchy 1976: 27-31, and Gerriets 1987.

2. Gerriets (1987), makes a valuable contribution to the evidence for royal demesne farming.

3. For further discussion of royal retinues see Ch. 12.

4. *CG* 435-6. This is pointed out by Charles-Edwards (1986: 61). In the tract, *Míadshlechta*, however, this distinction is blurred, for there *senchléithe* servants are attributed to all the ranks of the lords (*CIH* 584.21-9 = *AL* iv 351.12-23).

5. 'A *fuidir* does not sustain the offence of the kindred, until it is increased in wealth to five holdings. If they have five full holdings, they share their family lands.' See *SEIL*: 148-9.

6. Comyn (ed.) *Forus Feasa* i: 69. The translation 'tribal chief' is not satisfactory; 'head of a troop' is closer to the Irish sense.

7. *CIH* 1770.15-1778.33 = *AL* ii 195 - 221; ed. and German transl. by Thurneysen 1925b. The main features of the law-tracts' evidence on free-clientship are given by Kelly 1988: 32-3.

8. *DIL* notes *Leviticus xxv* as a source.

9. *CIH* 1776.3-5 = *AL* 213.2-6. See similarly '*sochur don flaith eside...*', that is profitable to the lord', *DRS*, ed. Crigger 1991: 339 #7.3 = 354-5 #7.3-4.

10. *NI SAOR NACH BEGCENEOIL NA BENAR .V.RAITH CETACH. (CIH 2010.37; 760.20).*

11. For cow and *sét* see Kelly 1988: 116.

12. *mo tic don aenciniud fognam do denum da curp don fhlaith, cid uad dech a thothcus.* more able is the single-person to do body-service for the lord, though his resources have gone. *(CIH 485.2-4 = AL ii 259.1-6).*

13. *AL* is actually helpful in understanding this tract, since the fief is throughout referred to as 'the proportionate stock' given for the renders.

14. Dissolution of the contract without good reason incurred double-payment of the food that was due *(IR III: 386 #52 = AL ii 319.36-321.8).*

15. Loyn 1962: 189-95. See also Brownbill 1925: 502.

16. Kenneth Jackson, *The Gaelic Notes in the Book of Deer* (Cambridge, 1972: cited by MacQueen 1979: 73).

17. *IM SCABUL CACH RAITHE. (CIH 371.1 = AL i 135.2).*

18. *Encyclopedia Americana*: 'Cattle'. Lisle, writing in 1776, noted that the farmers he had interviewed said that milk yield peaked in the sixth year. (Trow-Smith 1957: 31).

19. *TURCREIC AIGE LOIGE MEICH CONA FOSAIR...III.E TEORA SAMAISCI...IS E BES FOLOING FERDOMUN IN SIN NI TECHTA FAIR NI BES MO ACHT MA ROSA A ATHAIR RIAM AR NI RUCA. (CIH. 484.13-6).*

20. *CG* 106-8. This is Mac Néill's view: 'That land, too, is as means for him against it (i.e. against the service due from him)' (1923: 288). Charles-Edwards (1986: 70) rejects the idea that land was given, on the grounds that otherwise the details on land do not 'hang together' with those on livestock, given in *CG* (1986: 70). But, in addition to the objections given in this chapter to his views on the cattle-fief as the client's sole source of livestock, it should also be pointed out that his argument depends on the *a priori* ground that he could 'think of no other way to explain the pervasiveness of base clientship and its persistence from one generation to another' (1986: 70), and so was 'driven' to identifying the fief with the client's entire bovine stock. The difficulty of herd-expansion for the small farmer and the consequent difficulty of returning the fief, to say nothing of the political danger entailed in changing clientship, are

overlooked in this argument.

21. See, for example, the commentary to the tract on distraint, at *CIH* 1735.6-10 = *AL* ii 41.28 ff.

CHAPTER SEVEN

Rank

Kings, lords, free and base-clients were status groups of considerable structural fluidity; definition and solidity existed only at the cultural level in terms of legal concepts, social norms, and symbolic expression, while individual lives were lived out in the midst of personal and group change. Battles and raids were one element in social struggle, but far more salient and pervasive was the struggle for status within the framework of the legal system. Central to the conceptual organization of legitimacy was the division of society into named ranks, each having its honor-price. To outline this cultural framework I shall first indicate the scope of social action governed by the honor-price. The second part of this chapter will then explain how rank was allocated to individuals, focusing on the translation of wealth into status.

Honor-price (*lóg n-enech*; face-value)

Lóg n-enech, also known as *eneclann* (face-cleansing), was the amount payable to a person as *díre*, reparation, for any assault that lessened his/her social esteem. The amount of honor-price ranged, according to *CG*, from 14 *cumal*s (= 42 milch cows) for a provincial king, to a yearling heifer for an adolescent living on his father's land. Women's honor-prices were half that of male peers (typically, a brother). These amounts may seem to be small, but the honor-price was a resource that was to be always at hand, in order to meet obligations entailed by the various contingencies that might occasion payment. It was, then, surplus, over and above what the individual needed to meet his/her consumption and production requirements, as well as the surplus drained off by the lord or overlord.

Payments of honor-price were due when a person was the victim of physical assault (*guin*), assault on any of his/her social connections, both kinsmen and dependents, and assault on anyone who was

181

temporarily under his/her protection, and damage to personal property. Full honor-price was also owed to a person who suffered formal ridicule, satire (*áer*), without justification (Kelly 1988: 49-50). Honor-price was paid for the loss of social respect associated with any assault; restitution for the physical damage was another matter, often paid in addition to honor-price. It was dishonorable to be either the victim of offense without receiving honor-price as reparation, or to be accused of an offence and fail to submit to judgment of the charge. Someone who defied the law suffered loss of honor-price and was stripped of a large measure of social protection, since the various privileges governed by rank were no longer available to him or her. While he could not be assaulted at will, he could be insulted with impunity. This was a form of internal social exile; further lawlessness was sanctioned by further degrees of exclusion, which terminated in full, formal outlawry, along with physical extrusion from the territory (Kelly: 222-4).

Honor-price determined the scope of an individual's privileges and autonomy in society. As we have seen, the amount of fief given to a man was linked to his ability to make good his payments to the lord, and both were connected to the honor-price — the higher the honor-price, the higher the fief. Likewise, because the honor-price indicated social ability, it governed the value of the individual's word in a legal dispute. In early Ireland, as throughout medieval Europe, legal decisions were arrived at in part through compurgation — the oaths provided by plaintiffs and defendants. Often it was necessary for each opposing party to muster a group of people to swear a collective oath; the gravity of the issue determined what number of oath-helpers was needed to make the charge stick, or to deny it. But as the value of each man's oath in compurgation (*imthach*), varied with his status, an individual's helpfulness in this regard was entirely contingent on his/her honor-price. One great lord could succeed in overswearing (*fortach*) a number of farmers (Kelly 1988: 198-202). According to *CG, fíadnaise*, eye-witness evidence, was taken into account only if the person's honor-price was appropriate to the gravity of the charge to which he was testifying (*CG* 19, 26, 43, etc).

Honor-price also served as the delimitation of personal autonomy in social action. Unless a person had individually acquired wealth, over and above his share of family land and chattels, it was illegal for him/her to be a party to a contract (*fechem*), regarding amounts that exceeded his/her honor-price (Kelly 1988: 158). The point of this restriction was to prevent individuals from implicating their kin in liabilities, for kinsmen stood to suffer as involuntary sureties — *inmlegon* — for each other's debts and misdeeds, as is shown below. When a contract was in the offing, the principals had to bring forward men to act as sureties or warrantors, who would guarantee the principals' compliance to the terms of the contract — be it the legitimacy of a sale (for example, guaranteeing that an animal was not sick or stolen), or the future fulfillment of some agreement. It was clearly in the interest of these sureties that neither principal should contract for more than he could cover, in the event that a debt ensued.

Suretyship was, in effect, the formalization of the countervailing social pressures that tended to compel people to honor their contracts; but without the formal instrument these pressures would have been insufficient to compel people to compliance with the law, for competition and violence were rife enough to dissolve the larger social groups into feuding micro-units of society. The honor-price served as the gauge of the pressure that each party to the transaction could bring to bear upon the principals. To further grasp the social implications of Irish suretyship, however, it is necessary to understand the basic mechanism of social sanction — distraint. A brief digression into legal procedure is thus necessary here.[1]

Someone who had abrogated a contract or otherwise broken the law, was pressured into compliance by means of a carefully formalized legal action of self-help, technically known as distress or distraint, *athgabál* (literally, 'taking back'). This consisted of the seizure of cattle from the debtor or culprit in lieu of whatever he owed in debt or damages. There then followed well-demarcated stages of progressive attrition of his rights of ownership in these cattle. In the first stage, the plaintiff gave formal warning (*apad* or *airfócre*) of his grievance and intention to seize an appropriate number of livestock in a specified number of days. (The delay, *anad*, varied from no delay at all, up to ten days). If the accused failed to respond, the plaintiff was entitled to enter the accused's land early on the morning of the specified day (before milking?) and remove the cattle in question. (Not all cattle could be taken: sick or newly calved cows, or cattle belonging to the chief in clientship, were exempt — *nemed*[2]). The cattle were then impounded, either on the plaintiff's *faithche* (green), or if the amount exceeded his honor-price, on the green of a person of high rank, a *nemed* (*CIH* 1718.22-6 = *AL* i 291 (last line)-293.8). There then followed a period of 'delay in pound' (*díthim*), after which, if the accused had still not acted, the cattle were gradually forfeited to the plaintiff. At any point in this process, the accused could halt the progress of the 'decay' (*lobad*) of his ownership by giving a pledge that he would come to law. The longer he delayed, however, the greater the cost to him, for even before the forfeiture of his cattle began, he ran up considerable expense for the stall-feeding of the impounded cattle.

The actual implementation of distress might be undertaken by the plaintiff alone, if he were experienced in this kind of action. Otherwise he could turn to the sureties who had participated in the formalization of the contract, and others experienced in legal action. Such group action to take the distress seems to have been especially appropriate where the person being distrained was not the principal himself but a kinsman, being sued for vicarious liability as kinsman. In this case, the removal of the cattle was performed by the plaintiff along with a man versed in the law (*aigne*), who could guide the plaintiff as to correct procedure and statements, and a witness (*fiadu*). When the cattle were brought outside the accused's land two sureties were also to be present.[3]

Distraint was something of a catastrophe for a farmer, for not only was his daily food-supply threatened, but his honor-price was *ipso facto* reduced, thus curtailing his social privileges along the lines described previously. It was also a threat to his kin-group, whose economic interdependence was such that severe economic loss to one member was a threat to next of kin. (How economically interdependent these groups were is explained in Ch. 10). In this context, sureties may be understood as basically providing reserve credit; they saved the plaintiff from facing the dangers of directly distraining an embarrassed debtor (who might be strong in terms of domestic manpower, though short of chattels), and they also protected the creditor from total loss in the event that the debtor absconded with his family and movables. To this extent, suretyship facilitated exchange between people of different kin-groups and even different territories. The social impetus to suretyship, however, is probably not to be sought in inter-tribal social outreach, but in the defensiveness of social groups when they were obliged to enter such exchanges.

Sureties were often, and perhaps ideally, members of the same kin-group (see Ch. 12), who thus protected the group from attrition of resources by assuming the debt and keeping the payment of fines by the creditor down to the minimum. The debtor himself might end up paying large fines or even entering debt-slavery — but his property and person remained with a wealthier segment of his kin-group, rather than leaking out into the hands of strangers and enemies. There were three main kinds of surety in early Irish law:

1. *ráth*, a paying surety, who was liable to make good the value of whatever amount the principal owed.

2. *naidm*, an enforcing surety, who compelled payment from the principal, or the *ráth*.

3. *aitire* or *gíall*, a hostage-surety.

No one could serve in any of these capacities where the chattels at stake were of greater value than his own honor-price. When default occurred, the principal notified the *ráth* that he was now liable for the amount, plus a penalty of one third the value of what was due; the *ráth* was not in fact expected to actually pay at this point, but to offer a pledge that the amount would be procured.

The pledge consisted of a personal item, usually intimately tied to the *ráth*'s own social identity, which would be forfeit to the plaintiff unless the *ráth* succeeded in getting restitution within a stipulated period of time, normally a month. Kelly (1988: 166) gives the example of a lord who handed over a goblet as pledge; 'he is entitled to receive interest of one *sét* for every three days until nine days are up. After that, the rate of interest is increased and he receives three *séts* for every five days until a further fifteen days are up.'

During this time, the debtor should pay what he owed, plus one-third of the debt in order that the pledge be recovered by the *ráth*. He also had to pay interest (*fuillem*) to the *ráth*, for the length of time in which the pledge had been in jeopardy. If, however, the principal again defaulted, the *ráth* had to pay on his behalf; the principal now owed his surety double the amount of the debt and the value of his honor-price, and incidental expenses. The surety was entitled to seize the property of the debtor to make good what was now owed to him. Most contracts involved at least two *ráths*, one on each side of the transaction. In addition, because of the honor-price limitation on individuals' capacity to serve as *ráth*, the law acknowledged supplementary *ráths*; one *ráth* would be the chief *ráth* (*cetráth*), another the 'back surety' (*ráth íar cúl*, or *cúl ráth*) (Kelly 1988: 169).

The second kind of surety, the enforcer, *naidm*, had two functions: to memorize all the details of the contract, and to compel the party to the transaction to fulfil his obligations — by violence, if necessary. If the *naidm* failed to produce compliance by the principal, he himself lost honor. If the *ráth* himself defaulted, the *naidm* would compel him to his duty; if both *ráth* and principle defaulted, the *naidm* was liable, but could distrain both debtors to make good what was now owed him. Both defaulters would now be without honor. Each *ráth* was backed by a *naidm*, including the supplementary *ráths*, who required their own *naidms* to enforce their individual duties.

The final type of voluntary surety was the *aitire*, who guaranteed a contract by becoming liable to arrest, in person, as a temporary hostage, in the event of default. The *aitire* could not offer material restitution to stave off this indignity; the defaulter who occasioned his dishonor had to discharge the entire debt, plus a punitive fine, within ten days of the seizure of the *aitire*. He also owed the latter compensation for his 'disturbance' and incidental expenses; the 'disturbance' entailed several days of acute discomfort and humiliation, for the *aitire*'s oath bound him to submit 'to remain in stocks or in prison' with his foot in a fetter or his neck in a chain. If the debtor did not pay within the stipulated ten days, the *aitire* could then give a pledge that he would pay his own ransom (seven *cumals*). At this, the debtor owed the *aitire* the price of seven *cumals* of ransom, his honor-price, recompense for losses and expenses incurred during captivity, and twice the original debt to the plaintiff. The *aitire* could distrain the plaintiff of goods to the value of this amount (Kelly 1988: 172-3).

Aitire sureties were involved in treaties between different *tuatha*, and shade off into hostageship. A hostage (*gíall*) was given as a regular condition of political submission, and was often a son of the subordinate king or lord (Kelly 1988: 174). The *aitire*, on the other hand, seems to have been a volunteer, an adult of high status, who was offered in an *ad hoc* agreement, rather than an arrangement that was expected or supposed to be enduring. As with other sureties, the *aitire* could only guarantee contracts whose material principle did not exceed his honor-price. Any of these sureties (*naidm*, *gíall*, or *aitire*) might end up participating in the action of legal distraint against the debtor, the *ráths*, or the kinsmen of the debtor, and even the kinsmen of defaulting *ráths*, for the liabilities of the latter were hereditary.

Suretyship was organized and controlled compulsion, although the controls were not in the hands of authorities, but were parcelled out to all male land-holding members of clans, on the basis of their honor-price. In Ch. 2 it was pointed out that *Berrad Airechta* stated that before the acceptance of the *Senchas Már* throughout Ireland, low ranking men had been permitted to act as *naidm* in contracts involving seven *cumals* — a king's honor-price — but that by the time of the text, suretyship was restricted to liabilities not exceeding an individual's honor-price (*BA* #41). This limitation had the effect of protecting the assets of kin who were legally liable, as involuntary sureties (*inmlegon*), for any debts occasioned by a kinsman. Other laws also attempted to defend the *inmlegon* from some of the worst consequences of guilt by association (Kelly: 179-80). In general then, the honor-price restriction on individual expenditure, the institution of suretyship, and its restriction to the amount of honor-price, all worked to protect the group's assets from damages incurred by individuals.

The honor-price restrictions on contractual capacity are integral to *CG* and pervade the body of Irish law, but appear to have emerged only sometime prior to the writing of *BA*, during the classical Old Irish period of law-tract writing in the seventh century. *BA* #58 also shows that the restriction of eye-witness testimony to issues commensurate with the honor-price of the witness was aimed at ensuring that people of low status would not participate to any great effect in the legal process:

> The law of witnessing: Why is witness (*fíada*) so called?
> Because he is a lord (*fíada*), for witnessing cannot be done
> except by a conscientious person ....

The tract offers an alternative etymology, but since it proceeds to list all sorts of people who should not be allowed to offer legal proof its basic intention to restrict legal participation cannot be doubted:

> Unfree men, senseless men (i.e. without a head), lordless
> men (i.e without a leader) provide proof that is supported by
> [the responsible testimony of others]. (*BA* #59).

In contrast, men who belonged to the various ranks listed in *CG* and other tracts on status, could offer eyewitness that was valid, but only so far as their honor-price.

Binchy maintained that *CG* and comparable tracts that recognize many levels of honor-price were schematic, and *on that account* 'unreal' (*CG* xviii-xix), but these sources are better seen as requiring people to maintain specified levels of productivity if they wished to have social privileges, and making the latter commensurate with the success of the farmer in contributing to the economic organization of the polity. It is particularly interesting that sureties were *not* invoked in intimate dyadic relationships that established long-term inter-dependence (Stacey 1991). Such 'exempt' interchanges typically involved individuals of *unequal* status (such as lord and client, father and son, abbot and monk, teacher and disciple). Suretyship, in contrast, applied in relationships that were limited in content, and that involved men of broadly similar status — adult land-holders — with each therefore at risk of losing property and status to the other through fraud. Honor-price restrictions functioned to minimize these dangers, and the violent conflicts that would erupt when losses that occurred in a contract were interpreted as deliberate cheating.

Leaving conflict and turning to normal social interaction, we can see that in almost every respect, honor-price governed the social capacity to interact with others beyond one's domestic group. An important outcome was that social relations that were not inherently hierarchic (as were clientship and apprenticeship, for example) were confined to relations between peers. This produced a society that, in terms of sumptuary rules and general snobbishness, approached an almost caste-like condition — though lacking the rigidity of caste.

For lords, honor-price governed the number of people they could take 'feasting and guesting' with them during the winter coshering season, as explained in Ch. 6. During any season, however, all travellers required protection from human hostility, and from the elements. The traveller had the right to ask for *bíathad* (food and shelter were both entailed), for himself and his companions; anyone who turned him out into the night was guilty of the offense of *esáin*, for which the victim was owed his honor-price. On the other hand, he could not bring hordes of people with him; the number was determined by his honor-price. When taken into a house, the traveller and his company had to be supplied with food appropriate to his rank. An example of sumptuary specifications (and the virtual impossibility of satisfying them adequately all the time) appears in the Introduction to the *Senchas Már*. (The words in brackets are my interpolations):

> What is the ever-full cauldron? Answer. A cauldron which should be kept continuously on the fire for whatever party might arrive ... which, no matter what is put in it, (the meat) comes out again in perfect condition, though any other cauldron would dissolve it (while waiting for the guests) ... and everyone's own appropriate kind of food is got from it for everyone: as, for example, the haunch for the king, bishop and senior man of learning; a leg for a young chief;

heads for the charioteers, a steak for a queen ... (*CIH* 349.36-
350.2 = *AL* i 49.7 ff).

Rank also determined the number of visitors and the type of food
allocated to individuals under the provisions of 'sick-maintenance'. This
meant that someone who injured another was obliged to pay damages
for the injury, provide a replacement for the individual as regards work,
and also pay for the cost of nursing the injured back to health at the
house of a third party, with all expenses pegged to the injured party's
rank (Binchy 1938a; 1938b). Appropriate food, a peaceful setting away
from family cares, and good company were assumed to help speed the
healing process. A prosperous farmer (*mruigfher*), for example, was
allowed:

> three men (in) his company in the *tuath*, three men with him
> upon sick-maintenance; butter to him, with relish, always. He
> protects his equal in status. Salt meat to him on the third day,
> the fifth day, the ninth, the tenth, Sundays. (*CG* 204-6).

Travellers also required legal protection (*snádud* or *turtugud*). A guest
would normally come under the protection of his host for the night,
under the rules of 'precincts', *maigen* (Kelly 1988: 140-1). Needless to
say, the extent of the *maigen* was also proportionate to the honor-price.
But legal protection also applied to people who were being hunted down
in the course of some conflict, such as a blood-feud, and who had not
had time to arrange a proper legal response. (It was not legal to protect
someone from due processes of law). Protection beyond one's precincts
could thus be granted by one individual to another for periods of time
that varied with the protector's status — it was a form of sanctuary
without buildings. Various lords could protect for periods such as ten
or fifteen days, while even the lowliest clansman could protect another
until he had time to get out of the *tuath*. If the person under protection
was killed or injured during this time, the slayers were guilty of *díguin*,
and owed the protector his honor-price, as well as compensation to the
victim or the kin. The institution of *snádud* (often and angrily
mentioned in sixteenth-century English sources as 'comrik') survived
until the end of Gaelic independence (Kelly 1988: 37-8; 141).

Finally, the law-tracts show that honor-price governed aspects of
the most intimate contracts, the fosterage of children, and marriage.
Fosterage (*altram*) was a widespread and seemingly preferred way of
bringing up children, not only in Ireland but throughout northern Europe
during the early middle ages. Children were typically sent away to other

households, very often the mother's brother's, from the age of seven until seventeen (the main source, *Cáin Íarraith*, prescribes fourteen years for girls. [*CIH* 901.35-6; 902.4]). It provided for children's education and socialization by placing them in suitable homes with adult supervision, including teachers for upper class children, and the companionship of other children. Given the dispersal of the population, this concentration of children clearly had some advantages. Fosterage also distributed children in the community, offering them a wide network of social ties that supplemented and to some extent offset the competitiveness of agnatic kinship. Needless to say, it diffused the emotional ties within the nuclear family, which could hardly have existed as a stable constellation of relationships. Kelly points out, for instance, that in Old Irish the affectionate diminutives for 'mother' and 'father' (*muime* and *aite*) had been transferred to the foster-mother and father (Kelly 1988: 86-7).

Although fosterage could be undertaken without recompense, there was also provision for payment of a fosterage fee, which would be forfeit if the child were badly treated, or if the fosterers sent him or her back home without justification (*ibid*: 86-90). According to the commentary in *CI*, the fee was set at the honor-price of the grade *below* the father of the child, with slightly more paid for the nurture of a girl (in the eyes of the commentator because girls required more fastidious care, or because they were less support to their foster-parents after marriage [*CIH* 1760.12-4 = *AL* ii 150.19-152.2]). This works out to be the same amount as the honor-price of the father according to other texts, such as *CG*, however. Amongst the aristocracy, fosterage was a political instrument of great significance and prestige, to the extent that children of this class were fostered by several families sequentially.

During fosterage the child was entitled to a standard of living and education appropriate to the father's status; thus children of different rank were provided with different sorts of food, clothing and training, which instilled in them a strong sense of the class system and their position in it, as well as ensuring better health for upper class children. The commentary to *CI* observed that differences in clothing were a new custom, not mentioned in any law book, thereby implying that the differences in food were long-established. In the commentary these are specified as follows:

The food of them all is alike, until the end of (the first) year, or (other version), three years ... Stirabout (porridge) made of (oatmeal) on buttermilk or water is given to the sons of the *féni* grades (farmers), and a bare sufficiency of it merely, and salt butter for flavoring. Stirabout made on new milk (is given) to the sons of the chieftain grade, and fresh butter for flavoring, and a full sufficiency of it is given them; and barley meal upon it (i.e. is the basis). Stirabout made of new milk and wheat meal is given to the sons of kings, and honey for flavoring (*CIH* 1759.38 ff = *AL* iv 149.29 ff).

If the child's maintenance was sub-standard, the parent could retrieve it and reclaim the fosterage fee. If on the other hand, the parents reclaimed the child without cause, they forfeited the honor-price that they had paid. While the child was with the foster-parents they were responsible for his/her actions, including any fines that the minor was liable for. A child who made serious trouble, however, could be returned to its parents at once.

A similar use of the honor-price appears in regard to the marriage contract. This was initiated by payment of *coibche*, a pre-nuptial gift from the intended husband to the father of the bride. The amount was equal to the bride's honor-price, and its receipt bound her and her kin to fulfillment of the promise to marry. Like the fosterage fee, it was forfeit to whoever caused the relationship to break down at a later date. Marriage was ideally contracted between families of the same rank. *CG* refers to the higher-status farmer, the *mruigfher*, as living with a woman who was the daughter of a man of his own rank (*ingen a chomgráid*) in a full-marriage contract (*coir chétmuinterasa*: *CG* 199-200), as opposed to concubinage. Full marriage involved mutual contributions to the connubial property, with the spouses sharing household responsibilities and profits. Marriage across the main social barriers was possible, but if a woman of the farming ranks married a lord, the marriage required additional inputs of property from the woman's family to compensate for their lower prestige and poorer social connections (see Ch. 11).

The structure of the ranking system

The honor-price system was based on the extent of a person's holdings of productive resources. In other words, mere wealth alone — in captured women and stolen cows, for instance — was not sufficient to establish a person's prestige and honor-price. These were conferred on those who held assessable amounts of land as well as stock. Since birth, occupation, wealth, gender and age influenced the extent of a person's wealth (in addition to whatever was gained through personal efforts), the law-tracts on status distinguished many ranks. The outcome was a multiplicity of terms, whose rank-orders are not entirely consistent from source to source, and yet, following the great synthesis of customary law in the seventh and eighth centuries, there also existed broad categories. Some aspects of these social divisions were discussed in Ch. 2, where the focus was upon the diverse historical roots of Irish law. Here we shall survey the class system as it is represented in the homogenized laws of the classical Old Irish period.

Separate rank hierarchies obtained for secular society, the Church, and the *filid* (Charles-Edwards 1986: 54). The ranks of the Church are said in *Míadshlechta* to have been based on the writings of St. Augustine (*CIH* 588.6 = *AL* iv 363.17-20), but many aspects of all the rank systems, including that of the Church, were influenced by a social ideology that originated in pre-Christian Irish society. Common to these distinct hierarchies were two main types of status distinction. One was the difference between *nemed* — a word that basically meant 'sacred'[4] — and non-*nemed*. The *nemed* included all lords and kings, clerics, *filid* (poets), and the learned, essentially aggregating the various ranks of these groups into one privileged status-group. The non-*nemed*, land-holding members of secular society, were generally referred to as the ranks of the *féni*. The second distinction was between those who were *dóer* and *sóer*, bond or free (roughly speaking), a distinction already encountered in the context of clientship. Dependents of lords, churchmen and *filid*, might be both *dóer* and *nemed*. The *dóer-nemed*, as shown in Ch. 2, included the lower grades of the learned orders and a variety of functionaries who would normally be attendant on a lord or king.

Ranks of the Nemed. The most significant feature of the *nemed* group was that its members were held to be shielded from the indignities of the normal processes of law when these were implemented by their social inferiors. As we have seen, where a dispute existed between ordinary farmers, the correct procedure was for the plaintiff to give warning of impending legal action before proceeding to distrain the accused of his chattels, but in the case of a *nemed*, the plaintiff was obliged to preserve the dignity of the *nemed* by first symbolically invoking his or her high status in order to shame him into agreeing to satisfy the claims against him. The basic mechanism was the fast (*troscud*), whereby the plaintiff sat in front of the *nemed*'s door, apparently from sunset until dawn, thus missing the main meal in the evening (Kelly 1988: 182-3).

During the Old Irish period a further legal protection intervened between the *nemed* and processes of distraint. In a case where the *nemed* was amenable to settling a dispute the plaintiff dealt not with the high-ranking defendant himself but with an appointed substitute, the *'aithech fortha'* (churl of substitution), who was sued instead. A late commentary states that 'originally' all ranks of the nobility, the Church, and the learned maintained such substitutes, who were appointed from amongst their own kin (presumably low- status kin) or their base-clients (see Ch. 12). Binchy has described the role as comparable to the king's whipping boy (Binchy 1973: 84); it is interesting that though legally obsolete by the sixteenth century, it was still a social institution at that time, as is shown by the selection of young Bernard Fitzpatrick, heir to the lordship of Macgiollaphádraig in Leix, as king's whipping-boy in the court of Edward VI. Whether the *aithech fortha* had a close personal relationship with the lord seems unlikely, however, for the legal institution of substitution concerned the social control of adults, and probably worked in quite a formal way; that is, if a *nemed* were in default he would transmit to his 'substitute churl' the amount in question, which would then be passed on to the plaintiff without face-to-face confrontation with the high-ranking defendant.

It is clear that élite status was protected by several barriers; legal interaction was discouraged not only by the differences of procedure described above, but by the rule that men had to sue with the aid of pleaders of the same rank (so that their honor-prices would be commensurate, and they would be at equal risk of fine for malpractice if they should plead incorrectly).[5] Intermarriage, as we saw, was also discouraged, and upward mobility by members of the *féni* was circumscribed by a number of barriers. These barriers, and the evidence that upward social mobility happened anyway, will now be described.

Commoners: the féni. The ranks of the *féni* comprised holders of varying amounts of land within clan corporations. They were divided into *sóer* and *dóer*, according to the nature of their clientship with any of the ranks of lords (or *nemed*). The main text on status, *CG*, implies that all men of the *féni* would have been *dóer*, in base-clientship, but as was shown previously, free clientship seems well suited to men of moderate social standing in free clans. *CG*, then, although it provides the most systematic treatment of social status, seems to have restricted its discussion of the ranks of the farmers to those who were in base-clientship to lords, leaving members of other clans — non-noble 'freeholders' as they were known in later English sources — to one side, just as it omitted other social groups. It seems therefore that *CG* was intended not as an analysis of the abstract principles of rank as found in general in society, but rather with the branching divisions of a ruling clan, that extended from its king (in the tracts' scheme, a paramount king), through the ranks of lords and farmers, down to its lowest members, the young sons of base-clients. All of these acquired their rights to status in the first instance through the inheritance of some piece of the patrimonial estate; the analysis stops before it reaches *fuidri* because these people did not have status on the basis of shares in clan patrimony.

The implications of *CG*'s model are given more attention in Ch. 9, where the intersection of rank and descent in the conceptual models of kinship is considered. A more clear-cut treatment of social rank is found in *Fodla Fine*.[6] The author of this tract regarded a lord's kinship group, his *cenél*, as extending from himself, at its peak, down through his kinsmen, whose grade was established according to their genealogical proximity to him, all the way to his *fuidri* and slaves. *FF*, being concerned only with dependence, not general social rights, listed landless men as part of the chief's clan (*cenél*). Its treatment of the chief's clan as *the* clan of the *tuath* is validated by the survival of district names that combine *tuathcenél* (the *tuath* of the *cenél* of ...) with a personal name. (See Ch. 3 for examples). In another law-tract, where the billeting of a lord's servants and retainers is discussed, conflict between one *tuath* and another is equated with conflict between the *cenél* of one, and an 'outsider clan' (*echtarchenel*) *(CIH* 890.1-4). Several sources, then, took as an ideal structure for their analyses, a conical clan — a descent group that fully occupied a *tuath* territory, in which both birth and competition for status affected individual position in the group and the structure of the group.

Before we can proceed to consider the ranks of the *féni*, however, two problematic aspects of the Irish status system need clarification here. One is the question of 'freedom'; it is only too easy to regard clan-membership as coterminous with freedom, for certainly it was impossible to be *sóer* ('free') without being a *bona fide* member of a clan. But being a clan member was no guarantee of any sort of freedom. In fact, there is evidence that base-clientship was ideally undertaken between kinsmen, and that men could become *fuidri* and even slaves to kin, out of debt and criminal liability. Clan membership was so all-encompassing in its implications for social status that degradation within the kin would often have been preferable to running away. There is, then, nothing inherently suspect about *FF*'s references to *fuidri* and other servile categories as members of the chief's *cenél*.

A second caveat is that the descriptions of rank in *CG* and *FF* are of ideal types in the native model of social reality, imposed as a grid upon the untidy structures and disorderly lives of actual people. Thus for example, it should not be thought that because *fuidri* were people who gravitated downward in society, that they were 'typically' retained by their clans. The statistical picture is unobtainable; *fuidri* may typically have drifted away from their kin, for all we know. What is useful about these models in the law-tracts is that they enable us to recognize some of the types of processes that shaped social groups; but as to the actual outcome, in terms of average sizes and structural patterns, only very late data can be of any use, and much work remains to be done on the early modern sources for Irish social history.

Classification of social ranks. It will be useful at this point to survey the terms for rank that appear in the various tracts on status, for these show the extent to which a common conceptual structure had diffused throughout early Irish legal culture. (The reader may also consult the chart on status, which shows how *CG* and *CA* are in unison as to the main concern of the lords, namely their demands for food from the different ranks of farmers). Below I have listed the tracts that refer to rank, and indicated (by the tracts' number) in which tracts a particular term appears. I have omitted a number of terms that appear infrequently. For a full listing of the ranks in all the tracts, the reader should consult McLeod (1986), and for bibliography, Kelly (1988, Appendix I).

Tracts on Status[7]

1 *Críth Gablach* (1-7 deal specifically with rank order).
2 *Uraicecht Becc*
3 *Míadshlechta*
4 *Díre*
5 *Bretha Nemed*
6 *Uraicecht na Ríar*
7 *Córus Béscnai*
8 *Cáin Aicillne* (base-clientship)
9 *Cáin Sóerraith* (free clientship)
10 *Cáin Íarraith* (fosterage)
11 *Cáin Lánamna* (marriage)
12 *Bretha Crólige* (12 and 13 are on medical treatment)
13 *Bretha Déin Chécht*
14 *Bretha im Fuillema Gell* (pledging)
15 *Cetharshlicht Athgabálae* (distraint)

Incidence of terms for secular ranks

Kings: most of the tracts recognize two or three grades of kings, notably the king of one *tuath*; king of several *tuath*s, and sometimes an over-king (1-4, 5, 8, 12-3)

Lords: most tracts recognize four or five grades of lord, usually, in descending order, the *aire forgill, aire túise, aire ard, aire déso* (1-3, 5, 7, 11-3), with *aire échta* added in 1, 2, 5, 13, and *aire fine/coisring* (heads of non-noble kin-groups) added in 1 and 3. Each of the descriptive terms refers to a jural function, e.g. *aire échta* means lord of vengeance or slaughter. (Kings and lords are often merged as one category, *grad flátha*, or *nemed*.)

Farmers: there is more variety in the grades of farmer, but all tracts recognize the *bóaire*, many include the higher status *mruigfher*, and many have a lower status category, the *ócaire*. Also common is the *fer midboth*, and descending ranks of adolescent or unmarried males. Typically, where a tract acknowledged a large number of distinctions amongst lords, it also divides the farmers into many ranks (e.g. *CG* has

6 ranks in the class of farmer and six in the class of lord, with one clearly transitional status between them). A similar pattern appears in 12, but each class has four subdivisions. Many terms refer to 'age' or juniority in a descent system that gave rise to cadet branches; others relate status to types of property, such as cows (*bó* > *bóaire*) or land (*mruig* > *mruigfher*).

Since the following discussion is largely based on *CG*, I shall here give for reference a complete list of the ranks discussed in that tract. The order ascends from lowest to highest status:

Farmers: first and second *fer midboth*; *ócaire*; *aithech* 'who farms in tens'; *bóaire febsa*; *mruigfher*; *fer fothlai*.

Lords: *aire coisring*; *aire déso*; *aire échta*; *aire ard*; *aire túise*; *aire forgill*; *tánaise ríg*.

Kings: *rí túaithe; rí buiden; rí ruirech*.

Determination of rank. Although ascribed social attributes — rank by birth, age and gender — shaped an individual's fate, personal achievement and luck could significantly raise or depress status, as this depended on wealth and social function. The ascribed attributes were largely consequent on kinship relations, and occupy later chapters of this book. The remainder of this chapter examines the relationship between wealth and social prestige.

CG's lowest grades were the first and second *fer midboth*, who were young men, still dependent on their parents economically and probably still unmarried. Because the *fer midboth* did not cultivate on his own account he was not obliged, or even supposed, to offer hospitality to anyone (*CG* 77).[8] Such a status could be a life-long condition if more property did not accrue to him.

Even the main grades of the farming classes were men who were interdependent with others (in addition to their dependence on lords). The *ócaire* had only a quarter of a plow (*CG* 95), for example, and the *bóaire* had half a plow (*CG* 158). The latter, however, had most of the structures needed on a farm — a kiln, barn, sheep-pen, pig-sty and a share in a mill (*CG* 155-7), whereas the *ócaire* only had a share in each of these (*CG* 96-7). All these grades, from the *bóaire* down, were said to derive their honor from the number of cattle in their possession (*CG* 329).

The rank above the *bóaire* exhibits most clearly the compiler's economic criterion for rank; productive self-sufficiency. The *mruigfher* was distinguished as follows; he had a whole plow and six oxen, a share in a mill that was enough to let him grind not only for his family but for guests (*CG* 192, 239-40), and he had 'the tools for use in every season, each one of them unborrowed.' (*CG* 178-9). In his house he had all the cooking equipment he could need, 'including irons and trays and mugs, so that he does not have to borrow them' (*CG* 175-6). He had a whole plow with all its gear (*CG* 181-2), his own kiln, barn, and outhouses (*CG* 192), charcoal for iron-work when a smith came around, and sea-salt for preparing meat for storage (*CG* 190-1). His sheep pasture was supposed to be large enough to graze his sheep without moving them (*CG* 197-8) - in other words he did not have to get involved in joint herding with other farmers who moved their flocks around in the 'circuit of grazing'.

Another contrast presents itself between the *bóaire* and the self-sufficient *mruigfher*. The latter means, literally, 'land man', and *CG* represents this superior farmer as having one half as much more land as the *bóaire*. (The *ócaire* had 7 *cumal*s of land[9]; the *bóaire* had 14 *cumals*; the *mruigfher* had 21 *cumals*) Interestingly, though, the next rank above *mruigfher*, the *fer fothlai*, is not represented as having *more* land, but as having more surplus produce which he invested in clients. The *mruigfher*, on the other hand, seems to have been enriched directly by cultivating his land, having extra food with which to hire extra servants, and perhaps investing surplus grain in hog raising, for he is depicted as owning twenty pigs, two brood sows and four domestic boars. Pigs constituted the 'small change' of farmers who could not make risky capital transactions in cattle. Since the *mruigfher* lies at the very first stage of emergence from the status of borrower to that of agricultural creditor, it is highly likely that this low-risk method of expanding his circle of business dealings would be his first venture into creditorship.

Another feature that may be more significant than it appears is the *mruigfher*'s half-share in a mill. The occupation of miller does not appear in the Irish law tracts, which describe injuries caused by malfunctioning mills in terms only of the mill-owner, the builder of the mill, and 'the person who is grinding'.[10] Saints Lives also depict people taking their grain to the mill and grinding it themselves: St Maedoc, for example, was robbed of meal while he was grinding wheat in the monastery's mill, 'the brothers being all engaged in other business' (Plummer [1922]: ii 208). *CG* 238-9 established a fine of 5 *séts* and confiscation of the meal, to be imposed on anyone who ground grain at the *mruigfher*'s mill without permission.

The remains of many broken hand-mills (querns) have been found, especially at pre-Norman ecclesiastical sites (Hamlin 1981: 11). These have been explained as the result not only of wear and tear, but of punishment inflicted on households who failed to observe the taboo on Sunday labor as set forth in *Epistil Ísu*.[11] Breaking the small-farmers' querns, however justified, would also have had the effect of compelling the affected households to seek out the nearest mill, at least for a while. This, indeed, is what occurred on a much greater scale throughout early Norman England and in thirteenth-century France, where manorial servants sought out and broke the hand-mills of peasant households in order to compel 'suit of mill', and payment for the service (Bloch 1969: 153-9).

In Ireland, mills were generally owned by monasteries or free clans, who charged for their use. Although ownership was vested in groups, by far the most extensive rights in any particular mill belonged to one segment of the group, who would have taken most of the payments made for using the mill.[12] Since *Epistil Isu* also stipulated that kilns should be destroyed if they had been used for drying grain on the eve of Sunday (Hamlin 1981), these fixtures too may have been a source of revenue for those who owned them. The monasteries, whose legal grip on their unfree tenant farmers could be very strong (Poppe 1986), may have originated the practice of breaking household querns, but the advantage of doing so, and the easy pretext of sacrilege, would have encouraged lay mill-owners to follow suit. Since mills were not widespread in Ireland at the time when *CG* is thought to have been written, the tract again appears to have been an attempt to prescribe rather than describe the qualifications for rank in some early Irish community. In this case, the prescribed qualification was one that would have been lucrative in the same way that hog-farming was; not enough to eject the *mruigfher* out of his social stratum, but certainly enhancing his prosperity. Above the *mruigfher* came the *fer fothlai*. *CG* asked:

> The 'man of removal' (*fer fothlai*), why is he so called? It is he who takes precedence over the other *bóaires* (farmers), because he secretly withdraws from *bóaire*-ship by taking clients. The surplus of his stock, his cows, his pigs, his sheep that his own land cannot support, and which cannot be sold

for land, (and) which he does not need for himself he gives
in fief to clients (*CG* 248-52).

The tract implies, then, that increases in wealth led to increases in status *within* the same class of society, but that after a certain level had been reached, increases in agrarian output did not enhance status unless invested in social relationships.

After the *fer fothlai*, but still on the lower side of the divide between true lords and farmers, came the *aire coisring*. His status and function was essentially concerned with creditorship in the wider social sense, that is, in the jural sphere of suretyship. Above him came the first rank of true lord, the *aire déso*. Just as the *ócaire*, *bóaire* and *mruigfher* fell into one category as local, interdependent, farmers, all in base-clientship (in *CG*'s framework), so the *fer fothlai*, *aire coisring* and *aire déso* all constituted a marginal group between cattle-borrowers and true cattle-lenders. The precariousness of this borderline group is insinuated by this comment on the *aire déso* (*CG* 354-7).:

> 'Five *séts* (of honor-price is due to him) on account of his
> own house, firstly, and five for the five houses enfeoffed to
> him, as long as he does not diminish his lordship by small
> matters and large, lest from authority he be cast.'

Upward mobility seems to be the bait with which *CG* was trying to attract ambitious men to a life of industrious husbandry — promoting a social ideal of prestige attained through productive farming, not primarily through warfare. Although barriers faced commoners who sought the privileges of lordship, both *CG* and *CS* suggest the possibility that after three generations in which prosperous farmers extended credit to their kin and neighbors, the latest scion of the family could claim petty lordship as an *aire déso*. Basically, this meant he could lawfully demand the sort of food renders from clients that would enable him to throw proper feasts to which he could invite other lords, and where he could thus enhance his political relationships by arranging peer-marriages for his grown children, attracting offers from his superiors to foster their children, and so on. Being a true lord, *flaith*, also meant playing a defined role as surety in the political structure of the local polity, as shown in Ch. 12.

CG states that the lowest rank of true lord had to be 'the son and the grandson of a lord (*airech*)' (*CG* 335-6), but this apparently did not necessarily mean a true lord, *flaith*, for both *CG* and *CS* recognized that the superior ranks of the farmers, such as the *fer fothlai*, made loans and got repayments from debtors that verged on a form of fief-and-render system. Of the *fer fothlai*, *CG* 253-5 states that when he started 'secretly' to take other farmers as debtors, he was entitled only to:

> Profit in grain to him, the value of the dung of each cow in grains of corn for food; for a vassal is not entitled to malt until he be a lord.

This meant that the *fer fothlai* was legally entitled only to such profits as would feed his extra labor and bigger household, for without malt he could not feast clients with ale. Not only was the élite anxious not to admit upstarts into its network, but the demands of parvenu lords for renders would cut into the local supply of the most valuable foods — fresh beef and ale — which clients were obligated to supply first and foremost to their established 'lord of first contract'. *Cáin Sóerraith* likewise states:

> There are different types of fief, and different types of lord, i.e. a lord who is only entitled to butter and seed and live animals .... An inferior lord whose father was not a chief ... *(CIH 1772.24-5 = AL ii 200.9-10.11.)*

Above the latter came a lord entitled to ale and boiled salted meat, and above him was one who was entitled to 'red meat and fat without being salted'. These three grades of lord in *CS* probably correspond to the *fer fothlai*, *aire coisring* and *aire déso* in *CG*, though the latter source gives no information on the renders paid to the *aire coisring* in his capacity as farmer.

Social mobility across the barriers between the farming clansmen and the cattle-lending, military élite, was slowed down by the legal requirements of sustained economic standing and social responsibility. Moreover, prosperity gained from farming might be diverted altogether into a different function, namely the role of the *briugu*, the 'hosteller'. He invested his considerable agricultural wealth in a 'public service', not in a personal clientele, and was therefore dependent upon the recognition and protection afforded him by the dominant dynastic clan of the territory. The *briugu* was viewed as completely severed from military organization, for his symbolic personal possessions (given in pledge when he went surety), were his cauldron, his cows, or his walking stick. If, however, he gave a spear as pledge, and this was broken while out of his possession, he was not entitled to interest on its worth (*fuillem*), but only to its basic value (Kelly 1988: 36-7) — in other words, he should not pledge a spear because it meant nothing to him. Very often in the later middle ages, the role of *briugu* was played by members of the skilled or learned families (Kelly 1988: 37-8), who held estates as rewards for their professional services and thus had surplus material wealth to use in this way. Since a hostelry would have been a center of news, the role complemented the political aspects of the learned families' role in the élite.

The *briugu*, then, shows that not all wealth led to investment in clients — only membership in a militarily powerful group enabled a man to proceed to convert wealth into personal political power through the establishment of a clientele. The framework of patronage had already to be present for individual social ascent to be possible. Membership in the political élite was to a great extent coincidental with descent in the male line from the older generations of a ruling clan. The élite's objective, however, was to retain power, not to nourish genealogical veracity for its own sake, so that incorporation was always possible for groups that had become locally strong, even where the agnatic connection had to be faked. These, however, had to satisfy the cultural élite that they merited inclusion, for it was the latter who had sole power to legitimate claims to lordship 'as of right', i.e., through descent. The learned families' control of the process of legitimation was bluntly described by a twelfth-century poet-historian, Gilla in Chomded Úa Cormaic (I here cite the translation given by Ó Corráin 1985: 70):

> There are three ways of note that confound genealogy: intrusion of base families taking the place and name of noble families; the expansion of serfs; the withering away of noble families, a dreadful horror, and the expansion of vassal folk; mis-writing, in the guise of learning, by the ignorant of evil intent; or the learned themselves, no whit better, who write what is false for gain.

To merit the legitimative support of the learned families, the upstart nobility had above all to show respect to the cultural élite, pay them, and uphold their views and standards of social propriety. In as much as the cultural élite were not primarily warriors but arbiters of social order, their ability to influence the behavior of the secular nobility's most volatile elements — those who were sliding across the gulf between true nobility and commoner status, in either direction — lent great force to the implementation of legal sanctions.

As to the importance of wealth to the status of lords and kings, this is a matter that needs little elaboration. It has already been shown with regard to clientship that the ability to enfeoff clients depended on the lord's ability to distribute cattle and throw feasts provided by his base-clients, while the cattle that he could suddenly withdraw from his free-clients served to ensure him against punitive distraint at the hands of his own overlord, if he failed in some duty, or of a peer whom he had offended. The ranks of the nobility were assessed not by their wealth but by the numbers of their clients — which depended on actual wealth, reputation, degree of political competition and personal factors, such as good looks, bearing and 'charisma'.

CG took a tidy building-block approach to this subject, claiming that the *aire déso* should have five base-, and five free-clients, and adding an extra five of each type of client at each ascending level of the ranking scheme. Some confirmation that such a scheme could have been used in military organization is provided by the parallel between CG and the *Senchus fer nAlban*, mentioned previously. It is also worth noting that a ratio of one horseman to five foot was characteristic of military service in a number of northern lordships during the sixteenth century, such as the lordship of Niall O'Neill in Co. Down, O'Hanlon in Co. Armagh, MacMahon in Co. Monaghan, MacGuire in Co. Fermanagh, while a number of others came close to this ratio (Mac Neill 1941/3: 14). This suggests that some formal aspects of the assessment system described by CG survived for hundreds of years in the north-east, even though the actual political framework within which it was applied had changed in a number of ways by the late Gaelic period.

Just as the tract shows how a build-up in agrarian resources augmented rank, but only up to a point, after which wealth had to be transformed socially if further prestige were to be gained, so more clients ceased to enhance rank beyond the rank of the highest lord, the *aire forgill*. The gulf between him and the royalty was shown by the fact that an heir apparent, *tánaise rig*, had hereditary serfs (*senchléithe*), which implies that he held a share of the royal demesne lands of the territory. This was reserved to itself by the triumphant dynasty that held the kingship of the *tuath* or groups of *tuaths*. In the most powerful royal dynasties, *tuaths* were parcelled out as patrimony between the sons and grandsons of paramount kings; the descendants of these heirs fought it out amongst themselves as to who gained the paramountcy, and who retained which *tuath* as personal holdings.

Judging by the organization of *CG*, the compiler thought that there was a sharp divide between the dynastic royalty and the established hereditary lords. The grades of the latter are, like those of the transitional lords, three-fold; for beneath the *aire forgill* came the *aire tuíseo* and the *aire ard*. Below the latter, lay the *aire échta* (lord of vengeance), who seems not to have been a lord in terms of normal clientship, but to have been a professional fighter supported by the *tuath* élite as a whole, in order to prosecute feuds in other territories (McCone 1990: 211-2). The established lords, then, seem to be envisaged as three ranks coinciding (conceptually) with seniority in a three-generation descent group. If succession went neatly to the 'eldest and worthiest', such a ranked descent group would consist (coterminously) of the eldest son of the eldest son of the founder; (one of) his bothers; (one of) his cousins. Competition, however, determined the actual distribution of power and status, so that the main lines that emerged did not coincide with the genealogically senior line.

One further aspect of the rank system remains in need of comment, namely the question of how the honor-price was actually implemented. How was a person's measure actually taken? There is no information on how honor was formally established, but since it was related to the inheritance of family property, it is reasonable to assume that everyone in the kin-group knew each other's honor-price, and that the group as a whole was assessed in the course of contact between the head of the group and the rest of the *tuath*. An arrangement of this sort is documented for medieval Iceland, where members of local communities (*hreppr*), which were defined on the basis of propinquity, with or without kinship, evaluated each other's property every autumn, for the purpose of paying Church tithes. The evaluation was not based on produce, as was the case in the parent-culture, Norway, but as in *CG*, upon assets of all sorts, including precious objects that could be used as pledges during legal processes: 'brooches, silver belts, cups and casks' (Sawyer 1982 (b): 348-9).

It is reasonable to believe that in Ireland also, honor-price was fixed within the local community on the basis of intimate knowledge of people's resources, and was symbolically represented to the outside world through appropriate dress, equipment, manners, size of retinue, and reputation. All the material expressions of rank were codified as to their significance; for example, the *aire désa* displayed his rank by equipping his horse with a silver bridle, and having four other horses (for his family?) that had blue bridles (*CG* 345-6). Little wonder that in the sagas, early Irish heroes and heroines are depicted as greedy for status symbols and outrageously boastful.

Local communities did not have the last word on the question of rank, however. Modern scholarship has established that infractions of law were often dealt with in public assemblies, and indeed in quite formal courts, presided over by judges and kings (Sharpe 1986; Kelly 1986; Gerriets 1988). A person deprived of honor in this context would be known by the wider community to have lost rank. Similarly visible would be the attrition of a lord's clientele; if he could not produce the requisite number of followers, he could hardly claim the privileges of his rank.

If there were any doubt as to someone's honor-price, it would ultimately be a lord or king's duty to clarify the matter. *Audacht Morainn* states:

Let him (the king) estimate the proper honor of every grade
of free and base-*nemed* person. (*AM* 52).

The 'king's truth', *fír flathemon*, was held to be the ultimate key to social order, for if it failed, disintegration of the community was expected to follow ineluctably (Kelly 1988: 18-21). The king, however, was only the apex of a constellation of roles that guaranteed order, namely the high ranks of lords, such as the *aire forgill* and *aire tuíseo*, described previously; together these individuals carried out functions that constituted a proto-state organization. These roles, and the basis on which they were assigned to individuals are examined in the final chapter of this book. The efficacy of the great lords as defenders of social order depended to a greater extent upon the manipulation of kinship relations, however, than the use of institutionalized means of coercion; it was primarily pressure from kith and kin — who, amongst the commoners, were held liable and distrainable for each other's actions — rather than a lord's *comitatus*, that secured individuals' conformity to social norms. We turn next, then, to the complexities of the Irish kinship system.

Notes

1. The main discussions of distraint are found in Kelly 1988: 77-82; Binchy 1973; D'Arbois de Jubainville in *Etudes sur le droit Celtique*. Paris, 1895: I, 255-384.

2. Details of *'nemed* cattle' are given in *BB* #15 notes: 108.

3. *AFOXLU TRIAUR DO CETHRUR. (CIH 1717.7 AL i 289.21).* These commentaries are of varying antiquity, but the references to *naidm* and *aitire*, suggest the persistence of old legal tradition here, as *ráth* and *trebaire* sureties tend to predominate in late commentary, *aitire* in older sources. The link with distraint of a kinsman is suggested by the reference to this procedure in the immediately preceding heading: *CINTUCH IAR NELODH CACH FINE IAR NAPUD...*Every kinsman is liable after absconding... *(CIH 1716.23).*

4. Mac Néill 1923: 266; Kelly 1988: 9-10. The fullest discussion of the semantic field of *nemed* in the law-tracts is found in *BB*, notes to #15, pp 107-9.

5. *FEICHEAMNUIBH FO MIAD... (CIH 1718.31 = AL ii 295.7 ff).*

6. *CIH* 429.13 ff = *AL* iv 283.91. The tract also bears a late title, *D'fodlaib Cineoil Tuaithi,* under which is appears in *AL.*

7. The following analysis was aided by McLeod's compilation of the details of social classification by rank in the various tracts that deal with status (McLeod 1986, 1987).

8. For a discussion of the text's depiction of the *fer midboth,* see McLeod 1982, and McCone 1990: 203-5.

9. The *cumal* of land is not readily determinable, since it was a measure of the utility of the land. However, one realistic and texually justified reckoning is that it often denoted an area of 34.23 statute acres/ 13.85 hectares, comprising land of mixed quality (Kelly 1988: 99). This value cannot be applied with confidence to any particular law-tract, however.

10. *fer bunaid ar aird, 7 ata saer, 7 ata fer bleithi. (CIH 287.18 = AL iii 281-3). 'fer bleithi'* does not appear as a particular occupation in any of the tracts on status and presumably refers to whoever was milling when the accident happened.

11. *Epistil Ísu* 24, cited by Hamlin 1981: 11. For text, see O'Keefe ed. *Cáin Domnaig.*

12. Binchy 1955b; Baumgarten 1985; Patterson 1985.

CHAPTER EIGHT

Close Kin and Neighbors:
'Gelfhine' and 'Comaithches'

The most basic objective of élite political action in early Ireland was control of the productive units of farming society. In Ch. 4 it was shown how small units, though ideally composed of balanced ecological resources, were dependent on broadly distributed 'waste'. Therefore it required the concerted efforts of groups of warriors to control a productive area; only when a whole region, with its wastes, was secured to a military élite could areas be parcelled out for the support of individual nobles. As we have seen, a system of parcelling-out did exist: at least, there was a definite conception of how many farmers, in what kind of association, were required to support a warrior of the élite. There was, however, no *legal* system for deciding which warrior achieved how many clients — this was decided by competition.

Units of five (individuals, households or other groupings) are commonly encountered in the law-tracts. Both *CG*, and the similar text, *Senchus fer nAlban*, worked on the assumption that it took five base-clients and five free-clients to support the lowest grade of lord, the *aire déso*, and that to achieve an additional increment of rank, a lord had to obtain the contracts of an additional group of five base, and five free-clients. Tenants-at-will — *fuidri* — could achieve the legal status of base-clients if they established five households. This was the amount that could 'feed a lord' and generate enough surplus that the group could sustain its liabilities, which probably means that each member had at hand a reserve of wealth equal to their honor-price. 'Five' was also the number symbol associated with the *gelfhine*, the closest circle of kin, while four tenants, plus a leader, are commonly assumed by the law-tracts to comprise the adult male population of the *comaithches*, the agrarian commune. The *gelfhine*, while only part of the bigger kinship group of 'seventeen men' (see Ch. 9) was incorporated as a distinct unit, whose members were co-heirs to each other, excluding more distant kin.

In view of the recurrence of this number symbol, it has been suggested that the ostensibly indivisible, five-fold, client-group comprised a co-residential lineage;[1] this is a view with which I agree to some extent, and which will be examined in this chapter. What we will observe is élite penetration of the authority structure of small-scale agnatic kinship groups, *gelfhini*, through provision of temporary usufruct of extra land to the younger generations of farming families, and élite imposition of the social model of kinship onto agrarian cooperatives, *comaithches* groups, which lacked an actual basis in close kinship. In the analysis we observe both how élite power was achieved at the local level without direct threat of coercion, and the elaboration of kinship norms as a method of legitimizing the social control imposed by the élite. In the following chapters it is shown that this method reached levels of sophistication that approached state institutions of government, while yet retaining the forms of kin-group relationships and some degree of actual kin-group solidarity. Hence the illusion of archaism and primeval 'tribalism' projected by the Irish sources.

The gelfhine of the bóaires of a clan

'Gelfhine' is a term for the innermost circle of kin in the system of kinship classification employed in the Irish laws; *fine* is a more generic term, referring to agnatic kin of unspecified connection, but not exceeding agnatic descendants from an ancestor in the fifth generation above *ego*. Provisionally, I will use a working definition based on Mac Néill's hypothesis, namely that the *gelfhine* consisted of all the descendants of a common grandfather in male descent lines. A group of young adult first cousins and their fathers and grandfather should thus be envisaged as the members of a *gelfhine*.

It was in the *gelfhine* group and on its land that individuals received their shares of *fintiu*, patrimonial land. These they obtained directly from their fathers in partible inheritance with brothers. Women received a pre-mortem inheritance in the form of dowry for marriage; this approximated a half of a son's share, but *did* include land,[2] though probably land that circulated through female lines, rather than pieces of *fintiu*, the ownership of which was strictly controlled by agnatic groups. Men also inherited property from more distant kin who died without children; this was known as *díbad*. Its distribution was of great significance for the functioning of the large corporate lineage, the *fine*, and it is therefore discussed in that context (in Ch. 10).

No early texts on patrilineal inheritance have survived, but a maxim connected with the tract on collective liabilities in the *fine* states:

> Why is it said: sons move forward hereditary land? Because it is over (forward) the *fintiu* advances - while there is a family in front it is not back to antecedents it turns. (Commentary: If the person who is dead has a son, his inheritance is taken by him. If he has not [a son] it is taken by his father. If he is not alive it is taken by his [the deceased son's?] brother.)[3]

There were no strict rules governing the portions received by sons in early Ireland. The church, which generally tried to promote the operation of rules rather than competition and struggle, endorsed primogeniture, or at least preferential provision for the eldest son, by interpreting the customary reservation of the lord's share of *díbad* as a rule supporting the provision of the eldest son with the share of a 'senior'.[4] A legal struggle over rules of succession is reflected in an Old Irish passage connected to the tract on jural procedure, *Cóic Conara Fugill*. This takes the form of a dialogue between two jurists, Sogen and Fachna, the former supporting primogeniture, the latter decrying it as unjust; both cite various maxims of law and appeal to 'custom'; not only does Fachna have the last word, however, but Sogen is depicted as a false, partial jurist, intimidated by great princes. Fachna's 'summation' of his reasons for rejecting primogeniture includes a reference to the fact that kinsmen shared *fintiu* because they had to share liabilities for each other's offenses.[5]

The ideal that prevailed, then, complemented kinship solidarity in regard to legal liabilities, namely that there should be equal division of the father's estate between his sons, and reciprocal obligations to extend assistance and assume vicarious liabilities between brothers who were sons of the same father. A method of equalizing the division of land existed (presumably operative after the father's death), namely 'the youngest divides and the eldest chooses'.[6] Nevertheless, there were neither laws nor social mechanisms that bound a father, while he was alive, to make an absolutely equal division of his lands and chatttels amongst his children, nor even to committ all his estate to these heirs. Early Irish culture appears to have sanctioned his right to show favoritism and thus to promote unequal status amongst his offspring.

Fathers were also able, by means of the death-bed bequest, *timna* or *audacht*, to alienate a portion of their lands (to the extent of the father's honor-price value) from their heirs to the church (Kelly: 122-3). No copies of written wills exist, if such were made in early medieval Ireland, but it is striking that the *timna* attributed to the legendary dynast of Leinster, Cathair Már, shows an utterly unequal and partial distribution of patrimony (Dillon 1962: 159). This composition, the function of which was undoubtedly to explain and legitimize the distribution, status and claims of the ruling families of Leinster and Munster in the eleventh or twelfth centuries, would not have taken the form of a father's unequal bequest if such a disposition was not a fairly standard occurrence in élite families.

It was particularly significant for the emergence of unequal status between sons, that heirlooms, which were inherently indivisible objects, had the potential (perhaps even the normal) function of serving as pledges or other guarantees in contracts of suretyship. Swords, for example, seem to have been sworn upon, as proof of the truth of a statement (Gray 1982: 68-69). In the story of the sword of Socht, it is evident that this object was valued above normal swords because it itself was the *audacht* ('testimony') of the father, grandfather and *cenel* (clan) of its owner (Nagy 1990: 132).[7] Only one son at a time could have possession of such an *audacht*, or *sét* (treasure), just as only one son could attain to his father's rank, if the father held office or leadership. Since the capacity to perform suretyship was an aspect of rank (see Ch. 12), a father could tip the scales in favor of one son's promotion over another by assigning the important heirlooms to his favorite. The father had a life-long interest in keeping his sons guessing as to the disposition of heirlooms and chattels, for in this way he could command care and respect from them until his last moment.

Against paternal power the son was in a weak position. He could not normally sue his father for land nor take legal action to get a larger share when there had been favoritism as regards another brother. The basic rule was that there could be no suit for restitution of the lost value of shared property between father and son, mother and daughter, foster-parents and foster-children of the same gender, as well as other very close relationships:[8]

It was promised that whenever these suits should take place,
the great disasters would take place ... for these rules were

established from the beginning of the world to the end, against litigation.[9]

The only sanction that a son could use against his father was the threat of withdrawal of support and cooperation (*goire*). This he was legally entitled to do if the father had reduced him to base-clientship, left him without land, or deprived him of chattels (*séoit*), 'out of special hatred' while providing his other sons with chattels.[10] Given the presence of favored siblings, however, the victimized son's right of withdrawal from his father offered him little leverage in the domestic community.

The social grounds of discrimination are identifiable. The status of the mother in the marital contract was one criterion: sons of women who were slaves and serfs were legally restricted to small portions of inheritance, as were illegitimate sons (see Chs. 10-11). But favoritism between legitimate sons on grounds of personal attractiveness must also have been common because of the great cultural stress on individuals' appearance and bearing — an emphasis that may have been developed in response to the use of formal ridicule (*áer,* satire), as a standard instrument of social control. *Míadshlechta,* a tract on status that was especially concerned with personal abilities and qualities as factors influencing rank, states:

> There are seven things by which a man is judged: appearance
> and family origins, land and homestead, craft (or profession)
> and treasure, and lawfulness.[11]

Handicaps, poor or unattractive physique and deviant personality were likely to severely affect a son's chances of paternal favor. It is well known that the kingship was ritually prohibited to men who were disfigured — an obstacle surmounted by a number of vigorous, maimed rulers (K. Simms 1987: 11 n.12) — but a statement of values, nonetheless (Kelly: 19). *Míadshlechta* shows that not only kings, but ordinary men were also discriminated against socially on account of physical defects.[12] Here it is said that 'nine types' of men should not be allowed to play the basic jural roles of adult clansmen (going surety, giving oath, etc.).[13] The list includes men who were afraid of fighting;[14] men with 'bad nerves' (supposedly driven to this state by their wives);[15] effeminate or homosexual men;[16] vagrants and men with eating disorders;[17] and 'every man who brings distortion upon his face or body'.[18] The last category would have included, on the one hand, people involved in pagan cultic activities who learned how to go into the warrior's frenzy (like Cú Chulainn, *díberaig* and Viking *berserker*

[Sharpe 1979; McCone 1990: 213-4]), but also people with borderline personalities and neurological problems, such as Tourette's syndrome, epilepsy, ticks and stuttering.

In the list of criteria by which men were judged, cited above, it is clear that certain things went together: land was coupled with homestead, a profession was associated with rewards in precious objects. Likewise appearance was regarded as strongly linked to family identity. In fact this consideration (*fineguth, finechruth, finebes;* family voice, appearance and manners) was legally decisive as a method of determining which of two or more possible fathers was responsible for a particular illegitimate child (Kelly 1988: 103). In such a cultural context it must have been common for fathers of several sons to reject the less attractive ones, favoring, like Cathair Mór the beautiful warrior type, who enhanced the father's own social identity.[19] The high cultural value of male beauty is expressed in stories in which central actions in the narrative are attributed to aggressive lust on the part of women — Derdriu, for instance, chose Noisiu mainly on the basis of his looks (she had a definite type in mind: black hair, pale skin and high coloring on the cheeks). The tendency of women to make bad political decisions under the influence of male beauty is the subject of two of the most important narratives, the saga story of the elopement of Díarmait and Gráinne, and the mythological tale, 'The Second Battle of Moy Tura' (see Ch. 11). Such a reversal of the Helen of Troy situation in terms of gender roles in narratives, reflects a highly fluid society in which personal sentiments strongly influenced relationships and social action.

While the Irish patriarch could thus exercise favoritism at will, he had nothing comparable to the Roman *patria potestas*, the legal power of life and death over children, slaves and wife. His power was offset in a number of ways. One of these was the son's mother's family's interest in their kinswoman and her son's welfare and status, and the son's inheritance rights in his mother's property (see Ch. 11). Of more significance to sons of the farming class, however, was the role of the lord in providing him with a fief that could liberate him from his father's direct, immediate control. In addition, sons had another ray of hope as to autonomy from the father, for like all other members of the extended kin-group, the *fine*, they stood to inherit a share of *díbad*, the property of extinct, heirless, *gelfhini*. These shares were allocated by formula (see Ch. 10) and it is unlikely that fathers had the power to withhold from younger men their due shares of land. The lord also played a role in the circulation of *díbad*.

The best evidence on the internal structure of a farming *gelfhine* comes from the tracts on status, where these describe the attributes of the ranks of the farmers. (See the chart on rank at the end of the book.) The junior status positions, such as the second *fer midboth* and the *bóaire* could become lifelong positions - just as the English yeoman was both a young man with a young man's social position, and a class of farmer.[20] In other words, the various farming ranks were status-levels in the unfolding domestic devolution of property *and also sometimes* a social dead-end into which some individuals sank under some circumstances. For example, the small community that wielded a joint-plow could have consisted of four life-long *ócaires*, or a *bóaire* and an *ócaire* who expected to succeed him, plus a second *fer midboth* and other 'juniors'.

All the texts that discuss social rank begin at the bottom with the least important members of male society, the working children. (Of course, small girls worked also, but female rank is in all cases treated as derivative from the rank of the individual's father or husband). In *Uraicecht Becc* they were subdivided according to the degree to which they were answerable for their actions in the event that they hurt another child at play, or failed to care for the animals in their charge; these distinctions imply a division by age.[21]

CG's description of the 'first *fer midboth*' gives the best picture of the young adolescent working male's status in the family. He was *midboth*, between huts, because he had left his parents' or foster-parents' home, but had not yet reached manhood (*CG* 30-32). He could not entertain anyone, nor take a fief, and he could not take any companions visiting with him and expect them to be fed (*CG* 44). Since he could not 'retain speech' or be a legal eye-witness, he could not be a *roach*, a valid witness to a contract, nor could he be a surety. He thus corresponds to the *mac beo-athair*, 'son of a living father', with whom no one should make a contract of any sort without the father's permission, who had no 'power of hand or foot' (Kelly 1988: 80-1). He was also termed the *macc te*, the warm or filial son, who stayed home and took care of his father. The only qualification to the father's absolutist power was that a son in this position could annul contracts that threatened his status, such as alienation of family land. In the event that his father died before he came to maturity, he was not entitled to take on the responsibility of an heir, a *comarba* in the *fine,* unless someone was prepared to act as his surety and adviser (*CG* 36-8; McLeod 1982b). He could take over his own affairs at seventeen, however, if he had inherited his father's land.

The next stage in life was that of the second *fer midboth.* In age he overlapped with the young adolescent:

> What is the special age (for him)? From fourteen years to
> twenty years, to beard-encirclement.[22]

Like the younger adolescent this youth had not yet received a share of family land or livestock, and did not have a proper homestead:

> The hospitality of his house is not permitted (to be given by)
> anyone when a minor, until he is capable of separate
> husbandry and taking his own parcel of land.[23]

His ties to his parents were still close: according to the tradition of *othrus* (sick-maintenance) an injured 'second *fer midboth*' took his mother with him during convalescence (*CG* 63). His inexperience meant that he could not fully ascend to his father's status, even if the father died, until he passed the age of twenty (*CG* 67-9). Nevertheless, he was allowed to take a small fief of five *séoit,* or four milch cows (*CG* 71).[24] Someone, then, permitted him some usufruct of land. It also seems that he too typically lived in a little cabin of his own. This is suggested by the fact that the next rank up, the *ócaire,* is said to have a house that is more than a '*tech inchis*' (*CG* 98). The latter was a house allocated to an adopted son who was brought in to care for an old person.[25] But it was also the little cabin associated with the *óenchiniud,* another low-ranking category of young freeman, who appears, according to *CA,* to have had the same fief and render as the second *fer midboth* of *CG.*[26] *CG* explicitly associates the second *fer midboth* with the *óenchiniud,* describing both as, 'a man who does not cultivate personal property nor family land for himself'.[27]

Separate roofs permitted greater sexual and social freedom, but did not mean a separate economy. On the contrary, the renders given by the second *fer midboth* involved the produce of an established dairy and a woman's kitchen (including new milk, butter, and 'twenty-four loaves of woman-baking').[28] Since he was unmarried, he must have depended on someone else's wife's dairy and kitchen to meet these obligations, though his own cattle-fief provided the milk from which he supplied the dairy produce. He was also not expected to be involved with plowing, for he had no share of a plow. This status-level could be permanent:

> Though he does not take his inheritance until old age, his
> oath does not go from a *fer midboth*'s yet. His fief of
> base-clientship shall be five *sets* .... If he attains property
> qualifications of a *bóaire* or something higher, the legal
> stipulation of his fief increases ....[29]

This meant that some men remained at this level after the death of the
father. In law, the second *fer midboth* was not, then, a 'son of a living
father', in the strict sense, but was granted legal competence as a surety
and witness — though only to the extent of his honor-price, which was
based on his meagre property. Moreover, it is unlikely that he could
marry without his father's permission, for the father retained the right
to prevent marriage where the son had not been 'established in
householding'. If a young man went ahead and married a girl, paying
bride-price to her father and bringing her onto his *fine* land without their
permission, his father could return the bride with dispatch:

> Every unlawful act. Commentary: That is of marriage
> connection. If in the connection there be any warning (that
> the contract was not approved), whether the warning be made
> by the father of the son or the father of the girl, the
> connection shall not be made binding, and the use of the
> *coibche* chattels is offset by the use of the woman.[30]

It is, no doubt, because of such constraints on the desires of the young
by the will of the old that the laws are full of references to 'marriages
by abduction', elopement and even 'marriage by rape' (Kelly 1988: 70,
SEIL: 16-75).

McCone has recently suggested that the status-group that most
nearly resembled the 'second *fer midboth*' — the propertyless and
unmarried *óenchiniud* — consisted of young men unable to obtain
usufruct of *fintiu* yet, and living rather marginal lives, possibly not even
attached to their own kin group (McCone 1990: 204 ff). The *óenchiniud*
seems to have been viewed as the typical young warrior, living amidst
the retinue of some lord or leader of a *fían* band. The *óenchiniud* and
second *fer midboth* were very similar in this respect, for they were both
free of some patriarchal controls, and had small fiefs, but were
unmarried and unable to take up an inheritance yet, and had to be
attached to someone else's productive unit. Both would therefore be the
sector of society that was most available for warfare; the fact that
neither plowed on their own account left them free to undertake military
activities in spring and summer. (In this context, it is interesting that the

honor-price of the second *fer-midboth* was the same as that of the professional guardsman, the *seirthid* [McLeod 1987: 86] See Ch. 11).

The military calling of this stratum of the farming population may be the reason why *CG*, in the midst of outlining the status of *second fer midboth*, goes off at what seems to be a tangent into a long discussion of sick- maintenance for the wounded. Warfare was clearly in mind in this section:

> He is raised over the bloodstained soil to a high sanctuary (or
> high *nemed* person) for his protection; he shelters against the
> sudden surge of the host.[31]

The chief difference between the *óenchiniud* and the *second fer midboth* is that the former seems to have been physically away from his kin, while the *second fer midboth* was integrated into clan society through his various privileges, and was expected to have his mother at hand to nurse him if he were wounded. I would suggest, then, that when farming families in base-clientship had to provided their lords with 'a man for every heifer on a hosting', it was the *second fer midboths* who were the primary candidates for performing the duty. Many would not have come back, while others would have been rewarded for prowess — one way or another, warfare redistributed male heirs in relation to land.

The next grade up, the *ócaire*, had a small parcel of land, seven *cumals*,[32] and also a small herd of mixed livestock — seven cows and a bull, seven pigs and a domestic boar, seven sheep and a horse of general purpose. He also had a quarter share in a plow. He was certainly a married man with children, but though established as a farmer and better off than younger men, the *ócaire* was included with them in two respects:

> The hospitality of his house is incomplete, and he is not
> capable of being surety for them (others) ... like every *bóaire*
> due to the paucity of his means.[33]

This 'incompleteness' has something to do with the devolution of family lands, for as we have seen, the two *fer midboths* were also 'incomplete', and their signal characteristic was that neither of them had yet inherited. The *ócaire*'s wealth, in fact, differs from that of his juniors chiefly in that the tract specifies chattels for the *ócaire* but not for the two *fer midboths*, implying that the inferior ranks had none of their own. The question, then, is whether the *ócaire* was merely the highest rank of a group that was characterized by expectations of land-inheritance that had not yet been fulfilled, and that this is the reason why they were all 'incomplete' as to their ability to provide hospitality — a function that entailed being a land-holder and offering jural protection to one's guests.

Referring to the first and second *fer midboth* and the *ócaire* as a group, *CG* obscurely states:

> It is through land that these grades are pledged (to their lords): from land moreover is (reckoned) the value of the ten chattels that come to him (i.e. to each client from these ranks) as fief: moreover, that land shall be (taken) on account of grievance against him.[34]

This seems to suggest that these grades — all of whom had fiefs of cattle from a lord — were also temporarily using pasture that belonged to the lord. The meaning of the Irish text is hard to retrieve, however, and the above rendering cannot be taken too literally or precisely.[35] Moreover, if we are to understand these grades as holding land of their lord, then the *ócaire* seems to have had a better clientship arrangement than the *bóaire*, for both paid renders to their lord only for the fief of cattle (or other moveables). Binchy and Thurneysen both interpreted the above passage as implying that the ranks below the *bóaire* did indeed receive land in their fief from their lord, but neither resolved the problem of the disparity in the clients' repayments entailed by this interpretation of the text.[36] A possible solution, however, may lie in the lines that make a seemingly pointless and tangential reference to the rental of land by an *ócaire*:

> He has seven *cumal*s of land; that is a cow-land according to the Feni, seven cows are put on it for a year, that is, seven cows are driven on it, the seventh cow is left after the year as rent for the land.[37]

This suggests that the *ócaire*'s seven *cumal*s of land were held on a rental agreement with the lord, for which he paid a cow a year in rent, *in addition* to the renders due for the fief. Further support for this interpretation is offered by the reference to the lands of these lowly grades being somehow pledged to their lords. Elsewhere it is said that lords took pledges from their clients to ensure that they would not break the law (see Ch. 12). Men who held shares of *fine* land were able to pay fines for minor offenses with their own chattels, and fines for serious offenses with land. The lowest freeman grades, having little or no disposable property with which to pay fines, would naturally have been required to surrender the lease on the lands they held from their lord if they became subject to a mulct. (As to restitution for damages, either the kinsmen helped pay these or the low-status man became forfeit in person, as a penal slave.)

The balance of these considerations, then, favors the view that the ranks below the *bóaire* temporarily used pasture that belonged to their lord while awaiting inheritance. Ideally, the lord would be a senior member of their own *fine*, or of another *fine* in the same clan, *cenel*, and the land would thus be lineage or clan land. But this need not always have been the case, as is shown below, where the *comaithches* group is examined. In any case, whatever the social identity of the lord or his land, such rental agreements diluted the social power of fathers in the lower ranks of the freemen, tilting the allegiance of their sons towards patrons in the élite.

The lord's ability to supply the lower/junior ranks of farmers with usufruct of land until they inherited shares of clan-land was based on his right of disposition of part of the lands that went into circulation as *díbad*, under the provision referred to as *cumal senorba*. The fragmentary and somewhat conflicting evidence on this matter has been summarized by Dillon:

> It is regularly cited as one of the privileges of the *flaith gelfhine* [lord of the kin-group] ... this much seems certain: it was a portion of land, originally a *cumal*, later one-seventh of the whole, which at the distribution of an estate was not distributed amongst the heirs but reserved to some responsible person (*flaith gelfhine, primáige fine, áige fine*) who undertook certain liabilities on account of it. (*SEIL*: 141-2)

One gloss explains this liability in terms of the head of the *fine*'s obligation to entertain the retinue of a king or bishop. Elsewhere it is said that a woman-heir to a whole *gelfhine* estate had to meet military liabilities for it, or else she could only get a *bóaire*'s share of the land, 14 *cumals*.[38] The *cumal senorba*, then, was a provision enabling the head of the *fine* to interfere to some extent regarding the peopling and working of a stretch of land. Another gloss views the following as likely candidates for sponsored settlement by a lord on such land; sons of a woman who had held the land as a *banchomarba* (these men were non-agnates and were likely to be dispossessed after their mother's death); landless *fuidri*, and men who were '*gormac*' — sister's sons and 'filial sons' who for some reason could not be supplied with land in timely fashion by their father.

In addition to this right to a share of *díbad*, the head of the *fine* would also have access to lands through forfeiture by kinsmen on whose behalf he had paid a fine or debt. The lord's concern would be not only to punish irresponsible men who endangered the community of kin, but to put on the land reliable men who would furnish military services. Turning land over to the young adult sons of farmers who had too little land to endow them all at the right time, was of immediate benefit to all concerned. The advantage to the patriarch would be that his sons were partially provided from outside, allowing time, attrition of heirs, and intake of *díbad* to relieve the tensions of competition for inheritance, and allowing him to retain his status as *bóaire*, which would have been diminished if he had split up his estate while he was still active. The price for him was that he lost much of his authority over his sons this way. The price for many young males was that they had to fight in order to survive until they were able to inherit, and many would not live to see that day.

In the case of a prosperous family with few adult male heirs, the *ócaire* would go from being an 'expected *bóaire*' to being an actual *bóaire* himself. In *Uraicecht Becc*, for example, it is said that the equivalent of the *ócaire* is the *tánaise bóaire*, 'expected *bóaire*,' or heir to a *bóaire*.[39]

CG too indicates that the *ócaire* was the first stage in the adult phase of the life cycle:

> *ócaire*: Why is he called young *aire* (free man)? From the youthfulness of his noble rank still, because he is new since taking husbandry (*CIH* 778.22-3. Binchy 1941: 101)

During the transition from the rather footloose life of a second *fer midboth* to a *bóaire*, the *ócaire* acquired a higher honor-price, and with it, a greater degree of autonomy than the other junior ranks. As a married man, particularly, if he were living away from his father's lands, he would have been regarded as an emancipated son (*mac sóerleicthi*, or a 'raised son', *macc ailte*: Kelly 1988: 81). His autonomy vis-a-vis his father was such that he could freely undertake all the contracts required to operate a separate household:

> There are seven contracts which the son of a living father makes independently of the father, which the father cannot reverse against the son ... purchase of land when he cannot

> fit in the land with his father: contracts of *comaithches* in the
> land in which he is; ample purchase of goods; to purchase
> the furniture of his house since he is recognized in
> householding; the purchase of joints of flesh meat for his
> house, an agreement for reciprocal plowing when his father
> is not plowing, payment for fosterage for the increase of his
> children, lawful bride-price to a *cetmuinter* wife of equal
> family — because the advantage of these contracts is greater
> than the disadvantage ....[40]

It is noticeable that he was thought of as likely to be detached from his
father's estate and living in an agrarian commune, a *comaithches,* on
'purchased' land. His privileges, however, did not extend to making
contracts of clientship, for which the permission of his father or the
head of the *fine* was necessary. If, as I think may have been typical, the
ócaire held pasture-land temporarily from the head of the *fine*, there
could be no question of his taking a fief from another lord without
permission.

At this point a summary of the interdependence of farmers, lords
and farmer's adult sons, as I have reconstructed it, may be helpful:

Clients' inherited assets

bóaire	*ócaire*	*second fer midboth*
14 *cumals* land	land for tillage	
12 cows	7 cows	
small stock	small stock	small stock?
house	smaller house	a cabin
implements		

Clients' assets rented from lord.

12 cows	8 cows	4 cows
	pasture for above	pasture for above

Looked at this way, the power of the lord buttressed the status of the father in the society, but at the same time undermined the authority of the father in relation to his sons, and diverted their energies to further the immediate interest of the élite in warfare. Only in the highest reaches of society did patriarchy and lordship coincide entirely; but this was also the arena of internecine dynastic warfare where men killed their close kin for power and status.

The death of the father was ideally the occasion for the son(s) to be promoted to *bóaire* status, and their sons to ascend to the rank of *ócaire*. The importance of the grandfather's death to the grandson's status emerges in a vignette in the *Táin*. The episode concerns the appearance before the armies of Ulster and Connacht of a suicidal, age-crazed, Ulster warrior, Iliach. He had been left at home under the care of his grandson, who had thus been denied warrior status on account of the grandfather's lingering life. His appearance occasioned much mirth amongst the 'rabble', the various farm-lads and cheap mercenaries fighting alongside the regional nobility:

> So he came in this wise: in his shaky, worn-out old chariot, without rugs or covering, drawn by two old sorrel nags. And he filled his chariot with stones as high as the skin coverings. He kept striking all those who came to gaze at him stark naked as he was, long-membered, with his *clapar* (testicles?)[41] hanging down through the frame of the chariot. Then the host noticed in what manner he came and they mocked the naked man. Dócha mac Mágach checked the jeering of the rabble. And for that Iliach told Dócha that at the day's end, he, Dócha, should take Iliach's sword and strike his head off, provided only that Iliach had exerted all his strength against the host. At that point Iliach noticed the marrow-mash. He was told that it had been made of the bones of the cows of Ulster. So then he made another marrow-mash of the bones of the men of Connacht beside it, so that the two marrow-mashes are there together. Then in the evening Dócha struck off Iliach's head and carried it to his grandson. He made peace with him and Láegaire (the grandson), kept Iliach's sword.'(O'Rahilly 1976: 3366 ff.)

Only two generations, then, could hold adult male status at the same time, since both men had to be active. Often, however, it was impossible for a man to ascend to *bóaire* status, even when his father died. *CG* envisaged an intermediary status between *bóaire* and *ócaire*, the *aithech ara threba a deich* (the vassal, or base-client, who 'farms in tens'), whose position was attributed to insufficient land:

> What deprives this man of *bóaire*ship. Maybe it is that four or five men are in joint-husbandry as *bóaires* so that it is not possible for them all to be a *bóaire.*[42]

The 'four or five men' suggests a full-up *gelfhine* of 'five' or *comaithches* of 'four'. The status of such marginal *bóaires* was granted them only as long as they were properly married, continent on religious holidays and not involved in unlawful activities (*CG* 142-5) — rules that hint that men who were squeezed out of the farming life drifted towards the dissolute life of the *flan*, as McCone suggests (1990: 205).

These alternative positions within a *bóaire* family are closely analogous to the assortment of roles and statuses recorded in the later middle ages amongst upper-class Irish families. Simms notes, for example, that the *tánaiste* of a lord was usually a collateral of about the same age, who rarely succeeded himself and whose own sons stood even less of a chance of ascending to the chief position (K. Simms 1987: 56); these recorded outcomes of the transference of authority and possessions shed light on the assumptions on which *CG* seems to have been based, namely the presence at different levels of society of unequal rank positions, distributed between close kin. Broadly speaking, there was a main incumbent who headed the kin group, an unequal collateral (*tánaiste*), a highly ranked younger man, of competing status with the *tánaiste*, and declining collateral statuses in the younger generation. Just as the marginalized *aithech ara-threba a deich* (the 'vassal who farms in tens') was socially suspect (granted rank, in *CG*'s view, only if he comported himself as a Christian), so the junior collaterals of a king, the *meic riogh*, were particularly associated with brigandage and dissolute ways (K. Simms 1987: 58-9). These clusters of roles in descent groups at different levels of the conical clan are further examined in Ch. 12. Here I wish to emphasize only that status differentiation under the influence of élite interference in domestic economic organization, pertained between the closest of kin at all levels of society, and that the systemic outcome for society was the continuous drafting of marginalized males into the exchange of military services for sustenance.

Comaithches

A son released by his father from patriarchal control could take farmland within a *comaithches*, as we have seen. This agricultural cooperative was functionally equivalent to a residential kin-group on the scale of the *gelfhine*, in that members of small local groups, whether extended families or cooperatives, were obligated to enforce various social responsibilities, especially military and jural ones, upon one another. It is not likely that the harnessing of local populations to *élite* political needs through *comaithches* organization was a residue of prehistoric social organization, for the legal constitution of the *comaithches* is described in *BC* as an innovation (see below). Moreover, a very similar social institution existed in Carolingian France, where, in order to obtain military services from the free farming population, the authorities allowed 'groups of six men ... to form, five of whom would bear the cost of providing the sixth with the necessary equipment for military service.' (Mollat 1986: 35).

In many cases, a *comaithches* would have been composed of kin, or mostly of kin, but the group had no necessary basis in close kinship, as witness the adult son's departure from his father to join such a community, mentioned above. *Comaithches* organizations may also have included demesne farms worked by *fuidri*, for the main source, *Bretha Comaithchesa*, refers to members of a *comaithches* as ranging in possible status from a free clansman (*aire*) to a base-client (*aithech*), and from the head of a monastic estate, down to a shepherd.[43] It may be assumed that many a *comaithches* consisted of groups of tenants who were induced to settle on favorable terms by a lord, and that they had claims to clan status and to eventual inheritance which protected the lord from the sort of risks he incurred when he sponsored the settlement of *fuidri* in the local community. A probable context for the establishment of a *comaithches* would be the redistribution of the land of an extinct *gelfhine* as *díbad*, with surplus heirs from other *gelfhini* mixing together in newly formed local communities in which the ties of kinship were remote and diluted.

The absence of close familial ties of patrilineal kinship made for a different authority structure in the *comaithches*, for heads of households were here more independent of the community senior, their 'best *bóaire*', than were men in a residential *gelfhine*, bound by filial ties to their senior. The main difference is that in the *comaithches*, farmers provided pledges (*tairgille*[44]) to one another against future damage through negligence in fencing and other agrarian obligations. In the *gelfhine*, on the other hand, as long as the vertical ties from grandsons to grandfather existed, each son was bound to his father in a non-suable relationship. The *comaithches* was also physically divided, whereas the estate of the joint family was (probably) undivided — until such time that kinship relations became attenuated through group growth, demise of the patrilineal chains of command, and/or admixture of remote kin. *Gelfhine* and *comaithches* overlapped, then, for the estate of an extended family might devolve into a *comaithches*, while a *comaithches* founded as a pure act of colonization with no kinship base, could, through intermarriage, endowment of brotherless daughters, and some genealogical slight of hand, acquire a hereditary aspect and definition as a small *fine*. Moreover, both types of local community were subject to the same pressures in terms of relations to social superiors.

Members of the *comaithches* cooperative gave each other guarantees that they would make good whatever damages they inflicted on each other through negligence. These guarantees did not go through a third-party surety, a *naidm*, as described in Ch. 7, but were simply exchanged between the four parties. The avoidance of the *naidm* is described as a 'new custom'.[45] By proceeding this way the members of the *comaithches* were acting almost as if they were members of the same household. The social implication of this 'innovation' is very similar to the restriction of individual *fine*-members' capacity to take legal action to the extent of their honor-price; in both cases, personal autonomy as to the extent of the legal action that one man could take against another was strictly limited, and individuals were subject to controls generated within the group, whether the *fine*, or the *comaithches*. The purpose of the 'innovation' — which was obviously an early medieval one — was to establish the corporate solidarity and mutual liability of the *comaithches* members, with a view to safeguarding the provision of clientship services. Where groups of kin were co-residential these sanctioned each other's behavior; where men were established on a lord's land, the fellow-tenants played the same disciplinary role. Both types of social group were thus tied into the schemes of assessment of military contributions that are linked to clientship in *CG* and the *Senchus fer Nalban*, and to the later *trícha cet* system. These contributions will now be examined.

Military functions of the gelfhine and comaithches

The resources that civil society could marshal for warfare were slight in comparison to the efficiency of full-time professional soldiers, so that by the later medieval period the farming population was not regarded as the mainstay of a lord's military might. Whether it was more important in the Old Irish period is a difficult question, for the role of the *flan* in inter-dynastic warfare may have been very great, but is poorly documented. A piece of the puzzle seems to be missing, in part because of the church's unwillingness to even acknowledge the existence of *flan* bands, which reeked of diabolism (McCone 1990: 218-226). What we are left with is information on the military obligations of the ranks of clan land-holders as a sort of home-guard, on the one hand, and on the other, the emergence of military client-groups who served the aggressive, expansionist interests of dynasties by going to battle whenever needed. These had to be supported with rewards, and with provisions when on the move; here the role of the farming communities organized under the *trícha cet* system as townlands, quarters and ballybiattaghs was important.

Simms argues that the emergence of whole *tuatha* as military clients — *sóer tuatha*, as opposed to the food-providing *aithechtuatha*, who supported them — was a development of the ninth and tenth centuries, supplanting the old and limited provision of soldiery from within land-holding clans to the local king of the *tuath* (K. Simms 1987: 116 ff). The great upsurge in slaving that followed the advent of the Vikings is one pointer to how the costs of such a change in military organization could have been paid for (Holm 1986). On the other hand, warfare and war-lordship was also a pronounced feature of Irish society during the rise of the Uí Néill and Eóganachta in the fifth/sixth centuries, a process that must have cut right into the integrity of local polities, and must also have required a flexible and potent military force. It is perhaps the case that *flan* gave way to group military clientship when whole *tuatha* found that they could 'go *flan*' on a permanent basis and be supported by society through alliance with powerful over-kings.

During the pre-Viking period, the participation of the clans of the *tuatha* in warfare seems to have been restricted to a 'reasonable' contribution. *CG* states that the king of a *tuath* could legally impose a military muster at an *óenach* when this was to the 'benefit of the *tuath*'. This was defined as a muster to repel invaders, to support negotiations for peace or war, and to enforce 'rights' (demands for clientship tribute) in a tributary *tuath* (*CG* 501-13). Negligence in responding to the summons for a hosting was punished by distraint of property after three days.[46] The duty of 'hosting' (*slógad*) fell mainly on clan landholders, who had to supply both the required men and their provisions. These would have been organized through the various links of clientship extending down into the farming ranks, as described in Ch. 6. Although these restrictions on kings' demands for soldiers suggest a peaceable society, it is hard to tell how such restraints worked out in practice, or how many raids and forays were undertaken apart from full-scale musters for inter-*tuath* invasion. The tiny fief given to the *second fer midboth*, for example, could have secured his services to any rising young princeling. In Ch. 12, where the military functioning of a *tuath* is considered from the point of view of the interaction between inheritance and competition for status, clans appear as much more belligerent organizations than *CG* would suggest.

The best information that exists on the *bóaires*' duties regarding local organization for war concerns '*fuba* and *ruba*', the 'service of attack and defence', which a late gloss explains as protection of the territory from wolves, pirates and robbers.[47] An important aspect of this duty was that it complemented aristocratic warfare, for a territory emptied of its warriors away on expedition would have been an easy prey for other enemies. This aspect of clan provision of military functions is better documented than participation in large-scale warfare. A passage of Old Irish text from *BC* shows that the *comaithches* functioned as the agent for the lord in enforcing his duties on each farmer, by pressuring him or his next of kin (who need not have been in the same *comaithches*):

> Where there are two responsible landholders and an evader of duties, what is done with the evader? He shall be distrained until he fences, and if he has no fixed residence, let his next of kin in the *fine* be distrained until they make the fence for him, or forfeit the right to the grass for the year. If the *fine* forfeit the grass, let each of the two (adjacent) landholders erect a perfect fence, and they shall bring equal amounts of stock on it, and then each shall give the other an additional pledge.[48]

The person of no fixed residence, *foíndledach*, was a stock character in the law-tracts and a major target of social sanctions. The importance of getting him tied down to his house and fenced lands, lay in the fact that he could then be compelled to conform to normal social requirements by his next of kin and neighbors. In fact, vagrancy was equated with outlawry: 'he becomes a vagrant by non-observance of the regulations of the *fine*.'[49] The commentary to the passage cited above shows that performance of military service was one of the duties the absentee would evade:

> A man who is not able to perform *fuba 7 ruba*, or though he may be able to, is unwilling to ... what is done to him is to give him notice ... and make a distress upon him afterwards, and there is no certain restriction upon this distress, but (it shall be such) a distress as ... may be thought to be sufficient to induce him to come to law ....'[50]

This section of *BC* goes on to say that the person who neglected his *fuba* and *ruba* obligations could be deprived of the use of his land for the next agricultural year by his next of kin, who could use it themselves or rent it out.[51] If they failed to do so the other 'two solvent members' of the *comaithches* could distrain them in turn. The right of kinsmen to temporarily dispossess absconders of their land is also asserted in the Old Irish tract *Do tuaslucad cundrad*, where the commentary specified that the culprit, on returning, owed the kinsman who had fulfilled the obligation on his behalf 'honor-price and double the (value) of the grazing and crops' before he could reclaim his land, and compensation for anything planted (presumably by the kinsman).[52] The overlapping of the *gelfhine* and *comaithches* in military organization is made clear by a passage on female inheritance within the *gelfhine*, in which it is said that an heiress could occupy all the land of the heritage if she arranged for the performance of *fuba* and *ruba*, but if not she could only hold half the land.[53] The same doctrine appears in the Old Irish poem on inheritance, minus the proviso for military service, but with a useful detail about the link between the amount of a person's land-holding and their military duties:

> From right division by the *fine*, there comes to her by right of kinship only the right land of a *bóaire*, two equal seven *cumal*s, land of tenants that maintain a *bóaire* (*SEIL* 155 [xv]).[54]

The rule that a woman could not convey inheritance rights to her sons unless she married a close agnate is obviously to be understood in terms of the military functions of *fuba 7 ruba*, for any other arrangement would permit defense of the territory to fall into the hands of male outsiders.

Agricultural cooperation

By the post-Viking period it is fairly certain that the main burden of the military system on the farming strata of land-holding clans had been narrowed down to the economic contributions they made through clientship. In order to meet these obligations, local groups, whether agnatic *gelfhine* or *comaithches* groups, had to keep up levels of production commensurate with their fiefs, which, we have seen, were keyed to their ability to repay the renders and perform services, itself calculated on the basis of their inherited holdings of house, land and chattels.

Members of an agrarian community, whatever the basis of its internal relationships, were supposed to promote each other's prosperity by giving each other preference as trading partners:

> Every agreement to cooperate,[55] every reward, every purchase, every sale, every covenant, every contract, every tenancy, every (granting of) suretyship, every service is properly due to lawful relatives in the *fine* ....[56]

The later commentary adds:

> It is right that every litter of pigs which a member of the *fine* has should be brought to another member of the *fine* to fatten, so that he shall have the fourth of the benefit due to the owner of the land out of them.[57]

Nevertheless the predominant note struck by the laws is not labor cooperation, but vigilance in social relations. *Mruigrecht* (farm law) was proscriptive and emphasized individual property interests and responsibilities:

> Farm-law, why so called? That is the law of farms, that no-one may injure the farm of his neighbor, that he may not cut down the wood of his land, that he break not (the fences?), that he may not plow it, that he may not inhabit it; that every man shall give additional pledge for his cattle in

respect of every (any) trespass across a fence (i.e. into another member of the co-parcenership's land) or *tairsce* (trespass across an adjacent co-parcenership and into a third).[58]

Neighbors were obliged to erect proper fencing to keep stock out of areas of cultivation or reserved pastures. An elaborate system of fines was in force that regulated the compensation due from one neighbor to another in the event of trespass by an animal. These fines ranged from high to low according to whether the trespass had occurred in the presence of the neatherd (or owner) or not, whether the field was winter grass or summer, rich pasture or poor, and whether the animals had merely trampled and browsed a little, or had eaten to satiety and were discovered lying down and chewing their cud. (Kelly 1988: 142-4) To safeguard against quarrels over such liabilities the neighbors exchanged the *tairgille* pledges referred to above. In addition to keeping up fences, neighbors were supposed to provide 'lawful herding' for stock, namely the service of a neatherd during the day and proper enclosure at night. English commentators in the sixteenth century remarked that domesticated animals were all 'in bondage', as this legal commentary advocated:

> A yoke for the pigs: a hood for the hens: ties of leather for
> the goats: a spancel for the yearling calves: a shepherd with
> the sheep: a herdsman with the cows.[59]

It was also expected that within this group, individuals would jointly herd livestock. Each was therefore supposed to retrieve any lost animal he or she observed, and could claim no reward:

> There is nothing to the *gelfhine* man out of live chattels
> (found) on the four nearest lands (cethar-aird) ... because
> they are bound to mutual herding among themselves
> according to the laws of *fine* relations.[60]

Sometimes the people of the community would mingle their animals in a common herd that was taken out to pasture by someone from the community. This would obviously be convenient if people owned only few animals. If the herd were pastured on land owned by someone else, the land owner was compensated by services from the owners of the herd. Each person owed a labor contribution — for example, a day's herding for each head of cattle he had placed on the owner's land.[61]

Despite the obvious keenness with which private interests within the *comaithches* were safeguarded, the solidarity of the group against the outside world is manifest in the regulation of the agreements regarding control of animals. In the first place, the group settled its own internal disputes over such matters without involving outsiders as sureties or brehons. Moreover, if cattle strayed onto the lands of another *comaithches*, they came to terms as though there were one *comaithches* and tried to determine who was responsible for the weakness of the fencing and the neglect of the herd. But if the cattle strayed onto a third group's land (having passed across the second group's) the decision had to be made in some other way — presumably the case was then taken to the brehon. A legal maxim defines the scope of community self-government:

> Reciprocity of goods is not enforced by law in the case of neighbors exceeding eight persons, i.e. the four neighbors who are immediately about and the four non-neighbors who are nearest to them.[62]

There was one other limitation to the *comaithches*'s self-regulation in matters of farm-law. This was the case of trespass by horses. According to a late commentary, if their owners were known, the horses were impounded and the owners notified; if not formal notice was to be given at the *dun* (fort) of the nearest lord, at the *dun* of the brehon of the *tuath*, the forge of the smith, and at the principal church of the *tuath*, and the four neighboring 'lands'.[63] This was obligatory because the grazing of horses was the beginning of the ritual procedure for making legal claims to landownership (*tellach*) and could be a challenge leading to invasion (Kelly 1988: 186-7).

Cooperation in the arable sector of the economy also strikes one as lacking the sort of intense, inflexible communalism of English manorial villages. Despite the various checks on individual economic opportunism that have been described previously, social mobility amongst the ranks of the farmers was an important aspect of kin relationships; one of the factors that permitted this mobility was the rather low degree of integration between separate households in labor co-operation. Although harvesting parties worked the lord's fields, there is no definite evidence for the Old Irish period that amongst themselves farmers followed an equitable and reliable system, such as the sun-shift method characteristic of the bigger villages found in England and Scandinavia, described by Homans and Göransson. In the absence of some such method, reaping parties must have been organized by negotiations, the outcome of which would have been determined by bargaining power.

Plowing involved some cooperation for farmers at the level of *bóaire* or *ócaire*, since these held, respectively, half and a quarter of a plow. Joint-plowing is referred to in the law-tracts, but there is no evidence that the farmers habitually cooperated with each other within the *comaithches* as a whole to field a common plow. Even in *Críth Gablach*'s scheme of ideal social relationships, no such regularity is alluded to. *CG*, as we have seen, venerated self-sufficiency, ability to lend to others, and status within the hierarchy of agrarian creditorship — not cooperation. In the proverbs known as the Triads, this sentiment is expressed in the warning that there were three ventures that would surely bring sorrow: 'joint-plowing, vying in feats of strength, and marriage' (cited by Kelly 1988: 101).

The actual labor requirement for plowing was not great, amounting only to the plowman himself, the driver and the person who scattered the seed. A man who was able to maintain the oxen of a whole plow team could certainly have raised this labor from within his own household, especially if he owned slaves. People who were not self-sufficient entered into joint-plowing contracts (*comar*) for this purpose (Kelly 1988: 101). There was only one restriction on the choice of partners, namely, that a son who was 'established in farming' was obliged to team up with his father if the latter were still actively farming on his own account and needed the cooperation.[64] There was a general sentiment that men ought to cooperate with their kinsmen, for a contract of joint-plowing could be undertaken by either spouse when both had committed equal property to the marriage, and when the contract was undertaken with respectable kin.[65] But a late commentary added that if non-relatives offered a better deal, no one was obligated to plow with a kinsman.[66]

The impression given by the sources is that there was competition for plowing partners amongst those who needed this arrangement, rather than long-standing habitual partnerships. This is the implication of the only two surviving rules that describe *comar* agreements. One of these maintains that the agreement could not be reneged upon, even if one of the parties claimed he was drunk when he made it (Kelly 1988: 159). (This suggests that these agreements were made at fairs, as they were until this century.) The right to negotiate a contract of joint-plowing wherever the best deal could be obtained, reinforces the picture of a social life marked by considerable individualism in the management of assets, even at the lowest levels of clan society. Competitiveness and fear of exploitation by others was also reflected in the fine adjustments for damages that farm law permitted between neighbors and adjacent kinsmen. The outcome of severe competition was the many gradations of social rank that were acknowledged by the jurists. Such cooperation as did obtain was the result of the common political liabilities of members of a *comaithches* or *gelfhine*, which intensified cooperation and interaction between agnates and neighbors. In Ch. 10 we see the 'big' *fine*, the 'seventeen men', checking the activities of individuals in regard to clientship; the point of the localized *gelfhine* and *comaithches* was also in large part to keep people in each others' view and answerable to each other. Such surveillance, along with collective punishment of kin, served to ensure political compliance and social order in the absence of state mechanisms. These mechanisms of control through kinship will be examined in the remaining chapters of this study.

Notes

1. See Charles-Edwards (1972), who, however, views the minimal lineage as genealogically deeper (associated with the nine 'men' of the *derbfhine*). I have expressed disagreement with aspects of these views in 'Patrilineal groups in early Irish society' (1990).

2. See the references to a woman's 'land of hand and thigh', *orba cruib 7 sliasta, SEIL*: 133 (b); 137 (ii) 1; 139 (iii) 2; 150 (xii) 3; 152-4; 174-5, and especially the note on p.152, *muinchorach*. See also the references to marriage in which the wife brings the use of land in *Cáin Lánamna* (e.g. *SEIL*: 18.5; 32. 13).

3. *CIDH ARA NEIPER SCUICHIT MIC FINDTIUDH ARA IS ANUND ASAS FINNTIUDH CEIN BES FINNTIUDH AR CINN NI FOR CULU DOSAI. (CIH 2018.3-4)*. Commentary: *Ma ta mac agan duine is marbad ann, is a dibhadh do breith do; mana fuil, is a breith dha athair*. lines 9-10. See also *CIH* 2011.17.

4. 'in most recent days a father divides equally among all his sons and reserves to himself, as if to one of his sons, a part of the inheritance and whole substance, which he entrusts to his firstborn, and it shall be his inalienably, or it shall be divided after the firstborn's death between his heirs and his brothers and their successors.' *Can,. Hib.* xxxi, 18. See McCone (1990: 103), whose translation I have cited.

5. *Ara cinta condlat, ar conaracht selbha slechtaib aithre sceo senaithre... (CIH* 591.4-5). I am grateful to John Carey for drawing my attention to this passage and for sharing a working translation of the text.

6. ... *rannaidh ósor 7 dogogha sinnser (CIH* 1289.11 = *AL* iv 373. Note that the *AL* translation has 'the junior shares and the senior *is elected.* This is not the meaning of the proverb (see Kelly 1988: 102 n.15), but does reflect the intention of Donall O'Davoren, the compiler of 'Succession', who was trying to promote primogeniture (O'Grady 1926: 113 (15). See Patterson 1989: 59-60).

7. I wish to thank John Carey for drawing my attention to this story.

8. *CIS LIR CAIN IT(ER)NA BI IMACLAID...MAC 7 A ATHAIR, INGEN 7 A MATHAIR... (CIH 240.29-241.2 AL v 481.8 ff).* The nature of such legally corporate dyads (*lánamnus* relations) is discussed by Thurneysen in *CL #2, SEIL:* 3-16.

9. *IN TAN DONICFAT NA HIMACLAIDE-SEO IS AND DONICFAD NA DUBA DIGEANNA...AR ROSUIGIDEADH NA CANA-SO O TOSACH DOMAIN CO DIAIG CEN IMACLAID. (CIH 240.36-241.2 = AL v 481.25 ff).*

10. *MAC DIA TABUIR AITHIR SAINMISCUIS...MAC FONAGUIB A AITHIR CIN ORBA...MAC FONAGAIBH A AITHIR I NDAIRE DO FLAITH. (CIH 1817.22, 25, 30 = AL iii 63.13 ff).*

11. *CIH* 585.32-3 = *AL* iv 355.18-9.

12. *CIH* 582.32-589.32; 676.17-677.27; 1567.1-35. = *AL* iv 344-68.

13. '*Na nai ngrad deidinech-so...natat indraice nadma na raithe na haitire na naill na fiadnaise.*' These last nine grades ... they are not worthy of binding (contracts), going surety as *ráth* or *aitire,* nor to give oath, nor eye-witness evidence. *(CIH 585.1-4 = AL iv 353.8-13).*

14. *ni fuilet (?) re daim in fer-son ina fuil gnimiu laích lais...is gae greine dogairter.*' the man who does not have it in him to do a warrior's work does not belong (?) in a company (a lord's retinue) ... he is called a 'spear of sun(light)' (i.e. not a spear of iron). *(CIH 585.17-8 = AL iv 353.33-6).*

15. *'Oinmit: fer mitir im drochmnai 7 ona co ndentar mear 7 fonachtaide .i. fosgenigh...*' A fool: a man paired with a bad woman so that he is made crazy and unsteady, .i.e. moving (jumping around from one thing to another?). (*CIH 585.20-1 = AL iv 353.36-8).*

16. *Midlach i. fer na ragaib sealbh na horba ... arinni is mellach o deilbh 7 ciniul...* 'A *midlach* i.e. man who does not have his own property in stock, nor inherited land...for he is deceitful in his form and as to his descent'. *CIH* 585.22-4 = *AL* iv 353, n.2. *Mellach* had a range of meanings, including humped or bulging, pleasant and seductive. Whitley Stokes translated a definition of the *mellach* found in *Sanais Cormac* (Cormac's glossary, p.19): 'an effeminate person, not fit for war, a coward'.

17. *Sindach brothlaige i.e bruar cach bidh di iter dilis 7 indilis* 'A fox of the cooking-pit, i.e he gets bits of everything, proper and improper (food)' (*CIH* 585.30-1 = *AL* iv 355.16-7). The 'fox of the cooking pit' not only stole other people's food and left-overs (see Kelly 1988: 237), but also scavenged carrion and contaminated food. He is a reminder that the law-tracts were compiled shortly after a series of devastating famines, the greatest of which occurred in 664-6. A number of references are found in the Penitentials to the consumption of blood, urine, horseflesh, flesh of a dead beast, flesh contaminated by dogs, birds, cats and mice (*Can. Hib.* 12-21). Some types of contamination were of a pagan religious nature (e.g., eating horseflesh), but others refer to the breakdown of hygiene in the face of famine. During such times, only members of the strongest social groups would have had a normal food supply; the cultural emphasis on individual strength, and the growth in the legal power of kin-groups over their members, must be viewed against this background, as well as in relation to the militarism of the society, both of which must have contributed to the Hobbesian tendencies in Irish society of this period.

18. *Reimm do .i. fuirseoir no druth; nach fer dobeir remmad fo corp 7 a enech ni dligh dire, uair teit asa richt ar beluib sluagh 7 sochaide.* A contortionist now, i.e. a clown or fool; whatever man brings contortion upon his body and his face deserves no honor-price, because he goes out of his proper state before armies and crowds. *(CIH 585.25-6 = AL iv 355.7-10).*

19. Sheper-Hughes (1979: 142-3) discusses the 'low tolerance for physical deformity' in children found amongst rural Irish in modern Co. Kerry.

20. George Homans, personal communication.

21. *inol, flescach, gairid. (CIH 1609.4-6 = AL v 78.23).*

22. *In forcmai(d)ther ... ó chetheoraib blíadnaib deec co fichtig co cúairtulchaigi.* (*CG* 66-7) See Binchy's reconstruction of the text in the note to line 66.

23. *Ní dligther fothud a thige do neoch cein mbes maice combi túalaing saintrebtha 7 gabála[e] se(a)lb...(CG* 77-8).

24. The *set* of *CG* is taken to mean 4/5 of a 'great cow' (Kelly 1988: 116 n.116).

25. *DIL: inchis.*

26. Thurneysen 1925 b: 347-51 #8 = *AL* ii 257.24-26. Compare *CG* 76 ff.

27. *bes óenchin(n)eda insin, fer ná[d] tre(a)ba seilb ná ferann dó fadeisin (CG* 72-3).

28. *LEMNACH... IM ...CEITHEOR BAIRGENA XX.DO BANFUINE. (CIH 483. 29-37 = AL ii 255.2 ff).* 'Woman-baking' and 'man-baking' may have been conventional measures, but dairying was exclusively women's work.

29. *Cia beith cen gabáil n-orbai dano co críni, ní te(i)t a luige ó fhi[u]r midboth(a) beos* etc. (*CG* 69-70)

30. *CIH* 1003.25-1004.9 = *AL* ii 296. This is a late commentary, but *'innell'* was understood to refer to marriage arrangements by the glossator of *Cáin Aicillne* in MSS Copenhagen 261B (*CIH* 2223.32-2234.22); T.C.D. MS H 2 15A (*CIH* 492.1); T.C.D. MS H 3 17 (*CIH* 1795.22 ff). The simple exchange of the *coibche* for the girl could only be effected within the first ten days of the unlawful marriage.

31. *Atnaig tar fót crúach i n-ardnemed di[a] díte, dieim ar díantóla[e] slúaig.* (*CG* 53-4)

32. Seven *cumals* is given in Binchy's authoritative edition of *CG (91)*. Readers who consult Mac Néill's translation (1923) should note that it gives the land of an *ócaire* as 'thrice seven *cumals*' (1923): 286.77). *CG* is so internally consistent, however, that seven *cumals* is undoubtedly what its compiler had in

mind for the *ócaire*.

33. ... *húare nád n-óg fossugud a thige 7 nád n-inráith friu amal cach [m]boairi[g] ar lagait a fholaid. (CG 29-31).*

34. *Ar is di thír gíallaid a ngrád n-í; is di thír dano lóg a x. set dosom dia th[a]urche[i]c; bíd dano a tír sin for fola fris dó. CG 106-8.*

35. I have followed Mac Néill's translation which understands *folud* as 'duty', or in this case, dereliction of duty, whereas Binchy holds to the other meaning 'property qualification'. Binchy, however, was unable to arrive at an interpretation of the sentence on this basis. (See *CG* note to 108).

36. *CG*, p.28, notes to 108.

37. *Tír (trí) .vii. cumal les; is ed tír mbó la Feniu insin, foloing .vii. mbúu co cenn mblíadnae i fochraic in tíre. (CG 91-4).*

38. *SEIL:* 155 (xv) = *CIH* 217.20-22. The Old Irish text stipulated the restriction, while the later commentary adds that the heiress could hold more of the land if she provided the military and political services of *slóg, cis,* and *congbail.*

39. *CIH* 2327.15, 32 = *AL* v 87.26-89; 19-21. In this tract, the primary heir of a *bóaire* is described as the superior (out of three subdivisions) of the ranks of *ócaire.*

40. *ATAT .UII. CUIR FOCEIRD MAC BEOATHAR SECH A ATHUIR NACH TINDTAI INT ATHAIR UMA MAC. CINNI FORRNGARU INT ATHAIR IT CUIR* (etc.)...*COIBCE TECHTA FOR CEDMUINDTIR COMCINEOIL. (CIH 45.34-8 = AL v 285 [L]; CIH 1847.1 ff; 2193.10 ff).*

41. Kinsella's suggested translation, *The Tain* (1970).

42. *Cid nodmbrisi in fer so a bóairechas? Ar bes bid cethrar nó chóicer bíte hi comarbus bóairech con[n]ach assa[e] bóaire do cach áe. (CG 145-8).*

43. *ARINNI IS CUMA NODOGAIB AIRE FRI AITHECH 7 AIRCINDECH FRI BACLACH. (CIH 64.6-9 = AL iv 69.1-6).*

44. *CIH* 64.27-9 = *AL* iv 71.17. The fullest discussion of *tairgille* is found in *BB*, notes to #1, 3, 24-6.

45. *IMDINGAIB NAIDM NAESAIB...is eim dingbuithir do reir nua-feasa conach naidm nascaire uile ... (CIH 64.28-65.2-3 = AL iv 71.7, 22-4).* See also *CIH* 907.2.

46. *ATHGABAIL TREISI SLOIGED. (CIH 381.8 = AL i 157).*

47. *CONGBAIL...na tri fuba .i. fodiuba im loingsechu 7 um echtadait 7 im macu tiri.* Coigny...the three *fuba*, i.e. cutting off of pirates and aggressors and wolves (or bandits). *(CIH 381.33-4 = AL i 156.1-2).*

48. *OS AIRM I MBIATT DA COMORBU TREBAIRI IM EISERT CID DOGNITHER FRI HEISERT. GAIBET AIRE CO NIMCUA* etc. *(CIH 75.24-9 = AL iv 129.5-16).*

49. *Is ed doni faindlegach dhe, can tiachtain fo dliged corusa fine. (CIH 1157.14-5 = AL iii 410.20).*

50. Duine so risnach eidir fuba na ruba a feainn do denam etc. *(CIH 76.38-77.2 = AL iv 132.31-134.4).*

51. *CIH* 76.38-77.2 = *AL* v 132.31-134.4.

52. *CIH* 1876.3 ff = *AL* v 502.1-7. The Old Irish text on the liability of a defaulting kinsman is more fully given at *CIH* 245.26-9, but without details as to the kinds of duties in which the kinsman might fail.

53. '*Ban comorba so, 7 beiridh in ferunn uili co fuba 7 ruba re, 7 leth doib cen fuba cen ruba*'. *CIH* 1861.14-5. The same provision appears in a different tract, *CIH* 736. 30-1.

54. '*orba biatach mboaireach*' should probably be regarded as lands that supported a farmer's rank as a *bóaire* within a *baile biatagh/ballybetagh*, rather than lands occupied by tenants who supported a *bóaire*, for there is no evidence that the latter was typically a *rentier*.

55. *AL* translates *comsa* as litter of pigs, following the commentary, but Thurneysen understands this word to mean an agreement to cooperate in some task (*SEIL* 19 I [7]).

56. *CIH* 490.1-4 = *AL* ii 283.36-285.1-2.

57. *CIH* 490.5-7 = *AL* ii 285.4-6. See also *Cáin Lánamna, CIH* 506.22.

58. *MBRUIGRECHT ... RECHT MBROGA SON ARNA HORR NECH MBRUIG
A COMAITHIG. ARNA HEIBI FID A TIRE. ARNACH URBA. ARNACH ARA
ARNACH AITREIB. ARNA TURGELLAD CACH ARA CETHRA FOR CACH
NAILE 7 FOR CACH TAIRSCI 7 FOR CACH RUIRID. (CIH 75.3-6 = AL iv
125.12-19).*

59. *CIH* 68.28-31 = *AL* iv 85.37-87.4.

60. *Ni fuil ni d'fir geilfine a cethuraird na a culaird, uair dlegar comingairi
eturrud do reir corus fine* etc. *(CIH 1851.29-33 = AL v 323.25-32).*

61. *CIH* 1921.1-33; 576.24-577.24 = *AL* iv 101.5 ff. See Kelly's note on
comingaire, joint-pasturing (1988: 101, and App. I, 43).

62. *TAIRSCE.. TAIGACHT TAR SEILB NO TAR A DI... ar ní dlegar imuaim
folad do comiteach fri ni bes lia .uii.ur .i. na .iiii. comithaigh imabiad 7 na
.iiii.e comithaigh ada neasam doib-side. (CIH 198.14 = AL iv 127.33-129.1-4).*

63. *CIH* 193.27-33 = *AL* iv 105.40-107.1 ff.

64. *COMOL COMUIR IN TAN NAD NAIR LA ATHAIR. (CIH 45.37 = AL v
285.39-41).*

65. *comul comair fri coibne techta.* CL #5 *(SEIL: 19.2-3).*

66. *CIH* 1805.21 = *AL* ii 354.22-24.

CHAPTER NINE

The Forms of Irish Kinship

Introduction

Successful Irish clans expanded rapidly as a result of polygyny and expropriation of weaker neighbors' lands. This is the picture drawn by the traditional genealogist Dubhaltach MacFirBisigh in 1605:

> It is a usual thing in the case of great princes, when their children and their families multiply, that their clients and followers are squeezed out, wither away, and are wasted. Take Ireland, and even the whole world if you desire, and there is no limit to all the instances which you will find of that. (Ó Raithbheartaigh 1935: 26.44).

During expansion, such groups produced marked social differentiation amongst their own descendants. Hence it was proverbially remarked, 'seven generations from a king to a spade'. The most inclusive kinship group was the clan, but though 'clan' is actually a Gaelic word, the most common term in the Irish law tracts for this group was *cenél*. More precisely defined as a group was the *fine*; it was a branch of a *cenél*, but its relationship to the latter is not clarified by the sources. Within both clan and *fine*, there existed a gradation of power and autonomy, extending 'up', in terms of level of group aggregation and the status of the person with authority over the group, from the domestic patriarch of the farming commune to the *cenn fine*, or the chief of the *cenél*. Many of the ranks discussed in the last chapter have already been shown to be status positions within a descent group.

Social relations between *fine* members were referred to in early Irish law by means of a number of terms that were employed in different ways. That is, one term (such as *gelfhine*, encountered in the last chapter) signified rather different sets of relatives according to the classificatory scheme adopted by the writer. Since the law-tracts generally used these terms without offering clues as to the precise kinship model used by the writer, the interpretation of the kinship terms has long been one of the banes of medieval Irish history. In this chapter, therefore, we have to distinguish different aspects of the kinship system, and show how these were represented in the Irish law-tracts. This subject will be of more interest to specialists who encounter these terms in their source materials than to the general reader, but this survey will also be useful for readers when we deal with the organization of lineages. Medievalists and anthropologists may even be interested in the ways in which simple-seeming forms of expression were used to describe fluid and complex social subject-matter; the jurists maintained fidelity to form but stretched the frame of reference in all sorts of ways to encompass situations that were difficult to describe or legitimize.

Preliminary distinctions

The Irish law-tracts recognized the following types of kinship organization:

(i) *Cognatic or bilateral kinship* in which individual ties through both mother's and father's kin were important; this concerned payment/receipt of *díre* (honor-price), inheritance (pre- and post-mortem) of chattels and lands not tied up in agnatic corporate groups, and protection of the rights of women and their children against exploitation by the husband/father, or his substitute in the *fine*.

(ii) *Agnatic ties between individuals*, in which only connections through male ancestors were counted. This was important for payment/receipt of *cró* (wergeld), and inheritance of *fine* lands. Both (i) and (ii) were '**personal kindreds**', in that no one person's circle exactly overlapped with another's (other than with a sibling's before parenthood); for example, 'my first cousin' is only second cousin to 'my third cousin' (see *Fig*.1, below).

(iii) The *corporate agnatic kin-group, 'the' fine:* the important *fine* of the area, that of the local chief of the landowning clan. Such a structure is often referred to as a **descending kindred**, to distinguish it from the personal circles of kin.[1]

Since these different aspects of kinship were involved with different aspects of social organization, these distinctions are important for the understanding of early Irish society. The purpose of the descending agnatic kindred was to control the functions carried out in the personal agnatic kindred, acting as a watch-dog over individuals and branches of the whole corporate *fine*. Its most powerful members had internal and external jural roles that are described in Chs. 10 and 12.

The *fine* was hierarchical, one dominant lineage formed the central line, while others related to this 'spine' at varying degrees of distance — social, geographical, and genealogical. The genealogical principles of the *fine*, however, were a constant casualty of the competitive social system, so that no *fine* could consistently align actual descent with actual status, or real genealogical connections with actual social relationships. Genealogies, then, were faked (not all the time, of course), and served as the ideology of political relations which were legitimized through assertions of 'true' descent.

In the law-tracts, there is constant reference to the rights of members of a *fine* in each other and in *fine* resources. But such ubiquitous reference to the model in regard to *personal kindreds* does not mean that the descending agnatic *fine*, as a corporate group, was universally present on the social landscape. In other words, not everyone, even amongst the free, belonged to a corporate *fine*, for the simple reason that accidents of demography and political chance ruled out such regularity. The enduring structures were the *cenela*, and their package of human, animal and ecological resources, the *tuatha*; within these structures people 'belonged', even when their personal *fine* was incomplete, or its link to the chiefly *fine* not too clear. *Tuath* and *cenél* remained common words in early modern Irish, whereas *fine* became a bookish, technical term after the defeat of the native political order.

These different structures of kinship, taken together, amount to the total grid on which were plotted the relationships arising from the patterns of alliance and differentiation described previously. To a great extent, the claim to 'heritage' served as the oral title of possessions and status. Nevertheless, the power that enabled men to achieve and retain 'heritage' was not primarily based on alliance within the kin, but on alliances with other members of the élite — such as mother's kin and foster-kin — which enabled successful men to attract the loyalty of some members of their own agnatic kin and compel the submission of others.

The fact that political alliance was established at the level of social class, and not exclusively within the descent group, accounts for the prominent absence in the Irish law-tracts of any nomenclature describing levels of segmentation in kin groups. All we find are the generic terms, '*cenél*', for the composite 'clan' group, and *fine* for its local branches. The *gelfhine* did not 'nest' within a named, jurally defined, segment of the *fine*, nor did the latter constitute named, jurally defined, segments of the *cenél*. The *cenél* itself was not a major subdivision of the total frame of a kinship community, as its parallels would be in a more thorough-going organization of society on the basis of kinship. There were sprawling networks of élite agnates bearing collective designations, such as 'the seed (*síl*) of (ancestor)', or 'the descendants (*uí*) of (ancestor)', but these epithets did not necessarily signify distinct corporate structures, so much as eligibility on the part of those who claimed descent to have 'rights' vis-a-vis the other members of the group, or traditional vassals.

Given the depth of available genealogies in early Ireland, we would expect to find evidence of several levels of encapsulated, nesting segments, within lineages and clans, if indeed politics had followed the flow of kinship-group development, and if political roles represented levels of division in the total kinship community. One looks in vain for such evidence, however, finding instead that political roles were functions within the body politic, the *tuath*, which required definite capacities of those who played them, capacities for which the allegiance of the leader's kin group was only a necessary, not a sufficient basis. With these general considerations in view we may now examine the formal aspects of kinship structure.

Bilateral personal kindreds

Although the agnatic *fine* has a high profile in the law-tracts, actual emotional bonds were distributed across a broad social field. An individual life began in the intimacy of the relationship with the mother, but ideally moved out into the wider community at the age of seven, which was the ideal age at which children were sent to other homes to be fostered. At the completion of fosterage there followed, for males, a period of social limbo between physical maturity and admission into the ranks of the land-holders. Women typically married, however, and began raising children in late adolescence. On maturity (the death of the grandfather in all probability), men entered a structure which was agnatic and corporate, but until that time their lives were lived in a network of social relations that was not preponderantly agnatic.

The *maithre*, the mother's kin, had legal rights in their sister/daughter's children. If a child were neglected or abused during fosterage, the *maithre* as well as the agnates, could intervene to enforce its rights. Where a child was mentally handicapped there was a good chance that it was the mother's kin who would care for it, for the old Irish text on the care of the insane says that the family's share of the *díre*, honor-price, for injury of such a handicapped person was due to either the head of the *fine* that undertook his or her care, or to the mother or *maithre*.[2] Similarly, a woman's kin could protect the property she brought into marriage (Thurneysen 1928: 9 #23), which ultimately would pass in part back to them, and in part as heritage to her children (*SEIL*: 160 ff).

The bond between individuals and their *maithre* was strengthened by polygyny; plural sexual relationships were tolerated, and were probably typical amongst the secular élite (see Ch. 11). Residences, however were separate — it was such an insult to the wife to bring a concubine into the marital home that the wife was legally entitled to assault the concubine, and to divorce the husband with full economic penalties (*CL* #23 = *SEIL* 49). Permanent cohabitation between husbands and wives was not, then, an overriding norm. Women often retained close ties to their kin which strengthened the children's ties to them; this was especially true of concubines, whose kin retained a two-thirds share of their honor-price, but it was also true of chief-wives (whose kin retained only a third of their honor-price), since divorce or intermittent separation of the spouses was so likely to occur. Moreover, as many agnatic siblings were half-siblings, their basic allies in competition for dominance in the agnatic corporation were their non-agnatic connections, principally the mother's kin. Often this bond was reinforced by fosterage, for the mother's brother seems commonly to have been the foster-father; the foster-father was the person the child called 'dad' (Kelly 86-7).[3]

The claims of the *maithre* to a share in the social personality of women's children were legally recognized. Kelly summarizes the information on *díre*: '...a man receives *lándíre*, 'full payment' (presumably of his own honor-price), for the illegal killing of his father and mother. He gets half payment for the killing of his paternal uncle or maternal aunt, and one-third payment for the killing of the son of either of them, i.e. his first cousin on his father's or mother's side. He is even entitled to a payment (one seventh of his honor-price) for the killing of his fosterfather or fosterbrother.' (Kelly 1988: 126; *IR* 16-7, #15-#16; 19, #20; 20, #21. In addition, *maithre* claimed an *éraic* of one *cumal* for the killing of a sister's son, while the *fine* took its basic payment of seven *cumals*.[4]

Agnatic personal kindreds.

Because the term *fine* doubled for the corporate descent group, which had a legal head, and for each individual's personal circle of agnatic 'cousins' and 'uncles', *fine* was not a technical term, and did not explicitly allude to *descent*, let alone *agnatic* descent. Charles-Edwards observes that the root meaning of *wen* was 'love' or 'friendship,' exemplified in Latin *Venus* and Old English *wine*, as in 'winsome'. 'Kindred, kinship is an obvious development from friendship, as in Welsh *car*, a kinsman, compared to *caru*, to love.' (Charles-Edwards 1971b: 118). 'Alliance', then, seems to be the basic sense. There is no doubt, however, that by the sixth or seventh century, *fine* groups existed that were structured around agnatic unilineal descent. That is, no one could claim membership in a *fine* by right of descent traced only through a woman of the group. This is made clear both by the rules of descent and inheritance, and by the genealogies.

The exclusion of the children of women of the *fine* is most explicitly treated in the context of the rules relating to the *banchomarba*, a woman who inherited a life-interest in land in the absence of brothers. The oldest source for this subject is the 'poem on inheritance', edited by Dillon (*SEIL*: 134-59). This asserts the following points:

(i) The basic entitlement of women to receive lands. Women who inherited land, either from the father or from the mother's dowry property, are said to be under contract (*cor*) and are 'bound' to agreement with the *fine* from which the property stemmed as to its future disposition (*SEIL* 135-6, #9 [i]; 138, #9 iii).

(ii) The contract was formalized when the *fine*'s senior (*finnsruith*, or in commentaries, '*gelfhine* chief'), took securities from the heiress that the land would be returned to the agnatic descent line after she died (*SEIL* 137 [ii]).

(iii) Her son was prohibited from taking the land (though commentaries allow him a small amount, such as one-seventh), unless his mother and father were close agnatic kin, in which case his claims could be made through the father (*SEIL*: 150 [xii]).

The general rule, then, was that women did not transmit membership of their own father's *fine* to their sons, even though they conveyed dowry property to them (*SEIL*: 151-5 [xiii — xiv]). The exception to this was the case of a woman who was both an heiress and had been permitted by her kin to marry a landless foreigner; sons of such unions (who were classed as *glasfine*; blue-kin i.e. from out of the blue, the sea), were entitled to *orbae niad*, the inheritance of a sister's son (*CIH* 431.30-1). Limits were put upon both the heiress's holding and the *orbae niad*, however; the heiress' estate should not be more than the land of a *bóaire*, i.e. 14 *cumals* (*SEIL*: 155 [xv]), while a son by a foreigner should not get more than seven *cumals* of land, the holding of an *ócaire* (*CIH* 917.30-1; Kelly 1988: 104-5).

Genealogies also attest to the generally agnatic basis of Irish kinship. In the lists of historically or mythologically important women, the *Bansenchas*, the identities of each woman's father, husband(s) and children were usually given, but the woman's mother was rarely included (Dobbs 1930-2). Similarly, where a man's female relatives were named, these were his wife or wives, daughters and mother, but the mother's kin were not included. Each reference to a woman, then, indicated her personal importance and links to other agnatic *fini*, but did not show interest in the bilateral ramifications of cognatic relationships.

Within the agnatic set of kinship relations, the law recognized four categories of relationship and referred to these by means of a set of names; these are the terms which have caused historians so much difficulty. As shown in *DIL* (under '*fine*'), they may be translated literally as follows;

gelfhine	=	'bright or obvious kin'.
derbfhine	=	'true kin'.
íarfine	=	'side kin'.
indfhine	=	'end kin'.

Each term was symbolized by a number, as in the following passage:

> The *gelfhine* extends to five men...the *derbfhine* extends to nine men (Gloss: including the five of the preceding *fine*)... the *íarfine* extends to thirteen men (Gloss: including the two preceding *fine* groups)...the *indfhine* extends to seventeen men (Gloss: including the three preceding *fine* groups.'[5]

'*Fine*' itself was used to refer to the widest range of recognized agnates — the entire *fine* of 'seventeen men', and *also* to refer to each division within this group. Thus the whole *fine* is often referred to as 'the four *fini*' (*ceithirfhine*).[6] The terms for the various divisions of the *fine* (*gelfhine*, etc.), are also not consistent from source to source. O'Buachalla noted a contrast between the following usages:

(1) *derbfhine* = five 'men'; *taoibhfhine* = nine 'men'; *íarfine* = thirteen 'men', and *indfhine* = seventeen 'men'.

(2) *gelfhine* = five 'men'; *derbfhine* = nine 'men', *íarfine* = thirteen 'men', and *indfhine* = seventeen 'men'.

(O'Buachalla 1947: 49).

Finally, we should note that the term, *fine*, was not always used to refer to a genealogically distinguished group, but might refer to a category or division. For example, affiliated illegitimate sons were described as *dubfhine* (dark, or dubious, *fine*), while those who committed *fingal* (kin-slaying) were termed *dergfhine* (red, or bloody, *fine*).[7]

The only absolute consistency that underlies the method of representing kinship relations is that text and commentary from all periods recognized the central importance of a group of 'five men' amongst the kinsmen, namely the group examined in the preceding chapter. Generally, this group or class was termed the *gelfhine*. In some earlier passages, however, the five men were simply called the *cóicde*, 'the five'.[8] The other consistency lies in the persistence of the sequence of 'five men', plus three groups of 'four men', who follow each other in an order of postponement with regard to inheritance rights and legal obligations to fellow agnates, giving rise to the four-fold classification, the 'four *fini*'. This sequence is not elucidated by any Old Irish text material, but only by commentaries from various historical periods. In these, the sequence of terms and numbers are used to describe the two different types of agnatic structures indicated above — the personal (ego-focussed) kindred, and *also* the descending agnatic kindred, the corporate *fine*, with its ranked descent lines.

This has caused such confusion that for a long time it has been believed by some scholars that the Irish law-tracts preserve the remnants of a shattered prehistoric tribal system, preserved out of reverence for antiquity, but no longer understood and thus presented inconsistently in the texts (Binchy 1943; 1976b: 31, 45; 1984: 9-12; Charles-Edwards 1972a: 61-4; 1972b: 16-8). However, it is demonstrable that later medieval changes in kinship models account for some of these variant representations (Patterson 1990, and below). Irish kinship and society was evolving throughout the pre-Norman period and laws on kinship reflect these changes; but these are much later and quite different processes from the supposed collapse of a tribal kinship system in late antiquity deduced from the 'inconsistency' in kinship representation.

The most widely accepted interpretation of the categories and the numbers that denoted early Irish kinship classification is Mac Néill's, which regarded the *fine* terms as limited to the personal kindred. On this view, the *gelfhine* consisted of an individual's fist cousins (and their fathers and grandfather), the *derbfhine* consisted of second cousins, the *íarfine* were third cousins, and the *indfhine*, fourth cousins. The numbers for each category are explained thus: (see *Fig.* 1, below):

1. The *gelfhine*: the 'five men' of the *gelfhine* were five *categories* of patrilineal relationship, or five dyadic types. These were: (i) *ego* and his father; (ii) *ego* and his grandfather; (iii) *ego* and his father's brother(s); (iv) *ego* and his own brother(s); (v) *ego* and his cousin(s), i.e. father's brothers' sons.

2. The *derbfhine*: four more types of relationship are included, namely (i) *ego* and great-grandfather; (ii) *ego* and his grandfathers' brothers; (iii) *ego* and his grandfather's brothers' sons (father's cousins); and (iv) the sons of the latter.

3. The *íarfine* is traced in the same way (see *Fig.* 1), but the common ancestor, the great-great-grandfather is not counted because he could not be expected to be alive after *ego* reached the age of marriage.

4. The *indfhine* is reckoned in the same way, but two ascending ancestors are omitted from the count, also because of their presumed death or social retirement.

The main purpose of this classification, when it was applied to ego's personal kindred, was to establish (i) the order of postponement for kin-liability under rules of collective punishment (ii) the amounts allocated to different kin when wergeld was paid/received (iii) the allocation of different shares in residual inheritance (*díbad*) to categories of kin when a *gelfhine* died out. These were all aspects of the social control of individuals and groups by the élite through the medium of the corporate *fine* organization; these mechanisms of regulation are examined in Ch. 10.

The corporate *fine*; '17 men'

This organization preserved *fine* lands, *fintiu*, answered to society on behalf of its members, and controlled the weaker members with suffocating thoroughness. A corporate *fine* could conceivably have developed after initial colonization of land by a group of people, but in the inhabited landscape of the Ireland of the law-tracts it was far more likely that such a group arose from lineage fission, initiated by individuals of quite high social standing.

One context for lineage fission within an area of long-term habitation would be a shift in the balance of power within a lordship and the accession of a leader from another branch of the dynasty. Typically, each successful incumbent of a lordship or kingship would provide his close collateral kin and sons with lands and powerful roles in the polity. When the incumbency passed to another branch of the dynasty these men and their heirs were often dispossessed by the new chief to provide for his own close kin. Anticipation of such an outcome was a major factor contributing to the high frequency of internecine succession wars. One manoeuvre used to forestall seizure was for a weaker branch to declare its lands a separate lordship and attempt to pass them down to holders and heirs under the governance of their own *cenn fine*. Simms notes that the process was very common in the later middle ages, and that often the new sub-lordships involved only small estates. In some cases, however, the newly separated and defined kin-group challenged its collaterals for the chieftaincy and became the dominant branch, founding what would eventually become the new central line of the dynasty (K. Simms 1987: 58).

It is in the context of such fission that we must understand the term *'gelfhine* chief', for the *gelfhine* was precisely that unit that held its lands to itself and did not admit participation by other kinsmen on the basis of claims to *'díbad'*. The whole point of fission in the Irish context was to establish a new corporate identity; what is more, there is no sign that after fission new lineages ever 'merged' on the basis of kinship closeness with those kin from whom they had severed. Far from being each other's nearest allies they were inclined to be each other's most lethal competitors.

The chief of a fissionary branch of a dynasty was *'gelfhine* chief' to his own kin and dependents, though he was in varying degrees of relationship to his rivals in the dynastic kindred. The chiefly *fine* that

Fig. 1: *Old Irish terms and number describing patrilineal descent group structure*

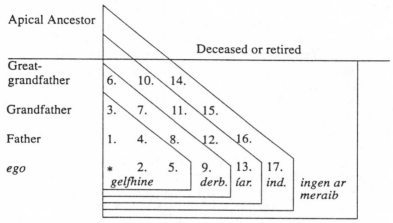

(Adapted from Mac Néill's *Celtic Ireland* (1921: 172). Note that each number represents a type of relative, e.g. an uncle; *ego* would probably have had several relatives at 4 - 17.)

stood at the head of this organization was often depicted in the law-tracts by means of the spinal cord (or '*truncus*') model of kinship; that is, the 'four *fini*' classification was applied not to *anyone*'s personal agnatic kindred, but to *the chief*'s. As this fissionary lineage developed, the 'four *fini*' classification could be applied to its newly sprouting branches, but in order to strengthen its separate identity its dominant group would continue to identify itself as '*the gelfhine*' of the new lineage. For this reason, there sometimes appear in the law-tracts, especially in late commentaries, statements that take '*gelfhine*' as a fixed reference point, and that assume that the *gelfhine* was the leading family of the area.

Some examples are:

> and those from whom it is right to avenge a man of the
> *derbfhine* are the five men of the *gelfhine*.[9]

and:

> the 'steward-bailiffs' (of the kings) came from the base-
> clients of the lord or the *gelfhine*, and the steward-bailiffs (of
> a bishop) came from the base-clients of ecclesiastical land or
> (base-clients of) the *gelfhine* (of the family that owned the
> church lands).[10]

The *truncus* model eventually became generalized to legal discussions
of issues other than a chief's relationships, as for example in the
following commentary upon the old text of the tract on fosterage, *Cáin
Íarraith*:

> the *gelfhine* in the direct line, as the father and son and
> grandson and great-grandson and great-great-grandson
> extending to five persons; and the *gelfhine* in the back line,
> that is, the father's brother and his son, to five persons
> again.[11]

Many of the legal passages that use the *truncus* model are quite late,
and I have suggested elsewhere that this model became popular with
Irish scribes when it became canonical in the late eleventh century
(Patterson 1990). Nevertheless, the model had antecedents in the Old
Irish period, for the tract *Fodla Fine*, displays the kind of social
formation to which the terminology of the *truncus* was later applied. In
FF, the lord (who seems to be represented as chief of the whole *tuath*),
had under him:

1. The landless *fuidri*.
2. His own kin.
3. *Gabail fodagniat* (no more information appears on these).

These were all designated members of the *flaith fine*, the chief's
kindred. *FF* gives few details as to the chief's *fuidri*, and it seems to be
immaterial whether these people were downwardly mobile (indebted or
otherwise disenfranchised) kinsmen, or drifters taken in from other
groups by the chief. From other sources it is known that they were
classified into many categories — as noted previously, those who had
kin verged on the lower reaches of clan land-holdership as base-clients.
This was not their *right*, however, but was contingent on the will of the
chief, whereas fully privileged kinsmen claimed shares of land by right
of inheritance. As the *fine* developed there would be tensions about

fuidri, as junior kinsmen claimed land, but seniors would want to retain demesne estates worked by *fuidri*.

The *fine* of the chief — his kin with claims to a share of the clan lands — was divided into 'four *fini*', just as was the case in regard to the circles of kin who radiated out from ego in the divisions of a personal kindred. The difference, however, was that in *FF* the chief was 'ego' (the reference point); genealogical distance from the chief signified lesser rights of inheritance within the clan estate. How this ranked kinship model was applied by the jurists will now be examined.

Kinship and rank

Since status and chieftaincy were determined by competition, political supremacy often had no inevitable dependence upon genealogical closeness to the line of recent chiefs. This fact could be disguised retroactively by genealogists and historians, who liked to make a successful king look like the heir in a straight line of father-son succession as far as possible, and also tried to make failed branches look like distant kin who should properly be claiming small estates on the far peripheries of the kingdom. But political realities had to be accommodated in the less ideological matter of the definition and description of the roles of important nobles and leaders within the *tuath*; as they did not inherit their positions directly, their roles could not be described in terms of kinship position. On the contrary, so politicized were kinship structures that the reverse held true: familial relations at different levels of society were assumed to be differentiated according to rank in the political system.

CG appears to have assumed a distribution of roles and statuses between kinsmen in a multi-generational devolved conical clan. I have delineated the conceptual plan of the tract as it seems to me, in *Fig.* 2. It will be noticed that I have amalgamated two positions, that of the *aire échta* (lord of vengeance) and *aire déso* (lord of clients), and that of the *ócaire* and the 'farmer who farms in tens' (*aithech ara-threiba a deich*, abbreviated to *a.t.d.*), because the tract provides little basis for distinguishing them. This interpretation of *CG*'s conceptual structure, while strictly hypothetical, was suggested by the general principle that powerful branches of families that temporarily lost the struggle for ascendancy were rewarded with another kind of recognized position of leadership, while sons too had to have some status and dignity during their father's occupancy of a position of leadership. The distribution of status in *CG* accords with the political realities of lineage competition as described by Ó Corráin: 'The office of *tánaise* or *rígdamna* was...an integral part of the system of segmentary opposition. It can be shown from the annals and genealogies that the *tánaise* was usually the leader of the most powerful segment out of power and his holding of the office of 'expected one' is, so to speak, an undertaking that he and his segment would get the next bite of the cherry.' (Ó Corráin 1972: 40).

Irish politics generally resolved into a struggle between two dominant factions, with third contenders getting eliminated as their followers lined up with one or other of the camps most likely to succeed (Ó Corráin 1972). *CG* clearly recognized and formalized this binary classification of status into 'incumbent', and 'possible incumbent', for one of the four considerations that ennobled any of the grades of lord was:

> ... his office in the *tuath*, including the position of leader or second in command, whichever of these offices (my emphasis).[12]

Here the tract uses *toísech*, leader/chief, to mean leadership at any of the levels of rank, for this statement in *CG* refers to the general attributes of all lords. Likewise, the position of *tánaiste* here refers to being second at any level of rank.

Competition extended even to the level of the *bóaires*:

> Whatever number of the divisions of the *bóaires* happens to be contending (for headship) though one of them be older than the others, the grade that is most venerable, as regards wealth, it is that takes precedence.[13]

This principle also applied to succession to abbacies, where the position of abbot was complemented by the *secundus abbas* (*secnab*), or *tánaise abbad* (K. Simms 1987: 54).

Basically, it seems that *CG* assumes that there would be in every family two generations and at least two descent lines competing for highest position at the family's rank-level. The high position could go to only one person, normally of the older generation, but competition determined which individual was successful. The system also recognized a 'second' level — thus we find named ranks for both a king's expected successor (*tánaise ríg*), and (in *UB*), an ordinary *bóaire*'s *tánaise bóaire*. Competition between the son of the incumbent and the strongest of the collaterals determined who in fact would play the role at any given time; thus there would not be two king's tanists at one time, but the position might well go from one collateral to another and then to a son of a king, all in one reign. For this reason, the terms for the secondary ranks tended to get used loosely for those who were regarded as eligible, likely or possible successors to the dominant position (K. Simms 1987: 53-9). In the case of royalty, there were usually too many of these for anyone's comfort.

To sum up: 'juniors' in the senior line held the same social position as seniors within the next most important junior line — 'junior' and 'senior' signifying greater and lesser power, and sometimes also age. I regard *CG* as carrying the ranking system all the way through clan land-holding ranks down from royalty to base-clients, because other aspects of social institutions (such as suretyship, hostageship, pledging, and even the formal aspects of base-clientship) had both their royal and their commoner forms, not only in *CG* but in other sources. On somewhat different grounds, other scholars have come to rather similar conclusions regarding the importance of complementary but unequal pairs of roles or 'offices' in the early Irish system of kinship and rank.[14]

As to the relationship between this model (as I have deduced it from *CG*) and actual social groups, I would expect that most royals would have fought to the death rather than be pushed down to *aithech* status within the *cenél*; further, that those who were degraded had their kinship ties expunged from recall. Nevertheless, the writers of the law-tracts seemed comfortable in assuming that related kin could belong to the ranks of the lords and commoners.[15] The notional distribution of rank and status in *CG* should be viewed as a *schema* for conceptualizing different levels of power in a long-established paramountcy. Where it may have come regularly close to reality was in small group relations — specifically, that personal kindreds at different levels of society were internally ranked according to the model. Discussion of this matter is resumed in the final chapter, where we examine the distribution of high office in the polity.

Kinship and territorial organization

Commoners appear at the far end of the clan spectrum in *CG* and other tracts on status, and in *Fodla Fine*. Social relations at this level of society were treated in the law tracts within a territorial frame of reference, for the purpose of organizing mutual liabilities between adjacent land-units. This was especially the case in seemingly late sources, emanating from a period when the kinship element in the relationship between petty land-holders and their lords was no longer emphasized. In this context the 'four *fini*' classification was imbued with a quite concrete numerical content that was even less related to genealogical structures than was the ranking system. The alignment of kinship to local territorial organization occurs in various contexts. One instance, deriving from the Old Irish stratum of kin occupying four adjacent lands (Patterson 1985). From late Gaelic Ulster comes a different kind of example of the application of the numbers associated with kinship classification to territorial units — the *trícha cét* system described previously. In this context, the lawyers seem to have treated sub-divisions of land as though they were subdivisions of a kinship group. How they refined these alignments is no longer apparent, but something along the lines set out below seems to have been assumed.

A territorial-kinship model was also used in the commentary to *BC*, where adjacent land-holdings of an agrarian community, *comaithches*, were treated as if they were the lands of a *gelfhine*, and the members' relations were also treated as if they were under obligations of kinship (see Fig. 3). The roots of this scheme lay in the fact that kin were generally neighbors, and most neighbors were often kin. But the blending of two types of social proximity in this model — the genealogical and the residential — served to put the obligations of neighborhood (*comaithches*) within the legal framework of obligations justified by ties of kinship, namely the collective liabilities for payment of wergeld and other obligations. The *comaithches*, as we saw in the last chapter, represents the fraying of clan structure at its peripheral margins, where insecure farming families in base-clientship barely held on to their lands, only to be displaced by the lords' preferred clients if they fell into debt and could not be redeemed by kin.

This survey, it is hoped, has illuminated more than the recesses of early medieval Irish academic thought about society, for casting a glance back at the different models, one may detect connections between them — a functional relationship within the juro-political system that shows that the lawyers were not simply indulging in play with legal forms when they used the 'four *fini*' terms in these

Fig 2. *KINSHIP AND RANK IN A PARAMOUNT ROYAL CLAN*
(based on CG)

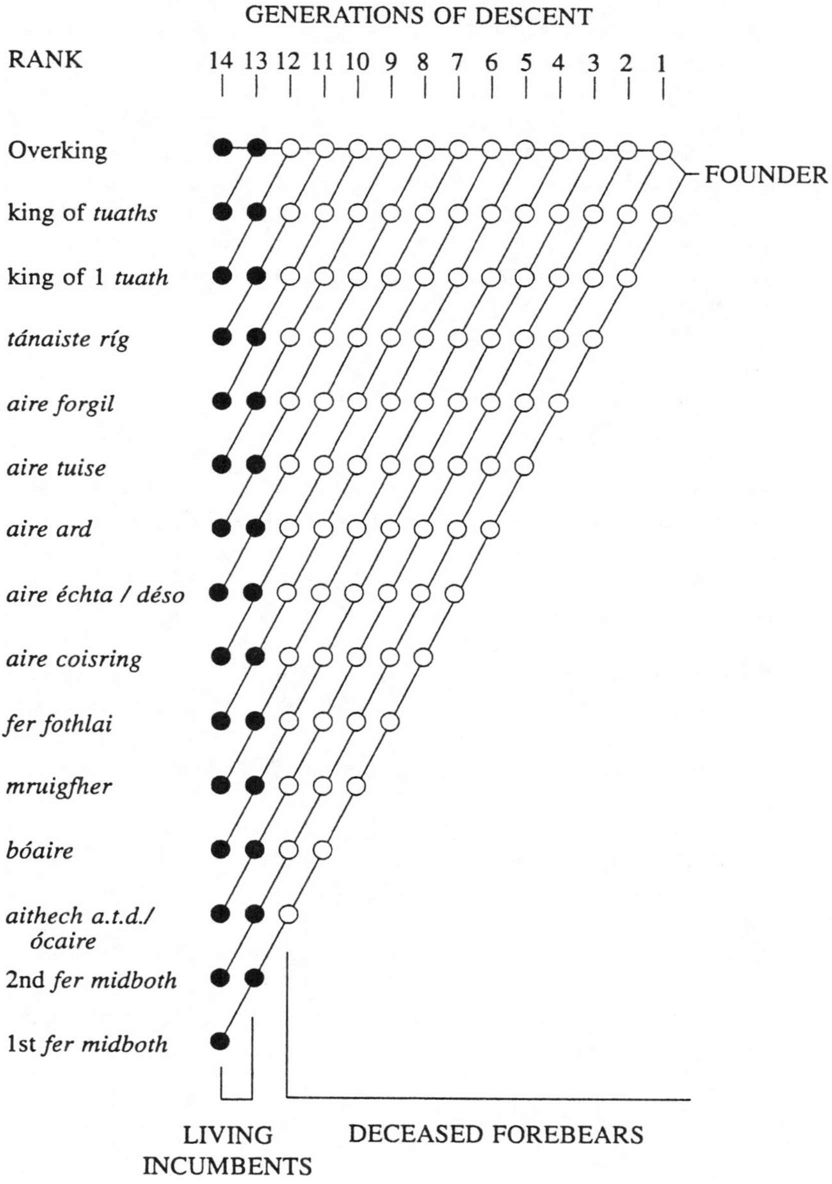

GENERATIONS OF DESCENT

RANK   14 13 12 11 10 9 8 7 6 5 4 3 2 1

Overking

FOUNDER

king of *tuaths*

king of 1 *tuath*

tánaiste ríg

aire forgil

aire tuise

aire ard

aire échta / déso

aire coisring

fer fothlai

mruigfher

bóaire

aithech a.t.d./
ócaire

2nd *fer midboth*

1st *fer midboth*

LIVING   DECEASED FOREBEARS
INCUMBENTS

divergent ways. The alignment of rank to kinship reflects the fact that the powerful dominated their kin. The genealogical calculus of the personal agnatic kindred was applied to measure degrees of liability for kin whose behavior had damaged the group. The territorial model describes social relations between kin who had slipped to the base of the clan structure and were interspersed with non-clansmen as neighbors and *comaithches* members — 'joint-tax-payers', cooperating in agriculture for the payment of renders and other services of base-clientship. Examples of the 'territorial model' of kinship are found in the law tracts in the context of problems of distributive justice, namely cases in which a number of neighbors wanted a share of some fixed resource — a bee-hive, a fruit-tree, or a water-mill. The lawyers treated the neighbors as if they were kin occupying adjacent lands.

Fig. 3 *Kinship classification and territorial divisions*

juniors (e.g. *ócaires*)	=	heads of the four family subdivisions (e.g. taths) of the plowland.
seniors (*bóaires?*)	=	the heads of 4 extended families in a townland.
4 *bóaires* + a surety	=	a quarter + a best bóaire = '5 men' of the *gelfhine*.
'9 men' of the *derbfhine*	=	a quarter + the next quarter + a senior as surety.
'13 men' of *íarfine*	=	as above + the next townland + plus one surety.
the *fine* of '17 men'	=	four quarters of the ballybetagh + the *aire coisring* (or equivalent).

Behind these various representations of kinship lay a straightforward concern — how to regulate and control the social groups whose produce and services were required by the élite. A kinship model was predominant, I have argued, because competitive lords had to permit 'rights of inheritance' to clients in order to retain their loyalty. Nevertheless, the existence of agnatic groups as an ideal type of organization in the eyes of the law would in no way have impeded colonization of depopulated areas on a piece-meal basis, nor the formation of associations which functionally substituted for kinship solidarity. Similarly, the dynamics of upper-class familial relations could hardly be described in terms of 'rules' of kinship, as Ó Corráin showed when he revealed the huge genealogical gaps between various successors to dynastic kingship (1971). It is because *actual* lineages were decimated by political competition and undermined by alternative sources of alliance and opportunity, that the *depiction* of kinship, attempting to keep at least half in touch with real goings-on, is so enormously complicated. Underneath this literary puzzle — a verbal equivalent of Celtic inter-lace — there lay some far less obscure social processes, however. We move on, then, to look at the details of social control in 'the *fine*'.

NOTES

1. Fox 1967: 164-74. See especially the discussion of the Kalmuk Mongol patrilineal personal kindred (pp 169-70).

2. '*do druthaib 7 meraib 7 dasachtaibh. (CIH 1276.18 ff)*. See Smith, 'Advice to Doidin': 68-72.

3. ...*ALTRUMA O MAITR*... (fosterage by mother-kin). (*CIH* 442.14-5). The literary characters Cú Chulainn and Bres were both sister's sons, fostered as children in the mother's group (see Ch. 11).

4. *CUMAL NAIRER*, 'the *cumal* of vengeance'. (*CIH 442.13-5*).

5. *GELFINE CO CUICER .... DERBFINE CO NONBOR (co nathgabail in cuicfhir na fini romaind) .... IARFINE CO TRI FERAIB DEC..(co. nathgabail na da fhine romaind) INDFINE CO .VII. FIRU DEC .... (co nathgabail na tri fini romaind). (CIH 429.27-430.18 = AL iv 283-5)*.

6. e.g. *dibad gelfine cobrannait na cetheora fine-so sis.* The four *fini* divide the property of an extinct *gelſhine.* (*CIH* 430.4. gloss 12).

7. See '*derggfine, dubſine, fine taccuir, glasfine*', etc. (*CIH 430.21-431.32 = AL iv 283 ff*).

8. e.g. *SEIL*: 137 (ii) (cf. *sese*, the 'sixth', who is excluded); SEIL: 144 (viii), *mad di cuicthe tormola* ('if it be a five-fold group that is destroyed'); *SEIL* 148 (xi) *muna cuic treba* ('unless [they maintain] five homesteads').

9.& *is doibh is digal fir derbhfine é do .u.er na gelfine.* (*CIH 2014.16 = AL iv 255. See similarly, CIH 744.8-14; 298.30-299.4; 2016.25-32; 1034.37-1035.5*).

10. '*7 do daercelib flatha no dia ngelfine a nathuigh forrtha, 7 do doermanchuibh eaculsa no dia ngelfine na hathuigh forrtha...*' (*CIH 1749.11-14 = AL ii 95.14-8*).

11. *in gilfine iar mbelaib, amail ata athair 7 mac 7 ua 7 iarmua 7 innua co .u.er, 7 geilfini iar culaib .i. brathair th' athar 7 mac co .u.er beos.* (*CIH* 1762.25-27). I cite O'Buachalla's translation (1947: 51-2).

12. *a dán i túaith, im dán toísig nó thánaisi, sechib dán di[i]b.* (*CG* 322-3).

13. *cidhbe d'foglaib boairech decma ima leth, cidh sine nach ae dibh arailiu, in gradh bes sruithiu .i. im tochus is é dofet.* (*CIH 1290.22-3 = AL iv 379*).

14. McLeod writes, 'Perhaps in the office of leader and of secondary leader we have two heads of authority ?' (1987: 52). O'Buachalla also configured Irish succession as based on the notional equality of the principal son of a chief and the principal collateral of the chief in his own generation (1947: 46).

15. *masa grad flatha is inbleogain do grad feine (CIH 366.12-3 = AL i 117.11-2*).

CHAPTER TEN

The Corporate *Fine*:
Control of Economic Behavior

Rank, we have seen, was tied to property, which was obtained in the first instance, through inheritance from the father and, to a lesser extent, the mother. Secondly, at various unpredictable points in the life cycle, individuals also inherited *díbad* — this was a collateral inheritance from heirless kin. Just as inheritance from the father was contingent upon filial behavior on the part of the son, so inheritance of *díbad* was contingent upon the individual's support of the kin group. Over and over again, the Irish laws tie these inheritance rights to the obligation of agnatic kin to band together in mutual economic and legal support, most especially in circumstances where wergeld was due for a member of the *fine:*

> Fines are shared after (the manner) of inheritance and
> wergeld. Inheritance and wergeld are divided after (the
> manner) of sharing fines.[1]

The interdependence of these claims, while 'fair', was by no means 'natural' behavior: it took compulsion from higher powers to enforce collective responsibility for *wergeld* and also to forestall seizure of *díbad* by those collaterals who happened to be resident near the deceased. The outcome of failure to pay wergeld would have been vengeance, falling possibly on innocent and distantly related people, if the culprit and his close kin ran away. On the other hand, without dependable support from kinsmen, a slayer would be inclined to do just that, for if taken in lieu of wergeld, as a *cimbid* — condemned person — his fate would have been death or slavery (Kelly 1988: 215). The rule making collateral inheritance of *díbad* contingent upon willingness to pay wergeld prevented those who might profit from their kinsman's disappearance into slavery from doing so. This rule not only promoted peace and proper 'brotherly' loyalty, the values upheld by the Church, but served the interests of the lay lords also who, as Keating explained, used entitlement to collateral inheritance of *díbad* as an inducement to their followers to remain in their lordship.

259

The personal agnatic kindred was invoked as a whole group — the 'seventeen men' — only to deal with wergeld or *díbad*. It was individual next of kin who enforced dutifulness on each other in other respects, such as care of dependents, economic responsibilities, and sexual restraint. Social control was complex: the right and duty to enforce proper behavior on others was divided between the next of kin (for example, a man vis-a-vis his brother, where both were free of paternal control) and individuals who had special authority in the situation in question. These might be voluntary warrantors in regard to certain contracts; ascriptive authorities, such as a father in relation to an unemancipated son, or a chief in relation to a base client; or individuals to whom special roles in the *tuath* were attributed. (Such 'offices' are discussed in Ch. 12.) All these were aspects of kinship organization, modified by rank; but the linchpin of kinship was the tie between inheritance of *díbad* and obligation to give wergeld support, for this supplied a positive inducement for kinsmen to stay together and cooperate across a broad spectrum of social behavior. For this reason we begin the analysis of the *fine* as an economic corporation by describing the inheritance of *fine* land under the rules of *díbad*, and the corresponding duty to share the burdens of wergeld payment.

Díbad and Cró

Fintiu was *fine* property which was conserved as such: it was only heritable by sons of *men* of the group. The outcome of such a restriction was to keep male heirs banded together as a residential group with a common perspective on local military and political affairs. *Fintiu* may have had physical characteristics, as is suggested by the following Old Irish passage on correct pounds for distrained animals:
level land, under the laws of the *tuath*, the homesteads of forefathers, excepting new *nemed* that have been ennobled by the *féni*.[2]
The glosses to this passage indicate that security and wealth were concentrated in these areas of
    'lands of father and grandfather'; here were no 'plunderers'
    or 'traders/purchasers'.[3]
Not all land was *fintiu*, for there are references in the old sources to the purchase of land, and to the endowment of women with land, either by the father or husband (see Ch. 11). It is reasonable, then, to think of

fintiu as sizeable blocks of good agricultural land, vested in the old families of the élite and their allies (the new *nemed* mentioned above; a new king or judge, according to a gloss[4]). As new estates, these would rapidly have become hereditary property, while the obligation to contribute to the military and jural functions of the *tuath* would also devolve through inheritance on subsequent occupants. Keeping *fintiu* together, as the land of a militarily capable group, was in the interests of these heirs and of their patrons.

Inheritance of *fintiu* normally proceeded from father to sons, but if a man died without sons his share reverted to his father for partition amongst his brothers; if there were no brothers it might be taken by a sister (who had to give sureties not to alienate it from the *fine*, however); if this family circle were deceased, the land would go to his uncles, each taking an equal share, with the sons dividing their father's share on his death. This is inheritance *per stirpes* (by descent lines) in the family. Imbalances in the family between land and heirs might readily arise, but unless the group grew as a whole, redistribution of usufruct through adoption, fosterage and cousin-marriage (described in Ch. 11) would often have relieved the ensuing tensions. Temporary imbalances were also offset by rental of land on the part of those awaiting inheritances, such as the ranks below the *bóaire* in *CG*.

In terms of inheritance, a legal boundary was drawn around the 'five men of the *gelfhine*', the first cousin group. If it died out as a whole, its property did not go exclusively to the nearest descent lines (the grandfather's brothers sons), to be shared by them *per stirpes*. Instead the property was treated as *tellach derlechta* ('derelict hearth'), which was subject to distribution amongst the 'seventeen men' of the four *fini*. Three-quarters of the heritage went to the *derbfhine*, three-quarters of the rest (3/16ths of total) to the *íarfine*, and the remaining 1/16th to the *indfhine*. These relatives were assembled and given shares, *per capita*. The sources that best describe this division are later commentaries, but the model which they use complements the more cryptic old Irish sources that also allude to inheritance of *fintiu*.[5]

Like inheritance of *fine* property, the Irish wergeld payment (*cró*, or *éraic*), was restricted to agnates and distributed according to the same method. Unlike the bilaterally distributed *díre*, honor-price, it consisted of a fixed penalty, regardless of rank or number of kin, and amounted to seven *cumals* — seven slave women — or twenty-one cows. Though universalized in principle, *éraic* was essentially a soldier's wergeld, for it was exacted by his lord no matter whether the man had kin in the land or not, and no matter what the birth of his father.[6] It is very likely that the wergeld of seven *cumals* was the rock-bottom payment, for references to actual payment in historical sources show huge herds of cows, or large tracts of land, changing hands to settle feuds amongst the élite.[7]

One of the main sources on wergeld (which was also Mac Néill's basis for his reconstruction of the four *fini* system), was the following passage, cited here in Mac Néill's translation. (I have emphasized aspects of the passage that are discussed below.)

Father and son in the first place, a half to them

exclusively. Father's brother and (his) son, they make a fresh division again to the extent of a half as long as anything remains. What remains over is then divided in three. One third to a brother, and what is still left is again divided in three. One third to the person who is nearest (of kin) to him (the deceased), *except that it goes by the number of 'heads of taking' (i.e. heads of branches)*[8] *and not by the number of heads of heirs* (my emphasis). And what remains over the thirds, that is when it has reached the grandfather backwards, howsoever little remains over the shares, goes *according to the number of heads of heirs* (my emphasis) up again in the opposite direction as far as father and son, and they come in, one like another, however small each man's share of it may be.[9]

The first step in the distribution, therefore, was that the wergeld was halved, then the remaining half halved again. Looked at from the point of view of the first category of heirs, as a whole, the victim/homicide's own *gelfhfine* of father and (own) son, and father's brother and his son, took three quarters. The remaining heirs got a quarter.[10] The rest of the wergeld was divided into three to be shared amongst kin beyond the *gelfhfine*. No details are given of the shares given to these further kin, except that the division was no longer *per stirpes* but *per capita* (see the underlined passages in the above translation). The extent of the whole group that participated is indicated elsewhere in the tract as extending to the 'nail kin', i.e. relatives who lay just beyond the boundary of the 'seventeen men' of the *fine*.[11]

The rules for wergeld thus generally correspond to those for inheritance of *díbad*; *ego*'s nearest kin (his *gelfhfine* in this case) took three quarters of the amount, distributing this *per stirpes*. Then the remaining quarter was subdivided, with the next class of collaterals taking the biggest share, dividing this on a *per capita* basis, as was done in the case of *díbad*. The need to provide for brothers (who were assumed to be alive in a case of wergeld settlement, but dead where *díbad* was involved), complicated the division of the last quarter, but yet it was divided into four (not quite even) parts. The sources on wergeld and on inheritance thus complement each other, as they are said to do by the law-tracts.

But despite the centrality of this distributive formula to *fine* structure, several aspects of the sources in which they appear suggest that they were not all purely indigenous secular customs. First, there is the reference to the 'nail kin'; this appears in an early clerical context, the *Old Irish Penitential*, as an aspect of the Roman cognatic method of calculating kinship (Bieler 1972: 271 V #2.7-8). ('Nail kin' in fact is a common expression in 'Germanic' kinship reckoning, which was bilateral, not patrilineal.) Secondly, the text cited above appears to be confused as to its kinship terminology, referring to the group of wergeld recipients as *'derbfhfine'* (which usually is understood to imply patrilineally related second-cousins only), but in fact attributing the obligation to participate in wergeld as far as 'nail kin' (fifth-cousins).

More telling, however, is that the distinction between *per stirpes* and *per capita* distribution corresponds in a rough but basic way to Roman laws of intestate succession. A principle of these, surviving from the Twelve Tables until the Empire, was:

> *Si intestatus moritur cui suus heres nec escit, adgnatus proximus familiam habeto. Si adgnatus nec escit, gentiles familiam habento.* If a man dies intestate to whom there is no *suus heres*, let the nearest agnate have the property. If there is no nearest agnate, let the members of the *gens* have the property. (Nicholas 1962: 247).

The *suus heres* (the first grade of heirs in the old law of the Twelve Tables) was the person or persons who inherited the whole social position of the deceased; if there was more than one (e.g. two siblings), they took aliquot shares *per stirpes*. In the absence of these, the nearest agnate, *proximus adgnatus*, succeeded; these shared the heritage *per capita*. (The rights of the *gens*, the further kin, were vague.) This basic distinction survived many changes in the Roman law of inheritance to emerge, modified, in the sixth-century Novels of Justinian (A.D. 543-

548). In this, the first class of heirs were descendants, but they were followed by a second class who also shared *per stirpes*, namely brothers and sisters of the deceased, and their children. Apart from its cognatic composition, this class of heirs corresponds to the Irish *gelfhfine*. Beyond this group, inheritance was *per capita* within the nearest grade of collaterals.

Though early medieval Irish lawyers apparently incorporated the Roman distinction between *per stirpes* inheritance within the *gelfhfine*, but *per capita* distribution among other kin,[12] they subordinated the foreign legal material to the overriding native cultural pattern. The Irish laws, for example, rejected both the cognatic element in Justinian's Novels, and the exclusion of distant collaterals by the nearest grade of kin. Obviously, then, this was no simple borrowing, but a purposeful evolution of law, the intention of which may be partly deduced from the implications of these rules: they sought to involve the largest number of *individuals* in the misadventures of *ego* by vesting residual heirship rights in these individuals.

The difference between a *per stirpes* and a *per capita* distribution boils down to the difference between letting the uncertainties of reproduction determine rights and duties, or fixing these so that everyone within the same kinship division had the same rights and duties. An example would be the wergeld obligation of the grandsons of two grandfathers in the *derbfhfine* category of relationship to *ego*; one old man might have only one grandson, the other many. Sharing *per stirpes* would unduly enrich the former where *díbad* was being shared, but unduly tax him where wergeld payment was concerned. The *per capita* rule must thus have been very helpful in mobilizing kinship relations for effective wergeld settlements, and it is probably for this reason that it became entrenched as a legal device for enforcing fraternal loyalty onto kinsmen who might otherwise have had little wish to be implicated in each other's affairs. Its introduction may have taken place between the writing of the two earliest sources (the poem on inheritance, published in *SEIL*, and *Fodla Fine*), i.e. in the later seventh century, for it appears only in the glosses to the former, whereas it is in the text of the latter.[13]

A final aspect of the laws on *cró* that suggest that these rules underwent modification during the middle ages is the comparison between the Irish rules on wergeld and those of the Norse *Baugatal*, 'ring-payment' for wergeld. A parallel to the Irish scheme for quartering the *cró* is found in *Gulathing* 223,[14] where it is shown that as in *Cró 7 Díbad*, there were three main heirs who shared the major part of the reparations (the *bauga*); the deceased's father and/or son, the father's brother's son, and the deceased's brother — the equivalent of coevals in the Irish *gelfhfine*. The division uses the same proportions as found in the *cró*: the Norse father/son received a half of the total, father's brother's son got a half of the other half (though he forfeited 1:20 to female kin), the remaining part went to the brother. Together then, the first grade of kin, *ego*'s father, son and brother took three-quarters, while the next grade (ego's father's brother's son) took a quarter. Provisions for further collaterals were different, since the Norse provisions included bilateral kin, in contrast to the patrilineal organization of the Irish *fine*.

These parallels are highly suggestive, for the Irish sources on wergeld are dated to the tenth or eleventh century (Greene 1973), and therefore stem from a time when interaction between Irish kings and the Vikings of Dublin was intense (Smyth: 1975/9). What is more, during the eleventh century, the Viking community of York, whose members were close kin and associates of those of Dublin, became involved in attempts to align the wergeld customs of different ethnic groups in the British Isles, under the leadership of Archbishop Wulfstan II of York (Whitelock 1981 V, IX, XII, XIII). The Irish sources, then, were written during a period when rationalization of wergeld customs was broadly underway in contiguous communities; given the convergence between *Cró 7 díbad* and *Baugatal*, it seems highly likely that these influences were operative in Ireland also. *Baugatal* is regarded by historians as an 'artificial' scheme, for there is no evidence of distribution of wergeld according to these provisions (Phillpotts 1913: 49-65, 72-3; Sawyer 1982: 44-5). In other words, like the Irish rules of *cró*, *Baugatal* was a deliberate attempt at manipulating customary social institutions, but is not less significant for that. On the contrary, the argument put forward here is that *cró 7 díbad* was also not a common 'folk' institution, but a juristic devices, which in the case of Ireland seem intended to induce people to cooperate in making reparations that would secure peace and salvage the political status of the local élite.

Since the Irish texts on *díbad* seem to be older than those on wergeld, and yet the later Irish sources on wergeld show a system of compensation well aligned to other medieval systems, it is possible that old rules were modified to fit in with the general rule amongst other ethnic groups according to which wergeld was divided into halves, quarters, eighths, etc. The extremely ambiguous nature of the oldest source on *díbad* (the poem published in *SEIL*), which is *compatible* with the later sources, but could also be interpreted in other ways, and the presence in the law-tracts of incredibly convoluted modifications of 'kinship rules' in conjunction with distributive schemes (Patterson 1985) show that a process of continuous reinterpretation and adjustment of basic jural forms was underway throughout the middle ages. But whatever the chronology of such adjustment — whether under later Viking influence or not — it is clear that *cró* was not a simple mechanism of self-help amongst people in an unregulated, feuding, and acephalous society. On the contrary, in *Cró 7 Díbad*, far more attention was given to the claims of kings, lords and posses, than to the claims of kin in the wergeld *(CIH 600.9-36)*.

Cró, then, was viewed as an indemnity which helped to establish peace at the highest levels of society. But it was at the lowest levels of society that loyalty had to be reliably enforced, or dynasties would crumble for want of support at the moment it was needed. As we have seen in regard to clientship and rank, there was great potential for fracture in alliances, as clients could realign themselves with new leaders. The first line of defence against loss of political support was the vesting of special privileges in a group capable of fighting for its patrimonial interests. *Fintiu* certainly constituted such a vested interest. In order to play the role of wergeld-payer, each member of the *fine* had to maintain his share of the patrimony. The role of patrimony as potential indemnity — the buffer that stood between a person and the danger of degradation to penal slavery — was explicitly recognized, as in the tract *Di Astud Chirt 7 Dligid* ('On the confirmation of right and law'), which states that a man, though still under his father's authority, could impugn the father's contract when the latter alienated property to the extent that the son's status was jeopardized. This included the alienation of 'choice chattels sufficient to redeem him from death'.[15] The connection between entitlement to *fintiu* and social protection against death in vendetta or slavery is also the theme of the *Saga of Fergus Mac Léti*, discussed below.

The inter-dependence of the *fine* group required that each individual act with economic and social prudence, or the wergeld would be unavailable for whichever of them needed it. This requirement gave rise to a system of restraints upon individual social action, which was implemented through the general rule that people could not alienate more than their honor-price in general social transactions. Thus kin were motivated to act as watchmen upon each other, and were legally empowered to veto each other's more dangerous transactions. This complex of norms was given clear articulation in passages such as the following excerpt from *Cáin Aicillne*:

> Every *fine* man has privileges as long as he preserves *fine* property, does not sell it, or alienate it, does not keep it private (i.e. prevent others from knowing what he's done with assets), or give it away to pay for offenses or contracts. He (the man in good standing with the *fine*) can impugn the contracts of his fellow *fine*-member, for whose offenses, fief-surety obligations, and contracts, he is liable, along with responsibility for his children, the (military) service for his lands, and support of the elderly of the *fine*.[16]

These restraints, which we shall now examine, served also to benefit the lords, not only because it was in their interest that feuds be settled through wergeld payments, but because fear of insolvency imparted to wealth a strong moral value; wealth came to be seen as socially generalisable protection, not merely something to be consumed while others suffered deprivation. Indeed, the most cogent statement of what amounts to the ideology of the *fine* comes from the clerically influenced (or written) tract, *CB (CIH 532.4-536.27)*, while similar statements about solvency and preservation of inheritance in *CA* and *CG* are accompanied by references to Biblical quotations as to Christian duties. In this social setting, there developed jural roles performed by those with adequate *folud* -means, or substance (Binchy 1976: 27-31). These roles further legitimized the differentiation of society, but also enforced certain norms of responsibility towards the community upon the wealthy — even if their wealth derived in large part from pillage of outside communities.

The functions of the corporate *fine* that are about to be described could have been performed by *fine* groups at any level of society that held land and were prosperous enough that their head was able to play the role of surety for kin. This restriction clearly excludes slaves and *fuidri*, who may have been quite numerous in some areas at some times. It should also be assumed that in all probability these controls did not apply within the kin groups of the dynastic royalty or even the upper nobility, whose relations were notoriously competitive and fratricidal, for though there existed cooperation and discipline within these groups too, élite males had a great deal of autonomy based on military capacity, and had to be reined in through military means, not the system of fines and deprivations that we are now about to examine. The élite probably operated at the level of the *cenél* of the *tuath*; the corporate *fini* were more likely to have been kinship groups controlling the middle levels of land-holding groups, i.e. the more locally embedded 'branches' of the *cenél*. The 'middle class' nature of the *fine* obligations described below, which are so concerned with regulation of mundane social transactions through suretyship, is well illustrated in the wisdom-tract, *'Advice to Doidin'*:

> Let not be surety for you a man who is too low or too high,
> for one is not able to constrain a person if he is too low.
> Anyone who is too high cannot be constrained. (Smith 1932:
> 77, #9).

Kin-liabilities and mutual surveillance

Every commoner with *fine* land was an involuntary surety (*inmlegon*; he who was 'milked out into'), for his immediate next of kin (Kelly 1988: 179-80). That is, where an individual defaulted on a loan, reneged on a contract, or was found guilty of a fineable offense and could not meet his liabilities, the plaintiff was permitted to take the coercive legal action of removing his cows — distraint — against the culprit's next of kin. The law permitted the innocent kinsman-surety a number of protections, such as an extension of the duration of the time between notice of the impending distraint and the action; this was twice the length of the interval permitted the actual debtor. Another qualification was that the liabilities of the *inmlegon* did not arise for every trivial obligation:

> And if he (the debtor) should have no calves, are the calves
> of his kindred taken instead? They are not taken, for ordinary
> oral contracts do not injure the kindred. (*BA* #47).

Nevertheless, every kinsman amongst the ranks of the commoners ran the risk of distraint of his animals under some circumstances. The principal context for such a fate was where the debtor had been accused of a serious crime, such as theft, arson, murder or rape, and had run away, or where he had defaulted in base-clientship. If the next of kin evaded their liabilities — for example, by hiding their animals in some remote glen (which was specifically forbidden in the passage from *CA*, cited above) — the liability passed on to the next circle of kin.

In the case of homicide, the obligation to help a slayer pay the wergeld was contingent upon the circumstances attendant upon the killing. If the slayer had acted with deliberation or with unusual carelessness, then the culprit himself bore the whole liability, even to the extent of being taken as a penal slave if his chattels were insufficient:

> In all cases of unnecessary crimes (deliberate or negligent) whether killing or not killing, his (the offender's) movables shall go first (to pay compensation) and himself afterwards. And if there is an excess (more to pay) this shall go upon the next hearth.[17]

This passage adds that the *fine* had the choice whether to hand him over and have his land to themselves, or whether they would give his land and retain the criminal as a *cimbid*, a man redeemed by his kin but enslaved by them.[18] Though late, this provision is in accord with the Old Irish story of Librán, a poor man who was redeemed by his rich kinsman but lost his freedom to him.[19] In this story, the redeemed man in fact ran away from the kinsman who had saved him, preferring the monastic life and penance to a life of slavery with a relative.

If the kin failed to bring the culprit to law, however, the guilt was transmitted in the following sequence to his relatives:

> (the liability) goes upon the chattels, living or dead (gloss: both land and chattels). As to him who has not these, his liabilities pass to his father (gloss: when he has no son, for if he has a son it is upon him it should go before his father ....) Where there is no father his liabilities go upon a brother and his *derbfhine* relations. If they have absconded so that they cannot be caught it goes upon his chief. If he has not (a chief), the liability passes to those who harbor him (those who provide bed, beasts — horses? — or refection). If the harborage (lit. 'bed') cannot be found, then the liability passes to the king. Hence the saying, 'every headless man to the king'. And so says the law of the *Féni* regarding any crime by any criminal.[20]

A late commentary on the fragmentary text of the tract, '*On the judgment of every crime*', goes on to say that no matter how many of the *fine* had absconded, the liability would pass as an undivided whole to 'the next hearth', and was not be divided (like wergeld) amongst the brothers and cousins of the *gelfhine*.[21] Liability for an absconding culprit was a serialized one, no matter what the nature of the offense.

In addition to bearing this responsibility for mutual surveillance, the *fine* was obliged to assist an individual who had committed an offense under legally mitigating circumstances (*deithbirse téchtae*: Kelly 1988: 97). In this case, the offender paid to the extent of his resources, but the *fine* paid the outstanding amount in the same manner as they shared *cró* and *díbad (CIH 2012.9-12 = AL iv 245.18-25)*. It was, then, only in those cases where the offender had committed an unjustified act *and* was able to pay for it, or stayed around and let himself be taken as a *cimbid*, that the kin were free of liability. If he ran away, or if the offense was serious but mitigated in some way, they were liable to help him redeem himself. In most cases the liability was serialized; that is, the next of kin had to exhaust their resources before the further next of kin became involved. Only in the case of mitigated homicide (and possibly other very serious offenses, also mitigated) did the entire *fine* share the burden. Even then, three quarters of the payment fell on the *gelfhine*.

Most of the evidence cited above is from late commentaries, but with the exception of the rules about mitigation, these fill out the terse statements of the old text. Certainly, the basic rule that the *fine* was liable for the debts of an offender who ran away is found in the old text.[22] Moreover, the Old Irish tract on suretyship, *Berrad Airechta*, shows that as in the case of kinsmen's liabilities, obligations of suretyship were also arranged as a circle of social relations of mutual compulsion, radiating out from the most immediately liable surety to the next one. Suretyship responsibilities, then, were *serialized*, not collectivized, in much the same manner as kin-liability. It is thus likely that from the time of *BA*, at least, sanctions were generally structured in such a way that those with the best opportunity to catch the offender (co-residential next-of-kin) and the least desire to see him caught or part with his chattels (their potential inheritance) were impelled to seize him by the next grade of kin beyond *them*, who would fear that the liability might devolve upon them.

The weakness in this system of sanctions was that the kin might *all* run away rather than surrender substantial amounts of livestock. Alternatively, they might fail to satisfy a kinsman's legitimate claims for wergeld assistance on grounds of poverty (hiding their animals, as

CB hints), and surrender him as a *cimbid*. Two safeguards were in place against these dangers. One was that the *fine* as a whole was meshed into the wider society through mechanisms of formal representation, described in Ch. 12. These consisted of pledges, given by *fine* representatives, that the group would uphold the regulations of the *tuath*. Secondly, there seem to have been restraints upon the *fine*'s power to turn over a kinsman as a penal slave; for example, a son still living under his father's control had the right to impugn contracts that alienated 'choice chattels sufficient to redeem him from death' (see Ch. 7). Proverbs state that 'a man is nobler than *díbad*', and 'better a man than land'.[23] This sparse information suggests that there existed mechanisms which protected weaker members of the kindred from being abandoned to slavery by their kin on pretexts of inability to pay the requisite fines. Again, these mechanisms are to be sought in the political organization of the *tuath* or local polity, and the way in which *fine* groups articulated with the wider community, as described later.

Control of expenditure

Loss of property was considered demeaning and disloyal to the *fine*, whether it resulted from criminal liabilities, or from making a poor agricultural bargain. Restrictions were placed on the amount that individuals could put at risk in their life-time, and the amount they could alienate from their *fine* at death. The fullest articulation of these restrictions is found in *Córus Bescnai*, where the author outlines the extent of individuals' rights to make bequests of land to the Church in return for *goire*, care, and spiritual salvation. As to transactions during life, the amount was set at the level of the person's *honor-price*. Those who had lost this amount lost their economic and social autonomy, while those who added to it acquired increased independence. The basic doctrine, cited below,[24] was summarized under the rubric that there were three types of holder of inherited land; one who relinquished and did not acquire more land, one who neither diminished nor added to his patrimony, and one who did not diminish his patrimony, but increased it:[25]

> The *comorba* (heir to *fintiu*) who preserves (*fintiu*) and the
> *comorba* who increases (*fintiu*) are similar with respect to the
> land of their fathers and grandfathers, but the difference

between them consists in their taking land outside. The *comarba* who has acquired a little may give out that little without asking permission if it be a case of little necessity (commentary: to buy a cow), and he gives more along with it in case of great necessity (commentary: a dearth), up to one third of (his) *fine* share. The *comarba* who has acquired little and who gives it without necessity, without asking permission, has it (his gift or contract) set aside, and he shall not give anything afterwards.[26]

In the interests of the Church, *CB* adds:

The *comarba* who takes without necessity cannot make a grant. If there be necessity however, he may give the value of his honor-price out of the *fine*'s third (part) to a church. The *comarba* who preserves (his inheritance) and the *comarba* who increases, may each of them give his honor-price out of the *fine*'s third part to the Church.[27]

Although this passage does not expressly prohibit individuals from risking more than their honor-price in ordinary transactions, it is clear that if they did and if they then lost cattle or land, they became a '*comarba* who gives out' — a clansman who was a loser, who required permission for his future transactions.[28] Honor-price, then, served as the marker of how a person stood in the eyes of his fellow agnates: it went up when a man strengthened the economy of the group and went down when he weakened it. The interdependence of the localized lineage's members is summarized thus:

... it is the same as if the *fine* had become extinct when it does not attend to its duties. It is one of the duties of the *fine* to support every *fine* man, and the *fine* does this when it is in its proper condition. The proper duties (of the individual) towards the *fine* are that when he has not bought he should not sell: that he does not wound: nor desire to wound or betray: although he be not wise, that his folly be not taxed (i.e. cause debts or fines), although he be not wealthy, but that he be not a plunderer of the *fine* or land. Every one is *trebar* (solvent) who keeps the *fine* land perfectly as he got it, who does not leave greater debt on it than he found on it.[29]

In addition to these restrictions, even the individual who had obtained private property, *tarcud fadessin*, was restrained from giving it all away as a death-bed bequest to the Church:

> It is lawful for the *bóaire* to make a bequest to the value of seven *cumals* out of the acquisitions of his own hand, but only if he leaves two-thirds of his acquired property to his *fine* ...[30]

Elsewhere, it is said that the property of a dying man could be legitimately divided in three, between his sons, the head of his *fine*, and the Church.[31] Two parts, then, went to his kin, and only one third could be alienated as a personal bequest. This division had ecclesiastical affinities elsewhere,[32] but it was rationalized in a thoroughly native, or at least Hibernicized manner, in terms of a doctrine which held that ownership of any item that was to be divided could be allocated to the providers of three factors of production: (i) the land, (2) the 'original stock' (in the case of animal produce) or the seed (in the case of grain produce) and (3) the labor.[33] It is very likely that the one-third of his property that a *bóaire* could alienate in a bequest, corresponded to the 'laborer's third', because the passage refers to the 'produce of his own hand'. Moreover, where the man's property had been augmented by rent for his land, or payment for his professional skills, the *fine*'s share was reduced, since their contribution was less.[34]

Just as an individual's *lóg imna* (the legitimate amount he could bequeath) constituted a third of his inherited assets (attributed to the value of this labor), so it seems that the *lóg n-enech*, honor-price, was also calculated by means of this tripartite division of shares in inherited property. But honor-price seems to have amounted to one third of his personal holding of livestock, whereas the bequest was a third of total assets, including land. A *bóaire's* legitimate bequest, for example was set at seven *cumals* in *CB*, which was one third of the land of the upper level farmer, *mruigfher* in *CG* (172), whose attributes are those of the standard *bóaire* in other tracts.[35] This is far higher than the honor-price of this rank.

In *CG* the honor-price of the *bóaire* was five *séts*, which in this text represented four milch cows: this amounted to one third of his dairy herd of twelve milch cows (*CG* 160-1; 157-8). Similarly, the *ócaire*'s honor-price was three *séts* (*CG* 120-1), or two cows and two-fifths of a cow (a beast worth less than a heifer).[36] This was very nearly one third of his own dairy herd, which was supposed to consist of seven milch cows (*CG* 90). Finally, the rank between the *bóaire* and *ócaire* had an honor-price equal to 3.6 cows, and a herd of ten cows. Since *CG* states that the commoners derived their honor-price from cows, it is apparent that the amount of each rank's honor-price was derived from the 'laborer's third' part of the value of the dairy stock that people of this rank had received from their *fine*. The kin group in turn retained the right to veto the individual's alienation of the remainder on grounds that they had provided the land that fed the stock, and the parent stock of the individual's cattle.

The Irish honor-price, then, represented simultaneously the degree of individual autonomy, and the economic inter-dependence of the individual with the *fine*. For this reason it is frequently said in the Old Irish law tracts:

> whatever takes away from a person's means or wealth takes away from his status and honor-price.[37]

Control of clientship

The general restrictions outlined above were buttressed by more specific ones, notably restraints on clientship contracts. The *fine*'s interests were involved in individual clientship contracts in that an acknowledged contract implicated them in liabilities for the defaulting client's renders. Naturally, then, everyone was anxious that his agnates did not exceed their productive capacity in what they promised to a lord. It was also important for individual contracts to be orchestrated so that one man would not bring more of his lord's cattle on the pasture than his due share. If he did, animals belonging to other *fine* members, and other lords, would suffer. The other danger was political: client lineages had to consider whether their various relationships with lords were compatible with each other. As a general rule of thumb, the main source on base clientship, *Cáin Aicillne*, stated that *all* contracts were valid when contracted with next of kin:

> Every work-arrangement (gloss: regarding pigs), every reward, every purchase, every sale, every economic contract, every social contract, every free clientship, every base-clientship, every contract of service, (is with) the nearest of kin in the *fine* ...[38]

The fief taken within the *fine* was distinguished from both free or base clientship. It was contrasted, along with several other relationships based on a gift of a fief, to free-clientship, thus implying that a fief in the *fine* would be long-term and not subject to rapid retrieval.[39] It is not clear what conditions were attached to such a fief, but they were probably less onerous than base-clientship, for according to the commentaries on *Fodla Fine*, base-clientship within the *fine* was reserved for marginal relatives, such a illegitimate sons fathered by lords upon women serfs. It is also noticeable that the upwardly mobile fief-giving 'lords' that occupied a status-niche between the peasantry and the nobility (e.g. the *fer fothlai*), and who would have been most likely to give fiefs to close kinsmen, were not entitled to the full *somoíne* (profits) of the fief. As for men of about the same rank, the 'loan of one commoner to another' received no legal sanction as a form of fief. As far as the ranks of the common *féni* were concerned, the general tenor of the law was that kinsmen were to support each other, not achieve prominence at each other's expense:

> The *fine* can mutually impugn (contracts) amongst themselves, mutually impugn (outside), they mutually swear oaths, they help each other, they support each other.[40]

At the same time, where the *fineráth* (kin-fief) was given by a genuine lord, it offered him certain protections, which again tended to promote the general solidarity of the *fine*:

> If a lord has a client who is good, who has 'original possessions' (heritage), and is of the native landowning *fine*, as a free client, this lord is able to remove (other) chiefs (i.e. send back their cattle-fiefs) ...[41]

Conversely, a lord had prior claims to the clientship contracts of his own *fine*, and could undercut unrelated lords who had placed cattle with his lower-rank kin. That is, if he could induce the client to abandon the other lord, the client was fined only a third of the honor-price of the rejected chief, as compared with the full honor-price due in the absence of such an excuse.[42] The other fines stood, however, i.e. double-restitution of the fief, to offset the inconvenience of terminating the contract prematurely; the rule, then, merely expresses a sense that it was dishonorable for men to align themselves outside the *fine*, rather than providing serious sanctions against the latter. Given the fluidity of Irish political relations inter-*fine* multiple clientship relations must have been commonplace.

The *fine*'s legal rights to repudiate clientship contracts are set forth in a commentary to *CA*:

> This fief is received by the tenant either with or without the knowledge of the *fine*, for if it was unknown to them they could impugn his contracts: but if it was with their knowledge, though the fief be ever so great it (the liabilities for the render) is fastened on them ... (If) ... they know the fief was received and do not know the amount of the fief ... and they were going to oppose it to the extent of their knowledge (*aititu*: recognition, or what they thought to be the case) there is fastened upon them that stock which the book mentions.[43]

In other words, if *fine* members claimed that they had intended to repudiate the deal, but had not done so because they said they did not know how much their relative had received, their excuse was not acceptable, but the lord on the other hand could not claim renders beyond the amount due for the proper 'stinted' fief — that which 'the book mentions'. It was the *fine*'s responsibility to discover the character of each member's contract, and warn the lord if they were going to return the cattle, and then do so promptly:

> warning (of the voiding of the contract) without returning (of the fief) incurs restitution.[44]

The implementation of these restrictions upon individual initiatives could be undertaken both by peers and by the *fine* chief. Interference by peers was usually undertaken by next of kin, as these were immediately liable for damages, and also normally in the best position to observe an individual:

> Every *fine* man ... is able to impugn the contracts of his kinsman for whose crimes and securities and contracts, fosterage liabilities (i.e. care of his orphans) and land-deeds (*gnimu orba* (commentary: *fuba* and *ruba*, i.e. military services), with support of old people that is due for *fintiu*, he is liable. (see n. 16 above)

These rights of restraint applied not only to base-clientship contracts, which threatened the pasture of the *fine*, but to free clientship contracts, which threatened its political character. The man who took a fief in free clientship without *fine* permission was punished by being obliged to repay under the terms of base-clientship.[45]

Obligations of the fine

Ideally, dependents were cared for by those who stood to inherit their share of property, either through filiation, adoption, or a contract for care which a man might make with a daughter. There was, however, a general obligation to care for helpless members of the *fine* where these people did not have enough wealth to compensate for the amount of care they would need.

The feeding and attendance of those who could no longer produce anything was regarded as a heavy burden: a man whose wife became an invalid was entitled to 'send her back if there is anyone to whom she may be sent' (*CIH 7.36-8.5 = AL v 145. 17-23*). (Otherwise he was bound to care for her, though he could take another wife to help him.) Productivity was so valued that kin could sue not only for the cost of the care of an injured person, but for replacement of the labor lost when a member of the household was bed-ridden from injury. A spouse could even sue for reparations for sexual deprivation occasioned by the episode; a woman, for example, could make oath as to how many periods of fertility had been wasted due to her husband's absence, and obtain damages according to the number of missed opportunities to conceive (*Bretha Crólige*: 102 ff). To be unproductive may have been unbearable for many in this society, and it is possible that in the story of the virtual suicide of the old grandfather, Ileach (Ch. 8), there is a reflection of idealized suicide by the elderly who had become a burden, as found amongst some circum-Polar Arctic cultures.

The Church, however, was deeply opposed to suicide on any grounds other than insanity,[46] and thus it is not surprising to find in the clerically inspired *Córus Bescnai* the fullest statements concerning the *fine*'s obligation to care for burdensome but deserving members. This duty was imposed first on the nearest of kin, who was penalized by loss of status if he or she failed to perform the expected duty. The *fine* itself, if it did not compel the liable person, or find some other way to care for the dependent, was under threat of being treated as 'extinct':

> ... it is the same as if the *fine* had become extinct when it
> does not attend to its duties. It is one of the duties of the *fine*
> to support every *fine* man, and the *fine* does this when it is
> in its proper condition.[47]

This must mean that their inheritance rights to communal heritage, *díbad*, would be suspended, along with claims to support for wergeld payments, while their own members' share of land would pass not to next of kin, but to the wider community as *díbad*. This passage appears in *CB* where the tract asserts the right of a church that had undertaken *goire* (sustenance and care) to have usufruct of the land of the dependent person, up to a third of the purchase-value of the land. (I have not found evidence, however, that the Church was prepared to care for the insane.) Since the Church was broadly concerned with the care of the sick, indigent and outcast, its intervention as surrogate kin — at a price to the *fine* — must have strengthened the sanctions upon correct behavior in kin relations by setting up competing claims to inheritance from neglected people. Below, where we examine the various offices by means of which authority was exerted in the public community, the *tuath*, it is shown that a *fine* group might (or should) have a jural representative, the *aire coisring*. One of his duties was to give a pledge on behalf of the *fine* to the synod as well as the *tuath* and king, to guarantee the lawful behavior of *fine* members. This shows that there was, in theory, a formal arena in which dereliction of duty towards dependents could be assessed and punished.

The image of the Irish Church as monastic may perhaps have diminished awareness of the degree of social influence exercised by the early Church. The literary record is now interpreted as showing far more cultural interaction between the secular and clerical literary networks than had hitherto been emphasized. But the early Church may also have performed many of the pastoral roles undertaken by diocesan churches in Europe. At any rate, an Old Irish passage from the law tract, *Do fastad cirt 7 dligid* states that every *fine* should have three men who perform legal functions on their behalf: one was a *conn*, a person of full legal capacity who could speak on their behalf; the second was a church which 'sustains' them; the third was a lord (*flaith*) who (according to the commentary) gave them fiefs of base-clientship and gave oath on their behalf that they would comply with the laws of the territory.[48]

Perhaps the most burdensome obligation of the *fine* was the care of the mentally ill or handicapped. Kin were expected to tie up the violently insane, but were not liable for the annoying but less lethal behavior of simpletons who, for example, threw stones at people (Kelly 1988: 92). The neighbors were expected to avoid the missiles and were not entitled to press legal claims if they got hit. As to the feeding, grooming and protection of the incompetent, kin were pressured into providing care by threat of fines and loss of land:

> at five *séts* has been fixed the fine for non-maintenance of every (type of) fool among the *féni*; with withholding of land from those who do not perform the maintenance; at ten *sets* has been fixed the fine for non-maintenance of every madwoman. The fine for non-maintenance of the latter is greater because no land supports her. Every fool who has no land has equal fine for non-maintenance with a madwoman. (Smith 1932: 68-72; *CIH* 1276.17 ff.)

'Withholding of land' was accomplished by carving out a man's share of *fintiu* on behalf of a madman and assigning it to sureties during his lifetime. The sureties were presumably the ones who would exact the fine in case of neglect and would bear witness as to the care that had been provided when the individual died and the land was to be assigned to heirs. In addition to these pressures, the king played a role in defending the insane, having an obligation to exact two-thirds of *díre* fine for injury to him or her, and assuming some responsibility for the recuperation of an injured 'fool' through the provisions of sick-maintenance (*ibid*: 70).

The *fine*, though broadly mutually responsible, had recognized limitations; not only could it formally repudiate incorrigibles at the local assembly when the grounds were sufficient, but certain categories of mentally incompetent or abnormal people were absorbed into the retinues of kings and nobles as entertainers, thus removing them from the local community and placing them in the more controlled environment of an armed retinue, where they could not do much harm, nor implicate their kin in their deeds. This solution seems likely to have been part of a pre-Christian social response to deviance. A more sinister aspect of this response was the disposal of incompetents outside the territory. In *Míadshlechta* one type of half-wit is described as someone fit only 'to go as a captive (*cimbid*) on behalf of the *tuath*'.[49] The penal captive could be kept in slavery, executed, or subjected to any conceivable fate; the feeble-minded who were handed over to vengeful enemies across the border could only have served as objects of hatred.

The early Irish church disapproved of slavery[50] and the maintenance of the mentally abnormal as entertainers, and seems to have been involved with the regulation of wergeld payment. It is possible that the great emphasis in *CB* and other law tracts, especially

CA, upon the *fine*'s duty to retain and care for its less valuable members, rather than selling them into slavery to settle feuds or alleviate poverty, constituted a new social pressure as society made the transition during the early middle ages to the classic Gaelic clan system. The purely materialistic and militaristic composition of the clans acquired a dimension of social altruism that would otherwise have received no formal sanction from any organized force in medieval Irish society. Though it is possible, as some scholars would stress, that such altruistic values were survivals from a pre-Christian past, it is still the case that only the Church had the power and authority to insist on these values in the early middle ages, doing so from the stand-point of a world-view that imparted a distinct meaning to charity within its own religious code. Charity required resources, *folud*, no less than did clientship, and so churchmen and lords converged in agreement upon the necessity for social groups to preserve their assets. Along with this economic discipline went sexual control, as we see in the next chapter. Here again Christian teaching was remarkably adaptable to the social requirement of the religious and lay *élite* that their followers and supporters conserve the economic base of the corporate groups that policed everyone's behavior.

Common property of the *fine*

In addition to nucleal agrarian land allocated to individual families and heirs, and common waste of all kinds, the resources of the *fine* included a number of indivisible assets. Many of these were listed in the tract on distraint, in conjunction with cases where the plaintiff was entitled to proceed with the distraint after a delay of only one day; the cases seem mostly to have involved distraint by one *fine* member of another for failing to perform a labor duty in regard to the common property. These are mentioned as a group in the Old Irish text as 'judgments about woods, judgment about the *fine*, water judgments (and) sea judgments'.[51]

These old tracts are lost, but commentaries shed a little light on their subject matter. They hint at interaction in activities that were not part of the mundane routine of subsistence farming, for which, it seems, most households were self-sufficient in labor. According to the commentaries, 'water judgments' concerned 'the rules of fishing nets', 'his share in the common net of the *fine*' (*CIH 369.9; 369.12-4 = AL i 131.1-3*); the problem envisaged here is that one kinsman had left his share of work at the fishing net (making or using it?) to another, who could distrain him of property almost at once, as a sanction against his laziness. 'Judgments of the *fine*' referred (in these glosses) to 'the common fort of the *fine*'; again, one kinsman could distrain another in regard to work that he had failed to do (*CIH 369.35-6 = AL i 131.38-9*). 'Wood judgments' concerned turbary rights: the *fine* is envisaged as building a bridge for the group's collective use from wood that was not normally to be used — the *nemed* wood near the fort (*CIH 1683.27-30 = AL i 135.26-35*). 'Sea judgments' dealt with various rights and duties vested in the *fine* who held shore-land, including the obligation to salvage wrecks, rescue the shipwrecked, take in beached whales, feed and protect arrivals by sea, and guard against marauders (*CIH 888.10-4 = AL i 129.25-31*). The *fine* also might own a 'common captive' (*CIH 372.19-20 = AL i 137.21-2*) or 'common *fuidir*', towards whom every *fine* member had a duty to ensure that he was not unlawfully seized by another on the pretext of distraint (*CIH 373.17-20 = AL i 139.30-33*). Propertyless individuals were distrained in person and fettered until ransomed by their lords (*CIH 363.23-8 = AL i 105.39-107.5*); in labor-hungry early Ireland a *fuidir* was a tempting target for unfounded distraint. The commentaries add other items to the list of common property, including a common barn, a common haggard and a common mill (*CIH 374.14-375.3 = AL i 141.11 ff*).

Other sources confirm that major fixed resources were held in common by groups that either were *fine* or *comaithches* groups. Usufructuary rights in woods, bee-hives, and water-mills were all modelled upon the distribution amongst agnatic kin of shares in wergeld and inheritance, as described above.[52] In other words, the main owner(s) took three quarters of the use or produce, their next of kin or nearest neighbors took three quarters of the remainder, the following category got three quarters of what was left, while the fourth category got next to nothing (one sixty-fourth part).

These common properties of the *fine* should not distract from awareness of the implications of clan and *fine* stratification, however. The clan chief had rights in poor clansmen, but they had only duties towards these common assets, from which at most they derived a small personal usufruct. The Irish distributive tracts that depict the allocation of shares in mills, fruit trees and bee-hives, in fact assume the presence of stratified kin-groups as their model, for the more 'distant' claimants received only almost worthless shares in the enterprise, while the 'inner' group took three-quarters of the total. Control was thus vested in a narrow segment of the *fine*, in all cases (except, for stylistic reasons, the water-mill [Patterson 1985: 60-65]) called the *gelfhine*. As we have seen, the chief of the *fine* came eventually to be termed the lord of the *gelfhine* ('*flaith gelfhine*'). Thus, while the restrictions on individual economic autonomy that have been described in this chapter *could* have been imposed by next of kin upon each other in small, genealogically close, kin groups (for the laws supported such interference regardless of the size of the kin group), the social origins of this system of constraint must be attributed to the pressures emanating from the élite, who were capable of destroying the integrity of small, weak clans by occasioning debt and seizing lands as restitution. The élite itself tended to reproduce and recruit low-status adherents in such a way that their own social groups tended to become stratified corporate *fine* groups. The reproduction of privilege and disadvantage within the *fine*, and society as a whole, is the next aspect of clan society to be examined.

Notes

1. *Confogluigther cion iar ndibud 7 croaib. confodlaither dibad 7 croidibh iar cintaibh. (CIH 1142.1-2; 1315.20 ff; 1926.3 ff.)*

2. *MIN TIRE COMINNULL TUAITHE TEALLUIGIB SEANAITHRE CINMOTHA NUANEIME RONUAISLIGTHUR. (CIH 1726.29-30 = AL ii 1332 ff.)* See also *CIH 1457.1; 1959.10.* I translate *cominull* after *DIL, comindell*, 'regulation of the territory'. The gloss to *CIH 1726.29 2*, adds *meodun na tuaithe*, 'middle of the *túath*'.

3. *no arna bet foghlada no cennaig. (CIH 1726.32 = AL ii 15.1.)*

4. *ri 7 fili. (CIH 1726.33 = AL ii 15.3-4.)*

5. See Dillon's remarks in *SEIL*: 146-7, citing *CIH 298.27-299.19*. See also *CIH 744.4-7, 8-10; 2016.22-39; 1034.34-1035.5*. The division of *díbad* is discussed in Patterson (1990).

6. *CIH 600.9-36.* See Binchy (1941: 86) on *éraic*.

7. Kelly (1988: 126 n.9), notes that in 1400, 126 cows were paid for the accidental killing of one of the learned family, Ó Maolchonaire. See Lucas (1989: 230-1) for further examples.

8. Mac Néill gives this translation for *linn cend ngabul*, which corresponds to *lin ngabul* in *SEIL* 137 [ii a], lines 5-6, translated by Dillon as 'number of branches'. The latter translation is preferable, since 'heads of taking' makes little sense in the context of descent group relations.

9. *athair 7 mac cétamus, leth doibh dinaisc. brathair: athair 7 mac rainnait aithraind atherrugh co leth ineth dohurrtét ann; a ndohurrtét ann iaram ranntair i tri; trian do brathair (?), 7 ranntar a mbis ann beus i tri; a trian dondi bes nesam do iarsan urd cedna, (ocu)s is i lín cenn ngabal tét 7 ni i lin cend comorbae; 7 a ndourrtét ann fa deoidh forsna treinibh .i. in tan rosaigh senathair for culo, a mbec dourrtét ann for rannaibh tét i lin cend comorbae suas aris i frithrusc corice aithir 7 mac, 7 tiagait ind amal cach cid bec cuit caich dibh de (CIH 600.39-601.6*; Mac Néill 1921: 119-20.9.)

10. Both this tract and *CIH* 742.4-9 provide for the brothers of the deceased out of the quarter assigned to further kin. The brother had been postponed by ego's son, but could not be merged with his father if he were an adult.

11. *Ocus an trian rosaigh in derb.f., cinnus ranntar? .ni., r. ótha athair 7 mac co senathair for culo, 7 frithrusc a frithisi coruici ingen ar meraibh ... (CIH 600.37-38 ff.)* 'And the third that the *derbfhine* has attained, how is it divided? The answer is certain. It is divided from father and son (of the deceased) backwards to grandfather, and in the opposite direction back again to *ingin-ar-meraibh* ...' (Mac Néill 1921: 119). *Derbfhine* is here used non-diacritically, signifying all agnates as far as 'nail kin'.

12. Dillon and Binchy identified the Roman origin of the Irish distinction between *per stirpes* and *per capita* inheritance, but did not consider its significance. (*SEIL*: 138, n. 2).

13. *DERBFINE CO NONBOR NI DABA HUAIDE COBRAIND FO LIN CENN COMOCUIS. derbfhine* to nine men. Their *díbad* is not divided according to the number of equally close kinsmen. *(CIH 430.5 = AL iv 285.4-6.)*

14. Seebohm 1902: 238-260. See also Phillpotts 1913.

15. *ATAIT .III. CUIR TINDTAI MAC BEOATHAR IMA ATHAIR, NACH AIRMEAD LIUBAIR NA FEINE ... FORGO SET AS TUALING GILL DE FRI BAS DO SANNAD. (CIH 227.7-10 = AL v 437.)*

16. *IS MESECH CACH FER FINE CONAE A FINTIU NADI REN* ... etc. *(CIH 489.8-33 = AL ii 283.7 ff;* Thurneysen 1925b: 370-71, # 33.*)* My translation is based on Thurneysen's, who points out that the reference to the care of the elderly is grammatically obscure, but the duty of *goire*, which normally devolved on direct heirs would, in the logic of *fine* relations pass to those who would inherit *díbad* from an heirless man who had failed to adopt a son or daughter. The obligations for land (*gnima orba* — literally 'land deeds', action on behalf of land) are explained in the gloss as referring to military duties. *Gnim* ('action'), often referred to military/coercive acts, for example a king's *fer gnia* was his champion (McCone 1990: 212). The *gnim* in fact became a land-measure, as did the 'horseman's bed', which also reveals the link between defending the land and entitlement to it.

17. *'a cinta indeithbiri uili, itir marbadh 7 gan marbhadh, a scuithi ind ar dus 7 se fein ina deghaidh-seicc, 7 ma ta imarcraidh air, a dul isin tellach is nessu'. (CIH 156.1-2. = CIH 2012.34-7 = AL iv 247.33-8.)*

18. *'.. no in e ín feronn doberad isin cinaidh, 7 a rogha na fine ata sin. '..* or whether they will give the land for the crime, and that is the family's choice'. *(CIH 2012.36-37 = AL iv 247* [last line].*)*

19. The story appears in Adomnán of Iona's eighth-century *Life of St Columba*. See Kelly 1988: 97.

20. *TEIT FOR INNILI DO BEODILIB NO DO MAIRBDILIB (.i. eitir tír 7 innile) DONACH BI SON ... ATHAIR IS A SUIDHIU ... INA BI ATHAIR ... TEIT A CIN FORA BRATHAIR ... MA 'SRULLAT-SIDE CONARUSTAR FORRO A CHIN FORA FLAITH. IS A SUIDIU NA BI LAIS ... BIDH A CIN FORA LEAPAID BRUIT 7 BIUD IS A SIUDIU MANA ARUSTAR FORA LEPAID..BID A CIN FOR RIGH. IS DE ISBEARAR CACH DICENN CO RÍ. ARACHAN FENECHUS DO UIDIB CINADH CACH CINTACH. (CIH 2011.14-29 = AL iv 241.)*

21. *Cidh fodera a cinta x.bire cen marbad do dul isin .t. is neso, 7 a cinta .x.bire marbhta do dul ar .u.fer na geilfine.* Why are (liabilities for) inexcusable crimes (not causing) death (attached) to the next of kin, and the (liability) for the inexcusable crimes (that do cause) death (attached) to the five men of the *gelfhine*? *(CIH 2013.1-12 = AL iv 249)*. This passage uses *gelfhine* to mean the

whole extended kin group. For this usage, see Patterson (1990). A somewhat similar distinction as to various kin-liability appears in the Welsh law books. See *LL. Ior*, # 106.

22. *EIRENTACH CACH FINE IAR NELOD CINTAIG.* Every *fine* is liable after the disappearance of a culprit. *(CIH 2011.33 = AL iv 243.14-5).*

23. *MAD DIBH DEITHBIRE. DEITHBIR CIA GELLTAR. GELLTAR GOLA. SRUITHE DAON DIOBHADH. FERR FER ORBA.* If it was excusable, it is excusable despite pledges (against breaking the law) - a pledge as to the pit (penal captivity). A man is nobler than inheritance rights. A man is better than land. *(CIH 2012.31-2 = AL iv 246.14-15).*

24. The following citations from *CB* are excerpts from commentaries. They are quoted because they are less terse than the old text but in complete accord with the latter, which the commentator obviously understood perfectly well.

25. *COMARBA RENAS NAD CREN COMARBA NAD REN NA CRENCOMARBA CRENAS NAD REN. (CIH 532.11-2 = AL iii 43.30-32; (CIH 1814.33; 1815.31.)*

26. *Inunn in comarba conae 7 an comarba doformaigh ... etc. (CIH 1815.24-10 = AL iii 49.7-18.)*

27. *In comurba reanus ni i nindetbirius, cid bec ... (CIH 1815.1 ff = AL iii 47.8 ff.)*

28. *INTI RENAS NAD CREN NI MEISECH-SIDHI IMNA ... (CIH 532.20; 1814.33 = AL iii 45.8 ff.)*

29. *AR IS CUMA 7 BID DIGBAD A FINE IN TAN NA NURNAIDEND A FOLTA IS DA FOLTAIB FINE GAIRE CACH FIR FINE ... (CIH 535.14-6, 23-4 = AL iii 53 (last line)-54.12).*

30. *IS TECHTA CIA IMANA BOAIRE CID LOG .UII. CUMAL DO TARCUD A CUIRP FADEISIN... (CIH 533.17-8; 1816 ff; 2038.21 ff = AL iii 49.19-22.)*

31. e.g. *BB* #49 (see notes, p.158 #3), and Appendix 5 (see p. 188).

32. For references and short discussion see Breatnach 1989: 38 #21.

33. *Caithchi bech*, an eighth or ninth-century variant of the tract on bees, states that 'the honey is divided in three, i.e. a third goes in respect of care, and a third goes in respect of the bees, and a third goes in respect of land' (*BB*: 187, App. 5). Similarly in *Cáin Lánamna* #10, spouses' rights in each others property were determined according to which of them had provided 'land, stock and service' (*SEIL*: 28. See also Ch. 11).

34. *MAD ORBA DOSLI IS LETH* ... if it is land that earns it, it is a half (to the fine). (*CIH 533.18-9 = AL iii 49.23.*)

35. Binchy remarks that *CG* split the standard *bóaire* category into a *mruigfher* (who had the render of the *bóaire* of *CA*), and a lower rank, *bóaire febsa* (*CG* pp 77-8). This may explain *CG*'s confusion over the *mruigfher's* honor-price, which is nowhere explicitly stated, though the tract states that various fines payable to this farmer for trespass were set at five *séts*, while his oath-value was six *séts* (*CG* 206-8). But given his much greater wealth, the difference between his honor-price and that of a *bóaire* should have been greater; perhaps, then, the *séts* paid for the honor of the *mruigfher* and other high status farmers was not paid in livestock (*bó-slabrae*; *CG* 120), but in other valuables not comparable to the *séts* of cows.

36. While the *sét* was often worth half a milch cow, in *CG* it was worth about four-fifths of a cow. Kelly 1988: 116.

37. *Ní tesban di fholtaib in bóairech tesban dia díriu* CG 169-70. *Folud*, of which *foltaib* is dat. sg., has a sense of property that could support a person's status.

38. *CORAI CACH COMSAI CACH FOCHRAIC CACH CREIC* ... etc. *(CIH. 490.1 ff. = Thurneysen 1925b: 372 #34 = AL ii 283 (last lines) - 284.)*

39. *CIA LIN RAITH DOCUISSIN FINERATH INERATH IARATH SOERRATH ... RATH NAICCILLE* 'how many fiefs are there? A fief in the *fine*, a fief not in the *fine*, a fief for fosterage, a free-clientship fief, a base-clientship fief ... *CIH 432-27-433.1-2.* (In her edition of DRS. Crigger [1991: 342 I.A.] offers 'the compensatory fief (?)' as translation on *inerath*.)

40. *IMUSFUICH FINE IMANEITIR. IMUSFUICHTE. IMUSCOITGET* ... etc. *(CIH. 489.8-9 = AL ii 281.34 ff.)*

41. *MAD CEILI DO FLAITH BE DECH CEILI BUNAID SELBA* ... etc. *(CIH 493.31 ff = IR III: 381 #44 = AL ii 307.19 ff).*

42. *MAD DO URGLAN RIA FLAITH AILE NABI AR DIUMUND ... (CIH 499.25 ff = IR III: 390 #57 = AL ii 331.4 ff).*

43. *in a fis no i nainfis fine ata in rath-so ... (CIH 1779.1 ff = IR III: 340 = AL ii 223.21-31).*

44. *FOEGIUM CIN INNARBA ... (CIH 1797.3 ff = IR III: 378 #41 = AL ii 301.25-31).*

45. *DAERRATH CACH TOTHLU SECH FINE ... (CIH 1777.30 ff = IR II: 252 #9 = AL ii 217.30 ff.)*

46. 'If anyone has killed himself in despair or for any other cause, he must be left to the judgment of God, for men dare not offer prayers for him ...' (Bieler 1975: 272 #5).

47. *AR IS CUMA 7 BID DIGBAD A FINE IN TAN NA NURNAIDEND A FOLTA IS DA FOLTAIB FINE GAIRE CACH FIR FINE FOGNE FINE INA FOLTAIB COIRAIB ... (CIH 535.14-6 = AL iii 53-5.)*

48. *CIS LIR TAIRGSIN CACHA FINE ... EACLAIS FOSUIGAIDTER ... (CIH 227.1-6; 1527.16-7 = AL v 437.16-24).*

49. *Midlach ... cona damna cimedha in sin tar cend tuaithe. (CIH 585.22-4 = AL iv 355.4-6.)*

50. *CB* proclaimed that 'the enslaved shall be free, the base born be raised up by (entering) the grades of the church and doing penitential service to God': *SAERFAID MUGO MOAICHFID DOCENEL TRIA GRADA ECALSA ... (CIH 528.5-6 = AL iii 31.1-6).* The founder saints, Patrick and Brigid, were both depicted as sympathetic to the plight of captives and hostile to the slave-raiding aristocracy.

51. *FIDBRETHA FINEBRETHA OSBRETHA MUIRBRETHA. (CIH 388.18 = AL i 182.1.)*

52. Patterson 1985: 49-86. A somewhat different interpretation appears in Baumgarten 1985.

CHAPTER ELEVEN

Marriage, Sexual Relations, and the Affiliation of Children

The coherence of the *fine* required that its membership be controlled; rules of affiliation existed, therefore, that distinguished the legitimate from the illegitimate child, but these differed from the general norms of European legitimacy in that affiliation was not strictly determined by the marital relationship between the parents. Another concern of *fine* members was the disposition of property vested in women of the *fine*, property which would pass beyond direct *fine* control when the woman married an outsider. Marriage to unrelated men also posed the problem of responsibility for the married woman's liabilities; if a woman in this position committed a serious offence, who should be distrained as her next of kin; those with whom she lived, or her family of origin? As with legitimacy, so with marriage: there were legally defined degrees of relationship, according to which a woman was more or less vested with rights in her husband's household and *fine*, or more or less attached to her natal kin.

These degrees of marital interdependence and gradations of legitimacy of children were associated with a system of sexual controls that differed from those that generally characterized medieval north European traditions. Though Irish women, like other European women, were disenfranchised as parents in that only men could transmit comprehensive social rights to offspring, they retained a large measure of personal social identity and sexual freedom since no single man ever had sole authority as regards a woman's social position. Given the apparent normalcy of divorce, widowhood and remarriage, especially amongst the élite, women might easily be connected to two or more *fine* groups.

Also tending to disperse the social interest of individual spouses in each other was polygyny, which was normal amongst élite males.[1] The usual pattern seems to have been that a high-status male contracted one principal marriage at a time, with a woman of similar rank, until divorce or the death of the spouse led to the next such union. Before and during formal marriage to a peer, he might maintain one or more mistresses in separate residences. Whatever temporary concubines were maintained near the first wife were probably not flaunted, for fear of the culturally approved, violent jealousy of the higher-status woman:

> The *cétmuinter* (first wife) is completely free from liability for anything she may do during the first three nights (after the concubine was introduced) short of killing ... The *adaltrach* (concubine) has (only) the right to inflict damage with her finger-nails and to utter insults and scratchings and hair-tearings and small injuries in general (*SEIL*: 87).

There was, then, nothing comparable to the large-scale, household-based polygyny associated with Oriental palace harems or African royal residences. In this respect, Irish marital norms are similar to the general European pattern as to élite male behavior. They differed, however, not only in that *fine* groups had an interest in the control and protection of women (as they did men), but as regards the determination of filiation; bastardy remained a matter in which the Church had a far less powerful voice than in the rest of Europe, the question of heirship being ultimately up to the *fine* to decide. The following analysis of marriage and kinship will focus first upon property interests, and then upon affiliation and the status of those children who had no clear-cut claims to *fine* membership. It will be shown that the rules reflected the interests of the élite in the essential features of the conical clan, namely conservation of the property and status of the powerful descent lines in the *fine*, and the retention of 'base' kin as workers and retainers.

Marriage and property management at household level

Marriage Preferences. Although in Ireland, as in the rest of early Europe (Goody 1983: 31-3), there were no hard and fast rules governing the choice of marriage partner (other than a taboo on primary incest), there was a preference for marriage between close kin (in-marriage), and for matches between children of fathers of equal rank (isogamy). Absent from the picture is evidence for child-betrothal, even amongst the upper classes, or evidence that women were customarily married in early adolescence.

Isogamous marriage is mentioned several times in *Críth Gablach* as one of the attributes of a man's social status. The *mruigfher*, for example, was supposed to be married to 'the daughter of one of equal rank, in a lawful marriage.'[2] Their parity and partnership was symbolized by the requirement that they both should have four complete outfits of clothing,[3] presumably to go together to quarterly festivals and winter feasts. The retinues appropriate to the ranks of the middle-level lords during the winter coshering season were specified in *CG* in terms of the numbers of married couples who attended on the lord (*CG* 334, 384, 399); these married couples must have been heads of important farming households, such as that of the *mruigfher*. Like him, the *aire déso* was supposed to be married to a woman who was 'suitable' (*comadas*) and of equal status by birth (*comchenél*).[4] She too had 'equal clothing' (or 'equipment'), matching her husband in dress (*óentimthuch*). The wife of the higher status *aire túise* is mentioned in a list of the accoutrements of her husband's household, which begins with 'the implements of every labor' and ends with 'a wife in the correct legal union, his equal in rank'.[5]

The wives of these ranks are all referred to in *CG* as having the status of *cétmuinter*, a term that was also applicable to the husband, and which may be translated as 'first-householder' or 'chief-householder'. Isogamous marriage preferences did not, however, mean that the marriage partnership was normatively based on equal contributions to the marital property fund, for the traditional dowry contribution of the wife's family constituted one third of *tinol*, the marriage property. According to a commentary to *Cáin Lánamna*, however, this ratio was reversed in the case of marriage between a woman of the farmers and a nobleman; in this case, the wife contributed two-thirds of the conjugal fund.[6]

This veritable 'entrance fee' for a woman who ascended through marriage to the nobility was levied because the higher rank of a nobleman's son required the resources of both parents. Hence it was said that a nobleman whose mother was a slave or serf was ineligible for high office, since 'his faults are as the mother's.' (see below). It was also obligatory that a woman who succeeded in affiliating an illegitimate child to a *fine* man (by bringing an oath as to paternity) pay a substantial amount to the *fine* as 'protection money', *séoit fóesma* (*CIH* 233.21-2 = *AL* v 457.30-31). The same payment was also sometimes demanded when a child was brought into the *fine* by adoption (Kelly 1988: 105). This payment was also intended to make good the deficit in the child's endowment due to the absence of the dowry that married women normally brought from their family of origin to their conjugal family.

Connected to the practice of dowering women was the preference for marriage with close kin; this tended to conserve property within the *fine*, or between pairs of *fine* branches that repeatedly intermarried. Clerical complaints offer indirect testimony to the Irish preference for canonically 'incestuous' marriage. The seventh-century source, the 'Second Synod of St. Patrick', records that the *Romani* — a faction of the Irish clergy advocating greater conformity to Roman Catholic practices — attempted to insist upon 'what is observed among us, that they be separated by four degrees', i.e. that men should not marry their first cousins (the fourth degree kinswoman). The nativists protested that they had 'never seen nor read' such a rule (Bieler 1975: 197 xxix; Hughes 1966: 131).

Again, in the eleventh century, churchmen singled out tolerance of 'incest' (marriage of kin) as a major fault of the Irish church.[7] Such laxity was still a scandal to Canterbury in the later middle ages, not only in cases involving famous families, but apparently amongst the general population. So weak were the sanctions against in-marriage, that incidents are recorded in which men were sexually involved with aunts and nieces — not in covert relationships, but marriages for which the parties tried to gain sanction and blessing (Nicholls 1972: 75). Even in the law tracts there survives a hint that Roman Catholic complaints were not without foundation, for *Córus Béscna* asks:

> What is the *corus fhéini*? (laws of the farmers) Joint-plowing, marriage, giving in charge, lending ... (Commentary) marriage — the daughter of each to the other, i.e., to such a one as is not cursed by the patron saint of the land.[8]

A curse from the local saint could be incurred on a large number of grounds, such as associating with the various categories of society tainted with paganism, not paying one's tithes, or simply belonging to a hostile group. The point is that a neighbor, even a close kinsman, was preferred as a husband because his exact social position was well-known — a sentiment shared by the Welsh and expressed in the proverb, 'marry in the kin and fight the feud afar.'[9]

One other practice completes the picture of customary marriage choices. This was the norm of patrilocal residence; since men were obliged to plow with their fathers when the latter required it, we may assume that a newly wed couple generally lived with or near the husband's father. Contiguity, however, probably did not amount to co-residence. As we have seen, ringforts do not suggest the existence of large domestic units, while the law-tracts on status hint that young adult males were housed in their own huts. Separate residences would have been facilitated by ownership of scattered plots of land.

Under these circumstances, and given the fact that women might bring land in their dowry and be resident amongst their own kin if the marriage were a 'close' one, the conjugal relationship tended more towards partnership between the married pair, than towards radical subordination of either the wife to the husband, or the younger couple to the parental generation. The virilocal emphasis in post-marital residence was probably most significant when a marriage was contracted between distant families. In that case, it was the wife who was expected to move away from her family of origin, for a man who moved onto his wife's property claimed honor-price on the basis of her honor-price -- and that was always half of what a man of the same rank and property as the wife would have been ascribed in law (*IR* I 64 #4). Many such marriages must have occurred, however, for women were entitled to inherit lifetime usufruct of the fathers' estate when he had no sons, and of the *gelfhine*'s estate when there were no male heirs (*SEIL*: 21, 151 ff., 174 ff). Where an heiress (*banchomarba*) married her close agnatic kinsman, children of the marriage were entitled to normal inheritance rights in the estate that derived from their maternal grandfather.

Marriages between kin of equal rank had the potential for linking leading families within the same descent group at the expense of poorer collaterals, whose disadvantaged position could thus be exacerbated and perpetuated over the generations. These marriage strategies would probably have been typical of families who had captured leadership positions in clan society — the men who filled the various ranks of *CG*, and their respectable *cétmuinter* spouses, mentioned above. On the other hand, amongst the highest and lowest ranks of society, status was not contingent upon making 'suitable, lawful' *cétmuinter* marriages. Kings and members of royal lineages married their counterparts, of course, but these relationships constituted alliances of a more directly political sort than did the 'proper marriages' of prosperous farmers. Part of the humor of the famous 'pillow-talk' episode in the *Táin* derives from the fact that the king and queen, Ailill and Medb, insult each other like peasants, she accusing him of being a 'kept man', living on property that she had acquired as a brotherless heiress, he asserting that the land was his through inheritance from his mother, and that he had married her nevertheless, for her noble blood. After this exchange, they both dragged out all their belongings, from their great herds of cattle down to their pots and pans, to see which one was the better spouse (O'Rahilly 1967: 137-9). If such scenes were played out during domestic brawls in early Ireland, they would have been more likely to occur in farmyards than on royal greens, where competition of a more lethal sort played a role in marital strife.

At the lower end of society, the connection between a man's social standing and his marriage was vague. The *ócaire*, though he was expected to have a son or daughter, was married to a plain 'woman' (*ben*).[10] A lifelong *ócaire*, whose inheritance was insufficient to raise him to the rank of *bóaire*, might have been economically unable to contract a *cétmuinter* marriage, with its pooled marriage property and legal interdependence between the spouses. *CG*'s grudging acknowledgement of distinct status in the case of the *aithech ara threba a deich*, whose status lay between the *bóaire* and the *ócaire*, was extended only upon the condition that such a man be united in a lawful union with a wife.[11] It is as if men who could not expect to attain *bóaire*-ship were also not expected to lead conventional domestic lives, but instead to content themselves with sexual associations with women of low rank. The only alternative to such relationships, amongst those who could not make a full marriage on account of their lack of property, was a life of chastity. As the monasteries expanded during the early middle ages, this must have become an increasingly feasible social option for non-inheriting males, but there is no trace in the early Irish record of a secular role comparable to the celibate *'onkel'*, a non-inheriting brother who remained in residence with the married heir on the father's farm in areas of medieval Germany (Homans 1941: 136-8). Instead of sexual prohibition, non-inheriting members of farming families in Ireland faced the likelihood that their children would sink into servile status; grades of landed status were accompanied by grades of marital status, shading off along a continuum of possibilities, rather than falling into sharply different categories.

Varieties of marital contracts

The information on marital relationships is found mainly in two Old Irish law-tracts, a tract on honor-price, *Díre* (Thurneysen 1931, *IR* I), and *Cáin Lánamna* (*SEIL*: 1-80), a tract on marriage, which was chiefly concerned, however, with divorce and the division of the marital estate. As regards women, *Díre* was concerned with establishing who was liable for a married woman's fines, and correspondingly, who was entitled to take honor-price for her (*IR* I:27 #27 ff). If a woman were contracted as a wife by her *fine*, these obligations passed largely to her husband and sons. The amount of her dowry had no bearing on this question. Accordingly this text produced a list of female marital statuses that depended on the degree of *fine* consent to the marriage; basically the lines were drawn between the *cétmuinter*, the *ben aititen*, an 'acknowledged wife', and the *ben bis for foxul*, an abducted wife (*SEIL*: 81). The first was married with the agreement of both her own and her husband's family, the latter was definitely a forbidden union, imposed on the *fine* (and perhaps the woman) against their will, while the 'acknowledged wife' was one whose status had been recognized *ex post facto* by the *fine*. Further sub-divisions were also made, but they are not important for the following discussion (see *SEIL*: 81 ff).

Quite naturally, the less the *fine* had been involved in establishing the marriage, the less they were prepared to acknowledge liabilities for the woman in the event that she was charged with some crime while out of their ken. Similarly, they retained greater legal entitlement to her property if she died, and to honor-price for the wrongs done to her. The reverse was true where the wife had been married to someone approved and trusted by her *fine* (*SEIL*: 160-74). The proportions for both inheritance and liabilities (given here in simplified form) were:

1 *cétmuinter* without a son: half to her *fine* — half to her husband.
2 *cétmuinter* with a son: a third to her *fine* — two thirds to her son.
3 *adaltrach* with a son: two thirds to her *fine* — one third to her son.
(Smaller proportions pertained in looser unions, varying with the degree of interdependence between the spouses.)

In addition to the degree of *fine* assent, marriage varied as to the degree of condominium in the relationship. For information on this subject we turn to *Cáin Lánamna*. Here a distinction was drawn between types of *cétmuinter* wife on the basis of the amount of the wife's dowry contribution; a woman who brought as much to the marriage as did the husband was termed a *bé cuitchernsa* — a wife of condominium. This distinction does not appear in *Díre*, and it has been asserted for this reason that the latter is an older text, reflecting an alleged 'original legal incapacity' of women.[12] Since the dowry was not critical to determining the receipt of honor-price for a married woman, however, it is hard to see why this tract *should* have referred to dowry, or any other aspects of women's property. As pointed out in Ch. 1, there also are no linguistic reasons for regarding *Díre* and other tracts that categorically deny women the right to make contracts, as older than other early sources, such as *CL*, which acknowledge the existence of women's property and the contractual capacity of women as proprietors. The 'disenfranchisement' texts do not *precede* the other texts, but simply differ from them. The question thus arises of whether the heavy influence of Old Testament and Patristic texts on early Irish legal writing (Ó Corráin *et al.*: 1984) did not give rise to a phase of theoretical legal disenfranchisement of women. Such a tendency, which elsewhere in Europe served to legitimize the exclusion of women from the Christian priesthood, actually ran counter to the general pattern of north European marriage in antiquity, as did the equally unsuccessful attempt by the Church to introduce into Ireland, exogamy ('incest') prohibitions on marriage.

For these reasons, and in the absence of definitive textual evidence in support of the evolutionary hypothesis, I see no reason to believe that the native tradition of Irish law in regard to marriage and the status of adult women changed profoundly in the early medieval period. It seems rather, that there existed chronologically concurrent, variant forms of marriage that were to a considerable extent dependent on the rank of the spouses and their status as heirs. Whatever changes took place occurred within this framework of alternatives — a shift as to cultural emphasis, but not the radical evolutionary hypothesis advanced by Binchy in *SEIL*. Below I suggest that it is likely that the status of married noblewomen was enhanced, in tandem with the increased power of the upper nobility in the phase of recovery from the Viking attacks, while the marital status of poorer women of the farming classes was in danger of being assimilated to that of the concubine, whose domestic power was highly circumscribed.

Cáin Lánamna lists all the possible arrangements that could form the basis of a sexual relationship that conferred social rights upon the child of the union (*CL*: #4).[13] In most of these relationships, there also existed a recognized bond between the couple who produced the child, to the extent that if one were injured or dishonored the other could claim some honor-price — if only a token fraction — from the culprit (*SEIL*: 98). These relationships are listed below in descending order as to the degree of connubium that prevailed between the man and the woman:

1. *lánamnas comthinchuir* — a connection of equal, or joint, property. *Tincor* had a general meaning of 'equipment', and also a special sense of household goods. The marriage property in this case was contributed by both partners (*CL* ##5-20).

2. *lánamnas mná for ferthinchur* — a relationship in which the woman was supported on the property of the man (*CL* ##21-28).

3. *lánamnas fir for bantinchur ... fer fognama* — a relationship in which the man was supported on the property of the woman, but the man performed 'service' (*CL* ##29-31). This situation would arise where a woman was an heiress in default of male heirs.

4. *lánamnas fir for bantinchur* — as above, but with no 'service' contribution (*CL* ##29-31).

5. *lánamnas airite for úrail* - a woman 'received by command'; the woman left home to cohabit with the man, but was not supported on his property and did not set up a household with him (*CL* #33). In this case she was probably incorporated into another household which supported her (perhaps at the inducement — pay — of the husband).

6. *lánamnas fir thathigte cen targud, cen urgnam* - a man who visited the woman 'without service, without command'. This was a woman's regular lover, whose visits were acknowledged by her family. The woman did not live with the man and he did not provide anything towards her support (*CL* #32).

7. A variety of illicit or unconventional unions are mentioned that had no standing in law, except that they created liabilities, such as responsibility for child-care if pregnancy ensued. They included unions initiated by abduction, a union of wandering mercenaries, and a union between mad people (*CL* ##34-6).

The ways in which these differences in property commitments to marriage affected the social relationship of the spouses and their children will be examined next.

Property and power in marriage

a) *Coibche: indirect bridal dower.* Irish law makes only scant, passing reference to a gift (*sicail*) made to a bride specifically for having preserved her virginity for the intended husband.[14] Such a contrast to Germanic morning-gift and Welsh *cowyll* has no obvious explanation, but one should not assume it stems from vastly different attitudes towards female sexuality.[15] It is perhaps more likely that the morning-gift emerged in England and Wales as an important source of personal endowment for a woman (and thus an inducement to accept a particular suitor), when the dowry became legally subject to the husband's control.[16] Since this was not the case in pre-Norman Ireland, and since the Irish woman in any case received *coibche*, a pre-nuptial gift contingent on fulfilling the obligations of *marriage*, not maintaining chastity, there was no special role for morning-gift in Irish marriage.

Coibche was paid by the intended husband to the father of the bride at some point after they had agreed upon a marriage.[17] It was payable for any of the socially approved sexual unions listed above, even very transitory ones, and essentially secured 'public' recognition that the woman's kin had agreed to the relationship. If the woman had no father, it was paid to her nearest agnatic kinsman or the head of her *fine*. Though the amount must have varied greatly amongst the wealthy, the Irish laws (like the Welsh law-books) upheld a legal standard payment. This was set at half the bride's father's honor-price,[18] which was the same as her own honor-price. The daughter of a *bóaire* in *CG*, for example, would have received a *coibche* of two cows; this was not too difficult an amount to raise, but not so low that a farmer could afford frequent temporary marriages to women of this rank.

Although *coibche* was given to the father or kinsman of the wife, she herself partook of it. There was no element of 'sale', in the sense of a market exchange, in the contract[19]; it was slaves who were exchanged for chattels. The best proof of this comes from an Old Irish passage on distraint that concerned the responsibility of a chief for the actions of people in his household; grouped together into one category were the runner (the messenger), the ship-wrecked person (here viewed as a type of retainer), the fool (mentally unsound), the lowest type of bard, and 'the purchased woman'.[20] Irish law consistently depicted marriage as a relationship requiring the willing participation of both partners; the woman, no less than the man, was expected to have sexual desire for the other spouse,[21] and could divorce a man for sexual inadequacy (grounds for divorce are described below). The function of the *coibche* was not recompense, therefore, but the establishment of a legal instrument.

After the marriage had been agreed upon, and after the *coibche*, or part of it, was handed over, the woman was described as *urnaidm*, bound by contract. Whether a woman could by contracted without a *coibche* is not clear, but the sort of people who would dispense with *coibche* (the very poor or very unconventional), would probably not have entered full, household-forming, marriages. There are no descriptions of betrothal or marriage ceremonies, though aspects of marriage ritual have been reconstructed. Mac Cana shows that the poet who presided at the marriage feast demanded a fee from the bride which was a commutation of the original gift of her marriage-gown. (Mac Cana 1970).

At the initiation of the relationship, *coibche* served to protect the husband from fraud. For this reason, it was illegal for a woman to take her *coibche* herself, privately, because the husband then had no protection against abandonment by the wife. The kin who took the *coibche* were supposed to compel the wife to stick to her agreement and not to 'flee the law of marriage', unless she had acceptable reasons; their duty would obviously be more difficult where the bride was reluctant. *Coibche* also protected the husband from another kind of fraud; if his relationship to his wife were repudiated by the wife's kin, they could claim ownership of her child and demand payment from the husband before restoring his paternal rights (*SEIL*: 88). *Coibche* presented before witnesses served as proof that a contract had been agreed upon.

After the marriage had been established, the *coibche* served as a pledge for the relationship. Whichever of the spouses caused the break-up of the marriage, that person forfeited the *coibche* to the injured spouse. In the event that an unoffending wife was abandoned or predeceased by her husband she retained the *coibche*; for want of specific information to the contrary, we should also conclude that if a woman died in marriage the *coibche* was merged with the rest of her estate, which passed to her nearest heirs, her son(s), rather than reverting to her husband, who might then transmit it to his children by another woman.

(b) *Tinol: the conjugal fund.* The basic pattern of family property devolution was that a daughter should get half of what a son got in endowment for marriage, and bring one-third of the marriage property (*tinol*) into an isogamous marriage. The prevalence of this custom is borne out by the fact that the honor-price of a daughter was always half that of her father and half that of her husband (*CG* 125-6), and that wives were entitled to feed only half the company that they would entertain if the husband were in residence (*CL* #24). The same ratio prevailed in Wales: 'A daughter should get no more of her father's goods than half of what a son gets'.[22] Judging by the ratio of the contribution of the maternal to the paternal kin to wergeld, the ratio was the same in Anglo-Saxon England also.[23]

Not all marriages were endowed in this way, however. Irish law vested a core of social rights in women who were in any of the following categories of marriage, notwithstanding differences in their economic constitution: (1) the *cétmuinter* with sons; (2) the *cétmuinter* without sons; (3) the 'woman of condominium', *bé cuitchernsa* (4) the *adaltrach* (concubine) with sons. In commentaries these were often referred to as 'the four lawful women' (*SEIL*: 44, 85, 229). What they had in common was the right to veto their husbands' alienation of property that he had committed to the marriage. Secondly, they had certain rights of disposition in a proportion of the property they brought to the marriage themselves, as well as complete control of any of their own property that had been withheld from the marriage or acquired independently of it.

The fullest rights were vested in the woman who brought an equal endowment to the marriage:

> In the *lánamnus comtincur*, if they (the couple, marry) with land and cattle and household stuff, and if their status in the marriage is equal as to rank (*sóer*[24]) and equally proper, the wife in this case is a 'woman of condominium'. The contract made by either party is not a lawful contract without the consent of the other, except in case of contracts that benefit their common-wealth; such as the alliance of co-tillage with appropriate relatives when they themselves do not have the means of doing the plowing; the taking (renting) of land; the collecting of meat (for winter renders), the collection of food for the festivals; the

> buying of breeding cattle; the filling of the house with
> furniture; a contract for cooperation at work; the
> buying of sacks (of grain) and other necessities. Every
> contract (should be) without concealment, it should be
> a fair conscientious contract, with justice to both
> (spouses), with acknowledgement of what is
> purchased, according to (which of them had)
> possession in the thing sold. (*CL* #5).[25]

It was also said:

> Nothing whose defects are a hindrance to husbandry
> may be sold without consultation, advice and
> compensation (to the owner), for the mutual
> advantage of a *lánamnus comtincuir* is not to be
> evaded without adjustment (*CL* #6).

In this marriage, each spouse stood in relation to the other rather as an emancipated son stood in relation to his father, for the list of contracts that both could make autonomously resembles the mundane, domestic decisions permitted the independent son. One of the most significant features of this marriage contract is that the husband apparently could not enter a clientship contract without his wife's consent. It follows that one way for members of the nobility to secure the loyalty of important clients would have been to endow their daughters well and establish them in marriages of this sort. Since it was not legal for a lord to give a daughter to a man in order to initiate a clientship contract,[26] and since the prolific Irish aristocracy must have bred as many daughters as sons (with more girls probably surviving to attain parenthood), matches between royal women and clients, or noblewomen and prosperous farmers must have been attractive.

As the power of the dynastic nobility advanced during the later middle ages, the demands of the bride-givers increased. Ó Corráin points out that married women of the dynastic nobility become much more prominent in status by about the mid-tenth century (MacCurtain & Ó Corráin 1977: 10-11). Whereas earlier wives of rulers were merely termed *uxor*, or 'queen of the king of (e.g.) Tara', the later wives are described as 'queen' of the territory into which they had married. Ó Corráin links the rise in status of royal women to the general increase in royal power in the later Viking period. The new wealth of the period (largely generated by the Viking slave-trade), helped consolidate royal networks of clients, vassals, allies, and mercenaries, and also made possible the emergence of formidably wealthy royal daughters.

The other type of *cétmuinter*, distinguished from the *bé cuitchernsa*, must have been the wife who brought the traditional one-third dowry contribution of a woman. It is difficult to imagine a wife who brought a smaller dowry than the *bé cuitchernsa* having the same economic powers as the latter, but it is not clear what were the exact rights of this other kind of *cétmuinter*. *CL* states only that a *cétmuinter* who was *téchta* (lawful) could oppose her husband's 'disadvantageous contracts' (*CL* #22), a weak power that is reminiscent, as Thurneysen points out, of the right of the 'son of a living father', whose permission was not required by the senior man in order to initiate contracts (such as clientship), but who could veto anything that would threaten his own standing in society, such as a pledge of heritable land (*SEIL* 47-8). *CL* treats this category of wife almost as an afterthought, after completing discussion of the *bé cuitchernsa*, and beginning to discuss the 'kept woman' — the woman on a man's property (*CL* #21). The tract seems to back-track, as though trying to insist that even without an equal dowry, the ordinary *cétmuinter* wife was nevertheless '*comaith*', as 'good' as her husband, so as to distinguish her status from that of the concubine. To make this point the tract states parenthetically that 'equal wealth' and 'equal birth' had the same force in the wife's entitlement to control her husband.

The vague differentiation of this category of *cétmuinter* from the *adaltrach*, concubine, suggests that the marital statuses of women of different social backgrounds were becoming more polarized during the time when *CL* was written (probably the eighth century). Lords evidently had the capacity to penetrate domestic life not only by giving fiefs of land to sons while their fathers lived (see Ch. 8), but by giving well-dowered daughters in marriages of condominium to clients. Many commoners would thus have found it as hard to place their daughters in *cétmuinter* marriages as they found it to resist the pressure of the descendants of growing *élite* lineages on their pastures. The *adaltrach* category is a virtual female equivalent to base-clientship, which itself was modelled on the restrictions operative in the patriarchal bond between a son and his 'living father'. *Adaltracha* must have been common wherever conditions prevailed that depressed free clans into base-clientship.

The precariousness of the status of the traditional *cétmuinter* is underscored by the nature of her rights in marriage. The compiler of *CL* shows what he had in mind by proceeding directly from referring to this type of female marital status in #22, to discussing in #23 her right to seize whatever her husband gave to a concubine as *coibche*, if he tried to bring the latter into the house against the wife's opposition. By stating that the wife had this right even if the husband paid the *coibche* from his own property, the tract emphasizes that the man's economic superiority did not entitle him to undermine the wife's status. If the husband persisted, however, the wife was entitled to beat up her rival, who could only defend herself, not counter-attack, as noted previously. If this did not succeed in getting rid of the newcomer, the wife could leave if she wished, taking her own dowry property, its produce, the concubine's *coibche*, and a payment of honor-price from the husband (*CL* #23). Thus, though the minimally endowed wife was not well positioned to interfere in her husband's decisions, she could protect her position as female head in the household. No *adaltrach* could protect herself from the threat of usurpation in this way.

The *adaltrach* may not have brought much property at all, since in many cases, the primary intention of the union was merely to achieve social acceptance of a sexual relationship and its progeny. Another goal was to set up a temporary working relationship, in which the man supplied the farm and the woman supplied labor. Where *CL* discusses spouses who were brought in to live on another's farm, it emphasized the labor aspect of the spouse's relationship (*CL* ##27-30); this was as true of a man supported on a woman's farm as it was of a woman supported on a man's property. *CL* #28 depicts the woman in this case as keeping half her handiwork, and one-ninth of the milk, corn and bacon produced during the time the couple lived together. The relationship was envisaged as likely to end at *Beltene*, the spring festival of May 1, which was also the time many women traditionally moved with the livestock to the summer pastures (see Ch. 5). The departing woman was supposed to have 'a sack (of produce) for every month' she had spent on the man's farm.

When we recall the lower grades of the farmers, who had not yet inherited much, and who were not expected in *CG* to be married to *cétmuinter* wives, it seems that it was to such men that women went in these kinds of temporary marriages. The Church regarded them as similar to second wives, calling them all 'adulteresses' (*SEIL*: 85; Kelly

1988: 71 n.16), but serial polygyny, as much as concurrent relationships, is implied by these customs. (For this reason, the commentary which refers to women receiving up to twenty-one *coibche* (nuptial) gifts — beyond this number didn't count — may not be as fantastic as it sounds.[27]) Without assuming the existence of a substantial female labor force that was distributed on a seasonal contractual basis, it is difficult to see why the laws should have distinguished between the *adaltrach* with and without sons, for unpregnant and childless concubines are not likely to have been a significant category, unless there were many whose main purpose on a farm was to work.

If, however, such a woman became pregnant (or maybe after she successfully bore a son), an *adaltrach* became a 'woman with rights' vis-a-vis the child's father (*SEIL*: 86). It was the *adaltrach* without sons who was compared to a base-client,[28] while the *adaltrach* with sons was assimilated upward in terms of contractual capacity, just as were the ranks of men beneath the *bóaire*, all of whom had jural capacity and membership of the *airecht*, the assembly, despite their slight holdings of clan land. As the mother of heirs to a man's *fine* the *adaltrach* henceforth had a vested interest in acting responsibly regarding the husband's *fine*'s property, and was therefore entrusted with some economic autonomy. It seems, then, that, regardless of endowment for marriage, all women with ongoing acknowledged conjugal relationships were attributed an amount of property that was commensurate with their honor-price and over which they had power of disposition:

> The woman of condominium and the *cétmuinter* with and without sons and the *adaltrach* with sons — these four women may alienate the amount of their own honour-price of their surplus in *ón* and *airlicud* loans, in contracts and transactions, in the presence and in the absence of their husbands, and they may receive that amount in deposit. And they may (similarly) alienate two thirds of the amount of their own honour-price of their contribution (to the marriage property) ... And they may alienate the whole of their surplus in order to release their friends from 'lock and chain' (captivity) and [for the same purpose] they may alienate their marriage contribution to the point of overburdening (the household) or utter poverty.

> And they may undertake *ráth* suretyships up to the
> amount of their honor-price in the presence of their
> husbands and up to one third of it in their absence.
> And their 'good' contracts are made fast and their
> 'bad' contracts are rescinded. (Binchy *SEIL*: 218).

These restrictions are similar to those imposed upon men of the *fine*.
The right of the *adaltrach*-with-sons to handle an honor-price share of
the domestic property reflects the fact that her 'laborer's-third share' of
the produce would not be removed from the estate, whereas the
adaltrach without sons might take her sacks of produce and depart on
May 1st. The woman who was only a sexual and/or a seasonal working
partner had few rights as a wife:

> The *adaltrach* without sons may alienate nothing in
> (her husband's) absence save a reaping hook (and a
> distaff and weaving implements). In his presence she
> may only alienate what her husband authorizes ... And
> if she has separate property she may go surety in her
> husband's absence one-third of her (or his)
> honor-price, and she may not go surety at all in his
> absence. And her 'good' contract and her 'bad'
> contract are alike rescindable .... (Binchy *SEIL*: 218-
> 9)

But even this distrusted mate could protect her economic survival; she
could invalidate her husband's sale of clothes, food, cattle or sheep —
her subsistence necessities. (MacCurtain and Ó Corrain 1979: 3).

The domestic economy

(a) *The composition of the dowry*. There seem to have been few
differences between the types of things brought by men and women to
the conjugal fund. *CL* assumed that a wife of condominium would bring
land, livestock and equipment or furniture as part of her dowry (*CL*
#5.1-2). Where arable was owned in scattered strips, the passing of
usufruct to a woman who might have been marrying into another *fine*,
need not have posed any practical difficulties for domestic economic
organization. Both spouses might own cows and sheep, and both are
assumed in commentaries to *CL* to have owned pigs (*CIH* 509.11 ff =
AL ii 367 ff). Women, however, were expected to provide the

implements of traditionally feminine tasks, such as the hook and distaff of the *adaltrach*, mentioned previously, and the buckets, churns, and other implements involved in dairying. Presumably, then, husbands supplied such items as hatchets, mallets, and so forth. A commentary to *CL* states that all married women received a larger share of the husband's milk than of his corn because, 'every woman is a great worker regarding milk' (*CIH* 508.21-2 = *AL* ii 367.1-2). Being a great worker was explained in a seemingly late discussion of marriage as a condition in which the woman supplied all the implements of her work (*CIH* 174.21-25 = *AL* ii 411.28). Between this text and the various commentaries to *CL* there was much difference of opinion as to whether the nature of the wife's dowry affected her claims to the part of her husband's produce which were based solely on her labor. The canonical text of *CL* does not make such distinctions, which again suggests that *CL* represents an early stage in the polarization in the status of women of different socio-economic backgrounds who brought different sorts of dowries.

(b) *The division of domestic labor (aurgnam)*. In *CL* #14 it is said that wives undertook plowing, reaping, enclosure (?) of livestock, feeding (of stock and people?), and fattening of swine. Thurneysen pointed out that women did not do this work alone, but helped with it, or their servants did. It is still to be remarked, nonetheless, that the division of labor was so unspecialized that work that became in other parts of Europe typically male labor was thought capable of performance by both genders. The basic pattern seems to have been that women were expected to be able to undertake any labor or craft that normally needed to be done on a farm (or to supervise it), so as to deal with periods when the husband was absent, but there were also certain activities that were only performed by women, even when men were available. Specialized male activities, however, seem not to have existed in the sphere of labor, but to have been confined to jural-military roles. Most of the information on the division of labor comes from *CL*, where the tract offers explanations for the share of each spouse in all aspects of farm production.

    Women's work: As was shown in Ch. 3, women played a paramount role in dairying, which was probably the most basic and universal of female tasks, for the large numbers of cows maintained by Irish farmers would have required more than one pair of hands in the morning to get the milking done. In the seventeenth century, Petty wrote that in Ireland 'three dairy-women will manage 20 cows and do much work of other kind between whiles.' (Petty 1719: 52). A commentary even states (humorously?) that in a certain Tulach Leis, the marriage contract of a wife only bound her to one duty — to be home in time to milk the cows.[29] Livestock required other types of care that were also assigned to women. In a commentary to *CL* the division of labor is rationalized in terms of a distinction between the husband's herding (*liasrad*), the wife's 'strewing' (*esred*), and the servants' 'minding'.[30] In the context of livestock farming, this suggests the strewing of straw to catch the dung on the floor of a cattle shed, and the hand-feeding of stock in pens during periods of fattening, bad weather, sickness, calving and impounding. A farmer's wife was also involved in the fattening of pigs (*CIH* 509.11 ff = *AL* ii 367 ff). Both of these activities could be done around the farmyard, with the fattening of pigs being almost an extension of work in the dairy and kitchen, since pigs fatten on scrap, and the whey left over when cheese and butter are made.

The other great female occupation was the manufacture of clothing. This included the processing of wool and linen through all the many stages required to produce cloth (*SEIL*: 36 #15). Linen was especially demanding: women picked the seeds, tended the growing plant, picked it, soaked it, beat it, and then subjected the raw flax to several stages of preparation. When the threads were ready there followed dying with home-made dyes and weaving or knitting. Women's textile work may have been quite rigidly segregated, as this incident from the Life of St. Ciaran of Clonmacnoise suggests:

> On a certain day Ciaran's mother was making blue
> dye-stuff, and she was ready to put the cloth in it.
> Then said the mother to him: 'Out with you, Ciaran!'
> They did not consider it proper or lucky to have men
> in the same house in which cloth was getting dyed.
> (Stokes 1890 ii: 266-7).

Linen clothing for the body was often cut, sewn and decorated, unlike wool cloth, which was more often draped; sewing was a skill to be taught during fosterage only to daughters of the nobility (Kelly 1988: 87), presumably because of the cost of the materials used in decorative embroidery. Idleness was not admired in women, even of the leisured upper class; it was said, for example, that Cú Chulainn chose his wife Emer from 'all the maidens of Ireland' because she had 'the six gifts', which included needlework (Cross & Slover 1969: 155).

The value of a woman's work to those with competing interests in her produce — herself, her husband, and her *fine* — was sufficiently important that overt recognition was given in the law-tracts and elsewhere to the value of female labor. *The Vision of Mac Conglinne*, for example, contains a list of 'futile things' which includes, 'housekeeping without a woman', and 'giving property to a bad woman' (Meyer 1892: 72.20, 26). The wife's position had social prestige amongst the middle and higher ranks of society in that the provision of entertainment for guests and for the lord depended very much on the quality of her domestic supervision. An established wife played an important role in local society, being expected to handle these responsibilities alone during her husband's absences:

> The woman may entertain half (the number of) the
> company of the man, according to the status of the
> husband of the woman (*CL* #24).

In the absence of large households, the mobility of men depended upon the skills and reliability of their wives. Such 'housework' tied the domestic division of labor directly to the performance of broad social functions and explains why a woman's labor, and her property, were so important to the rank of her husband in early Ireland.

Men's work: a man's share in his wife's cows' milk was rationalized in terms of his general contribution to cattle care, described as *liasrad*, or herding. Since the care of animals out at pasture was often attributed to neatherds and children, however, the husband's responsibility seems to have been to supervise the depasturing of the animals, to ensure that the cattle did not cause damage to others' crops, and that they did not get lost. By far the greatest direct labor contribution of the husband must have been cultivation. Men had special claims to grain and unless they had servants, they would have been involved with all facets of tillage from plowing, sowing, harrowing, weeding, and reaping through to threshing, kiln-drying and storing. Fencing is also depicted as men's work, as is the construction of buildings, roads and fortifications.

But perhaps the most important contribution of the husband cannot be considered direct labor input. This was his assumption of managerial responsibility for the household's productivity, the most basic element of which was his liability for clientage services and military obligations. This role only receives direct mention in *CL* #29, which ascribes a higher share of produce to a man who helped manage his wife's farm than to a husband who did not. In a society where encroachments and raids were far from rare, the husband's ability to take appropriate legal and political action was essential to the family's survival. This meant that he had to belong to an effective political organization. Much of the husband's 'work' may thus have consisted of talking with other men at meetings of the local *airecht*, and performing legal acts that ratified contracts. It also included participation in the military obligations of clientship, which, as I pointed out above, would have thrown the burden of household and family management on the wife during the periods when he was away, at least until the couple's children matured.

(c) *Division of profits.* While the marriage lasted, each spouse was supposed to share the use of his or her capital contribution with the other, and also to share whatever was required for consumption. The detailed sumptuary rules that appear in conjunction with status provided a standard set of expectations of 'fair feeding' for each rank of society. Presumably, whatever surplus was produced was also committed to replacing the depreciation of the original stock and equipment. If the marriage was productive, however, and produced actual growth in the couple's resources (the *somoíne lánamnus*[31]), it also produced the possibility that each would acquire personal surplus — new *forcraid.* For example, a woman who was a skilled worker with wool had ownership rights in the finished products. If she exchanged some of these for an animal, its subsequent produce would be her own, either wholly, or in part, if she fed it on her husband's land. The process of generating personal wealth would have been slow, hedged as it was by rules that protected the interests of both parties. These rules, which will now be described, indicate how early Irish society viewed the economic aspect of marriage.

As described previously, early Irish jurists employed a doctrine of ownership based on the division of a product into three equal parts, according to who supplied the land, the seed or stock, and the labor that generated the wealth. In the division of the marital estate, either physically at divorce or death, or notionally during marriage if the couple kept an eye on their respective shares, the increase of each product at the end of the agricultural cycle was divided into three parts according to this scheme, which was outlined in *CL* #27. The workers' third part was subdivided, again into three parts. One part went to the husband, one to the wife, and one to the slave/servant(s). (If one of the spouses owned the slave or servant, that spouse took that share). Thus, one ninth of the total product was given to each spouse, no matter which of them had contributed the capital that had generated that product. For instance, the husband's one-ninth of the total increase of his wife's cattle, grazing her land, was attributed to his droving, as mentioned above (*CL* #22). The wife's similar share of her husband's calves and milk was attributed to her stall care.

The scheme is depicted in the canonical text of *CL*, but the details to be described now are depicted only in commentaries. There the scheme was applied with thoroughness to the spectrum of produce discussed in *CL*. Pigs, for instance, were owned in proportion to who owned the corn and milk that they were (a) bought with and (b) fattened on. If a woman had only 'milk of a ninth' (i.e. only obtained milk from her husband's cows by virtue of acting as her husband's milk-maid), and if she then bought a pig and raised it, she was entitled to only one ninth of the bacon. Moreover, if the husband had bought the pig and she had only fattened it (or vice versa), she only got one-eighteenth part of the bacon (*CIH* 179.21-11-4 = *AL* ii 412.14 ff). These rules can be seen to have taken the wife's share of the milk as a ready-reckoner for calculating her share of other items (*CL* 15); it was applied to shares in other produce such as garlic. Labor-intensive products, such as wool, flax or dye, however, were divided according to how much processing had been accomplished; the more labor the woman had invested in the work, the more she took away with her (*CL* #15).

Marriage seems to have been intended to blend the resources and output of the spouses, so that each had a bit of everything made on the farm and even the poorest spouse received one-ninth of the produce of the other in return for a labor contribution. But later commentaries to *CL* sought to adjust this claim according to the nature of the dowry, claiming that a woman could obtain half (not a third) of the entire worker's third were she a 'great worker' with milk. The same question came up regarding the wife's share in her husband's corn and calves and other bovine products. These commentaries should not be regarded as evidence for marriage agreements in pre-Norman Ireland, but they do reflect the increasing importance of (and the increasing variability in) the quantity and composition of a woman's dowry to her economic claims in marriage, a trend that had already begun as far back as the eighth century, when the canonical text of *CL* was composed.

Termination of marriage

Where spouses agreed to part without contention, the division of the property was undertaken according to the shares of the partners in the farm, as described above. The same provisions governed division of rights in the farm when one of the spouses died, for spouses were not each other's primary heirs; these were sons, daughters, and the *fine*. The decision was a private one, in that no clerical or secular authorities seem to have had any entitlement to participate in, much less prevent, divorce. Theoretically, after an amicable divorce each spouse would be in a position to remarry, or to maintain a child (or give a bequest to a church), in return for support in old age.

Penalties were incurred, however, if either spouse abandoned the other without cause, or if one gave the other good reason to end the union. The laws indicate some of the grounds upon which a man could divorce his wife without having to make a full property settlement with her. These included adultery, aborting a fetus, abusing (or killing) a child, frequent theft, general domestic incompetence, shaming the husband, and, of course, deserting him (*CIH* 2198.24-6 = *IR* V 7: *Gúbretha Caratniad* #44 [gloss 1]). The wife could leave the husband at the inception of the marriage, keeping her *coibche*, if there had been fraud in the contract, especially as regards the man's ability to give her legitimate children. The laws list physical incapacity due to impotence, or being 'too fat for the work', and social disqualification, such as holy orders and landlessness, saying, 'a child on the road is not proper' (*CIH* 4.33-5.52 = *AL* v 133 [III].) After the establishment of the marriage, the wife could leave with her dowry and *coibche* if (i) her husband slandered her, (ii) repeated a satire about her so that people laughed at her, (iii) her husband punished her 'unlawfully' and left a scar on her, no matter how small, (iv) her husband supplanted her with another woman, (v) he rejected her sexually, preferring to sleep with grooms in the stable (i.e. homosexual preference), (vi) he was found to have given her a love potion to seduce her into marriage, (vii) he deprived her of use of her fair share of the food and goods (*CIH* 47.21-48.26 = *AL* v 293 [LII]). A separate passage adds, regarding the latter complaint, that 'where there is not fair feeding they separate.'

There existed, then, a legally enforceable set of expectations in marriage concerning mutual respect, fair economic treatment, and an adequate sexual relationship. The law acknowledged that a man might try to bully his wife, for it provided protection for the wife against the husband, in terms of her *fine*'s duty to serve as sureties for the enforcement of her rights, even without appointment. On the other hand, if a wife ran away from her husband without good reason, they were also bound to return her. Where the compact was broken, the offending spouse forfeited property to the other:

> If either of the two parties be 'unqualified' (at fault)
> the service of the 'unqualified' is forfeit to the
> qualified. (*CL* #13)

'Service' means here the part attributed to the provider of labor — one ninth (at least) of the product of the farm. The other penalty was forfeiture of the *coibche* by the guilty party. Theoretically, an aggrieved wife, no less than a husband, received a property settlement that was adequate to re-establish her outside the marriage.

In the looser unions that had no significant marital fund there was no question of sharing the profits of one spouse's capital with the other; *CL* does not even discuss this subject. There was, however, according to one commentary, an exchange of shares in handiwork, which were calculated by comparison with the exchange that would take place between a man and his chief woman (*primben*). For example, between a man and one of the various types of concubines distinguished by the laws (the distinctions are not clear), there lay claims to a fraction (a fifth or a fourth) of the woman's handicrafts that would have pertained in a normal marriage. (*SEIL* 92-3). The egalitarian exchange of produce between men and women upon separation seems to be a legal fiction in this case, for there is no evidence that men undertook craft work of the same importance as cloth manufacture. Even in these loose unions, however, there was protection against the economic consequences of separation, for the temporary wife kept much of what she made.

Heirs and bastards: the boundaries of the fine

It follows from the marital norms described above, that there were no rigid bastardy conventions in early Ireland. Nevertheless, there existed potential conflicts between the reproductive goals of individual men, who were strengthened socially by the birth of many children, and those of their *fine* and their wives. Since *fine*-membership entailed rights to shares in *fintiu* and all the social supports described in the last chapter, *fine* members were no more willing to countenance a kinsman's untrammelled production of heirs than they were prepared to let him take inordinate fiefs from an overlord. Wives and their kin were also averse to the competing claims of concubines' children. These recurrent sources of friction in the closest of relationships led to the development of restrictions on the acceptance of children into the *fine* when there had been no marriage contract between the parents and their kin.

Affiliation was most difficult where the relationship between the parents had been secret, so that paternity was questionable. Secret affairs were generally referred to as taking place 'in the woods':

> honor-price is diminished by furtive sexual union;
> 'belly- kin' get no share of land; the son of the dark
> cannot sue for land according to the *Féni*; the son of
> the woods is doubted (as a kinsman) even though
> acknowledged for, she (a woman who acted this way)
> consents to receive each night anyone in her embraces
> ... the stealthy conception of each harlot belongs to
> the mother's *fine* .... [32]

A daughter's sexual independence was considered similar to a son's general disobedience — both threatened the status of the father, and the *fine* as a whole, because children conceived in unsanctioned liaisons were ascribed to the mother's group. Fear of potential social damage gave rise to sanctions on unmarried women's sexual behavior:

> For it is the rule according to the *féni*: half the honor-
> price of everyone of each grade in the *tuath* (to) his
> wife and his son and his daughter unless she is a
> *dormun* or the son is an evader of filial duties — a
> quarter (honor-price) to them. [33]

A '*dormun*' was a 'woman with a strong crotch',[34] who had secret affairs 'in the bushes'.

Against the categorical exclusion expressed in the old text, however, the gloss provided that 'respectable' women could make an oath to convince the rest of the *fine* as to the child's paternity. This was needed even if the father of the child acknowledged the relationship:

> If she be a worthy woman, and the man

> acknowledges connection with her, what she needs is
> an oath of testimony to bring her son into
> (possession) of land: but if an unworthy woman she
> requires *arra cuir* (an oath by fifteen men.)[35]

That there was much flexibility as to affiliation is not in doubt, but the
law empowered the *fine* to include or exclude illegitimate children at
will whenever the woman's oath was inadequate, and to demand any of
the following proofs or recompenses:

> Every woman who has secret sexual relations is a
> *'baitsech'*, as is every woman who runs away from
> her marriage without acceptable reasons; the belly-kin
> cannot settle with the *fine* without invitation, or
> security payment, or the ordeal of the cauldron or
> holy expurgation.[36]

The security payment (*séoit fóesma*), is described in a commentary as
ranging from 2 *cumals* for a son of the farming grades, to seven *cumals*
for the son of a king (*CIH* 431.22-4 = *AL* iv 280.35-8). Its purpose may
be deduced from the situation in question: an unmarried woman's son
would have no entitlement to property from his mother's kin as they
had not given her in marriage. His ability to settle his own liabilities
would thus be diminished, and the danger of kin-liability falling on the
fine would therefore be greater than if his parents had been married.
The 'security payment' substituted for the lack of dowry; without it, the
rights of an unaffiliated child to wergeld and collective inheritance were
not supported. This point, and its potential danger to the mother's status,
is dramatized in the Old Irish *Saga of Fergus Mac Léti*, which appears
in the law tracts as part of the preface to the tract on distraint.

The story has as its setting the pseudo-historical landscape of
a time of struggle between the Ulstermen, the *Féni* of the midlands, and
the men of Leinster. It relates that a warrior of the *Féni*, Eochu 'yellow-
lips', went into exile with the king of the Ulstermen, Fergus mac Léti,
after a fight with his own king, Conn 'of the hundred battles'.
Eventually, Eochu decided to go home and sue for peace, but on re-
entering his native land he encountered six men of the *Féni*, who slew
him. The slayers consisted of a son of Eochu's old enemy, Conn, and
four brothers, sons of one Buide. The group also included Fotlinne, son
of Dorn, who was Buide's daughter. Since the slain man had been
under the protection of Fergus mac Léti, the latter was now dishonored.
He mounted a retaliatory attack on the *Féni*, who then sued for peace,

offering Fergus restitution for his damaged honor in gold and land from each of those who had helped slay Eochu. Fotlinne, however, was unable to come up with a wergeld payment. In both recensions of the tale, he was formally repudiated by his mother's brother's sons on the ground that he was a 'trespasser' on them — he had been conceived as a result of a relationship with an outsider, *deorad*, which the mother's *fine* had specifically forbidden. His mother, Dorn, was surrendered into slavery as a pledge against his eventual return with a proper wergeld to redeem them both. In the surviving recensions of the tale, Fotlinne vanishes, and Dorn was taken into captivity in the north, where she was killed by Fergus after she insulted him.

Even after affiliation, sons born out of wedlock might be second-class citizens in the *fine*. Though invested by the father as heirs to his own land, their rights to *díbad* might be diminished: :

the fourth of the share of each legitimate man when he had been begotten in secrecy.[37]

In like manner, as the *indfine* obtains the fourth of the *díbad* property of (an extinct) *gelfhine*, the *dubhfine* obtains the fourth of a man's share of the *díbad* (property) and all his father's land.[38]

Marginal legitimacy, then, was translated into marginal genealogical connection, which served to allocate lower status and property claims to such kin. Since such sons would often have been born to slaves, servile concubines, and poor women, these restrictions effectively channelled the inheritance of high status to descent lines emanating from wives who were of equal rank to the husband. Degradation within the kindred, rather than severance from it, was also the possible fate of children of incestuous relations, and those who committed *fingal*, kin-slaying. The child of incest, known as *macc scríne*, 'son of a shrine', was towed out to sea in a leather 'shrine' as far as a white shield was visible from the shore, and left to the whims of nature. If the child in its 'shrine' washed back to shore, it was reared as a servile member of the *fine* (Kelly 1988: 220-1). Acknowledged sons of women slaves or serfs and their masters, were also slighted in status:

What three sons do not receive the status of chieftain according to the *féni*? The son of a slave-woman, the son of a '*mucsaide*' (gloss: daughter of a *senchléithe* or a bond-*fuidir*), the son of a slanderer (?) ... his vices are like his mother's.[39]

A glossator added that the son of a lord and a woman of the serfs (*senchléithe*) should get only land under the obligations of base-clientship.[40] Another gloss explains their degradation thus: 'their faults are as their mother's, i.e. lack of wealth'.

These restrictions must sometimes have been relaxed, however, for when *fine* membership was too low, it is evident that outsiders were incorporated who were only vaguely reputed to belong.[41] Adoption of children from outside was also possible when an individual lacked heirs. Later commentaries, which discuss these provisions in detail, show that this was accomplished like affiliation of illegitimate children, either with or without payment. When there was no payment, the adopted child was a 'kinsman by invitation'. Otherwise 'protection' was paid for him, in a contract bound by sureties and ratified by the head the *fine* (Kelly 1988: 105).

Why patrilineality?

From the preceding survey it would be easy to conclude that marriage and the affiliation of children were governed mainly by the economic norms of the *fine* — that it was a question of controlling the timing of marriage, the numbers of child-bearing women in the group, and the economic contribution of the latter to the solvency of their children, so as to ensure that the *fine* maintained appropriate numbers and resources. But issues of allegiance and identity were also involved in *fine* membership — this was a group that might call on the individual to make sacrifices, including undertaking vengeance or paying wergeld. There existed a strong ideology of patrilineality that went far beyond mere economic interests, reaching down to the foundations of political security and gender identity. This is expressed in another story found in the law tracts:

> Lomna the druid of Find, son of Cúmall, saw Find's wife going to meet another man. 'Well, my girl!' said Lomna. The girl said, 'Let Lomna be called to us, and let us give him money not to tell of us, or let us kill him.' They call Lomna and said to him, 'Do not tell anyone what thou has seen.'... One day, Find took his wife's son in his arms. Lomna gave a rod into Find's hand, and carves this accusation on it: 'A wooden

stake in a fence of silver, hellebore is the son of a
lecherous woman who is pressed to the bosom of a
kinsman(?). But ... he is a false warrior in the opinion
of the *féni* (Dillon 1932: 58 = *CIH* 2115.38-2116.6).

In this story, the *féni*'s concern with warriors and loyalty outweigh other
objections to women's sexual independence. The equation of a weak
agnatic bond with a weak political bond was also found in *The Saga of
Fergus mac Léti* (above), where the sister's son was deprived of
assistance by his mother's kin and was left to pay the wergeld alone —
in the event, causing his mother to be given into slavery as a substitute
for the land and chattels that he was not entitled to bring to a wergeld
settlement.

In opposition to these norms, an alternative structure of social
relations — one in which the sister's son is not rejected, but is
welcomed and politically advanced by his mother's group — is explored
in the great mythic tale, *Cath Maige Tuired*, 'The Second Battle of
Moytura' (Gray 1981/3), which was briefly mentioned in Ch. 5. In this,
the men of the divine tribe, the *Tuatha Dé Dannan*, were persuaded by
the women of the group, to accept the rule of Bres the beautiful, who
was the son of a woman of the *Tuatha Dé* by Elathu, a strange man of
the rival powers (the *Fomoiri*), who spent only one night with Bres'
mother. Bres proved to be a bad king, whose behavior cause his people
to revoke their allegiance. He then turned to his mother and demanded
to know how he could get help from his father. The mother, who was
more interested in her son's status than her kinsmen's, produced the
ring left by Bres' father against such a day, and the pair departed to
find Elathu. When they met up with the father, he was unsympathetic,
pointing out that Bres had behaved badly and deserved rebellion.
Nevertheless, Bres secured military forces amongst the *Fomoiri* with
whom he confronted the *Tuatha Dé*. The latter prepared for battle, and
finally defeated Bres at the second battle of Moytura, in which they
were greatly assisted by Lug, the son of one of their own men by a
Fomoiri princess. Here filiation worked as it was supposed to — Lug
was a member of his father's people, supporting them against his
mother's group. Bres showed patrilineal loyalties, but against his
residential kin group, his *maithre*. Patrilineal loyalties between warriors
are here depicted as 'natural', and matrilocal residence is concomitantly
'unnatural'.

The ideologically 'unnatural', however, seems to have been

quite commonplace in practice. As we have seen, *CL* recognized the validity of a number of types of marital union that would have resulted in children growing up in the mother's residence, whether amongst her own *fine*, or in a household that supported her. Fosterage would have led to some of these being relocated in other households, but probably not amongst the father's close kin, since these were the natural rivals of young male heirs; indeed, children seem to have been ideally fostered amongst their mother's kin. The sister's son was often referred to by the expression *gormac* (the warm, or filial, son), as well as by the genealogical description, *nia* (Ó Cathasaigh 1986: 136-41). *Nia* and *gnia* ('sister's son' and 'warrior/hero') became virtually interchangeable in Old Irish.[42]

The archetypal 'good' sister's son was Cú Chulainn, warrior-hero of the Ulstermen, devoted nephew of the king, Conchobor, and son of the king's sister, Dechtine.[43] The *Cattle Raid of Cooley*, which is told from the Ulstermen's standpoint, presents matrilateral kin in a very positive light, for not only Cú Chulainn, but Erc, Conchobor's daughter's son, joined the battle, 'without his father's permission'. These ties of purely consanguineal kinship were thought to heighten warriors' valor:

> Bravely will the warriors of Ulster roar as they hew down the army before them, rushing to rescue their beloved lad. They will all feel the ties of kinship (*condalbae*) ... Cú Chulainn will cast up three ramparts of (dead) men around the battle as he rushes towards the little lad. Mindful of their *condalb* with the boy, the warrior of Ulster will attack the vast host.[44]

Matrifocal residence, and with it a bilateral inheritance pattern (in which sons of women of the group had heirship rights), must have been a greatly tempting cultural option in early Ireland, for it provided a solution to the problem of household security posed by the mobility of either gender.[45] A recent example of the connection between mobility (especially sea-faring), dispersed conjugal residence, and bilateral inheritance, was found on Tory Island, off the coast of Donegal. Here the working male population led a maritime existence which encouraged young married women to stay at home with parents and siblings, rather than live alone for much of the time. Descent on Tory was fully bilateral (Fox 1978). The islanders preserved a special term for the mother's bother, *amnair* (*ibid*: 73), which is found in the Old Irish life of St Brigid and the St Gall Priscian glosses (M. O'Brien 1938: 364).

The existence of this special term, not paralleled by a term for the father's brother, has been interpreted as evidence for the 'avunculate' (Ó Cathasaigh 1986: 134) — the special tie between a man and his uterine nephew found in many patrilineal societies (Radcliffe-Brown 1952: 15-31) — but clearly it is compatible in Ireland with the early existence of a purely bilateral kinship system. Dispersed conjugal families (often described as 'visiting relationships') may have had old historical roots on Tory, for Herbert and Ó Ríain cite a legend that appears in the Irish Life of Columcille, which reflects Christian disapproval of the close sibling bond that exists in societies with residence patterns like the Tory Islanders'.[46] The legend concerned a woman from 'India' who died and was buried on Tory, where her body is said to have rejected the same grave as contained the bodies of her bothers.[47] A similar tension in the brother-sister relationship is expressed in the story of the body of the pregnant sister of Molaise of Leithglenn, which could only be buried when she had been forgiven her transgression.[48] St. Patrick, too, is depicted as showing a harsh attitude to his sister's illegitimate pregnancy.[49] These Christian stories tend to reject the brother-sister relationship and to cast the brother in the role of censor of his sister's sexuality — a reaction, possibly, to the counter-model of marriage and family formation presented by pagan society during the early period of the conversion.

At this point, we may recall *Cáin Lánamna*'s list of types of marriage, many of which were visiting relationships. It is easy to assume that these were necessarily confined to low-status individuals — because the latter would have found dowered marriages difficult to establish, because the Church disapproved of such relationships and depicted all but the 'proper' wife as 'adulteresses', and because analogies drawn by scholars between *CL* and a simplified model of the Brahmanic prestige-hierarchy of marriage has furthered this impression.

Nevertheless, narrative literature not infrequently depicts adult daughters of the nobility, living at home with elderly parents, and sometimes entertaining lovers with the full cognizance of the father.[50] Before assuming that the divinity of these characters (which is often evident) explains the sexual behavior depicted in narratives, it should be realized that aspects of the laws support the view that this was a real social pattern (such as the provision that a woman might contract with a parent to provide care, *goire*), while comparative evidence lends further support to 'loose unions' as a possible correlate of the very high rank of the women in such relationships. Amongst the *highest* subcastes of the Rarhi brahmans of Bengal, for example, unmarried women whose caste-position was too high for them to readily make a marital match were permitted a form of marriage in which 'the girls stayed with their families and were visited by their roving husband, and the children were brought up by their mothers'.[51]

Of course, there was no systematic hypergamy in Ireland, just as there was no true caste system, and therefore the phenomenon of rank-related female unmarriageability is not to be found there. But other factors, outlined above, were present to produce a similar outcome in terms of the legal acknowledgement of visiting relationships between upper-class women and their lovers. For example, there would have been a severe conflict of values in early Ireland between filial devotion and fertility, if a woman was required to live at the parental home but could not find a suitable husband to move in and assume the role of 'a man in a woman's place'. Since it was permissible (i.e. not grounds for divorce), for either spouse in a barren marriage to temporarily depart in order to attempt to conceive a child with another partner (Kelly 1988: 75), it is justifiable to conclude that a father who required the assistance of an adult daughter would be obliged to permit her to form a family of her own by means of a relationship with a non-residential spouse.

Visiting spouses would have been easy to find: in early medieval Ireland and western Britain, mobility seems to have characterized the life of at least the upper social stratum of male society in 'heroic age' Britain in general. Picts and other roving maritime groups based in Scotland constituted the archetypal progenitors of illegitimate children; they were known as *cú glas* (blue- or sea-dog/wolf) and were sometimes specifically described as an *Albanach*, a Scotsman. In *Fodla Fine*, one of the low-status categories of the *fine* was explicitly linked to such ancestry:

> 'Blue-kin'; a son that a woman of the *fine* bears to an
> *Albanach* (Scot); he gets but the inheritance of a
> sister's son, or of a *duthracht*, severed from the *fine*.[52]

Not only were men from what was later known as Scotland active along the coasts of early medieval Ireland, but numerous young men dwelled in the interior, hunting and living by the sword as members of *fían* bands. At least one of the mobile 'ethnic' groups, the Picts are well known to have permitted royal succession to pass to the sons of sisters or daughters in dynastic lines (Smyth 1984: 36-83).

The general patterns of marriage, child-raising, male mobility, and the probable labor-shortage of Ireland and the western British Isles make the adoption of exclusionary patrilineal descent rules seem rather gratuitous, especially in view of the general bilaterality of kinship in other areas of medieval northern Europe. Are we then to fall back on the idea that patrilineality is more 'natural', or an inert survival of Indo-European culture? A more immediate explanation is at hand, however. Smyth has recently pointed out that the Picts' peculiar kinship 'system' correlates with another even stranger historical fact — the Picts' astonishingly complete disappearance as a cultural and political entity. He points out that what appear to be matrilineal *'rules'* of succession amongst the Picts, may have been nothing more that the repeated imposition of sons of foreigners — Bres-types — especially of the Irish *Dál Riata*, into the Pictish kingship, as the Picts' power-structure gradually crumbled (Smyth 1984: 59-72).

The demise of the Picts underscores the implications of the Irish tales about sisters' sons and the ruin they were thought likely to bring to their mother's people, or themselves, if they tarried too long with the latter. The depiction of Bres in the *Second Battle of Moy Tura*, has indeed recently been shown by John Carey (1989/90), to be a ninth-century expression of Irish fears that the Vikings would destroy traditional culture. Carey points out that Bres's mother was none other than Ériu, the Irish sovereignty goddess, who in this story — and in no other story of the sovereignty goddess — is seduced by a foreigner from beyond Ireland. While Irish-Norse alliances offered advantages to some Irish leaders, the society as a whole came to suffer from the depradations of the sons of Viking men and Irish women, the *Gallgoidil*. (Carey 1989/90: 58-60). (Archaeological findings suggest that relatively few women accompanied the Dublin Vikings from Norway. [Edwards 1990: 182]). Looking beyond the terminus of the period in which the Irish law-tracts were written, to the Irish relationship with the Normans during their initial period of success, we find again that marriage between an Irish princess and a powerful immigrant foreigner was a sinister political omen from the point of view of those Irish who were not party to the alliance; Strongbow's Norman heirs claimed Leinster through the daughter of Mac Murrough. Within a few generations of the Norman semi-conquest, however, the Irish were on the political offensive, and the Normans had adopted Gaelic clan-organization; both were 'strictly patrilineal', shutting out the descendants of further in-marrying adventurers.

It is probably nearer to the truth, then, to regard strongly enforced 'patrilineal rules' as an *outcome* of political success in the context of the highland zone of the British Isles, and signs of 'matrilineality' as the result of advancing vassalage[53] amongst politically endangered groups *of the same or similar ethnic background* as their 'patrilineal' opponents, rather then seeing either as 'systems' transmitted inertly from a prehistoric past inhabited by patrilineal 'Indo-Europeans' and matrilineal 'others'. A rule or custom of patrilineal descent was the expression of a political aim: political groups sought to supply each of their male members with dominions and clients, and if possible to impose their daughters as strong wives in marriages to clients. A break in the patrilineal transmission of legacy was shameful because it implied political rejection and/or penetration by another group — a daughter's son had failed to receive a paternal legacy and had to be integrated into his mother's group, or (looked at the other way), another man's son had succeeded in securing a piece of his mother's brothers' rightful legacy.

The laws stressed patrilineality at all levels of society, not merely because the equation of patrilineality with political dominance imparted a sort of snob-appeal to the agnatic tie, but because clans and *fine* groups were readily dissolved at their social boundaries — for example, downwardly mobile members of clans might be sucked into base-clientship relations with other groups, and then further alienated by inter-marriage with their clan's competitors. If the latter could claim inheritance rights through their mothers in their neighbors' lands, political relations would have lost what little normative content and definition they had. Lawyers (and possibly churchmen) seem to have seen clans as agents of social stability; as part of the élite, the lawyers had their own interests in reducing the possibilities of conflicts, which were abundant enough as it was.

Militarism, then, not residential or productive patterns, appears to be the key to the stress on patriliny in social groups in early Ireland; the sons of sons were retained, but the sons of daughters were dispersed *as heirs*, even though in terms of residence, the opposite was often the case for substantial periods of the life-cycle. The patrilineal rule was ultimately a defense against the sister's son's connections with outsiders — principally his father's people. As such, patrilineality was a counter to clientship, designed to limit the options that individuals had as to where to place their loyalties. It is therefore not surprising to find that the ingrained ambivalence expressed in early Irish literature towards the sister's son had, as its counterpart, the suspicion levelled at the incoming wife — she too came trailing other ties and cherishing her own agenda. These bad-wife stories, in which the wife usually betrays her older husband with a younger man, who is either the husband's son or close companion, came from a milieu which, though it cannot have been too happy, gave to literature (from the British Celtic tradition) the cycle of Arthurian romances in which is found 'the only European myth of adultery'. But whatever the dreams of individuals, the goal of clan society was not romance; its fundamental ideal was to minimize danger by avoiding intercourse of all sorts with outsiders, as far as this was possible. For the upper stratum of society, marriage was an aspect of politics and could in no way be confined to in-house alliances; but for the middle ranks, sexual confinement went hand in hand with economic restriction as the price of clan membership.

Notes

1. The pattern is best documented for the later middle ages, but accords with evidence from Old Irish law-tracts as to marital norms. See K. Simms 1975.

2. *A ben, ingen a chomgráid inna coir chetmuinterasa. (CG 199-200.)*

3. *cethard[e] ndíllat(a) leis 7 a ben. (CG 198-9.)*

4. *Cetmuinter dligthech comcheníuil comadas for óentimthuch. (CG 346-7)*

5. *Cetmuinter co córus lánrechta lánamna comcheníuil. (CG 410-11.)*

6. *AR MAD INGEN IN BÓAIRECH GU MAC IN AIRECH FEIBI / DA TRIAN CETHRE UAITHE. MAD INGEN IN AIRI FEIBI TES CO MAC IN BóaireCH. DA TRIAN CETHRE O MAC IN BÓAIRECH 7 AEN TRIAN O INGIN IN AIRECH FEIBI. AR IS MO DLEGAR CETHRE DO BOAIRIB OLDAS DO AIRECHUIB FEIBI.* If it is the daughter of a *bóaire* (wed) to the son of a lord 'of worth', two thirds of the livestock from her. If the daughter of a noble 'of worth' to the son of a *bóaire*, two thirds from him and one third from her. For

it is more correct that livestock (come) from the *bóaires* than from the lords 'of worth'. *(CIH 46.2-7; 1511.5; 1847.23; 1811.33-37; 504.11-14 = AL ii 351.14-7.)*

7. Lanfranc's letter to the King of Munster, Turlough O Brien. See Watt 1972: 1-8.

8. *CAIR CAITE CORUS FENE COMAITHCESA LANAMNAS ... ingen caich dib da ceile, in neoch arna fuil briathar erluma. (CIH 523.27-33 = AL iii 17.15-6; 21-2)*

9. *Dyweddi o wnc, galanas o bell.* Evans, *Proverbs*, cited by Lloyd (third ed., 1939), I: 290.

10. *di fhorcur a mná, a ingine.* the rape of his wife, his daughter. *(CG 124).*

11. He had to be properly married and chaste on Fridays, Sundays and the three Lents. *Os he cona lánamnas choir 7 denmai i n-aínib 7 domnachaib 7 chorgasaib. (CG 144-5.* See notes, p.29)

12. See Binchy, 'The Legal Capacity of Women in Regard to Contracts' *(SEIL:* 210, 207-34). Binchy's theory is reiterated by Ó Corráin in 'Women in Early Irish Society', in Mac Curtain and O Corráin (1979: 1-25), and by Christopher McAll, 'The Normal Paradigms of a Woman's Life in the Irish and Welsh Texts', in Owen and Jenkins (1980: 7-22).

41 Parallels between this list and the variety of legally recognized sexual relationships in medieval Welsh law are discussed in T. M. Charles-Edwards, '*Nau Kynywedi Teithiauc*' (Jenkins and Owen 1980: 35-8).

14. See Thurneysen's comments *(SEIL:* 124-1), and McAll 1980: 8-10.

15. McAll's speculation (ibid: 9-10) that fosterage was hazardous to Irish maidenhood is unconvincing; had morning-gift been important, virginity could have been singled-out for special protection as part of the fosterage contract. It was in any case probably assumed that foster-parents protected children from sexual harm as well as other dangers.

16. The Welsh Laws, for example, emphasize morning-gift from the husband to the wife *(cowyll)*, and a woman's divorce settlement *(agweddi)*, again from the husband to the wife. This was arranged before marriage and ostensibly governed by legal convention, being linked to the father's rank. The wife's

dowry, however, is shadowy, and its disposition during and after marriage, vague. A wife could only be sure of leaving a marriage with her *cowyll*, since the other types of private property that might come to a woman were contingent, no matter the size of her dowry. The clear-cut identity of the Irish dowry is absent from the Welsh laws, but morning-gift (stemming from the husband) emerged as a woman's unchallengeable private property. (See D. Jenkins 'Property Interests in the Classical Welsh law of Women' in Owen and Jenkins 1980: 69-92.)

17. Less common terms for a nuptial gift were *tinnscra* and *tochra*, the latter surviving in Scots Gaelic. How these differed from *coibche* is unclear.

18. *letheneclann a hathar no trian eneclainni a senathar i coibchi cach mna.* *(CIH 46.12-3 = AL v 288).*

19. McAll's statement that 'virginity did not affect a girl's market-value in Irish society' is misleading: there was no 'market'. See Singer 1973; Goody 1990: 13-6.

20. *DO MNA FOCHRAICE, DOR FIR TAISTIL, DO MUIRCHURTI,* etc. *(CIH 382.18; 890.10.)*

21. *toil 7 genus 7 bangnim uaithe-si do-som 7 fergnim uadh-sum di-si.* Will and desire and female-deed from her to him, and the male-deed from him to her. *(CIH.504.9-10 = AL ii 351.5-7).* This is late commentary and is reminiscent of theological doctrine on the 'marriage debt'.

22. *Ni dyly merch o da y tat namyn hanner ran braut.* Jenkins 1963, *Llyfr Colan* # 39.

23. *Leges Henrici Primi,* ed. and transl, L. J. Downer (Oxford, 1972) and F. Liebermann, *Die Gesetze der Angelsachsen,* 3 vols. (Hall, 1903-16): 75.8,9; 76 1a.

24. Thurneysen translates *sóer* as *adel,* (equal in) nobility *(SEIL:* 19).

25. This is a close paraphrase of Thurneysen's translation *(SEIL:* 19-20). See also *AL* ii 357.37-359.9 for a similar translation into English.

26. *TAIT .UII. NECMACHTA RATHA LA MUG. CUMUL. CIMID. BEN A LANAMNUS. CELL CONA HINCROD ...* Seven things are impossible to give as stock: a male slave, a female slave, a captive, a woman in marriage, a church

with its contents ... *(CIH 27.9-10 = AL v 222.1-6.)*

27. *CIH* 294.40-295.2; 295.20 = *AL* iii 317. The commentary's defense of the father's right to his daughter's first *coibche*, and its insistence that the chief was entitled only to shares in subsequent ones, may imply that lords in the later middle ages tended to usurp this payment, as they did others that were traditionally associated with authority in the extended family, such as the heriot due to the *cenn fine*.

28. *adaltrach cin macu..7 im daercheli. (CIH 45.29 = AL v 287.32).*

29. *amail robattar mna tulcha leis ... acht gu toirsidis do bleogain a mbo im eatra, a slainti doib. (CIH 43.14-6 = AL v 277.27-9.)*

30. *CIH 508.11-12 = AL ii 365.23-27; CIH 174.7 ff = AL ii 410 ('Appendix to Cáin Lánamna').*

31. The concept of *somóine* is usually linked to clientship. But a Heptad states: *IT E .UII. MNA INSO ... NADI TUALUING SOMAINE LANAMNUIS.* There are seven women (i.e. seven cases) ... who are not capable of (demanding) the profits of marriage. *(CIH 43.10-12 = AL v 272.)*

32. *DOCIALLATHAR LOGH NEINEACH IN CELAD BAINFESA NI TAIGI TARRFINE TORANNA MBRUIGHE NI SAIG ORBA LA MAC DOIRCHE IS BRECHT CE ROITHNE MAC MUINE ARFAIM CACH NDOIRCHE CACH INA COMFOGAIL. (CIH 232.5-8 = AL v 453.14 ff; CIH 1299.37 ff; 915.2.* See likewise the black-kin, *dubfhine. (CIH 1880.23-4; 430.26 ff).*

33. *Acht is breth la Feniu: leth díri cach gráid túaithe fora mnaí 7 a mac 7 a ingin, acht ma[d] dormun nó mac bes elódach ria ngoiri — cethramthu for suidib. CG* 124-7.

34. *ben trensliastach. (CIH 42.35 = AL v 274.27).*

35. *Mad bean indric 7 adaim in fer comrag fira, 7 is fir tesda uaithe do breith a meic a norba. (CIH 232.18-19 = AL v 455.16-8)* (The oath, *arra cuir*, may have involved more, up to sixty, men. See Kelly 1988: 205 n.105.)

36. *BAIDSEACH CACH BE TAIGE NO CACH BEN DEIRAIG A LANAMNUS CEN DEITHBIRE AR NI SAIG A TARRFINE FINE CEN TOCUIRID NO CIN LOG FAESMA NO GEN FIR FOGERRTA NO COIMPERTA NOIME. (CIH 233.20-22 = AL v 457).* See *SEIl*: 99-103 on the classification of various kinds

of 'harlots'.

37. *IARUM CUNRANDA CETHRUIMHTHIN FRI HINDFINE. (CIH 1880.31 ff = AL iv 295.16-7)*

38. *amuil beirius indfine cethraime do dibad ghelfhine, beridh dubfhine cetruimhe chota fir do dibad 7 tír a athur uile. (CIH 1880.35-6 = AL iv 295.25-7).*

39. *CISNE .III. MIC NA GAIBEAD URTECHTA FLATHA LA. MAC CUMAILI MAC MUCSAIDE MAC BIRIDE ... AR ID CUTRUMA A DOAILCHE FRIA MATHAIR ... (CIH 233.4-12 = AL v 457).* The *'biride'* is obscure; the glossator understands 'female satirist', yet the other two categories are women who are in the possession of a lord.

40. *is cora lim ... do beith fo cis daeraicillnechta na ferand do tabairt do.* 'it is more correct in my view ... that he be under the obligations of base-clientship than that land be given him'. *(CIH 233.16-7 = AL v 457. 21-2).*

41. *INGEN AR MERAIB ISUIDE DODINDNAIG CLUAIS DO CLUAIS. DOCOM CENIUIL.* The nail-kin; it has passed from ear to ear that they are of the clan. *(CIH 431.35-432.1 = AL iv 287.1-5).*

42. *DIL, nia* and *gnia*.

43. Different versions of the story diverge as to Cú Chulainn's parentage, but in all cases his situation is depicted as irregular — he was not incorporated amongst the men of Ulaid as an heir, *comarba*, but as a champion. For discussion in this context see Ó Cathasaigh 1986: 136 ff.

44. *Táin Bó Cúalnge* I, 3837 ff. Cited and discussed by O Cathasaigh 1986:156.

45. Fox (1967: 100-114) discusses the relationship between mobility, household formation and uterine kinship (sometimes matrilineal, sometimes matrifocal).

46. The best-known example of brother-sister (non-incestuous) family formation is that of the Nayar, described by Gough in Schneider and Gough (1961).

47. *Beatha Colum Cille* 102 (#113), cited by Herbert and Ó Ríain 1988: 76 n.129.

48. O. Bergin, C. Marstrander, ed, *Miscellany presented to K. Meyer* (Halle 1912), cited by Herbert and Ó Ríain, *ibid.*

49. *Bethu Phádraig* 2774-81, cited, *ibid.*

50. See the story of Trusc and the daughter of Mac Rethe (Dillon 1932: 57-8); the story of the conception of Cormac mac Art at the house of his mother's father, Olc Acha the smith (Dillon 1946: 23); the incident(s) in the *Táin* in which Medb offers her daughter as a reward for a warrior's services.

51. S. J. Tambiah, 'Dowry, Bridewealth and the Property Rights of Women in South Asia', in Goody and Tambiah 1973: 67, citing J. H. Hutton, *Caste in India.* Cambridge 1951: 53.

52. *GLASFINE MAC MNA DIR FINI BERES DO ALBANACH NI GAIB-SAIDE S ORBA NIAD, NO DUTHRACHTA DEDLAID FRI FINE. (CIH 431.30-1).*

53. In both Welsh and Irish legal culture, the status of wife was literally modelled on that of the male vassal in relation to his lord. (Patterson 1988).

CHAPTER TWELVE

Kinship and the Proto-State

The early Irish élite, which placed such a high value on keeping clan lands inhabited, farmed and defended, was unwilling to sanction unlawful behavior by inflicting severe punishment on individuals. The tortures associated with medieval feudal law are not a striking part of the Irish legal tradition, either in the corpus of law-tracts, or in historical documentation (Kelly 1988: 221-2). The impression created by this negative evidence is supported by the numerous complaints made by Tudor officials as to the indulgence shown by Irish lords towards their own followers. Sir John Davies, who implemented the official suppression of brehon law in 1603, attributed some of the difficulties encountered by the English crown in changing Irish society to the weak sanctions imposed by Irish law:

> For, whereas by the just and honourable law of England...murder, manslaughter, rape, robbery and theft, are punished with death; by the Irish custom, or Brehon law, the highest of these offences was punished only by fine, which they called an eric.[1]

Capital punishment, mutilation, flogging and incarceration were fates reserved primarily for those who were not native members of the local polity, such as slaves, or hostages who were forfeit on account of the treachery of their lord. But as to landholding members of the clans, punishment normally consisted of fines and social degradation within the kin.

Such weak social sanctions against individual delicts are often associated with 'feuding' — a term which signifies nothing more specific, however, than the existence of norms of conduct and reaction to their violation without the benefit of state regulatory institutions. As we shall see in this concluding chapter, early Irish law reveals not only elaborate norms of conduct, but also a set of jural institutions that positively sanctioned adherence to these norms. The difference between such a system and that of a centralized government, like that which the Tudors eventually imposed upon the Irish, is that the latter controlled through the fear of punishment, while the former controlled through a system of prevention and frustration of individual autonomy, which limited the social damage that any one person could do. This system of social control was embedded in the kinship group, and a good part of the structure of restraints has thus already emerged in the last two chapters. Its effectiveness, however, did not depend merely upon kinsmen's disapproval, or even concerted action by them, such as the return of an unlawfully large fief, but was enhanced by a focussed mechanism of enforcement, namely suretyship between kinsmen and on behalf of kinsmen.

Suretyship, which was described in a general way in Ch. 7, was far from being a socially simple relationship, for it involved a group of people on each side of the transaction — the principals themselves, and the different types of surety. In the case of inter-personal contracts within the same polity — the sale of a cow to someone in a neighboring townland, for example — it seems that anyone whose honor-price was equal to the liabilities that might arise from the contract could serve as surety. But suretyship that concerned transactions that had the potential to disrupt a broad field of social relations was far more structured. This mainly concerned relations between people who belonged to different *fine* groups, and relations between members of different *tuatha*. In both contexts, suretyship was representational, to the point that we can speak of office in conjunction with rank, even though the office in question was allocated not by a state administration, but by competition and agreement within a dynastic kin group. Moreover, these offices show signs of division of labor and complementarity which followed a similar pattern in the case of a *fine* of the commoners and in a *cenél* of the upper nobility of a *tuath*. It is justifiable, then, to speak of these offices are functioning in some ways as a system of government, in the absence of centralized power.

Rank and suretyship within the *fine*

Since the law-tract that described relations within the *fine*, the *Córus fine*, is no longer extant, the information on representational suretyship on behalf of members of the *fine* is meager. Nevertheless, scattered throughout the law-tracts are references to a number of positions of responsibility within the *fine*, positions which were aspects of the total social position, the rank, of the holder, rather than short-term, *ad hoc* roles. These were:
(i) involuntary *naidm* suretyship within the *fine*.

(ii) two types of elective sureties who guaranteed the *fine* to unrelated people.

(iii) the *aire coisring* as surety for the whole *fine*.

i. *The involuntary naidm.* The *naidm*, as described in Ch. 7, was essentially an enforcer of contracts, rather than someone obligated to be a surrogate for a defaulting party to a contract. The involuntary *naidm* was honor-bound to protect the weakest individuals in clan society from the dangers of punitive distraint. The *naidm* in this case was someone who was qualified (in terms of property and legal standing) to act as such, and who also stood in a relationship of temporary or permanent responsibility for someone else. The role is described in *Berrad Airechta*:

> There are *naidm* sureties that fulfil the responsibilities (of their office) though they have not been appointed as *naidm*-sureties, for instance a *naidm* surety for the cattle of a woman — the *derbfhine* and non-*derbfhine* kin enforce it. etc.[2] (*BA* #23).

In most of the relationships named below as examples of this position, the surety was depicted as the 'head', and the dependent as his 'limb'.

> Moreover, one man of a kindred as against another, a father for his son, a teacher for his pupil, an abbot for his *manaig* (monks and monastic tenants), a lord for his client — [namely] every 'head' for his proper 'limbs' — are ... *naidm* sureties ...they are not impugned on account of him over whom they are entitled to exercise authority. Therefore it is said 'enforced and not appointed.' (*BA* #24)

These relationships were *'lánamnus'* relations, in which neither party could sue the other, but the relationship could be terminated if either violated the trust and dependence essential to the bond, i.e. if the junior person dishonored the senior, or the senior threatened the vital interests of the junior. Where a 'junior' person's rights were in danger, it was not necessary for the party with claims to have agreed to the appointment of a particular individual as the junior's *naidm* in order for the latter to assume the responsibilities of the role. The rule protected the junior person from distraint, when he or she was liable for debt or offense, by placing the 'head' in a position to settle claims before distraint was made of the junior's property. In the case where it was the weaker person's rights that needed enforcement (as in the example of a woman's control of her marriage property), any kinsman could intervene on these grounds, not merely the appointed *naidm*.

Most of the relationships in which a man could be an automatic *naidm* for another person were long-term and multifunctional — *full* relations (*lán* = 'complete' or 'abundant'), so that the *naidm* could expect eventually to receive restitution where the junior person was the debtor, and was better served himself by being allowed to be *naidm* than have the junior person socially damaged by distraint or penal captivity. Similarly, in such relationships, the senior person had a vested interest in enforcing the rights of the junior, and was entitled to act, even though not appointed. In a *lánamnus* relationship (as was shown in regard to the father-son relationship), the minor person was quite severely restricted in his or her legal capacity to make contracts; these usually required the permission of the 'head' and could be abrogated by him if his permission had not been granted.

(ii) *Elected sureties in the fine*. Two types of elected sureties served to deal with conflicts between members of the *fine* and outsiders. One was the *ráth forngartha fine*, a surety 'authorized (or commanded) by his kin'. This is referred to in an Old Irish heptad, where the gloss indicates that the *fine* in this case chose someone who was not a lord to perform this function on their behalf. The contract was approved (or at least 'not forbidden') by the lord, and was solemnized at the (local?) Church.[3] Kelly suggests that in this case, the group as a whole offered a collective surety, and that the 'commanded surety' formally represented them (Kelly 1988: 169).

In the same category was the *ráth forsaigi fine*, 'the surety that sues his *fine*'. The gloss explains him as 'the best *bóaire* of the *fine*, who served as *ráth* surety on behalf of non-kin'.[4] It was his obligation to actually distrain a debtor within his own *fine*, for which he received four cows in compensation, four for his honour-price (which shows that he belonged to the upper ranks of the farmers, according to *CG*), and four as another compensation.[5] Since the debtor presumably owed no more than his honor-price and was of about the same rank as the surety, it seems that the surety stood to get back what he had paid out to discharge the principal, plus twice its worth. The gloss envisaged the 'best *bóaire*' who distrained his kinsman performing this duty with the support of four ordinary men (not craftsmen) of his group (or household).[6]

The social character of such a 'best *bóaire*' is depicted in the Old Irish tract, the '*Advice to Doidin*', where an ideal surety is described as 'a true *bóaire*, a *bóaire* of the first rank', who owes 'no more than ten cows' (in clientship presumably), and has 'original possessions' (i.e. not purchases, rented or *díbad*).[7] This sort of person corresponds to the upper ranks of the farmers of *CG*, who held fiefs of ten or twelve cows, and the upper rank of *bóaire* in *Míadshlechta (CIH* 584.27 = *AL* iv 351.24-6). He was also supposed to be a big, hard-fighting, smart-talking, shrewd fellow, with 'his four *fini*' alive. The last point referred to the fact that surety liabilities were hereditary, so that default by the principal, having passed to the surety, passed on if he too defaulted to the next of kin, like any other liability.[8]

Precisely how these two sureties differed or perhaps complemented each other is unclear, but the existence of such roles shows that low-ranking *fine* groups were organized to limit the damage that might be done to each other by individuals of the group who got into trouble with outsiders. The importance of this mechanism may be appreciated when we consider the alternative; if an outsider served as *ráth* or *naidm* and the debt began to 'run', not only would the culprit's property be jeopardized but so would that of his next of kin, under the rules governing the high rate of compensation to sureties when the principal defaulted. The protective functions of these roles are thus analogous to that of the 'automatic *naidm*' described above, for in both cases close kin were legally entitled to assume a role that permitted them to fend off distraint of a relative by outsiders. Thus the jural structure of suretyship — itself a defense against social aggression — made it necessary for every kin group to promote the concentration of wealth in the hands of those men who would be able and willing to act as sureties.

(iii) *The aire coisring.* At the summit of responsibility for the commoner *fine*, representative suretyship was quite complex. The best information comes from *CG*, but a rather different tradition, preserved in the tract on distraint, also alludes to 'the man who is responsible for the offenses of a *fine* in a *tuath*'.[9] According to *CG*, a senior member of the *fine*, the *aire coisring* — 'freeman of obligation', literally, 'of drawing together' (*Kelly* 1988: 14, n.91) — offered a pledge on behalf of members of the *fine* to the *tuath*, the king and the church synod (of the *tuath* presumably). The pledge was to be of semi-precious substance (i.e. some object not in normal circulation), such as silver, bronze or yew.[10] (Such exceptional objects are likely to have been imbued with mystical properties, to have been hereditary *fine* property, and perhaps kept on deposit at the local church.) This function elevated the *aire coisring* to the ranks of the lords, so that he was also termed *aire fine*, freeman of a *fine* (*CG* 280) — privileged *because* of his role in the *fine*, just as other men were honored on account of cows (*bó aire*) or clients (*aire desa*).

The *aire coisring*'s suretyship was voluntary, in that he did not have to assume this degree of liability, but it was a position open only to someone of wealth and prestige. If a kinsman became liable to someone outside the *fine* and was unresponsive to demands for legal satisfaction, the first step taken against the *aire coisring* would be that his pledge would be taken in hand on behalf of the suitor. The debtor faced a fine of a cow for every day that the pledge was outstanding, up to ten days, plus compensation for the *aire coisring*'s honor (*CG* 284-94), for during this time his whole social *persona* was in limbo, literally in another's hands. If the debtor were an ordinary *bóaire*, he would have used up his own livestock and be looking to his nearest kin for the additional fines by the time the ten days were up. After the first ten days, the daily fine increased, until at the end of two months the *aire coisring*'s pledge was forfeit, he was dishonored (perhaps permanently), and the defaulter was now taken as a *cimbid* (penal captive), or proclaimed an outlaw.

Since the *aire coisring* could have distrained the culprit's next of kin, a pledge that was forfeit presumably implied that this circle of kin had absconded, leaving liabilities greater than the *aire coisring* could meet. This, in effect, would mean that the whole *fine* was on the point of crumbling, taking the *aire coisring* down with it. His status depended, then, on control of those for whom he was the standing surety to the outside community in the *tuath*. This was effected through the forces described above — the general structure of economic restraint, organized on the basis of the honor-price; the patterning of reciprocal liabilities in an ego-focused 'circle' of liable next-of-kin and sureties; and the functions of the paying and enforcing sureties appointed by the *fine*.

The *aire coisring* was someone who had specifically entered into an agreement to represent the *fine*. He was not *necessarily* the chief of the *fine*, the *cenn fine* (or *ágae fine*), for Irish surety structures tended to involve multiple sureties, with the whole *rath-naidm-aitire* combination serving to protect the actual chief, who held the lion's share of the group's property and held together the group's structure of power, legitimacy and possession. This point comes across most clearly where we examine noble suretyship. As to the headship of non-noble *fini*, however, the most we can say is that while direct evidence is wanting, the logic of suretyship suggests that the *cenn fine* was not necessarily the *aire coisring*.[11] The *cenn fine* was ultimately liable for defaults by his 'members'. He had therefore to be a pillar of morality and a bank of wealth:

> Every head defends its members, if a good head, of good deeds, good morals, exempt (from liabilities), affluent, competent. The body of every head is his *fine*, for there is no body without a head. The head of every (*fine*) according to the people, should be the *fine* man who is most experienced, noble, wealthy, wise, learned, truly popular, most powerful in opposing (others), (and) most steadfast in suits regarding profits and losses. [12]

A special form of suretyship existed which exploited the *cenn fine*'s sensitivity to attacks on his reputation. A man could in some circumstances secure a transaction by getting a satirist to offer a pledge for the fulfillment of his promise (*CIH* 466.5-9 = *AL* v 389.1-9; Kelly 1988: 50-1). If he defaulted, causing the pledge to become forfeit, the satirist would then produce some stinging rhyme about the *cenn fine* of the liable person. This would be chanted around in his presence, and later picked up and repeated by all those beyond fear of his wrath. (Fear of ridicule by children is voiced by the character Manchín in the middle Irish satire, *Aislinge meic conglinne*: 'little boys will sing those verses unless those words are avenged on him who made them' [Meyer 1892: 16.17-9]). The psychic pain was believed to cause outbreaks of boils or acne (Kelly 1988: 44). In this case, the chanting of the *ben rindas*, the woman-satirist, was particularly dreaded.

The use of satire against the *cenn fine* is reminiscent of the use of ritual against the *nemed*, the élite; in both cases, sanctions worked through symbolic dishonor rather than material dispossession. This suggests that the *cenn fine* of a commoner *fine* was sometimes also its *flaith*, its lord of clientship, who was only able to supply a few of the fiefs needed by his people, however, who were largely in base-clientship to other lords. This assumption was also made by Lúcás Ó Dalláin, who glossed a copy of *Bechbretha* in the early fourteenth century. Explaining the right of the head of a *fine* (*áge fine*) to a share of a bee-hive found on his *fine*'s lands, Ó Dalláin attributed it to 'the right of his headship, i.e. the fief of base-clientship'.[13] Such a *cenn fine* would have been a low-ranking lord, not included in the 'septenary grades' on account of his lack of free-clients. How typically a commoner *fine* was headed by a solo *aire coisring*, or a chief, together with an *aire coisring*, is indeterminable, however.

Despite the sketchiness of the evidence, it is apparent that the structure of suretyship within the commoner *fine* was complex; the 'layering' of sureties, each enforcing liabilities on the other, seems to parallel the 'circles' of the agnatic kindred, where more distant kin obliged the closer kin to control individuals. The formal, representational roles of suretyship were distributed in the *fine* on the basis of status, with the *aire coisring*, coming from the most prominent family of the *fine* (the chief's *gelfhine*). The two sureties seem to have been at about the level of *mruigfher*, while heads of families acted as involuntary *naidm*s. There is a good chance, then, that these offices were distributed within the framework of the ranked model of the lineage (se Ch. 9), which, as we must constantly keep in mind, was the outcome of the impact of political competition upon family and lineage relations.

Rank and office in the *cenél* of a *tuath*

Kinship and tuath structure.

The laws offer evidence for the existence of high-ranking offices within the *cenél* of a chief or king. The only way to describe these roles in relation to society is to analyze the quite schematic treatment of these offices in the law-tracts. Before proceeding, then, it will be useful to recapitulate some points made in earlier chapters, so as to outline the probable relationship between the neat social hierarchy depicted in tracts such as *CG*, and the political bricolage unearthed by historical research into non-legal materials.

The tightly controlled kin-groups of farmers — the *fine* groups described previously — were connected by ties of clientship and kinship to lords of various rank in the *tuath*. Some of the commoner *fini* were local groups belonging to the larger, less structured and less localized group, the *cenél* or clan; many such *fini* would have been downwardly mobile branches of ruling or former ruling clans. The relationship of *fine* to *cenél*, and *cenél* to *tuath* is hard to specify, since each overlapped, but only partially. In the early medieval period, each *tuath* ideally had a king — but only one, so that we may assume that there was only one acknowledged royal descent group in the *tuath*. This is also the assumption of the tract *Fodla Fine* (the divisions of the *fine*), whose later medieval title was *D'fodlaib cineoil túaithe*, 'on the divisions of the *cenél* (clan) of a *tuath*'. The correlation of *cenél* with *tuath* is also reflected in place names. At the same time, the fluidity of medieval Irish society meant that other clans were present in the *tuath*. Similarly, at the core of local political society was the *fine* of the chief, but other *fini* existed within the chief's *cenél*, that had been grafted on, or had devolved to lower status. For example, in one (admittedly late) commentary, base-clients are assumed to be *indfhine* to the *fine* that owned their land.

Stratification was not confined to the internal processes of a *tuath*. Evidence from the late pre-Norman period shows that paramountcies were controlled by ruling dynasties, which were divided into competing branches, usually two or three, with their own subdivisions. Allied with these different branches were separate clans, under their own heads. The latter did not compete for the kingship, but played an essential role in electing the king from amongst the candidates of the dynastic clan. Katharine Simms points to examples of the chiefs of non-royal clans turning to outsiders and offering them the kingship of their territory; such was the case in the mid-twelfth century, where the Cineal Eóghain repeatedly offered their kingship to the king of Airghialla, Donnchadh Ó Cearbhaill (K. Simms 1987: 45). Sometimes, the election of a local king was accomplished by means of consultation and agreement between the chiefs of subordinate clans, and the over-king of the province. It was not the case, then, that royal lineages spread down into all the intermediate levels of power that held together the paramountcy of a large kingdom or province. The political situation was more complex than that, with fractures and discontinuities of genealogy occurring within small areas, including single polities, while conversely, genealogically connected groups spread into distant, and even non-contiguous territories.

The survival of independent clans in the interstices of the domains of dynastic clans was due to the role they played as allies to branches of dynasties in the competition for kingship. This competition was perpetually stimulated, like a series of chain reactions, by the tension between alliance based on kinship at the expense of vassals, and alliance with vassals at the expense of kin. On the one hand, as Mac Firbisigh observed, great families were forever multiplying and squeezing out their followers. This process was played out at the lower edges of royal clan structures where the hopelessly downwardly mobile accepted the slide down into farming and clientship. At the upper levels of royal dynasties kinsmen nudged each other into the lower ranks of the nobility. Nicholls provides a very clear example of the process, still operating in the sixteenth century:

> The case of Clanmahon, where we find the sept in possession first weakened by the loss of eligibility for the central chieftaincy, eventually losing local political headship and thereafter suffering intrusion and displacement by three successive groups of the sons of current rulers ... may well stand as a classic example of the pattern of displacement...
> (1978: 8).

Such pressure could readily produce violent dissension, with rival agnatic kin finding allies in matrikin, foster-kin, and so on. The result was that the hierarchy of rank and status at any given time and place was the outcome of struggles and accommodations whereby the rewards of participation in a successful political faction were distributed amongst its leaders — some close kin, and others not. Thus, some of those who held the ranks to be described below must have been close kin to the local ruler,[14] but equally it is probable that some offices were assigned to leaders of independent clans, and to genealogically distant branches of the chief's *cenél*.[15]

Lordship and office

To the world outside his clan and polity the Irish king and his noble relatives and clients were at best devious allies, and at worst dangerous war-lords. But within their community these men were, when things were going well, bulwarks of order and security. *CG* supplies the basic ideology of good lordship, for *déis*, the 'vassalry of a lord' — both his clients and his rights in them — included his *dán*, or office in the *tuath*

(Binchy 1941: 82). An 'office' was a function or role in the political organization of the *tuath*; men competed for rank, and so decisions as to the allocation of these offices could only have been made in the *tuath* (or regional) assembly, when all men who were eligible to have a voice in politics appeared, along with their retinues of clients and kin. Promotion and demotion was essentially the result of political consensus and was formalized through acclamation; though functionally similar to an appointment by a king within a state administration, the incumbency of Irish offices was achieved only when clients supplied adequate support. Office could readily be disputed by other factions, and lost. Many of the roles that we now examine are probably best understood as assigned to more than one person at a time, and to have been held but for periods of time while the holder was in his political prime. Moreover, where a polity was weakened by raiding and tribute-payment, there would not have been lords capable of performing these offices.

Two functions of the offices of the ranks of the lords may be distinguished: one was to safeguard outsiders who entered the *tuath*; the other was to deal with claims made by outsiders against the *tuath*. Broadly speaking, the distinction boils down to protecting, and answering for, those who occupied the rather narrow public domain in society, and warding off hostile take-overs motivated by outstanding claims (or pretexts) against the *tuath*.

Public domain

In a society in which, ideally, everyone was meshed into corporate kin groups, the outsider, *deorad* or *ambue*, occupied an anomalous and dangerous position. As we have seen, the normal social position of such detached individuals was that of the *fuidir* and similar serfs, and slaves; all these were attached to lords who were obliged to cover what damages they caused in society. But other, even less assimilable, social categories existed — individuals who could not be tied into the normal framework of society on a servile basis, but who could not be eliminated from society either. These were, on the one hand, skilled itinerants, whose services and mobility were beneficial to the élite, and social deviants who could not be made responsive to the pressures of social control through fines and dishonor. These two extremes of articulation with mainstream society were both accommodated by the lords. In addition to marginal individuals, there coexisted in *tuath* society, almost on another social plane, the Church communities. I shall briefly discuss these three facets of the 'public', to whom lords owed protection:

(a) *Protection of the Church*: *Córus Bescnai* states that chiefs gave pledges to the local churches to guarantee that the people under their control would pay tithes, first fruits and alms to the Church; if they failed to do so the chief's pledge would be forfeit until the dues were made over, and the indebted parties would owe the chief the heavy fines that accumulated when a nobleman's pledge was outstanding. According to the text, every lord, *flaith*, gave pledges on behalf of his *fine* and his base-clients, and every 'great lord' (*márflaith*) gave a pledge for the *tuath* as a whole. Holding together this structure of responsibility was the king, towards whom the whole *tuath* was bound in duty, while the king was supposed to support the *tuath* in performing its duties to the Church.[16] In time the monasteries were to become mirror-images of noble, landholding clans, to whom the monastic families were often distantly related. By the eighth century, for example, the larger monasteries were able to field armies, composed of their own clients and tenants, against threats emanating from other monasteries. To what extent, then, their relationship with secular society continued to be based on these formal engagements for protection by the secular élite is a question that raises many complex issues regarding the medieval Irish Church, questions that lie beyond the scope of this study.

(b) *Protection of itinerants*. A lord had the right to protect craftsmen and professional specialists.[17] Craftsmen were in a peculiar legal position regarding their customers, as Stacey points out, for the law did not treat their exchanges like ordinary transaction that required sureties, but instead modelled the relationship between craftsman and customer on that of the *lánamnus* — the 'full bond' pertaining, for example, between a lord and client, father and son, teacher and pupil. As noted above, such exchanges were immune from all claims; in the case of craftsmen, this meant that once they completed the work they had agreed upon, their payment could not be withheld from them on any grounds — not even, for example, if the goods made over in payment were stolen.[18]

A number of factors must have contributed to the special treatment of craftsmen's contracts; as Stacey notes, long-term interaction between families and craftsmen might have made the high level of formality in suretyship inappropriate. Another factor must have been the mobility of craftsmen, some of whom at least, were peripatetic and had to cross *tuath* boundaries. These people would have been unable to obtain normal sureties within the local area. Of all people, however, those who travelled with valuables and without large armed retinues needed protection. The willingness of craftsmen to enter a territory, which would have been of great concern to the élite, would have depended on their confidence in their security.

Stacey suggests that the social response to this situation was that in the case of commoners belonging to a proper, 'capable' *fine*, the *aire coisring* served as a standing surety for all individuals of the *fine* (Stacey 1991). *CG* states that the *aire coisring* pledged his kin to lawful behavior in relation to 'king, synod and people of crafts'.[19] Thus if a craftsman ran into trouble outside his own territory, he would not have to wrangle with individuals and their kin, but could deal with someone who undertook the responsibility to sort out the problem. In view of the high development of laws connected with the treatment of craftsmen before the emergence of the synthetic legal system of the seventh-eighth centuries (see Ch. 2), it is probable that these provisions were an adaptation of older forms of ritual protection that had guaranteed the safety of craftsmen as they travelled. Higher levels of lords had further obligations towards craftsmen:

> every craftsman who makes the artifacts of a lord or a
> church is supported (on sick-maintenance) with half the
> maintenance of each person whose things he makes.[20]

This passage appears in *CG* where the tract describes the obligation of the highest king, 'the inherent king of every chief'[21] to provide *folog*, care of those who had been injured. The emphasis is upon the king's ability to preserve law and order, for 'ever *cenn* (head of *fine*) who could not be controlled by another chief came under his power'.[22] The tract lists a number of people who were likely to need maintenance when injured; apart from ordinary people, it lists mercenary soldiers, their wives and sons, stewards, couriers and craftsmen (*CG* 472-89). These provisions were probably not a digression, as Binchy suggested, but were made here because these people were thought likely to get hurt, either because they were mobile, and therefore away from their kin, or because they interacted with the public in circumstances such as assemblies, where people became drunk and aggressive. (Other aspects of meetings were also dangerous. Kelly [1988: 150] points out that 'by attendance at a fair (*óenach*) a person is evidently felt to have willingly exposed himself to the risk of being killed or injured by horses or chariots, and there is consequently no recompense for such accidents.) The king, as ultimate authority, imparted some social protection to these people. Since the role of protector of the rights of craftsmen was assigned to the entire set of lords (*CG* #23), it is fair to assume that intermediate ranks of lords had similar responsibilities at their residences.

(c) *Containment of sociopaths.* Early Irish kings and nobles maintained 'fools' as entertainers[23] — a relationship best known to English literature from the character of poor Tom, King Lear's fool. A blurred line separated the genuinely mad from the buffoon, who imitated insane behavior, and from other uninhibited, dishonorable types who entertained in upper class households, such as the farter and the prattler. These men may not have been mad but must have had abnormal personalities which in the litigious, stressful and honor-conscious culture of early Ireland would have put their kin at risk of legal action by others. Irish law recognized a great variety of socially handicapping disorders (Kelly 1988: 91 n.194). For example, men who suffered from priapism and compulsive masturbation were not allowed to stay in other people's houses without their own 'women-folk' (*Bretha Crólige* #29); the rule is stipulated in the context of sick-maintenance, but no doubt such men were viewed with general suspicion once their reputation was known. People with borderline personalities might thus have been turned loose by their kin, even at the price of loss of land or payment of fines.

It was, then, a social convenience that some types of deviants be included as 'entertainers' in royal and lordly retinues. This custom probably accounts for the surprising level of detail in *Cáin Lánamna* on the question of responsibility for the upbringing of a child conceived by a fool. It comments, for example, on the case of two fools brought together to copulate for the amusement of onlookers; whoever instigated this was liable for the child's upkeep, but its honor-price went to the king, the Church or the child's father's *fine* (Kelly 1988: 93; *SEIL* 74 # 36). A similar exploitation of abnormality is found in Giraldus's reference to the entourage of a king of Limerick which included a women with a beard to her waist and a crest down her spine, but who was otherwise 'sufficiently feminine'. Giraldus wrote that 'she followed the court wherever it went, provoking laughs as well as wonder' (O'Meara 1982 #53). A monstrous male was similarly reputed to have been maintained by Maurice Fitzgerald until killed by local yokels who had been taunted by the soldiery that it was they that begat such monsters on their cows. (*ibid* #54). Apocryphal or not, these stories are consonant with Irish social attitudes towards marginal members of society.

The uncompassionate ethos of the warrior stratum, which is well-known from saga literature, is further borne out by casual asides in the law-tracts, such as the passing reference to the game of scaring the type of half-wit known as *omnaig*, whose frailty was extreme timidity. The game, called 'the battle of the sticks', involved putting a mask or piece of cloth on a pole to startle the *omnaig* — even to the extent of frightening him to death, although such excess was fineable.[24] CB contains a remarkable passage on 'the devil's feast', which included amongst the devilish revellers, fools and prostitutes, showing that the Church was well aware of the possibilities of indecency inherent in the maintenance of 'fools' as entertainers (*CIH* 526.15-9 = *AL* iii 25.6-12). The description of the fictional retinue of the *fian*-leader and prince, Áed Allán shows the Church's view of such entertainment:

There were clowns and satirist and whores and begging poets
and louts, roaring and bellowing there. One lot drinking,
another asleep, another vomiting, another piping, another
whistling... (Radner 1978: 60-3; McCone 1990: 222).

But such disapproval never quite obliterated the traditional inclusion of amusing half-wits in noble retinues. John Derricke's *Image of Ireland* (1581), for example, includes an illustration of a lord feasting in the open air after a cattle raid. In the fore-front, a harpist and a singer perform, while behind them two *braigetóir*, farters, are bent over (keeping time to the music?), performing with their breeches down.[25] (Skeptics may view Ingmar Bergman's *Fanny and Alexander* for an example of this traditional European form of clowning.)

'Policing' the tuath

Responsibility for the rather minimal public functions described above, when conjoined with a king or lord's need to enforce his own rights upon his clientele, created a need for a body of armed men capable of enforcing the social order of the polity. Such roles evidently did exist, but have a low profile in the law-tracts, as well as the secondary sources, because the most comprehensive source on status and office, *CG*, was influenced by the anti-militarist ethos of *Cáin Adomnáin*, and admitted only one military specialist, the *aire échta*, amongst the ranks of a *tuath*. But another tract on status, *Míadshlechta*, offers a less bucolic picture of the lower ranks of the Old Irish farmers, while even the clerically-inspired *Córus Bescnai,* upheld the military function as a valid aspect of society, provided that war served God:

> What is the human feast? Everyone's alehouse feast for his lord according to his entitlement... Mutual obligation of the *féni* in feasting (and) refection. The propriety of service regarding hosting, encampment, pledge, assembly, vengeance, posse and vigilante action, serving God, furthering the work of a lord and of everyone for his lord, for his kin, for his abbot. Protecting his lord...warding off every loss from his lord... [26]

Míadshlechta was concerned with the personal qualities which enabled people to perform the roles associated with the offices of the various ranks. It produced therefore a classification that did not have the full scope of jural rank (for example, *díre* and *éraic* are not systematically keyed to rank in this list), but does indicate what society valued in men who were soldiers, scholars or priests. Scholars had to be skilled in literacy to varying degrees, and priests were required to be chaste, also to varying degrees.[27] As to the soldiery, the different qualities of soldier were rewarded in terms of the different numbers of companions they could have with them on the support of the *tuath*, and the amount of the fine payable for violating their protection, or for refusing them shelter and food while travelling. These privileges were clearly related to the performance of their military duties. The following categories were named, in ascending status.

The *seirthid*, literally, a heel-man, or rear-guard, appears not only in *Míadshlechta* but in *CG* 583. There he is depicted as one of four body-guards of a king, and both sources agree that his function was to stay close to the king as he entered and left his house (*CG* 583-5). But *CG* refers to him as an *amus*, a henchman, and describes the ideal *amus* as a man rescued by the king from capital punishment, slavery, or serfdom (*CG* 578-80; Kelly 1988: 66). *Míadshlechta*, on the other hand, emphasizes the man's good attributes: he had come from a 'good family', or his father had been a leader, or he had talents as a body-guard.[28] Nevertheless, his honor-price was much less than that of the lowest clan member (*tánaise bóaire*), suggesting unfree origins, with low status offset by military capacity.[29] Kelly points out that unfree bodyguards also figure in the Old Irish tract on leechcraft, *Bretha Déin Chécht*, where it is said that the reparation payment due for wounding a king in his temple was an unfree bodyguard with a breastplate (Kelly 1988: 66 n.214; *Bretha Déin Chécht*: 26).

Above the guard came the *úaithne*, a 'pillar' of the community. This role entailed the protection and supervision of 'the destitute and the needy', and the avenging of (their) honor 'without action by the *fine*' (*CIH* 584.32-4 = *AL* iv 351.33-7). It was, of course, the duty of the *fine* to care for such people, but it seems that where there was no *fine*, or the latter could not be compelled to do their duty, a mechanism existed for passing the responsibility to someone who was compensated for assuming the supervision and protection of dependents. Like the 'heelman', the *úaithne* was listed as lower in status than the lowest clan landholders, but he had higher legal protection as regards performance of his special function, i.e. a higher fine was incurred for violating his protection or refusing him hospitality.[30] In fact, his right to protection was guaranteed to the same extent as that of a middle-rank commoner (*CIH* 584.23-4 = *AL* iv 351.18). He was, then, of low hereditary status, but was enhanced in some respects by his role. It is possible that he was supported by the king, for as we have seen, the king was involved in the social security of others for whom the *fine* could not fully provide, such as the mentally handicapped. In their case, *ráth*-sureties were appointed to care for their land and exert pressure on their *fine* to fulfill their obligation: the *úaithne* would probably have exerted pressure on next of kin also, as well as protecting the rights of the 'wretched' against non-kin.

Both these offices seem to have played a 'police'-like role within the *tuath*. The low status of their incumbents is further demonstrated by the fact that fines paid to them were made only in '*séts* of the cow', while the higher ranks were entitled to fines in *cumals*. Above them, in

Mladshlechta, came several ranks that had no special military function at all, but were simply included as clansmen; of the main category, the *bóaire*, it is said that 'he wounds no man, but in a day of battle; he swears only one oath a year'. In other words, his main military virtue was to stay out of trouble and accept the authority of the military officers and leaders of the *tuath*.

Above these ideally pacific commoners came the lowest ranks of the nobility; in *Mladshlechta* these were dignified by their military function, just as were the lowest ranks of the commoners. The lowest office was that of *dáe* (a wrist, or forearm?); someone who fought on behalf of another's cause, particularly when the latter had no *fine* (*CIH* 584.15-20 = *AL* iv 349.40-351.7). Of higher status was the *ánsruth*, whose duty it was to protect the whole territory (*crích*) 'to its four points', making expeditions with up to twenty men over the border into a neighboring territory, and conducting attacks on enemies up to four times a year — once per season; after a seasonal assembly? (*CIH* 584.9-11 = *AL* iv 349.29-39). Finally, the tract names the rank of *idhna*, whose status was attributed (perhaps fancifully) by the tract to his being the father or senior kinsman of a large group (up to thirty) of swordsmen (*CIH* 584.3-8 = *AL* iv 349.19-28).

Of these various ranks of warriors, only the *ánsruth* (*ánrad*) is familiar from other legal sources. According to *BA* 45, this officer was entitled to protect a debtor or an offender at law from the coercion of a *naidm*, who was seeking to seize him; the *ánsruth* had the same powers as a court of law or an assembly, and thus was representative of the polity as a whole, but he was also a capable warrior, for defense against a *naidm* might require force.[31] He did not protect the accused against the course of the law, but seems rather to have protected him from being seized or beaten up when, for some reason, neither *ráth* sureties nor the next of kin could be sued in his stead. (Perhaps the 'ordinary oral contracts' in question were not warranted, so that fraud would be sanctioned by an 'automatic naidm' — e.g. the plaintiff's lord.) *BA* states that his status was ideally hereditary, so that the *ánsruth* of a king should be 'the son and grandson of an *ánsruth*'(*BA* 45). The *ánsruth* seems to have had a distinct role, focussing on protection of members of the polity against aggression and the promotion of peaceful resolution of conflict.

In other sources there appear various terms for types of fighters and strongmen, such as the previously mentioned 'cowless' *ambue*, the *amus* (*CG* 577; glossed by Cormac as 'he who has no rest, but moves from place to place... from lord to lord'. Stokes 1869: 2 *amos)*, the 'man of deeds', *fergnia*,[32] the *fénnid* (*fían* member), the 'man of feats' *caimper* (Stokes 1869: 47 *'caimper'*), the warrior, *galgat* (Stokes 1869: 87), the 'border-combatant' (*caithchid crích. CIH* 476.10 = *AL* v 419.17-8), the *carr* — whose role it was to obtain from each landholding (*orba*), the fat cow due to the king when he went to negotiate inter-territorial treaties,[33] the runner of the *tuath*,[34] and 'the man who collects the food tribute of the chief'.[35] *Míadshlechta* is the only tract, however, to offer any amount of detail regarding the social status of those who held office as enforcers. These details reveal a broad pattern of disparity between their social position and that of clan landholders.[36] On the one hand, the enforcers had greater rights of protection and refection than clansmen of roughly similar social standing, but on the other hand, the latter had higher honor-price, indicating stronger social connections in the polity.

It seems likely, then, that these warriors were somehow marginal to clan society (hence *CG*'s relative lack of interest in them), either because they originated as captives, as mercenaries, or in noble vassal families that had assumed special military functions while withdrawing from competition for the chieftaincy of the polity. The use of the term *fénnid* (a member of a *fían* band) to describe such roles underscores the alienation of such military specialists from their own natal clan and/or region, for the *fían* had a strong connection with life on the fringes of society, as noted previously. McCone has also drawn attention to the link between the social category *ambue* and the *fénnid*: *ambue* had a literal basic sense of 'cowless', but came to double as a term for a stranger and/or outlaw, a sense reflected in Cormac's gloss on the term, 'without foundation' i.e. a base for social identity (Stokes 1869: 10 *ambue*). The personification of the goddess Brig as a war-goddess (coming to the assistance of kings in battle) took the form of *Brig ambue*, suggesting that the *ambue* fought with even greater valor (borne of desperation) than a mercenary *fénnid* (McCone 1990: 162-3). While *fían*-members might eventually return to settled society, and in any case belonged to a group that was organized enough to take fiefs of cows from lords (a *'fíad-rath'*, or 'wild fief', grazed in forests [*ibid*: 211]), the 'cowless' *ambue*-men were members of broken clans, or men who had severed their own ties with settled society.

The details provided in *Míadshlechta* suggest the existence of at least a rudimentary division of political function during the Old Irish period: just as the *aire échta* usurped the 'natural' role of the kinsman as avenger, so the 'outsiders' that were incorporated into the *tuath* to serve as enforcers, were able to function in their special roles because they were not affected by feelings of loyalty or obligation arising from ties of kinship or clientship with members of the community. In a much less obvious way, *CG* also reveals that the foundations for a system of government that transcended clan particularism were already present in Ireland before the Viking age. *CG* provides a picture of jural function, which reveals a split in the organization of power between those whose office it was to control the distribution of wealth and those who deployed force; the former held higher status than the latter, ultimately standing to cover the costs to society of using force. The enforcers described above, however, were mainly used *within* the *tuath*, but were recruited from outside the clan whose chief they served. The reverse is the case regarding the offices that we shall now examine; these were distributed amongst high-ranking members of the *tuath*, and were aimed at fending off dangers from external forces.

Ensuring the tuath against outsiders

Just as kings and lords had to be warlike, so they were supposed to be capable of warding off hostilities through jural action where this was appropriate. In the legal formulation of representative roles performed by high-ranking individuals, pre-Norman Irish society laid the foundations of indigenous state development. These roles display continuity with the institutions of suretyship that operated within kin groups, and it is appropriate therefore to end this analysis of early Irish social structure with a consideration of the ways in which kinship institutions and pre-state governmental institutions dovetailed into one another, both conceptually and sometimes in actuality.

At the head of the polity, whether *tuath*, *mór-tuath*, or larger unit, stood the king. He was elected from amongst the pool of royal 'king-material' — *rígdamnae*, eligible members of the royal *cenél* — on the basis of the strength of his faction in the dynasty and his personal qualities:

> How is chieftaincy obtained? By virtue of appearance and
> family descent and knowledge, by virtue of hereditary right

and eloquence, by the strength of fighting and an army it is taken. (Meyer 1909 # 13).

One of the king's prime functions was the arrangement of inter-territorial meetings at which treaties, *cairde*, were made. According to the commentary to *Bretha Étgid*, however, *cairde* agreements were concluded by kings but most usually broken by members of the *tuath* (*CIH* 258.27-8 = *AL* iii 133.8-18, 20). The notorious fragility of the Gaelic polity was the result of the continuous dissipation of power through growth of the entitled cadet lines within ruling clans. Nevertheless, there did exist a system of response to potential crises, so that when power structures were strong and coherent, emergencies could be dealt with quite expeditiously. The system was based on a delegation of responsibility through various types of representational suretyship. It demanded resources — economic and military — which the rank-holder had first to acquire, then be able to marshal effectively in a crisis.

The essence of these offices was that the incumbents were not only in command of adequate wealth, but also had the social capacity to retrieve it at once and deploy it immediately. Previously it was shown that in late Gaelic Ireland, free-clients enabled a lord to gain rapid access to cows that they maintained for his emergency needs. There are many signs that the rapidity of a lord's response to crisis was crucial to his political standing in early Ireland also. The law, for example, structured the time-frame of response to legal challenge with such detail that it is evident that delay was interpreted as a token of probable impending default and intentional insult. (See the provisions for *anad* [delay] between the various stages of legal actions against plaintiffs [Kelly 1988: 178-79]).

Conversely, it was possible to formally embarrass a person by making a demand that could not be met with the required speed. Under circumstances no longer well understood, society could unleash upon someone the horror of a visit by a professional satirist, the *cáinte* referred to previously. Amongst this person's skills was the capacity to come up with 'an extempore request which causes a blush' (Kelly 1988: 49-51). Kelly gives an example from the *Táin*, where Redg Cáinte demanded that Cú Chulainn hand over his spear whilst in the midst of battle — a request that he had to refuse, but which nevertheless privileged the satirist to proceed with the verbal assault (O'Rahilly 1976: 1513). The satirist had been sent to Cú Chulainn by his enemy, Ailill, suggesting that such 'extempore demands' were probably not legal acts, but malicious, war-like challenges, connected to the martial rituals and psychological tricks developed by the Druids.[37] The point of the 'extempore request which causes a blush' is that status depended on being able to meet demands for loans and help without hesitation; in the case of Cú Chulainn, a high ranking warrior was probably expected to be able to find an extra weapon in his chariot to lend to another warrior in a battle.

Because it was the free-clients who held the ready-access fiefs of cattle, a lord's ability to offer suretyship on behalf of the *tuath* ultimately depended on his contracts with free-clients. It is probably for this reason that *CG* stipulated that all lords should have free-clients, and that even the lowest level of response to problems arising from breach of treaty required the action of a lord. From the *aire désa* up, all lords were bound to protect clients' interests and to uphold the norms of social relations in the following areas:

the rule of the *fine*, the *tuath*, the lord, the Church, ordinances, and *cairde*. (*CG* 341-3).

In contrast, the head of the *fine* (unless he also happened to be a true lord) and the *aire coisring* took no formal part in relations over the *tuath* border, nor in enforcing treaty agreements on his kin. The technicalities of how lords 'bound' their clients are obscure, but since all the lords were said to serve as *ráth*, *naidm* and *aitire* it is probable that clients offered pledges to observe treaties, and that their lord served as surety (*CG* 375, 397, 424, 441, 452, 469-70). (It is not likely that the *fine* head, even where he was an *aire coisring*, would offer a collective pledge in this regard, because members of a *fine* might be in clientship to several lords.) In the event of a breach of treaty, it is likely that the lord was responsible for quickly obtaining *éraic* and *díre* from the liable parties, or from his own resources, in order to immediately settle an impending feud. With the emergency taken care of, he would enforce restitution and payment of honor-price to himself, sometimes backed by other lords in the role of *naidm* and *aitire* of the treaty agreement. If the lord failed to enforce compliance on his clients he would have been in default of his suretyship and would suffer loss of honor and rank.

If these mechanisms of suretyship failed to restore inter-territorial peace, the next level of response was limited revenge, agreed upon under treaty. Significantly this action was undertaken by a specialist, the *aire échta*; the existence of a special officer for this role shows that it was recognized that those with personal ties of kinship or lordship to a victim would be unlikely to restrict themselves to limited retaliation, but would set in motion an uncontrollable vendetta. The *aire échta* had the same status as the *aire désa*, in terms of honor-price, but whereas the latter was merely a 'lord of clients', the *aire échta*'s title meant 'lord of slaughter'. McCone has recently rendered a translation of the lines in *CG* that describe the *aire échta*'s function:

> ... he is the lord of a band of five that is left to perform slaughter in an allied territory until the end of a month to avenge the dishonour of a kingdom against whom recent homicide is committed...[38]

When there had been a murder involving individuals of different *tuatha* who were under treaty, the *aire échta* was charged with the duty of raising a posse of five men who were entitled by treaty to search for the slayer for up to a month. Elsewhere this officer was termed the 'man of remedy', *fer lesaighthi*, whose signature property (his pledge) was a horse, symbol of his mobility,[39] or the war-dog,[40] symbol perhaps of the man-hunt. No doubt, a man elected to this role was qualified primarily by personal qualities. McCone has drawn attention to the texts' conflation of *aire échta* with *fénnid*, member of a *fían*, but there is no support for regarding him as an actual outsider, hired from a forest *fían*-band, rather than that he was someone with the attributes of a *fénnid*, and possibly a distinguished and prolonged background in that way of life.

It appears, in any case, that there was more to the *aire échta*'s role than martial prowess, for he drew on social resources within the *tuath* to perform his function. The text refers to the role of his *car*, friends and/or kin, in accommodating the other members of the posse as they made their way home. The *aire échta* must have known the trails across the borders and had standing arrangements (perhaps covered by the usual pledges and sureties) with householders *en route*; without such understandings ordinary families would probably have been frightened to admit a company of armed men, sometimes bearing enemy heads as proof of a mission accomplished.[41]

Another responsibility of the *aire échta* involved the distribution of token compensation for injury or death inflicted during the expedition — presumably involving innocent kin of the culprit. How easily injury might come about is illustrated in a story which prefaces the tract, *Bretha Étgid* (*CIH* 250.1 ff. = *AL* iii 83-5). This relates how an *aire échta* named Angus entered the territory of the Luighne to avenge an injury to his *cenél*. He performed the basic act of distraining a kinsman of an accused person (*inmlegon*) by forcibly drinking milk in the house of a woman of the territory, at which the woman reproached him with the fact that while he was merely drinking her milk, his kinswoman had been abducted and had not yet been avenged. It was such back-talk that got the enslaved Dorn murdered in *The Saga of Fergus mac Léti*; the narrator of the present tale implies some surprise, therefore, that 'no book mentions that he (Angus) did (any further) injury to the woman'(*CIH* 250.7 = *AL* iii 83.14-5).

CG says that the *aire échta* ensured that his companions, even if they slaughtered people while seeking the killer, did not stand to lose their own land or bronze cauldrons as wergeld. Instead, he was supposed to be able to 'pay on their behalf ... vessels to the value of a cow' (*CG* 362-5). This was a standard chattel and unit of worth, and odd though it may seem, *CG* implies that the *aire échta* and his party set off with enough of these vessels to offer this obligatory restitution to bystanders who were injured by the posse as they worked their way through the other territory. One probable function of the tokens was to prove that the group were not merely brigands, but were on duty. The vessels may also have served as tokens of future amends when treaty relations were restored, or even as tokens entitling victims to restitution from the kin of the culprit in their own *tuath*; but there is no further information available on this subject presently. The *aire échta* met these costs — the worth of a few cows — put his life at stake, and took care of the liabilities and the safety of the other men in the posse. This contribution to social order conferred on him the status of the lowest rank of lord.

Although the ranks of the lords begin with the *aire échta* and *aire déso*, who were at the same status-level in terms of honor-price, these two low-ranking types of lord lacked the common characteristic of the higher grades of noble, all of whom were 'able to pay, if sued, without borrowing, without surety'.[42] The higher nobles could thus go before an *airecht*, a court, and settle at once, before any debts or mulcts began to 'run up' the amount that was owed. They could be *naidm*, *ráth* and *aitire* sureties to the amount of their honor-price. Not only were they capable of defending themselves from the consequences of insuring an unpaid fine or debt, but if a client were in trouble, the lord was entitled to come forward as his 'automatic *naidm*' and sponsor an agreement on his behalf (*BA* 24). The lowest ranks of lords, the *aire déso* and *échta*, who were not self-sufficient in the performance of their jural role, are thus analogous to ranks such as the *ócaire* and second *fer midboth*, who were also 'incomplete' as to their particular function, namely providing 'hospitality' in clientship. Perhaps, then, *aire désa* and *aire échta* were status roles occupied by younger and junior members of lordly families, as I suggested in the model of *CG* put forward in Ch. 9.

The next rank up in *CG*, the *aire ard* ('high freeman/lord') seems at first sight to have been without a special function; the tract proceeds to specify the jural and military roles attached to the rank above him, the *aire tuíseo* (freeman or lord of leadership). Just as there are parallels between the jurally 'incomplete' ranks at both lordly and commoner level, so here we find a parallel between a lordly and commoner head of kindred. The *aire tuíseo* represented a whole clan (*cenél*) in dealings beyond the *tuath*, in a manner analogous to the *aire coisring's* representation of a lineage (*fine*) to the *tuath*. As part of his role, he assumed responsibility for whatever *ráth*-suretyships his father and grandfather had undertaken, if these still required enforcement (*CG* 414-5). This lord, then, maintained the order of long-term and wide-scale social relations. Finally, again like a high-ranking commoner (the *mruigfher*, whose qualifications an *aire coisring* would have probably exceeded), this high lord is described as having an elaborate and complete house and farmstead, able to offer appropriate hospitality to companies of people. The *aire tuíseo's* wealth was such that he was

> of complete assistance to the *tuath* with regard to representations, oaths, pledge and hostage, (and) treaty on behalf of a *cenél*, over the border and in the house of the lord.[43]

The parallel between the roles of *aire coisring* and *aire tuíseo* was not just a feature of *CG*, for *Córus Bescnai* refers to a similar division of levels of representations, juxtaposing the lord (*flaith*) who gave pledges for his *fine*, with a great-lord (*márflaith*), who gave pledges for his *tuath* in regard to payment of tithes.

CG next describes the role of the *aire forgill* ('freeman of superior testimony'; *CG* p.72). Though placing him above the *aire tuíseo*, the tract treats this status rather like that of the *aire ard* — that is, seemingly devoid of functional content.[44] It is interesting, therefore, that *Míadshlechta*, with its emphasis on men of action, regards the role of *aire ard* and *aire forgill* as identical, describing both as someone chosen by the *tuath* to represent it when *cáin* and *cairde* agreements were at issue. This rank of lord, however, did not 'bind' the *tuath*, i.e, he did not take pledges from them or offer one on their behalf, thus putting his own honor and hostages at stake in regard to the *tuath*'s behavior. That was the role of the king; the role of this officer was to enforce the agreements of *cáin* and *cairde*.[45] *Míadshlechta* uses the same term to describe the function of the *aire ard/forgill* as is elsewhere used to describe the *aire échta* — both officers were men who obtain 'remedy' (*les*) for the *tuath*.[46] This suggests that the *aire forgill*'s role was to cross the border, like the *aire échta*, but with the difference that the *aire forgill*'s duty was not to take vengeance for a killing, but to enforce the terms of the treaty upon the sureties of the other territory. Since one of the defining attributes of this officer was that he could overswear all the grades beneath him (*CG* 417-9) — presumably no matter how many assembled to bring a counter-oath — it is likely that this role evolved as a way to avoid contention with a large group of angry farmers in the other territory, which would tend to produce a brawl, and to restrict the interaction at a delicate point in inter-territorial relations to two high-ranking officers of equal status. The non-binding representational role is stressed in *Míadshlechta* with regard to both the *aire tuíseo* and the lower-rank, the *aire ard*:

> *aire tuíseo*: he (i.e. they, men of this rank) leads (or represents) a *fine* of equal lineage (as himself) to the king and speaks for them.[47]

and:

> *aire ard*: a man on behalf (?) of *tuatha* of equal standing as regards common (matters?) and treaty.[48]

The language of the passages and the general thrust of the tract suggest that the important part of the *aire tuíseo*'s role was not so much to represent other people, but literally to lead to the assembly, men of a *fine* or *tuath* that had a legal problem and there to present them to the king and court, 'speaking for them' in the sense of announcing them and explaining their problem, rather than putting their case for them. Elsewhere we are told that the *fine* should have a *conn* who could speak on its behalf,[49] and even the *fine* of base-clients had its own representative at law, the *aire coisring*. Much of *Míadshlechta* is given over to describing the size of the retinue, the amount of free feeding, and the extent of protection accorded to each officer — all attributes that suggest that their main role was to actually get hold of individuals who were involved in feuds and disturbances of treaty agreements, and then accompany them to an assembly where legal processes could be instigated. Since the feuding parties would have had to leave their own territory, the logistics of simply getting them to the assembly without further violence taking place, must have been formidable. (This point is made, unfortunately not for Ireland, but for Iceland, in Vápnfirdinga Saga, in which the chieftain Brodd-Helgi physically bars his rival, Geitir, from the site of the court where Geitir had intended to charge him with violations of the law [Byock 1988: 213]).

Here again, the parallel between the *aire ard/forgill* and *aire échta* is meaningful, for a large part of the latter's special role was also to protect his own posse and accompany them out of the feuding territory until they reached home safely. The significance of the parity of rank (*comcenél* and *comsaer*) between the *aire ard/forgill* and those he accompanied is also intelligible if we envisage his role as analogous to a sheriff rather than a legal representative of a party to a suit; he could not accompany men of higher rank because he did not have the resources to protect them from their own peers. (For example, if a skirmish occurred, the *aire ard/forgill* who accompanied a party to a quarrel might become liable for an opponent's honor-price; this should therefore not exceed his own.)

The ranks of *aire ard* and *forgill*, then, were not without office in the *tuath*. As we shall now see, they were complementary to other jural offices outlined in *CG*; the man of lesser rank implemented and enforced the jural process, while the man of higher rank put his honor and property at stake, through provision of pledge or hostage, to guarantee that such enforcement would take place if treaty-law were broken. The basic paradigm of political organization thus resembled at all levels the voluntary suretyship which secured *ad hoc* transactions. As D.B. Walters remarks, 'the strategy underlying Irish suretyship at the time of *BA* is to separate the function of discharging the debt from that of enforcing it' (Walters 1986: 100).

In *ad hoc* suretyship, the primary enforcer (*naidm*) tried to compel the accused to meet his obligations, but if he failed, and the debtor's sworn substitute (the *ráth*) also reneged, the *naidm* of the latter would move in to compel the *ráth* to answer the charges. In representative, standing suretyship, which served 'governmental' functions, this complementary dyad of payer and enforcer was also present, but the social structure of the relationship differed. Although the king or lord provided a hostage and/or pledge, compliance to the treaty was enforced not on the king, but on the people of the polity by one of the enforcers of the treaty, the *aire forgill* or *aire ard.* (If the king himself broke the treaty, there was no legal action against him, but his hostages were forfeit.) These officers would go, along with a group of armed supporters, across the border to seek out their counterparts in the other territory, and there come to agreement or fight it out. References to 'the champion of a territory' suggest that fighting, like the jural process itself, might be narrowed down to involve only representatives of the two polities. If both sides agreed to mend the treaty, one mechanism available to them (in the case of a quarrel involving murder) was to admit the *aire échta* of the offended side into the culprit's territory. Another mechanism was for the *aire forgill* or *aire ard* of both territories to seek out the *aire coisring* of the *fine* of the trouble-maker(s), who had given a pledge on his people's behalf regarding observance of treaties. The *aire coisring* could then summon the two sureties of the *fine* described above, and dispatch them into the backwaters of the *fine*'s lands to procure the culprits and/or their possessions, or their next of kin.

At all levels of society, then, social security in relations with 'outsiders' was achieved through the cooperative action of a dyad consisting of (i) a higher status man or senior kinsman who, as representative of the group, could put substantial and symbolic property at risk in suretyship of agreements that bound the entire group in compliance, and (ii) a lower status man or junior kinsman who took physical action to enforce compliance. The ideal-type of the most basic building-block of the entire system would seem to be a father-son relationship, in which the father made decisions and the son carried them out for him. Where power had been lost, this relationship appears in its crudest, starkest form: a son was the typical hostage demanded of a lord who submitted to another.

The previously cited statement that the *ánsruth* should be the son and grandson of an *ánsruth* suggests that these high offices were distributed between close kin in élite families, and moreover, that branches of a *cenél* might specialize in the role of enforcer, so that an *aire forgill*'s 'best' son might be an *aire ard*. Evidence for this kind of role distribution comes from a version of the previously cited *Saga of Fergus mac Léti*. After Dorn was killed in slavery in the North, her father and one of her brothers claimed honor-price for her according to their rank. The father was described as 'an *aire forgill* of the middle rank', and his son as an *aire ard*.[50] The incident in which they had been involved (and which had led to their kinswoman's captivity) is an example of the kind of action attributed to the *aire échta* in *CG*. In this incident, the leader of the group that had caused the trouble (by slaying Fergus mac Léti's client, Eochaidh) was Asal, son of Conn of the Hundred Battles. Asal is described in the text as a *fénid*, leading a band of five.[51] As was shown above, the *aire échta* was often regarded as a *fénnid*, and his posse consisted of five men.[52] Like the posse described in *CG*, Asal and his gang were operating over the border of their own territory, in this case in the Fews Mountains in south-east Ulster (*CIH* 354.33 = *AL* i 71.11). The five men of the posse consisted of middling-level members of the nobility; one was an *aire ard*, but his other brothers were probably of lower rank. However, Dorn's son, Fotlinne, evidently shouldn't have been involved at all, as he had no official rank in the *tuath* on account of his lack of agnatic connection, and therefore was unable to pay wergeld when the course of events brought down the wrath of the more powerful king of Ulster on these Leinstermen. Fotlinne's fate, and that of his mother, underscores the necessity that men of rank be able to ward off the fines that would redound upon warriors when military action resulted in political failure. In other words, high lords underwrote their 'representational' or 'public' functions with their own personal wealth; there was no public treasury to support their activities.

In the event that the *tuath* was liable for some serious breach, the officers described above stood between the king and dishonor. Kings, as ultimate guarantors of each polity, depended on these lords to function as *naidm*-enforcers, who compelled the various lower ranks of lords and *cenn-finni* to make sure that their troublesome underlings answered for their misdeeds. Default would cause the king himself to be liable to an over-king, or to a powerful enemy. The role of the high ranks of lords as a buffer to the king of the *tuath* is depicted in a fragment that appears in the tract known as '*Succession*'. The compiler of these proverbs expressed puzzlement over the old maxims, cited below; these, however, seem to reflect the fact that these lords' duties consisted primarily of readiness to respond to a crisis and stave off enemy attack:

> The *aire forgill* deserves chieftaincy or abbacy; even though
> he has only his weapons or clothes he has the honor-price of
> a king or *aire forgill*. And also the *aire ard* saves the high-

ranking lord and his *tuath*; the price of his death protects his
king and prevents them being plundered by outsiders (*CIH*
1291.13-6 = *AL* iv 383).

When all else failed, and plundering was inevitable, the rules of status
still, in theory, protected the élite. Normal distraint, as we have seen,
was undertaken only against commoners; where a noble was subject to
distraint after other procedures had failed, it was not his high-ranking
next of kin who undertook the liabilities of the kinsmen-sureties
(*inmlegon*) — for these had probably already played their hand,
economically and politically, in the roles described above. Distraint was
inflicted instead on distant, low-status kin or quasi-kin in the clan. As
was shown in the last chapter, low-status members of the *fine*,
especially the illegitimate sons of *fine* men and slave or serf women,
tended to be assimilated to this category of 'distant' kin. These people,
then, were tolerated as property-holders in the *fine*, as caretakers of a
reservoir of expendable resources — in terms of chattels and their own
persons.

The basic principle was that men of the upper stratum of the
chiefly ranks (the so-called 'seven grades') were exempt from liability
to be distrained on account of their kin, as *inmlegon*. The exemption
was not absolute, but the order of priority was changed, so that low-
status and distant kin were distrained before genealogically closer,
higher-status kin. Although most of the references to this privilege
appear in commentaries of various periods,[53] early references are found
in *Bretha Nemed*, where the Church is exempted (Breatnach 1989 #3),
in *Uraicecht Becc*,[54] where the smith is exempted, and in a legal
glossary, where the scholars and poets (*filid*) are said to be exempt.[55]

The exemption of the élite, and the substitution of poor kin where
distraint was unavoidable, received its most formal expression in the old
provisions that allowed a king to be distrained through a low-status
substitute, rather than in person. This 'substitute churl' (*aithech fortha*)
would certainly not have been next of kin to a king or lord. The oldest
reference to this institution specified that if the king had no appointed
aithech fortha, then one might be picked, *ad hoc*, from the king's *fine*
(Binchy 1973: 81, #9). The whole *fine*, moreover, should join in to raise
the amount required to free the king of his liability (*slán*). Binchy points
out that *fine*, in this case, might include all the unfree dependents of a
chief, as listed in *FF* (*ibid*: 84-5).

A passage from another Old Irish law-tract, *Do fastad cirt ocus dligid* ('On the confirmation of right and law'. *CIH* 224.1-244.22 = *AL* v 426-92), which was concerned to protect farm production from the damage that could arise from excessively inconvenient distraint, refers to men in base-clientship as remote kin (*indfhine*) of the *fine*.[56] Their oxen were not to be taken in distraint during the plowing season; the implication is that they were liable to distraint at other seasons on account of the debts or delicts of the higher-status members of the *fine*.

The same point is made in the tract on the procedure for impounding distrained cattle.[57] Here the basic text states that the 'exempt' cattle[58] of the chiefly ranks should not be seized; the commentary adds that this referred to distraint on account of kin liability, and applied where there were members of the lord's group (*aicme*) who were of commoner status — implying that these should be distrained instead.[59] According to another commentary, clients of a chief who were being distrained on his account were deprived of some of the protections normally extended to kinsmen in this situation; for example, the client could be seized in person, even though he had land which could cover the debt (*CIH* 1736.3 = *AL* ii 45.24-7). In this case, the liability occasioned by a man's chief was treated in law as identical to his own personal liability. *Fuidri* too could be seized instead of the cattle of a noble.[60]

Some of the late commentaries seem to be describing rules of *realpolitik*, not law, for if a chief were subject to distraint his power had gone, *ipso facto*, and nothing could preserve his weaker dependents from being expropriated. But during the early medieval period there existed a formal procedure of gradual distraint that only slowly escalated to full-scale plundering of the chief's dependents. As we have seen, other lords protected the king of the polity by taking political risks to enforce treaties, risks which they secured with their own personnel and their own wealth. Since many of these lords would have been kin to the king, successful aggression against the ruling *cenél* of a polity would have been like gradually peeling an onion. When these outer layers of lordly kin had been removed, enemies could press their claims directly against the king. He, however, would first liquidate the assets he had parcelled out to underlings, allowing in the first instance a chosen low-ranking representative of his *fine* to pay for him. If the reserves held by the latter were insufficient, the whole *fine* would have to contribute, including base-clients. Some serfs would evidently be handed over as slaves. With the entire structure crumbling, a king could still sometimes brandish one trump card to save his skin, namely his personal sureties, for treaties, like other contracts, were guaranteed by sureties who were not principals to the transaction. In the case of inter-territorial *cairde* treaties, sureties were drawn from beyond the local clan-structure; often they consisted of prominent churchmen and relatives through marriage and fosterage. These would be expected to step in to save a king from captivity and death.

Such a gradual process of political destruction through 'fighting with property' (the combatants often coming from competing branches of the same dynastic clan) reveals a society in which the dissipation of power from its temporary nodes of concentration had the paradoxical consequence of permitting continuous factional competition, and at the same time promoting reverence for the legitimacy of claims to rulership. The low levels of coercive power available to the military élite stimulated their appetite for validation of their claims to loyalty and subordination from the potential clientele, while the continuous circulation of the élite through dispossession and recrudescence meant that 'title' was not hard for anyone to find in some remote corner of his genuine genealogy. The thirst for title created for the literary élite a great demand for their services and enormous potential for political interference on their part.

Conclusion

The ultimate social purpose of the 'public' suretyship associated with rank and honor-price in the *fine* or *tuath* was nothing so abstract or altruistic as the maintenance of a system of law and order. Preservation of social order was the outcome — a rather haphazard one at that — of legal institutions whose immediate motivating purposes were narrowly self-promoting. Suretyship, if it could be fulfilled, warded off the danger of punitive distraint of members of the group, be it the patriarchal household, the *fine*, or the *tuath*; the lord preserved his underlings from distraint by 'outsiders' the better to enjoy their services himself. Furthermore, if distraint were inevitable, it was levied from the chattels of the low-ranking members of the clan, sparing the nobility, and only when these too had been despoiled, reaching high-status members of the élite. What looks like 'group solidarity', then, turns out to be a protective cocoon of kinsmen's chattels, lands and bodies, surrounding at its heart, the local ruler and his nearest kin. The relationship is perfectly expressed by the customary designation of a clan chieftain by the name of his clan — *the* O'Néill, *the* O'Donnell, and so on.

These circles of defense around members of the élite were the exact opposite and counterpart of the circles of constraint and pressure by next of kin which surrounded the individual low-ranking clansman. For the latter, 'kinship' was oppressive; for the former, kin were useful. Understandably, then, the Gaelic élite promoted such rules as *'cin comfocuis'* (kin liability) until the collapse of Irish independence. Great lords who were accustomed to think of themselves as 'the O'Néill', etc., were not socialized to think of the body politic as something separate from their own bodies; they were, as Simms has argued, little more than warlords by the later middle ages, and seem not to have commanded general popular support, no matter what their paid panegyrists may have said.

In Scotland, where the end of the Gaelic political structure came about at a later date and more abruptly than in Ireland, the lords found themselves suddenly plunged into the cash economy and real estate market of the recently united kingdom of Britain. Their response was to sell their clan-lands and move to London, with the consequence that clansmen were dispossessed by new landowners, assisted by the British army, and the Highlands cleared of people, cattle and forest, to make room for sheep and game reserves. The destruction of clan-based society came about because the far western lands of the British Isles were finally exposed in the early modern period to a new economic world-system; the actual end, however, was only the apogee of a centuries-old series of endings, as polity after polity succumbed to the inveterate narcissism of its political élite, and each new dynasty brought forth only the seeds of new struggles for personal pre-eminence.

Notes

1. Sir John Davies, *Discovery*: 165 (See Maxwell 1923: 352).

2. Translated by Stacey 1986: 213. I have not followed Stacey in interpreting *'fine-derb'* and *'inderb'* as close and remote kin, because I think the difference is not one of genealogical degree, but of type of relationship — the 'uncertain' kin, could include close social relations of a woman, including her own

husband. (See Patterson 1990.)

3. *RAITH FORNGARTA FINE. (CIH 61.9-10, 16 = AL v 341 [lxv]).*

4. *in boaire is ferr,* 'the *bóaire* who is best' (most reliable, lawful, prosperous, etc.) *(CIH 61.18-9 = AL v 343.15; see also CIH 790.26 ff.)*

5. *7 cethru ba aithgena 7 cethre bai diabalta 7 cethre bai eineclainni. (CIH 61.20-21 = AL v 343.17-8).*

6. *cethrar aneladhnac do muindtir (CIH 61.21-2 = AL v 343.19-21).*

7. *Gab so dot ae friut fer selba bona : beo a ceithir fine...Ní dlegthar de dechde a buar; bo aire fír, in cetna bo aire.* Smith (1932) 75 #14 a, #15 a.

8. See Binchy 1984: 11; Kelly 1988: 157. In the *'Advice to Doidin'*, the liability is imputed to the 'four *fini*', not the four generations of the *derbfhine*.

9. *Fer bis fri folug (?) chinaid fine i tuaith. (CIH 899.33 = AL ii 127.19 ff).*

10. *CG* 277 ff. Binchy commented that this surety for the *fine* gave a pledge 'which he might be summoned to give on their behalf', but the text implies no such contingency, and Binchy himself describes the *aire coisring* as an 'automatic surety' once he gave his pledge (see n.36). Stacey has recently interpreted the *aire coisring*'s pledge as a 'standing gage' put up to ensure lawful behavior in relations between the members of the *fine* and those other *tuath* members with whom they would have regular, on-going interaction, such as craftsmen (Stacey 1991). *Ad hoc* sureties would have been ineffective as a means of securing general order.

11. Kelly differs, maintaining that the *aire coisring* would have been the *cenn fine* (1988: 13-4).

12. *IMDICH CACH CORP A MEMRU MAD SOCORP SOGNIMACH SOBESACH SLAN SOFOLTACH SOCUMAIS CORP CAICH A FINE NAD BI NACH CORP CEN A CENN. CEND CAICH IAR NDAINIB A FINE. BESA SRUITHIU. BESA UAISLIU, BESA TREBAIRE, BESI GAITHIU. BESI ECNAIDE. BESI SOCHRAITI CO FIR. BESA TREISI FRI IMFOICHID BESI FORASTA. FRI URNAIDE SOMAINE 7 DOMUINI. (CIH 488.25-6, 33-5 =* Thurneysen 1923: 369 # 30, 31 = *AL* ii 279.27-35*).*

13. *dualgus cennachta* .i. *in daerraith*. *BB* # 49.f. On Lucas Ó Dalláin, see *BB*: 4.

14. See the remarks to this effect of McLeod 1987: 53-4.

15. See Ó Corráin's remarks (1972: 40), on the vesting of the position of king's *tánaiste*, not in close kin of the incumbent, but in heads of segments of the royal *cenel* who had been elbowed out of the contest for chieftaincy. In other words the 'second' was 'second in command', not next in line for the chieftaincy.

16. *DLEGAIT FLAITHE ... FORA FINE 7 FORA NAICGILLNE. CACH MARFLAITH FORA TUATHA... (CIH 526.20-527.13 = AL iii 25).*

17. *comditen dána CG* 320-1. This is Mac Néill's interpretation (1923: 296.105).

18. *CIH* 591.15-17, 592.13-15 = Thurneysen 1928, *Burgschaft* #2, #16. See the discussion of immunities from claims in Stacey (1991).

19. *tobeir gell tar cenn a fine do ríg 7 senud 7 óes cherdd... (CG 280-81).*

20. *Cach dán dogní aicdi flatha nó ecalsa folongar lethfholug a míad cháich asa aicde dogní. (CG 486-7).*

21. *Rí bunaid cech cinn... (CG 472).*

22. *Ar indí as fo chumachtu a chundrig bíid cech cenn nád timmairg a choimdiu... (CG 472-4).*

23. *DO DRUTH* .i. *Masa druth ac rig a aonur...druth iter rig 7 tuaith ...a coimedacht acin righ.* 'If it be a fool with the king alone...(or) a fool shared by the king and the *tuath* ...on circuit of entertainment (coigny) with the king.' *(CIH 1688.16-19 = AL i 162, n.1).* See also DIL, *óinmit*, for references to 'wise fools' in the retinues of Conchobar mac Nessa and other saga heroes.

24. *I FUBTUDH CACH OMNUIDH. (CIH 1692.4 = AL i 179.1-2).*

25. *The image of Ireland* (London, 1581; another ed. with notes by Walter Scott, ed. J. Small. Edinburgh, 1883). A reproduction of the woodcut appears in M. E. Collins 1980: 6. On the historical value of these engravings see Edwards and O'Dowd 1985: 126-8.

26. *CIH* 524.18-526.19. I cite the translation by McCone 1990: 221-2.

27. The same doctrine as to qualification for clerical rank appears in the Introduction to the *Senchas Már. (CIH 1225.7-17 = AL i 57.30-7).*

28. *oclach do daghcenel. (CIH 584.35 ff = AL iv 353.1-7).*

29. *CIH* 584.31, 37-8 = *AL* iv 351.32, 353.6-7. The *tánaise* of a *bóaire* had an honor-price of two *séts* of bovine stock, usually worth between 1 to 1 3/5 cows; the *seirthid* had an honor-price of one three-year-old heifer, and one two-year-old heifer, together worth 5/6 of the four year old 'great cow', *bó mór*.

30. Five *séts* in the case of the *uaitne*, but only three in the case of a *bóaire. (CIH* 584.34; 584.29 = *AL* iv 351.36-7; 351.28.30.24.) The text, however, is cryptic, giving 'u.s.' for the *uaithne's* honor-price, which may be taken as 'v *séoit'*, but leaves room for doubt.

31. Stacey translates *ansruth* as 'high noble', but a secondary sense of *ánrad* is 'warlike, valiant' (*DIL, ánrad* [c]) The military function of this noble is emphasized by the fact that the honor-price for both the ordinary and the noble *ansruth* included 'a trusty sword'. *(CIH* 585.12, 14 = *AL* iv 349.35, 39).

32. The *fergnia* ranked with the master-smith in the Old Irish text, *Bretha nemed toísech*, both apparently holding a special rank in the *tuath*. (Breatnach 1989: 16-17, #18.)

33. *IN FOSUITHER CAURRU. (CIH 1683.38 = 372.1 ff = 888.31 = AL i 135.39-40).*

34. *FIR TAISTIL... (CIH 382.18 = 890.10 = 1688.13 = AL i 156-7, 185).*

35. *FIR CONGRENN FLED FLATHA. (CIH 393.36 = AL i 199.35-6).*

36. The tract's provenance has not been identified. If it is connected to the *nemed* school, as Byrne suggested (1971: 176), its distinction between military functionaries and members of farming clans would match the existence of special functional 'castes' for artisans, the learned, priests, entertainers, etc., and would tend to further sharpen the distinction drawn in Ch.2 between the dominance in the north of agro-pastoral clans, which *combined* military and economic functions, and the lesser social importance or lower degree of development of these multifunctional, 'total' social formations in the archaic system of the south-west.

37. The *cáinte* operated under pagan supernatural protection and was loathed by the Church. See Sharpe 1979: 82; McCone 1990: 220-3.

38. *CG* 358-61. McCone (1990: 211) supports Mac Néill's original view, as against Binchy, who argued that the *aire échta* operated within his own *tuath*. (*CG*, pp 70-71).

39. *EACH FIR LEASAIGTHI. (CIH 32.5, 11 = AL v 241-3).*

40. *Cia lasa coir árchú? .ni. ic airi echta. (CIH 2128.28).*

41. Head-taking in warfare is attested mainly in the saga literature; see the entry *cendail*, in *DIL*. The practice was connected to the widespread north European veneration of the severed head. The evidence on this subject is surveyed by Ross 1967: 61-126.

42. *cen air[r]ech cen airliciud (CG 398-9; 425; 442-3; 453-4; 470-1)*

43. *combi lánchongnam i túaith do aidbdenaib, do noillechaib, do gi[u]ll, do gíall, do chairdiu tar cenn ceníuil tar crích 7 i tech flatha. CG 411-3.*

44. McLeod has analyzed the various textual references to *aire ard* and *aire forgill* and concluded that the former probably did not signify a special rank of lord, but was a generic name (high *aire*) for the ranks who had special positions, not merely clients. McLeod 1986: 62-5.

45. *7 atguidhet-som na tuatha, 7 is rig ardonaisc. (CIH 583.23-4 = AL iv 347.24-6).*

46. *Dligid a saerbiathad coruice .xxx. oc lesugud tuaithe. (CIH 583.24 = AL iv 347.27-8).* Compare *CIH* 32.11. Kings and bishops maintained retinues for the *les* of the *tuath* and the Church (*CG* 598-10); presumably, then, the action concerned the rights of the *tuath* against a similar social group, and not primarily action within the *tuath*.

47. *Aairi tuisi, dofet fine comcinel do co rí 7 arrolabrathar. (CIH 677.8; 583.28 = AL v 347.34-5).*

48. *fear tair ceann tuatha comsaera fris coit(chenn) 7 a cairde. (CIH 677.3; 583.22 = AL v 347.22-3).*

49. *CIS LIR TAIRGSIN CACHA FINE. CONN ARDOLABRAIDTAR... (CIH 227.1 = AL v 436.13-4).*

50. *CIH* 1666.9-11 = *AL* i 77.26-9.

51. *CIH* 354.33 = *AL* i 71.12. *AL* translates *fenid* as 'champion', obscuring the link to *fían* and the role of the *aire echta*.

52. A middle Irish passage shows that the role and function of the *aire échta* might be more flexible; he might be a single-combatant, or the leader of a group of up to thirty men. *(CIH 2128.28-33).*

53. e.g. *gradh flatha ant aithir 7 isaer he ar cinaidh ninbleogain. (CIH 63.36-7 = AL v 351.10-12. See also CIII 63.24, 39; CIH 255.7-25 = AL iii 113.23-115.22).*

In goba...is saer he ar... cinaid inbleogain. The smith .. is free of kin-liability. *(CIH 1593.18-20).*

55. *Cad saorus in filid ar cinaidh ninbleogain. (CIH 954.5).*

56. *CIDBE IMDIROIBRE DFIND FINE IS DO ANFUIGLIB AIRECHTA FUIGEALL IMPU. (CIH 229.15-6 = AL v 443.36-9).*

57. *'Do coimed dligtach annso' (CIH 1723.11-1755.16; 1368.1-1370.31; 1455.33-1465.20 = AL ii 1-118.6).*

58. In the context of distraint, 'exempt cattle' included cows that were sick, newly calved, or in heat. See *BB*, p.108.

59. *NI GAIBTHER ATHGABAIL NEIMHE GRAID FLATHA 7 ECULSA .i. im cinuidh ninbleogain cein bet graid fheine don aicme. (CIH 1736.23-4 = AL ii 49.4-9).*

60. *IN daer, mas im cinaid nurraid rogabad i nathgabail he.. (CIH 364.36 = AL i 109.41-111.4).*

Social Ranks of the Farmers in Early Ireland

Source   *Crith Gablach*

Term	Honour Price	Own Property	Fief	Render[1]
First *fer midboth*	'from a needle to a *dairt*'			
Second *fer midboth*	*colpdach* (yearling, female calf)	a cabin	5 *séts*[2]	wether
Ócaire	3 *séts*	7 cumals land; 7 cows + 1 bull; a house; 1/4 plow; etc.	8 cows	*dartaid inite* (Shrove tide male calf) pig's belly; 3 sacks malt; half sack dried wheat; etc.
Aithech arathrebe a deich	4 *séts*	same as *ócaire* but 10 of each animal; house and outhouse	10 cows	pick of yearlings; bacon; 4 sacks of malt; platter of grain etc.
Bóaire	5 *séts* (= 4 cows)	14 *cumals* land; 12 cows; 2 horses	12 cows	*colpdach fírend* (male yearling calf) with *imthach* (bacon malt, wheat, etc.) *twice* a year etc.
Mruigfher	6 *séts*	21 *cumals* land; 20 cows; 2 bulls; etc.	2 *cumals*	Cow, etc.

1. The 'chattels of subjection' are not included
2. The *sét* in CG = 4/5 milch cow (Kelly 1988: 116).

Social Ranks of the Farmers in Early Ireland

Source	*Cáin Aicillne*	
Term	Fief	Render
fer domun	3 *séts*	*Ág* (animal) or *miach* (sack of grain)
Óenchiniud	6 *séts* - 3 cows	wether
Fer midboth	12 *séts* - 6 cows	*dartaid* plus produce
Ócaire	16 *séts* - 8 cows	*colpdach* plus produce
Bóaire	30 *séts* - 15 cows	Cow plus produce

The Theory of Population Growth and Social Instability in Early Christian Ireland.

It is widely maintained that early Irish society was profoundly affected by population growth in the early medieval period. One of the main pieces of evidence marshalled in support of this theory is a statement in the tract on status, *CG*. Regarding this, Charles-Edwards has written: 'During the seventh century the Irish system of hierarchical social grades was changing, probably under the influence of a growth in population. Status in Ireland depended upon wealth, and some kindreds were finding it impossible to find enough land and stock to maintain the status of their members.' (Charles-Edwards 1972b: 9-10).

The evidence on which this major historical proposition rests is the statement in *CG* that the rank of *aithech a.t.d.* (see chart) was given to the sons(s) of a *bóaire*, when 'there may be four or five men who are heirs of a *bóaire* so that it is not easy for each of them to be a *bóaire*.' Charles-Edwards concludes therefore: 'What this meant is plain: the seventh century in Ireland saw a loosening of the tie between wealth and status' (*ibid*).

It is indeed interesting that a man who had not inherited a 'man's share' of clan-land was granted the basic social franchise of a land-holder, but whether population growth is the explanation is a matter to be proven, not inferred. Without further evidence *CG*'s statement can only be taken as showing that in Ireland as everywhere else, some lineages expanded, and some contracted, and that individual status went up and down within these volatile structures, depending on circumstances.

Charles-Edwards has recently reiterated these views, this time emphasizing that population growth in the late seventh century, though not necessarily incremental in absolute terms (since the context of the trend was a previous decline, due to plague), was relatively sharp as a growth trend (Charles-Edwards 1993: 473-6). This contention still does not rescue the argument that *CG* reflects unusual frequencies of status-

depression, however, for sharp rises in an emptied landscape would lead to *migration* (with and without lineage expansion) into vacant territories. Charles-Edwards' insistence on demographically induced changes in social structure is tied more to the theory of kinship contraction (which it supposedly explains) than to any facts of medieval Irish demography.

The only other documentary data on population pressure at this time are an anecdote and a morbidly humorous legend about 'the sons of Aed Slane'. The legend is found in a Life of St. Gerald of Mayo, and also in the Preface to Colmán moccu Clúasaig's hymn, which is cited here:

> 'God's blessing'. Colman Mac Uí Cluasaig, lector of Cork, made this hymn to save himself from the Yellow Plague which was in the time of the sons of Aed Slane. For numerous were the men in Ireland at that time, and such was their multitude that they used to get only thrice nine ridges for each man in Ireland, to wit nine of bog, nine of arable land and nine of forest. So the sons of Aed Slane...and many others fasted together with the nobles of Ireland, for the thinning of the people, for scarcity of food had come because of their multitude. Wherefore the Yellow Plague was inflicted on them, and there died in that year the sons of Aed Slane... (Stokes and Strachan 1903, II: 298).

Kenney states that on linguistic grounds the Preface to Colmán's hymn is generally regarded as falling between 800-850 (1929: 727), and its account of the *causa scribendi* thus belongs to a type of narrative which placed a text into a *literary* context by providing it with a pseudo-historical context (Kenney 1929: 464). Such material cannot be taken as evidence of actual events unless corroborated. But the Annals, which do refer to the Yellow Plague at 664-5, make no comment as to the numerousness or otherwise of the population at this time, although references to natural phenomena such as extremes of weather, the condition of the harvest, the quantity of mast, and animal growth, are commonplace in these sources.

The anecdote is even weaker evidence. Purporting to explain how a charioteer was able to traverse a vast expanse of land in a very short time, the text asserted that he could do so because at that time there were no fences in Ireland. These were put up, the author continued, only in the time of 'the sons of Aed Slane', because there were too many heirs on the land at this time. The anecdote clearly replicates a motif in the story of the Yellow Plague. It is undermined by archaeological evidence of pre-Christian fences and ditches (Norman and St. Joseph: 59-72), and by the fact that population growth within local settlements is historically associated with open-field farming, not with enclosure (see Ch. 4).

The weakness of the documentary support for the theory of population growth is not surprising, for the theory is generally linked to the development of monasticism during this period, and is in fact an inference from this development, on the assumption that monasticism stimulated the revival of grain production in early medieval Europe after the agrarian slump of late antiquity. Recently, however, other views have come to the fore on this subject. Georges Duby, while acknowledging that before the end of the first millennium, most of the big farms in France were in the hands of the king's agents and monastic communities, also shows how unproductive were the latter in terms of cultivation, and how the communities depended on their use of the *saltus*, the grazing lands (Duby 1974: 5-6). In any case, the role of agriculture in the development of higher levels of wealth and production in Europe is now seen by many scholars as secondary to external forces, such as the flow of bullion from the major sources in the east, which made possible the restoration of currency and markets (Van Bath 1963: 29-39).

Nevertheless, monasteries and grain production are assigned pride of place in the theory that early Christian Ireland *must* have experienced significant natural population growth. An early statement of this position was put forward by Father John Ryan (1931: 364): 'Agricultural, as distinct from pastoral pursuits were ... favored by the great increase in population during the sixth century (which led to the enclosing of lands in the seventh century) and by the fact that corn (rather than butter, milk and meat) was the staple article of diet of the monks.'

But it is very doubtful if the ascetic aversion to protein — the monastic ideal of life on bull's milk (thin porridge and water) — offers any evidence as to staple consumption. The monastic influence on population growth has been often repeated,[1] however, most influentially perhaps in Ó Corráin's *Ireland before the Normans*: 'The phenomenal expansion of Irish monasticism from the middle of the sixth century led not only to an expansion of agriculture and horticulture but also to the introduction of more sophisticated techniques...All this activity points to a steady rise in population. Ireland in the ninth and tenth centuries, far from being a country of wandering pastoralists in which property was owned tribally, was a land of settled mixed farmers with a developed sense of private property.' (1972: 49).

As evidence Ó Corráin pointed to such facts as, 'the high frequency of the element *dísert* 'waste land' in monastic place names and the almost equally common *clúain*, which may mean pasture land won from forest'; 'references to the reclaiming of waste land and the clearing of woodlands in secular texts which date from about 800 or before'; a statement in an early law-tract to the effect that 'a holder of an estate deficient in open ground, moorland (rough pasture) or water may supply the defect from such unappropriated land as may be available'; the glossing of the term *dírainn*, 'which means unappropriated land originally' by later scribes as 'waste or economically worthless land'; and the existence of 'a highly developed and sophisticated law of trespass'.

These are all interesting pieces of evidence for early agrarian organization, but none supports the specific contention of population *growth*, let alone growth to the point of either human saturation of the landscape, or social stress prompting change in class relations, as proposed by Charles-Edwards. As to *dírainn*, since no examples of a clear-cut change of meaning are given, it remains possible that this word signified the same complex of meanings in early and later texts and glosses, namely land that was used for purposes other than cultivation and winter grazing, comparable to Latin *vastus*, whence English 'waste' ('vast, open' country, not 'waste, worthless' country), in which people had only contingent and latent rights of usufruct. Such land was not carved up into individual portions and therefore had no fixed worth to any individual — but certainly had worth to the community. In any case, the definition of 'economically worthless' must be questioned in this context. In a society short of labor, valuable land would be that which is already under cultivation, while potential arable land might be viewed as of little worth because of the costs of clearance.

As to *clúain* (meadow), and its association with early monastic sites, Ó Corráin seems to imply that the term can only refer to primary clearance of virgin land. But under the extensive land-use regimes found commonly throughout Atlantic Europe, land was cleared by burning, cultivated until weak, then left to regenerate naturally for a long time. In such a context, *clúain* might well refer to re-clearance of secondary growth. The extent to which monasteries were superimposed on existing farming communities is only just beginning to be investigated and until definite findings are obtained it is reasonable to suppose that religious communities were granted rights in areas that were already or had recently been in production. On this point, we may note that the Saints Lives do not depict the sanctified as heroic woodsmen; unless they were hermits (in which case they were supported by others), the saints are usually depicted toiling away in an established agricultural routine. And, for what it is worth on this kind of question, *The Book of Invasions* and *Dindshenchas* onomastic tradition ascribe the creation of the great cleared farming areas of Ireland, the 'plains', to the activities of ancient goddesses.[2]

The historically specific circumstances of early monasticism should also be considered: the first monks, unlike the twelfth-century Cistercian sheep-farmers who sought pasture to escape mankind, were engaged in the conversion of a pagan population. This they did by extending networks of dependent communities throughout the countryside, eventually establishing large confederacies. Many of the earliest central foundations were placed on very good agricultural sites in the east midlands, such as Tallacht, Finglas and Kildare, which were areas of ancient occupation. Moreover, Bitel writes, 'the obsession with donations and endowments in all types of ecclesiastical literature suggests that monks and nuns were forced to seek land from those who already owned it' (1986: 17). It was only after repeated Viking raids that the remote monasteries of the lower Shannon overtook the old, centrally-situated, foundations in importance (Ó Corráin 1972: 109-110). The interior monasteries, though sited on islands of fertile land, were not positioned there in order to open up the farming potential of the boglands, but rather to take advantage of the social and economic opportunities afforded by control of water and overland long-distance routes through the interior wilderness.[3]

While some monasteries must have made serious efforts to improve agricultural production so as to feed their many visitors, we have no proof that whatever efforts they made actually resulted in greatly enhanced production. For one thing, the period of monastic growth coincided with the onset of a sustained period of bad weather, as compared with the warmer and sunnier Roman period. In this changing environment there occurred a series of devastating plagues (MacArthur 1948-9), poor harvests, and animal diseases.[4] Another consideration is that the monks — the very sector of society supposedly in the van of agricultural improvement — were the least committed to sexually reproducing their own kind.

Even where robust fertility was likely to flourish, around the homes of the nobility, it is doubtful that extra food systematically found its way into the mouths of lower-class pregnant women and their small children, those who would have to get more in order for population levels to rise rapidly. There were other things to do with additional foodstuffs: more grain could mean more alcohol, and more meat and cheese could simply mean a better diet for the powerful, and increased capacity to support slaves, craftsmen and mercenary soldiers. It is quite conceivable that Irish society grew more comfortable at the aristocratic level during the 'golden age' of the seventh and eight centuries, while levels of nutrition, hygiene and fertility remained low for others. Indeed, whether population change in antiquity is attributable mainly to changes in the quantity of available food is questioned by modern research (M. E. Jones 1979: 232-9); sanitation, hygiene, endemic morbidity, poor shelter and clothing, insecurity and anxiety may depress fertility, notwithstanding improvements in nutrition. In all probability, Ireland during the first millennium conformed with population trends in the rest of Europe; that is, there was population decline c. 545-700, spurts of growth between 700-850 that were possibly correlated with the drier, calmer weather of this period (Manley 1962: Ch. 12), during which some expansion into unoccupied land was possible, and stagnation thereafter, possibly continuing in Ireland well past the eleventh century on account of chronic warfare (Russell 1972: 37-41).

The arguments reviewed above are inferential ones. The only attempts to supply direct evidence of population growth have come from archaeologists. One finding that formed a plank in the theory of population growth was derived from pollen analysis, which suggested that in some parts of early Christian Ireland, grasslands expanded and forests retreated (Culleton and Mitchell 1976: 120-79). This has been taken to indicate the advance of tillage. Newer methods of soil analysis cast doubt on earlier findings based on this method, however, and the extent of deforestation and increased tillage during the early historical period is now questioned (Hirons 1983: 111). Even granted that primary forest clearance for tillage took place in some areas, it is far from proven that this was a widely distributed trend, and that it coincided significantly with the expansion of the monasteries; for example, the pollen diagram from Red Bog, Co. Louth, showed clearance preceding the Christian conversion, namely between A.D. 1-600 (Edwards 1990: 52). On this subject all that can be said is that data does not yet exist that would permit the sort of aggregate analysis required to shed light on the theory under discussion here.

The other type of physical evidence of expanding human occupation of the land is the distribution of settlement sites. As was shown in Ch. 4., the difficulties of dating ringforts and determining their functions make it impossible to estimate population sizes, let alone changes in specific centuries, on the basis of the numbers. Archaeological evidence, because it cannot fill in the whole social picture, doesn't rule out the theory of population growth, but does make it look less credible. Historians of agriculture, looking at the material remains of the historical period, have suggested that low population densities were common in Ireland throughout the middle ages (Butlin 1978: 33-4).

Further detracting from the plausibility of the theory are two facts of historical geography. One of these is that dynastic groups often survived after defeat on marginal lands. The other is that the Normans entered a country, heavily wooded, thinly populated and hard to farm. Lydon has shown that a factor in the failure of the Normans to permanently tilt agriculture towards crop production was the difficulty of securing labor (1972: 1-7). Although Norman lords offered advantageous conditions to both their immigrant English workers and native Irish farmers (many of whom accepted inducements to return to lands they had vacated during the immediate post-invasion period), the manorial estates were chronically short of labor. Kenneth Nicholls makes the same point regarding economic conditions as late as the end of the sixteenth century: 'The lack of people in this period is borne out by the frequent reference in documents to the shortage of tenants and cultivators, for whose services landlords competed and who wandered around from place to place and master to master, apparently driven not by want, but by restlessness and the inducements held out to them' (1987: 409).

A strong bargaining position on the part of the potential labor force, as we saw, was one of the hallmarks of the clan system during the early Christian period, in which lordship possessed an unusual contractual aspect. Another sign of chronic agrarian labor shortage is that even burgesses, quite honorable English dependents of manorial lords, had to pitch in with menial work, an unusual stipulation that resembles the Irish free clients' manual services (see Ch. 6).

Only a very general conclusion can be drawn from these considerations, but it is not one that favors notions of radical population growth in the early middle ages. One must conclude that there were strong constraints against sudden natural increases in aggregate population levels that could be sustained over the long-run. Short-term local increases would inevitably have occurred in the context of temporarily favorable conditions, notably a period of sustained good weather and political successes, but these would inevitably give way during reverses of natural conditions or when an expanding political group had fully occupied its new niche. In this respect Ireland was no different from medieval and prehistoric Europe in general, for which recent research on agrarian output and population levels shows no simple causal relationship between one variable and the other — no simple equation, such as 'more grain, hence more people'. (Grigg 1982: 43; Barker 1985: 260-2). But whereas Britain and France went through periods of stasis and even regression, there was nevertheless a long-term gradual movement in these regions towards higher levels of economic production and associated social complexity. In Ireland, however, periods of crisis, when the agricultural system collapsed in the agrarian sector, seem to have plunged society back to a low level of economic organization marked by great paucity of material remains in the archaeological record and later, in historical times, by desertion of nucleated settlements and regression to greater dependency on livestock and wilderness (Aalen 1983: 368). Such stasis partly explains the persistence of the clan system, as analyzed in this book, throughout the medieval period, for the clan was essentially a people-keeping device — an organization that promoted group coherence, conserving the services of its members for each other, and for its lords.

Notes

1. De Paor 1958: 53; Mitchell 1965: 121-32; J.G.Evans 1975: 71-2.

2. For example, *Tailtiu*, a princess of the defeated mythological group, the *Fir Bolg*, was said to have chopped down the woods to make the meadow-lands around Telltown in Meath (Gwynn 1924: 149-51, 155, 161).

3. Smyth 1982: 26-32; 84-100. Smyth notes that Melville Richards makes the same point regarding the location of early Welsh monasteries at remote sites on important routes (1970: 337-8).

4. Some scholars interpret plagues as evidence for population growth, on the model, perhaps, of the fourteenth-century crisis. Mac Niocaill, for example, suggests that the plague of 664-5 'was the outcome of famine (for which read malnutrition), itself caused by overpopulation' (1972: 66). The evidence, however, is derived from the Life of Gerald of Mayo.

GLOSSARY OF TECHNICAL TERMS

Agnates : kin reckoned only through males, e.g., father's father's brother's son's son. Warning: father's father's brother's son's daughter is an 'agnate', but her son is not.

Agnatic : adjective from above, describing a kinship system, or a relationship traced in this way.

Bilateral : kinship traced through all ancestors and all their descendants, regardless of gender.

Cognatic : same as 'bilateral'.

Descending kindred : the on-going set of relationships in a kindred over several generations, not necessarily confined to patrilineal relationships, though these may be the dominant ties, as in the Irish and Scottish clan. Sometimes termed a 'ramage' in bilateral systems.

Dyad : a relationship between two people only.

Ego: the point of reference ('me') adopted to describe a person's kindred, as in 'ego and (my, or anyone's) cousin'.

Fief: any advance of wealth given to secure political allegiance and/or repayments in a decentralized political system; originally cattle in Germanic as well as Celtic culture.

Matrilineal : kinship traced only through the female line - in formal terms a mirror image of agnatic kinship, but with important social differences.

Patrilineal : alternative term for agnatic.

Personal kindred: a circle of kin, focused on *ego*; a group that only coheres in relation to this reference point.

377

Polity: a non-committal term for any unit of political significance in whatever context (used to avoid the connotations of words like 'kingdom', 'tribe' etc.)

Wergeld : a Germanic word for an indemnity paid by a slayer and his kin or other associates, to relatives and sometimes the lord and associates of the slain man; a payment to ward off vengeance.

GENERAL GLOSSARY OF IRISH TERMS

Only the nominative singular form is supplied. Definitions are working definitions only; for the semantic field of any word, see the *Dictionary of the Irish Language*.

aire: freeman, and/or lord.

aithech: rent-payer, commoner, client, ordinary farmer.

banchomarba: woman-heir, usually of high status, inheriting life-time usufruct of *fintiu*.

bóaire: a farmer, often used of the several grades of farmer, or specifically, a 'strong-farmer'.

cairde: a treaty between two independent polities.

ceile: client; also (especially later), spouse (m. or f.)

cenn: head or chief, e.g. *cenn fine*, lineage chief.

cenél: a descending kindred, in-marrying, and so 'bilateral' in many aspects of kinship, though patrilineal in descent; usually had a chiefly agnatic group at the core. Parallel to Welsh *cenedl*, a bilateral descending kindred.

coibche: 'engagement present'; a pre-nuptial gift from the intended husband to the bride and her father.

comaithches: 'joint tax payers'; a community of neighbors with some of the mutual obligations of kin.

cró: wergeld, worth seven *cumal*s regardless of rank.

cumal: (i) slave-woman (ii) the main unit of 'currency' or measure of wealth, worth three 'great cows' (cows having calved three times and in full milk-production).

derbfhine: in a personal kindred, ego's second-cousins and their ascendents; also used loosely for kin, as compared with other associates.

díbad: *fintiu* land that passed into collective inheritance when a *gelfhine* died out.

díre: honor-price, paid according to rank (see chart on rank). Fractions paid depending on gravity of offence.

dóer: dependent, attached, ignoble.

fer midboth: junior ranks of farmers, generally without having received inheritance (two subdivisions existed).

fine: a classification of kin, usually of agnatic kin. See Ch. 8.

fintiu: land inherited through the *fine*.

flaith: a lord, ruler or king.

fuba (and) ruba: 'home-guard' — the obligation of neighbors to secure territory from human and animal predators.

fuidir: tenant without claims through inheritance to a share of clan lands, i.e. without *fintiu*.

gelfhine: in an agnatic personal kindred, ego's first cousins and their fathers. Also used to indicate a single line of descent for several generations. Also used to refer to the prominent descent group, especially that of a chief (later termed *flaith gelfhine*).

goire: obligation to care for dependent kin, especially a parent of the same sex as oneself.

íarfine: in an agnatic personal kindred, ego's third cousins and their ascendents.

indfhine: in an agnatic personal kindred, ego's fourth cousins and ascendents.

inmlegon: a surrogate, usually a close kinsman, penalized on behalf of another.

lánamain: a pair or couple, in the relationship of a *lánamnas*. Eventually signified a married couple, but in early law indicated a legal relationship in which exchanges were 'immune'.

lánamnas: dyadic relationships, generally long-term, interdependent but unequal, e.g. father and son, lord and client, teacher and pupil. Husband and wife not originally included.

maithre: mother's kin.

naidm: an enforcing surety

nemed: privileged persons, usually but not always of the élite, often skilled professionals, including craftsmen, clergymen and poets.

ócaire: a grade of farmer below the *bóaire*, lacking certain social privileges.

rath: a fief, or advance of property, usually cattle, given to a client by a lord to secure his services.

ráth: a surety who promises to pay on behalf of another (a *fechem*), if he/she defaults on a contract.

rí: a king

senchléithe: 'old house-posts'; hereditary serf, unable to leave.

sét: valuable, treasure or jewel: a unit of 'currency'

sóer: independent, 'free', sometimes 'noble' - always better than *dóer* (q.v.); in compounds, e.g. *sóercheile*, client at liberty to terminate contract.

trícha cét: the largest unit assessed for military capacity, probably originating during the Viking age.

tuath: the basic polity; a people; a petty kingdom or lordship.

AALEN, F. H. A. (1978) *Man and the landscape in Ireland.* London. (1983) 'Perspectives on the Irish landscape in prehistory and history', in Reeves-Smyth and Hamond, 1983: 357-72.

ALCOCK, LESLIE (1987) *Economy, society and warfare among the Britons and Saxons.* Cardiff.

ANDERSON, J. G. C. (1938) ed. *Cornelii Taciti: de Origine et Situ Germanorum.* Oxford.

ARENSBURG, C. M. (1959) *The Irish Countryman: an anthropological study.* Gloucester, Mass. (first pub., 1937).

ARNOLD, BETTINA, AND GIBSON, T. BLAIR (1994) eds. *Celtic Chiefdom, Celtic State.* Cambridge.

BAILLIE, M. (1980) 'Dendrochronology — the Irish View', *Current Archaeology* 73: 62-3.

BAKER, A. R. H., and **BUTLIN, R. A.** (1973) eds. *Studies of Field Systems in the British Isles.* Cambridge.

BANNERMAN, J. (1974) *Studies in the history of Dalriada.* Edinburgh and London.

BANKS, MARY M. (1938) '*Na tri mairt*, the three marts and the man with the withy', *Études Celtiques* 3: 131-43.

BARKER, Graeme (1985) *Prehistoric Farming in Europe.* Cambridge.

BARRETT, G., and **GRAHAM, G. J.** (1975) 'Some considerations concerning the dating and distribution of ring-forts in Ireland', *Ulster Journal of Archaeology* (Ser. 3) 38: 33-45.

BAUMGARTEN, ROLF (1985) 'The kindred metaphors in '*Bechbretha*' and '*Coibnes uisci thairidne*', *Peritia* 4: 307-327.
(1986) *Bibliography of Irish Linguistics and Literature 1942-71.* Dublin.

BEST, R. I. (1969; orig. 1942) *Bibliography of Irish Philology and Manuscript Literature 1913-41.* Dublin.

BEST, R. I., and **BERGIN O. J.** (1929) eds. *Lebor na Huidre: Book of the Dun Cow.* Dublin.

BIELER, LUDWIG (1975) ed. and transl. *The Irish Penitentials. Scriptores Latini Hiberniae*, vol. 5. Dublin (first pub. 1963).

382

(1979) ed. and transl. *The Patrician texts in the Book of Armagh.* Dublin. *Scriptores Latini Hiberniae.* 10.

BINCHY, D.A. (1936) ed. *Studies in Early Irish Law.* Dublin.

(1936) 'The family membership of women', *SEIL*: 180-6.

(1936) 'The legal capacity of women in regard to contracts', *SEIL:* 207-34.

(1938a) ed. and transl. *Bretha Crólige, Ériu* 12: 1-77.

(1938b) 'Sick-maintenance in Irish law', *Ériu* 12: 78-136.

(1940) *'Aimser Chue'* in John Ryan ed. 1940: 18-22.

(1941) ed. *Críth Gablach.* Dublin.

(1943) 'The linguistic and historical value of the Irish law tracts' [The Sir John Rhys Lecture of the British Academy. Separate publication, paginated 3-35]. Also in *Proc. Brit. Acad.* 29: 195-227, and reprinted in Dafydd Jenkins ed. *Celtic law papers.* Brussels 1971: 73-107.

(1952) ed. and transl. 'The Saga of Fergus Mac Léti', *Ériu* 16: 33-48.

(1955a) *'Bretha Nemed', Ériu* 17: 4-6.

(1955b) ed. and transl. *Coibnes Uisci Thairidne, Ériu* 17: 52-85.

(1958a) 'The fair of Tailtiu and the feast of Tara', *Ériu* 18: 113-137.

(1958b) 'The date and provenance of *Uraicecht Becc*', *Ériu* 18: 44-54.

(1961) 'The background of early Irish literature', *Studia Hibernica* 1: 7-18.

(1962a) 'Patrick and his biographers', *Studia Hibernica* ii: 7-173.

(1962b) 'The Passing of the Old Order' in *Proceedings of the International Congress of Celtic Studies.* Dublin: 119-32.

(1966a) ed. and transl. *Bretha Déin Chécht, Ériu* 20: 1-66.

(1966b) 'Ancient Irish Law', *Irish Jurist* 1: 84-92.

(1967) ed. 'Prolegomena to a study of the Ancient laws of Ireland, by Eóin Mac Néill', *The Irish Jurist*, 2: 106-15.

(1970) *Celtic and Anglo-Saxon Kingship.* Oxford (*The O'Donnell Lectures for 1967-8*).

(1971) ed. and transl. 'An archaic legal poem', *Celtica* 9: 152-68.

(1972) 'Celtic suretyship; a fossilized Indo-European institution?' *Irish Jurist* 7: 360-72, repr. in Cardona, Hoenigswald and Senn eds. *Indo-European and Indo-Europeans* (1970): 355-67.

(1973a) 'Distraint in Irish law', *Celtica* 10: 22-71.

(1973b) ed. and transl. 'A text on the forms of distraint', *Celtica* 10: 72-86.

(1975-6a) 'The Pseudo-historical Prologue to the *Senchas Már*', *Studia Celtica* X-XI: 15-28.

(1975-6b) 'Irish history and Irish law : I and II,' *Studia Hibernica* 15: 7-36; 16: 7-45.

(1978) ed. *Corpus Iuris Hibernici* i-vi. Dublin.

(1981) 'Brewing in eighth-century Ireland', in Scott ed. (1981): 3-6.

(1983) '*Corpus Iuris Hibernici — Incipit* or *Finit Amen*?' in G. Mac Eóin ed. *Proceedings of the Sixth International Congress of Celtic Studies (1979)* Dublin: 149-64.

(1984) 'The original meaning of *co nómad náu (nó)*; Linguists v. Historians?', *Celtica* 16: 1-12.

BITEL, LISA M. (1986) 'Women's monastic enclosures in early Ireland: a study of female spirituality and male monastic mentalities', *Journ. Medieval History* 12: 15-36.

BLAIR, P. H. (1962) *An Introduction to Anglo-Saxon England.* Cambridge.

BLOCH, MARC (1969) 'The advent of the water-mill' in *Land and Work in Medieval Europe.* New York: 136-68. (repr. from *Annales*, 36 (Nov. 1935), Vol. vii: 538-63).

BONNEY, D. (1972), 'Early Boundaries in Wessex', in Fowler ed. 1972: 168 ff.

BRADLEY, JOHN (1988) *Settlement and Society in Medieval Ireland: Studies presented to F. X. Martin.* Kilkenny.

(1988) 'The interpretation of Scandinavian settlement in Ireland', in Bradley ed. 1988: 49-78.

BRADY, CIARAN, and GILLESPIE, RAYMOND (1986) *Natives and Newcomers.* Dublin.

BREATNACH, LIAM (1984) 'Canon law and secular law in early Ireland: the significance of *Bretha Nemed*', *Peritia* 3: 439-59.

(1986) 'The ecclesiastical element in the Old-Irish legal tract *Cáin Fhuithirbe*', *Peritia* 5: 36-52.

(1987) *Uraicecht na Ríar*. Early Irish Law Ser. 2. Dublin.

(1989) *Bretha Nemed Toísech* ('The first third of *Bretha Nemed Toísech*') ed. and transl. *Ériu* 40: 1-40.

(1990) 'Lawyers in Early Ireland', in Hogan and Osborough, eds. 1990: 1-14.

BRINDLEY, A.L., LANTING, J.N., AND MONK, W.G. (1989/90) 'Radiocarbon dates from Irish *fulachta fiadh* and other burnt mounds', *Journal of Irish Archaeology* 5: 25-33.

BROWNBILL, J. (1925) 'The tribal hidage', *Eng. Hist. Rev.* 40: 497-503.

BUCHANAN. R. H. (1973) 'Field systems of Ireland', in Baker and Butlin, eds. 1973: 580 ff.

BUCHANAN, R. H., JONES, E., and McCOURT, D. (1971) eds. *Man and his Habitat: Essays presented to Emyr Estyn Evans*. London.

BUSH, M. L. (1988) *Rich Noble, Poor Noble*. Manchester.

BUTLIN, R. A. (1976) 'Land and people, c.1600', in Moody, Martin and Byrne eds. 1976, vol. 3.

(1977) *The Development of the Irish Town*. London.

(1978) 'Some observations on the field systems of medieval Ireland', *Geographia Polonia* 38: 31-6.

BYOCK, JESSE L. (1988) *Medieval Iceland: Society, Sagas and Power*. Berkeley.

BYRNE, FRANCIS J. (1971) 'Tribes and tribalism in early Ireland', *Ériu* 22: 28-66.

(1987) *Irish Kings and High Kings*. London (first publ. 1973).

CAMPBELL, BRUCE M. S., and OVERTON, MARK, (1991) *Land, Labour and livestock: historical studies in European agricultural productivity*. Manchester.

CAREY, JOHN (1989/90) 'Myth and mythography in *Cath Maige Tuired*', in *Studia Celtica* xiv/xxv: 53-69.

(1990) 'The Two Laws in Dubthach's Judgment', *Camb. Med. Celt. Stds.* 19 (Summer): 1-18.

CARNEY, JAMES (1955) *Studies in Early Irish Literature*. Dublin.

CASEY, P. J. (1979) *The End of Roman Britain*. B.A.R., British Ser. No 71. Oxford.

CASSANELLI, LEE (1982) *The Shaping of Somali Society.* Philadelphia.

CAULFIELD, SEAMUS (1983) 'The neolithic settlement of North Connaught', in Reeves-Smyth and Hamond eds. 1983: 195-216.

CHADWICK, NORA K., (1958) ed. *Studies in the early British Church.* Cambridge.

CHAMPION, T., GAMBLE, C., SHENNAN, S., and WHITTLE, A. (1984) eds. *Prehistoric Europe.* London.

CHAPMAN, MALCOLM (1978) *The Gaelic Vision in Scottish Culture.* London.

(1982) 'Semantics' and the 'Celt', in David Parkin ed. *Semantic Anthropology.* London: 123-143.

CHARLES-EDWARDS, T.M. (1970-72) 'Some Celtic kinship terms', *Bulletin of the Board of Celtic Studies* 24 (May): 105-22.

(1972a): 'A note on common farming', in Kathleen Hughes, *Early Christian Ireland: an Introduction to the Sources.* London and New York: 61-4.

(1972b) 'Kinship, Status and the Origins of the Hide', *Past and Present* 56: 3-33.

(1980) 'The *Corpus Iuris Hibernici*' (review article), *Studia Hibernica* 20: 141-62.

(1984) **'The Church and settlement'**, in Ní Chatháin and Richter eds. 1984:160-75.

(1986) '*Críth Gablach* and the law of status', *Peritia* 5: 53-73.

(1993) *Early Irish and Welsh Kinship.* Oxford.

CHARLES-EDWARDS, T. M., and KELLY, FERGUS (1983) ed. and transl. *Bechbretha.* Dublin.

CHARLES-EDWARDS, T.M., OWEN, MORFYDD M., and WALTERS, D.B. (1986) eds. *Lawyers and Laymen.* Cardiff.

CLANCY, EILEEN, and FORD, PATRICK (1980) *Ballynaglera Parish.* Dublin.

CLARKE, D. L. (1972) ed. 'A provisional model of an Iron Age society and its settlement system', in D. L. Clarke ed. *Models in Archaeology.* London: 801-69.

CLUTTON-BROCK, JULIETTE (1989) ed. *The Walking Larder. Patterns of domestication, pastoralism, and predation.* London.

COLLINS, A. E. P. (1966) 'Excavations at Dressogagh Rath, Co. Armagh', *Ulst. J. Arch.* 29: 117-129.

COLLINS, M.E. (1980) *Ireland, 1478-1610.* Dublin.

COMYN, DAVID (1902) *The History of Ireland by Geoffrey Keating; Foras Feasa ar Eirinn* vol i. London.

CONDIT, TOM (1992) 'Ireland's hillfort capital', *Archaeology, Ireland* 6. n.3: 16-20.

COSGROVE, ART (1987) *Medieval Ireland, 1169-1534.* Oxford. Vol ii of *A New History of Ireland* (10 vols), edited by Moody, Martin and Byrne.

CRAMP, R. (1986) 'Northumbria and Ireland' in Szarmach and Oggins eds 1986: 185-201.

CRIGGER, BETTE-JANE (1991) ' "A man is better than his birth": identity and action in early Irish law', *Unpublished doctoral dissertation. University of Chicago, Departments of Anthropology and Linguistics.*

CROSS, TOM PEATE, and SLOVER, CLARK HARRIS (1969) ed. and transl. *Ancient Irish Tales.* New York (first publ. 1936).

CULLETON, E.B., and MITCHELL, G.F. (1976) 'Soil erosion following deforestation in the Early Christian period in South Wexford', *Journal of the Royal Society of Antiquaries of Ireland* 106: 120-79.

CUNLIFFE, BARRY (1974) *Iron Age Communities in Britain.* London.

(1988) *Greeks, Romans and Barbarians.* New York.

CURTIS, E. (1910) 'The clan system amongst English settlers in Ireland', *Eng. Hist. Rev.* 25: 116-20.

DAHL, GUDRUN and HJORT, ANDERS (1976) 'Having herds: pastoral herd growth and household economy', *Stockholm Stds. in Soc. Anth.* 2.

DANAHER, KEVIN (1964a) *Gentle places and simple things.* Cork.
(1964b) *In Ireland long ago.* Cork (first ed. 1962).
(1972) *The year in Ireland.* Cork.

DAVIDSON, T. (1958-9) 'Cattle-milking charms and amulets', *Gwerin* ii no. 1: 22-37.

DAVIES, R. R. (1979) *Historical Perception: Celts and Saxons.* Cardiff.

DAVIES, WENDY, and FOURACRE, PAUL (1986) eds. *Settlement of Disputes in Early Medieval Europe.* Cambridge.

DAVIES, WENDY, and VIERCK, HAYO (1974) 'The Contexts of Tribal Hideage: Social Aggression and Settlement Patterns', *Frühmittelalterliche Studien.* Band 8: 223-93. Berlin and New York.

DE PAOR, M. and L. (1958) *Early Christian Ireland.* London.

DILLON, MYLES (1932) 'Stories from the Law-tracts', *Ériu* 11: 42-65.

(1936) 'The relationship of mother and son, of father and daughter, and the law of inheritance with regard to women', *SEIL*: 129-79.

(1946) *The Cycles of the Kings.* Oxford.

(1954) *Early Irish Society.* Dublin.

(1962) ed. and transl. *Lebar na cert. The Book of Rights.* London.

DILLON, MYLES, and CHADWICK, NORA (1967) *The Celtic Realms.* London.

DINNEEN, P. S. (1908 - 1914) *The History of Ireland: Forus Feasa ar Eirinn, by Geoffrey Keating*, vols ii-iv. London.

DOBBS, MARGARET E. (1930) ed. and transl. *'Banshenchus'*, *Revue Celtique* 47: 282-339; *ibid.* (1931) 48: 163-234; *ibid.* (1932) 49: 437-89.

DOCKÈS, PIERRE (1982) *Medieval Slavery and Liberation*, transl. A. Goldhammer. Chicago (first publ. France, 1979).

DODGSHON, ROBERT A. (1980) *The Origin of British Field Systems.* London.

DOHERTY, CHARLES (1980) 'Exchange and trade in medieval Ireland', *Proc. Roy. Ir. Acad.* 110 (C): 67-89.

(1982) 'Some aspects of hagiography as a source for economic history', *Peritia* I: 300-28.

DOWN, KEVIN (1987) 'Colonial society and economy in the high middle ages', in Cosgrove ed. 1987.

DRISCOLL, STEPHEN T., and NIEKE, MARGARET R. (1988) eds. *Power and Politics in Early Medieval Britain and Ireland.* Edinburgh.

DUBY, GEORGES (1974) *The Early Growth of the European Economy: Warriors and Peasants from the Seventh to the Twelfth Century.* Ithaca (first publ. Paris 1973).

DUFFY, P. J. (1981) 'The territorial organisation of Gaelic landownership and its transformation in County Monaghan, 1591-1640.' *Irish Geography* xiv: 1-23.

DUIGNAN, MICHAEL (1940) 'On the medieval sources for the legend of *Cenn (Crom) Croich* of *Magh Slecht*' in Ryan, J. ed. *Feilsgribhinn Eóin Mhic Néill*. Dublin.

DUMÉZIL, GEORGES (1968), *Mythe et épopée. vol 1. L'Idéologie des trois fonctions dans les épopées des peuples indo-européens*. Paris.

DYMMOCK, JOHN (1600) 'A Treatise of Ireland', in *Ir. Arch. Soc. Tracts* (1842).

EARWOOD, CAROLINE (1989/90) 'Radiocarbon dating of late prehistoric wooden vessels', in *Journal of Irish Archaeology* 5: 37-44.

EDWARDS, NANCY (1990) *The Archaeology of Early Medieval Ireland*. Philadelphia.

EDWARDS, R.W. DUDLEY, and O'DOWD, MARY (1985) *Sources for Early Modern Irish History*. Cambridge.

EMPEY, C.E., (1985) 'The Norman period, 1185-1500' in Nolan ed. *Tipperary: history and society*.

ETTLINGER, ELLEN (1952) 'The association of burials with popular assemblies, fairs and races in ancient Ireland', *Études Celtiques* 6: 30-61.

EVANS, D. ELLIS (1981) 'Celts and Germans', *Bulletin of the Board of Celtic Studies* 29 pt.2: 230-55.

EVANS, D. ELLIS, GRIFFITH, JOHN G., AND JOPE, E. M. (1986) eds. *Proceedings of the Seventh International Congress of Celtic Studies, 1983*. Oxford.

EVANS, ESTYN (1939) 'Some survivals of the Irish openfield system', *Geography* 24: 24-36.

    (1940) 'Transhumance in Europe', *Geography* 25: 172-80.

    (1942) *Irish Heritage*. New York.

    (1956) 'The Ecology of Peasant Life in Western Europe' in W. L. Thomas, Jr., ed. *Man's Role in Changing the Face of the Earth: an International Symposium*. Chicago.

    (1957) *Irish Folk Ways*. New York.

    (1967) *Mourne Country*. Dundalk.

EVANS, JOHN G. (1975) *The Environment of Early Man in the British Isles*. London.

EVANS-PRITCHARD, E. E. (1940) *The Nuer*. Oxford.

FITZGERALD, ROBERT, ed. and transl. (1963) *The Odyssey*. New York.

FLATRÈS, PIERRE (1958) 'Rural patterns in Celtic countries: a comparative study', in 'Ancient agriculture in Ireland and North-west Europe', *Advancement of Science* xiv (56): 365-73.

FLEMING, A. (1972), 'The Genesis of Pastoralism in European Pre-history', *World Archaeology* 4: 179-91.

FLOWER, ROBIN (1979: first pbl. 1947), *The Irish Tradition*. Oxford.

FORTES, MEYER, and EVANS-PRITCHARD, E. E. (1940) *African Political Systems*. London.

FORD, Patrick (1977) *The Mabinogi and other Welsh Medieval Tales*. Berkeley.

FOWLER, P. J. (1972) *Archaeology and the Landscape*. London.

FOX, CYRIL F. (1933) *The Personality of Britain*. Cardiff.

FOX, ROBIN (1967) *Kinship and Marriage*. Harmondsworth.
    (1978) *The Tory islanders*. Cambridge.

FRANKLIN, T.B. (1953) *British Grasslands*. London.

FRASER, J., GROSJEAN, P. and O'KEEFE, J. G., (1931-3) *Irish Texts*, 8 vols. London.

FREEMAN, A. MARTIN (1970) ed. and transl. *Annala Connacht, The Annals of Connacht*. Dublin.

FREEMAN, THOMAS W. (1972) *Ireland: A General and Regional Geography*. London.

FRIED, MORTON (1959) *Readings in Anthropology II*, New York.
    (1967) *The Evolution of Political Society*. New York.

FRIEDRICH, PAUL (1966) 'Proto-Indo-European Kinship', *Ethnology* 5: 1-36.

GERRIETS, MARILYN (1981) 'The organization of exchange in Early Christian Ireland', *Journal of Economic History* 41: 171-6.
    (1983) 'Economy and Society: Clientship according to the Irish Laws', *Camb. Med. Celt. Stds.* 6: 43-61.
    (1985) 'Money in Early Christian Ireland according to the Irish Laws', *Comparative Studies in Society and History* 27: 323-39.

(1987) 'Kingship and exchange in Pre-Viking Ireland', *Camb. Med. Celt. Stds.* 13: 39-72.

(1988) 'The king as judge in early Ireland', *Celtica* 20: 1-24.

GIBSON, D. BLAIR (1990) *Tulach Commain: a view of an Irish chiefdom.* University Microfilms: Ph.D. dissertation, University of California, Los Angeles.

GIBSON, D. BLAIR and GESELOWITZ, MICHAEL N. (1988) eds. *Tribe and Polity in Late Prehistoric Europe: demography, production and exchange in the evolution of complex social systems.* New York.

GILBERT, JOHN (1979) *Hunting and Hunting Reserves in Medieval Ireland.* Edinburgh.

GLASSIE, HENRY (1982a) *Passing the time in Ballymenone: culture and history of an Ulster community.* Philadelphia.

(1982b) *Irish folk history: texts from the north.* Philadelphia.

GOODY, JACK. (1969) 'Indo-European kinship', in Goody ed. *Comparative Studies in Kinship.* Stanford: 235-9.

(1973a) *The Character of Kinship.* Cambridge.

(1973b) *Bridewealth and dowry in Africa and Asia.* Cambridge.

(1983) *The Development of the Family and Marriage in Europe.* Cambridge.

(1990) *The Oriental, the Ancient and the Primitive.* Cambridge.

GÖRANSSON, S. (1961) 'Regular open-field pattern in England and Scandinavian *Solskifte*', *Geografiska Annaler* xliiib: 80-101.

GRAHAM, J.M. (1953) 'Transhumance in Ireland', *Advancement of Science* x no. 37: 74-9.

(1972) 'South-west Donegal in the seventeenth century', *Irish Geography* vi no. 2: 136-52.

GRAHAM, P. ANDERSON (1893) *All the Year with Nature.* London.

GRANT, ALEXANDER (1985) 'Extinction of direct male lines among Scottish noble families in the fourteenth and fifteenth centuries', in Stringer, K. J. ed. *Essays on the nobility of medieval Scotland.* Edinburgh: 210-231.

GRAY, ELIZABETH (1981-3) '*Cath Maige Tuired*: myth and structure', *Éigse* 18: 183-209; *ibid* 19 (1982-3): 1-35; 230-262.

(1982) ed. and transl. *Cath Maige Tuired: the second battle of Mag Tuired.* Dublin. Irish Texts Society 52.

GRAY, H. L. (1915) *English Field Systems.* Cambridge.

GREENE, DAVID (1973) '*Cró, Crú* and similar words', *Celtica* xv: 7-8.

GRIGG, D.B. (1982) *The Dynamics of Agricultural Change.* London.

GUYONVARC'H, CHRISTIAN (1961), '*Notes d'etymologie et de lexicographie Gauloise et Celtiques*', *Ogam* 13: 470-80.

GUYONVARC'H, CHRISTIAN, AND LE ROUX, FRANCOISE (1986) *Les Druides.* Rennes.

GWYNN, AUBREY (1913) *Metrical Dindshenchas.* Part III. Dublin.

(1940) 'An Old-Irish tract on the privileges and responsibilities of poets', *Ériu* 13: 1-60.

HAMLIN, ANN (1985) 'The archaeology of the Irish churches in the eighth century', *Peritia* 4: 279-99.

(1981) 'Using mills on Sunday', in Scott ed. *Studies on Early Ireland*: 11.

HAMP, ERIC P. (1979-80) '*imbolc, oimelc*', *Studia Celtica* xiv/v: 106-113.

HANCOCK, O'MAHONY, RICHEY, HENNESSY and ATKINSON (1865-1901) eds. and transl. *Ancient Laws of Ireland* 6 vols, Dublin.

HANDFORD, S. A. (1951) ed. and transl. *Caesar: The Conquest of Gaul.* Harmondsworth.

HANDLEY, J. E. (1953) *Scottish Farming in the Eighteenth Century.* London.

HANLEY, ROBIN (1987) *Villages in Roman Britain.* Haverfordwest.

HARBISON, PETER (1988) *Pre-Christian Ireland.* London.

HARDING, D. W. (1976) *Hillforts: Late Prehistoric Earthworks in Britain and Ireland.* London and New York.

HARRIS, MARVIN (1968) *The Rise of Anthropological Theory: a History of Theories of Culture.* New York.

HARVEY, A. (1987) 'Early literacy in Ireland: the evidence from ogam', *Camb. Med. Celt. Stds.* 14 (Winter): 1-14.

HECHTER, MICHAEL (1975) *Internal Colonialism: The Celtic Fringe in British National Development, 1556-1966.* Berkeley.

HEERS, JACQUES (1977) *Family clans in the Middle Ages: a study of political and social structures in urban areas*, transl. Barry Herbert, in Vaughan, Richard ed. *Europe in the Middles Ages. Selected Studies* No. 4. New York.

HENNESSY, MARK (1985) 'Parochial organisation in medieval Tipperary' in Nolan ed. 1985.

HERBERT, MAIRE (1988) *Iona, Kells, and Derry: the History and Historiography of the Monastic Familia of Columba*. Oxford.

HERBERT, MAIRE, and O RÍAIN, PÁDRAIG (1988) *Betha Adamnain. The Irish Life of Adamnán*. London.

HICKS, S.P. (1972-3) 'The impact of Man on the East Moor of Derbyshire from Mesolithic times', *Archaeol. Jnl.* 129: 1-21.

HIGHAM, C. F. W. (1967) 'Stock Rearing as a Cultural Factor in Prehistoric Europe', *The Prehistoric Society* 6.

HILL, LORD GEORGE (1887) Facts from Gweedore, (5th ed.) ed. Estyn Evans.

HILTON, R.H. (1954) 'Medieval Agrarian History', *Victoria County History of Leicestershire* ii.

HIRONS, K. R. (1983) 'Percentage and accumulation rates: pollen diagrams from east Co. Tyrone', in Reeves-Smyth and Hamond eds. 1983.

HILZHEIMER, M. (1936) 'Sheep', *Antiquity* 10: 195-206.

HOGAN, EDMUND (1910) *Onomasticon Goidelicum*. Dublin.

HOGAN, DAIRE, AND OSBOROUGH, W. N. (1990) *Brehons, Serjeants and Attorneys: Studies in the History of the Irish Legal Profession*. Dublin.

HOGAN, J. (1929) 'The *tricha cét* and related land measures', *Proc. Roy. Ir. Acad.* xxxviii C: 148-235.

HOLE, CHRISTINA (1976) *British Folk Customs*. London.

HOLM, POUL (1986) 'The slave trade of Dublin, ninth to twelfth centuries' *Peritia* 5: 317-45.

HOMANS, GEORGE C.(1941) *English Villagers of the Thirteenth Century*. New York.
(1957) 'The Frisians in East Anglia', *The Economic History Review*, 2nd ser. 10: 189-206.

HOSKINS, W. G. (1979) *The Making of the English Landscape*. Harmondsworth.

HUGHES, KATHLEEN (1958) 'The distribution of Irish scriptoria and centres of learning from 730-1111' in Chadwick ed. 1958: 243-72.

(1966) *The Church in Early Irish Society*. London.

JÄGER, HELMUT (1983) 'Land use in medieval Ireland: a review of the documentary evidence' in *Irish Econ. and Soc. Hist.* 10: 51-65.

JAMES, E. O. (1961) *Seasonal Feasts and Festivals*. Norwich.

JENKINS, DAFYDD (1963) ed. *Llyfr Colan*. Cardiff.

JENKINS, DAFFYDD and OWEN, MORFYDD (1980) eds. *The Welsh Law of Women*, Cardiff.

JENKINS, GERAINT (1969) ed. *Studies in Folk Life: Essays in honour of T. Iorwerth Peate*. London.

JOHNSON, T. B. (1848) *A Sportsman's Encyclopaedia*. London.

JOHNSTONE, PAUL (1980) *The Sea-craft of Prehistory*. London.

JONES, G. R. J. (1972) 'Post-Roman Wales' in Finberg 1972: 281-382.

(1976) 'Multiple estates and early settlement', in Sawyer 1976: 15-40.

(1983) 'Nucleal settlement and its tenurial relationships: some morphological implications', in Roberts and Glasscock, 1983: 153-67.

JONES, MARTIN K., (1991) 'Agricultural productivity in the pre-documentary past', in Campbell, Bruce *et al*: 78-94.

JONES, MICHAEL E. (1979) 'Climate, nutrition and disease: an hypothesis of Romano-British population', in Casey, 1979: 232-9.

JOYNT, MAUD (1936) *Feis Tighe Chonáin*. Medieval and Modern Irish Series 7. Dublin.

KARP, MARK (1960) *The Economics of Trusteeship in Somalia*. Boston.

KAVANAGH, RHODA M. (1988) 'The horse in Viking Ireland', in Bradley ed. 1988: 89-121.

KELLEHER, J. V. (1963) 'Irish History and Pseudo-History', *Studia Hibernica* 3: 113-27.

(1971) 'The Táin and the annals', *Ériu* 22: 107-27.

KELLY, FERGUS (1976) *Audacht Morainn*. Dublin.

(1986) 'An Old-Irish text on court procedure', *Peritia* 5: 74-106.

(1988) *A Guide to Early Irish Law*. Early Irish Law Ser. Dublin.

KELLY, JOAN GADOL (1984) *Women, History and Theory*. Chicago.

KENNEY, JAMES F. (1929) *The Sources for the Early History of Ireland: ecclesiastical. An introduction and guide*. 1966 ed. New York.

KINSELLA, THOMAS (1970) transl. *The Táin*. London.

KIRCHOFF, PAUL (1959) 'The Principles of Clanship in Human Society' (repr. in Fried, Morton, ed., *Readings in Anthropology* II: 370 ff. (originally pub. 1955: *Davidson Journ. Anthrop.*)

LAING, LLOYD (1975) *The Archaeology of Late Celtic Britain and Ireland*. London.

(1977) ed. *Studies in Celtic Survival*. B.A.R. No. 37. Oxford.

(1985) 'The Romanisation of Ireland', *Peritia* 4: 261-78.

LAMB, H. H. (1966) *The Changing Climate*. London.

LANGDON, JOHN (1986) Horses, Oxen and technological Innovation. Cambridge.

LASLETT, PETER (1971) *The world we have lost: England before the industrial age* (2nd ed.) New York.

LATOUCHE, ROBERT (1961) *The Birth of Western Economy*. New York (first ed., Paris, 1956).

LEACH, EDMUND (1961) *Pul Eliya, a Village in Ceylon: A Study in Land Tenure and Kinship*. Cambridge.

(1962) *Rethinking Anthropology*. New York.

LEGGE, A. J. (1981) 'The agricultural economy' in Mercer (1981b).

LEHMACHER, G. (1950) 'The ancient Celtic year', *Journal of Celtic Studies* 1: 144-7.

LEISTER, INGEBORG (1976) *Peasant openfield farming and its territorial organisation in County Tipperary*. Marburg.

LE ROUX, FRANCOISE (1961) '*Études sur le Festiaire Celtique: I Samain*', *Ogam* 13: 481-506.

LITTLETON, C. SCOTT (1966) *The New Comparative Mythology*. Berkeley and Los Angeles.

LLOYD, SIR JOHN E. (1939) *A History of Wales*, 2 vols. (3rd. ed.) London.

LOYN, H.R. (1962) *Anglo-Saxon England and the Norman Conquest*. London.

LUCAS, A.T. (1958) 'Cattle in ancient and medieval Irish Society', *The O'Connell School Union Record*. Dublin.

(1960-62) 'Irish food before the potato', *Gwerin* III, no. 2: 8-35.

(1966) 'Irish-Norse relations: time for a reappraisal', *Jrn. Cork Hist. and Arch. Soc.* 71: 62-75.

(1967) 'The plundering and burning of churches in Ireland, 7th to 16th century', in Rynne 1967: 172-229.

(1969) 'Sea Sand and Shells as Manure', in Jenkins ed. 1969: 184-203.

(1972-4) 'Irish ploughing practices', *Tools and Tillage* 2/i 1972: 52-62; 2/ii 1973: 67-83; 2/iii 1974:189-60.

(1989) *Cattle in Ancient Ireland*. Kilkenny.

LUDWIG, MARY A. (1986) 'Friendship and Kinship in Irish Society: Ancient and Modern Parallels', in *Proc. First North American Ann. Cong. Celt. Stds.* ed. Gordon W. MacLennan: 309-317.

LYDON, JAMES (1973) *Ireland in the later Middle Ages*. Dublin.

LYNN, C. J. (1983) 'Some early ring-forts and crannogs', *Journal of Irish Archaeology* 1: 45-58.

(1993) 'Navan fort — home of gods and goddesses?', *Arch. Ire.* 7 no.1 (Spring): 17-21.

(1992) 'The Iron Age Mound in Navan Fort: a Physical Realization of Celtic Religious Belief?' *Emania* 10: 33-57.

MAC AODHE, B. (1962) 'Seasonal stock movements in the Sperrins', *Gwerin* iii (5) 1962.

MACARTHUR, W. P. (1948-9) 'The identification of some pestilences in the Irish Annals', in *Irish Historical Studies* 6: 169-88.

MAC CANA, PROINSIAS (1955-6) 'Aspects of the Theme of King and Goddess in Irish Literature', *Études Celtiques* 7: 76-114, 356-413; *ibid.* 8 1956: 59-65.

(1970a) *Celtic Mythology*. London.

(1970b) '*Elfennau cyn-Gristionogol yn y Cyfreithiau*', *Bull. Brd. Celt. Stds* 23 prt. 4 (May): 316-320.

(1970c) 'The Three Languages and the Three Laws', *Studia Celtica* 5: 62-78.

(1971) 'Conservation and Innovation in early Celtic Literature', *Études Celtiques* 13: 61-118.

(1974) 'The Rise of the Later Schools of *Filidhecht*', *Ériu* 25: 126-46.

(1979) *'Regnum* and *sacerdotium*: Notes on Irish Tradition', *Proc. Brit. Acad.* 65: 443-75.

(1980) ed. *The Learned Tales of Medieval Ireland.* Dublin.

MAC CURTAIN, MARGARET and Ó CORRÁIN, DONNCHA **(1979)** *Women in Irish Society.* Westport.

MACDOUGAL, HUGH A. **(1982)** *Racial Myth in English History: Trojans, Teutons, and Anglo-Saxons.* Montreal and Hanover.

MACFARLANE, ALAN **(1978)** *The origins of English individualism: the family, property, and social transition.* Oxford.

MAC NÉILL, EÓIN **(1911)** 'Early Irish population-groups: their nomenclature, classification, and chronology' *Proc. Roy. Ir. Acad.* 29 C: 59-114.

(1919) *Phases in Irish History.* Dublin.

(1921) *Celtic Ireland,* Dublin.

(1923) 'Ancient Irish Law: the Law of Status or Franchise', *Proc. Roy. Ir. Acad.* 36 C: 265-316.

(1935) *Early Irish Laws and Institutions.* Dublin.

(1941-3) 'Military Service in Medieval Ireland', *Jrn Cork Hist. and Arch. Soc.,* Ser. 2, 46-8: 6-16.

(1967) 'Prolegomena to a study of the Ancient laws of Ireland, by Eóin Mac Neill', (ed. D. A. Binchy), *The Irish Jurist,* 2: 106-15.

MACNEILL, MÁIRE **(1962)** *The Festival of Lughnasa.* Oxfords (repr. 1982, Dublin).

MACNEILL, MARIAN F. **(1957)**: *The Silver Bough* 4 vols. Edinburgh.

MAC NIOCAILL, GEARÓID **(1971a)** *'Tír Cumaile',* *Ériu* 22: 81-6.

(1971b) Jetsam, treasure trove and the lord's share in medieval Ireland', *The Irish Jurist* 6: 103-10.

(1981) 'Investment in Early Irish Agriculture' in Scott (1981).

MAC NIOCAILL G., and WALLACE,P., **(1988)** eds., *Keimelia: studies in medieval archaeology and history in memory of Tom Delaney.* Galway.

MACQUEEN, JOHN **(1979)** 'Pennyland and Davoch in South-west Scotland', *Jrn. Scott. Studies,* 23: 71-5.

McALL, CHRISTOPHER (1983) 'The Normal Paradigms of a Woman's Life in the Irish and Welsh texts', in Jenkins and Owen (1983): 7-22.

McCONE, KIM (1984) 'Notes on the text and authorship of the early Irish Bee-laws', *Camb. Med. Celt. Stds.* 8: 45-50.

(1986a) 'Werewolves, cyclops, *díberga* and *fíanna*: juvenile delinquency in early Ireland', *Camb. Med. Celt. Stds.* 12: 1-22.

(1986b) 'Dubthach maccu Lugair and a matter of life and death in the Pseudo-Historical Prologue to the *Senchas Már*', *Peritia* 5: 1-35.

(1990) *Pagan Past and Christian Present.* Maynooth.

McCORMICK, FINBAR (1983) 'Dairying and beef production in Early Christian Ireland, in Reeves-Smyth and Hamond (1983)

(1988) 'The domesticated cat in early Christian and medieval Ireland', in Mac Niocaill and Wallace, 1988: 218-28.

(1991) 'The dog in prehistoric and early Christian Ireland', *Archaeology, Ireland* 5, no 4: 7-9.

McCOURT, DESMOND (1971) 'The dynamic quality of Irish rural settlement', in Buchanan, Jones and McCourt, 1971: 126-64.

McERLEAN, THOMAS (1983) 'The Irish townland system of landscape organisation', in Reeves-Smyth and Hamond (1983).

MCGRAW HILL (1982) *Encyclopaedia of Science and Technology.*

McKITTERICK, ROSAMUND (1990) ed., *The Uses of Literacy in Early Medieval Europe*, ed., Cambridge.

McLEOD, NEIL (1981-2) 'Parallel and paradox: Compensation in the legal systems of Celtic Ireland and Anglo-Saxon England', *Studia Celtica* xvi-xvii: 36-9.

(1982b) 'The two *fer midboth* and their evidence in court', *Ériu* 33: 21-71.

(1986) 'Interpreting Early Irish Law: Status and Currency. I', *Zeit. Celt. Phil.* 41: 46-65;

(1987) *ibid.* II, 42: 41-115.

(1992) *Early Irish Contract Law.* Sydney.

MAINE, H. S. (1861) *Ancient Law.* London.

(1875) *Lectures on the Early History of Institutions.* London.

(1887) *Village Communities in the East and West.* London.

MAIR, LUCY (1965) *An Introduction to Social Anthropology.* London.

MALLORY, J. P. (1984) 'The origins of the Irish', *Journal of Irish Archaeology.* 2: 65-69.

(1986) 'Silver in the Ulster Cycle of Tales', in Evans, Griffith and Jope, eds, 1986: 31-78.

(1992) ed., *Aspects of the Táin.* Belfast.

MARTIN, MARTIN (1695; 1884) *A description of the Western Islands of Scotland, circa 1695.* London (1884)

MATONIS, A., AND MELIA, D. (1990) *Celtic Language, Celtic Culture: a Festschrift for Eric P. Hamp.* Van Nuys.

MAXWELL, CONSTANTIA (1923) *Irish History from Contemporary Sources, 1509-1610.* London.

MEGAW, J. V. S., and SIMPSON, D. D. A. (1979), eds, *Introduction to British Prehistory.* Leicester.

MEITZEN, A. (1895) *Seidelung der Germanen*, 3 vols., Berlin.

MERCER, R. (1981a) *Farming Practice in British Prehistory.* Edinburgh.

(1981b), ed., *Grimes Graves, Norfolk: Excavations 1971-2*, vol i, London.

MEYER, KUNO (1892) ed. and transl. *Aislinge Meic Conglinne: The Vision of Mac Conglinne.* London.

(1894) ed. and transl. *Hibernica Minora*, Oxford.

(1904) ed. and transl., *Cró ocus Díbad, Ériu* I, pt. 2: 214-2.

(1905) ed. and transl., *Cáin Adomnáin*, Oxford, *Anecdota Oxoniensia.*

(1909) ed. and transl., *Tecosca Cormaic*, R.I.A. Todd Lecture Series 15. Dublin.

(1910) ed. and transl., *Fianaigecht*, R.I.A. Todd Lecture Series 16. Dublin.

(1912) ed. and transl., *Sanais Cormaic: an Old Irish Glossary. Anecdota from Irish Manuscripts.* 4, ed. Osborn Bergin, *et al.* Halle.

MITCHELL, G. F. (1976) *The Irish Landscape.* London.

(1965) 'Littleton Bog, Tipperary: an Irish agricultural record', *Jrn. Roy. Soc. Antiq. Ire.*, 95: 121-32.

MOLLAT, MICHEL (1986) *The Poor in the Middle Ages*, transl. Arthur Goldhammer. New Haven and London (orig. *Les pauvres au moyen age*, Hachette. 1978)

MONK, M. A. (1985-6) 'Evidence from macroscopic plant remains for crop husbandry in prehistoric and early Ireland', *Jrn. Irish Arch.* 3: 31-6.

MOODY, T. W. (1978), ed., *Nationality and the pursuit of national independence*. Belfast.

MOODY, T. W., MARTIN, F. X., and BYRNE, F. J. (1976 —) *A New History of Ireland*, 10 vols. Oxford.

MOORE, D. (1970) ed., *The Irish Sea Province in Archaeology and History*. Cardiff.

MORRIS, HENRY (1939) 'Reliques of the Brehon law and other ancient usages in Ulster', *Bealodeais*, 9, pt. 2: 288-95.

MORRIS, JOHN (1975, rev. ed.) *The Age of Arthur*. London.

MULCHRONE, K. (1936) 'The rights and duties of women regarding the education of their children' in Binchy, ed., *SEIL*: 187-205.

(1939) ed. and trans., *The Tripartite Life of Patrick*. Dublin.

MUNRO, JEAN (1981) 'The Lordship of the Isles', in Maclean, L., *The Middle Ages in the Highlands*, ed., Inverness.

MURPHY, GERARD (1933), ed. and transl., *Duanaire Finn*, ii London.

MURRAY, ALEXANDER C. (1983) *Germanic Kinship Structure*. Toronto.

MURRAY, HILARY (1979) 'Documentary evidence for domestic buildings in Ireland c.400-1200 in the light of archaeology', *Med. Arch.* 33: 81-97.

MYERS, JAMES P. (1983) *Elizabethan Ireland: A Selection of writing by Elizabethan writers on Ireland*. Hamden, CT.

MYTUM, HAROLD (1992), *The Origins of Early Christian Ireland*. London and New York.

NAGY, JOSEPH, F. (1985) *The Wisdom of the Outlaw*. Berkeley.

(1990) 'Sword as Audacht', in Matonis and Melia, 1990: 131-6.

NÍ CHATHÁIN, PROINSIAS (1978-9) 'Swineherds, Seers, and Druids', *Studia Celtica* xiv-xv: 200-211-xv: 200-211

NÍ CHATHÁIN, PROINSIAS, AND RICHTER, M., (1984) eds, *Irland und Europa: die Kirche im Frühmittelalter. Ireland and Europe: the early Church*. Stuttgart.

(1987) *Ireland and Christendom: the Bible and the Missions*. Stuttgart.

NÍ DHONNCHADHA, MAIRÍN (1982) 'The guarantor list of *Cáin Adomnáin*', Peritia 1: 178-215.

(1988) ' 'An address to a law student': a Mac Egan poem (*CIH* 1584.1-1585.8) of the late thirteenth century', in Ó Corráin et al., eds: 159-77.

NICHOLAS, BARRY (1969) *An Introduction to Roman Law*. Oxford. (corrected reprt. of 1962 ed.).

NICHOLLS, KENNETH W. (1972) *Gaelic and Gaelicised Ireland in the middle ages*. Dublin.

(1978) 'Land, Law and Society in Sixteenth-Century Ireland.' *O'Donnell Lecture*, Dublin.

(1983) ed., *The O Doyne (O Duinn) Manuscript*. Dublin (Irish Manuscripts Commission. Survey of Irish lordships: special volume).

NOLAN, WILLIAM (1979) *Fassadinin: Land, Settlement and Society in Southeast Ireland 1600-1850*. Dublin.

(1985), ed., *Tipperary: History and Society*. Dublin.

NORMAN, E. R., and ST. JOSEPH, J.K. (1969) *The Early Development of Irish Society: the Evidence of Aerial Photography*. Cambridge.

O'BRIEN, DAVID (1932) 'The *Féni*', *Ériu* xi: 182-3.

O'BRIEN, M. A. (1938) '*Miscellanea Hibernica*', *Études Celtiques* 3: 362-73.

O'BUACHALLA, LIAM (1947-48) 'Some Researches in Ancient Irish Law', *Jrn. Cork Hist. and Arch. Soc.*, 2nd. ser., 52: 41-54, 135-48; *ibid* 53: 1-12, 75-81.

(1952) 'Contributions Towards the Political History of Munster, 450-800', *Jrn. Cork Hist. and Arch. Soc.*, 2nd. ser., 57 no. 186: 67-86.

Ó CÁTHASAIGH, THOMAS (1986) 'The sister's son in early Irish literature', *Peritia* 5: 128-60.

Ó COILEÁIN, SEAN (1989) '*Mag Fuithirbe* revisited', *Éigse* 23: 16-26.

Ó CORRÁIN, DONNCHA (1971) 'Irish regnal succession: a reappraisal', *Studia Hibernica* 11: 7-39.

(1972) *Ireland before the Normans*. Dublin.

(1974) 'Aspects of Early Irish History', in B. G. Scott, ed. *Perspectives in Irish Archaeology*: 64-75. Belfast.

(1978) 'Nationality and Kingship in pre-Norman Ireland, in Moody ed., 1978.

(1981a) ed., Eóin mac Néill, *Celtic Ireland*. Dublin.

(1981b) ed., *Irish antiquity: essays and studies presented to Professor M. J. O'Kelly*. Cork.

(1983) 'Some legal references to fences and fencing in Early Historic Ireland' in Reeves-Smyth and Hamond, eds, 1983: 247-52.

(1985) 'Irish origin legends and genealogy: recurring genealogies', in T. Nyberg, et al., eds., *History and heroic tale. A symposium.* Odense (1986).

(1986) 'Historical need and literary narrative', in Evans, Griffith, and Jope (1986).

Ó CORRÁIN, D., BREATNACH, L., and BREEN, A. **(1984)** 'The laws of the Irish', *Peritia* 3: 382-438.

Ó CORRÁIN, D., BREATNACH, L., AND McCONE, K. **(1988)** *Sages, Saints and Storytellers: Celtic Studies in Honour of Professor James Carney.* Maynooth.

Ó CUÍV, BRIAN **(1961)** ed., *Seven Centuries of Irish Learning.* Dublin.

O'DONOVAN, JOHN **(1843)** *The Tribes and Customs of Hy-Many.* Dublin.

(1845-51) *Annals of the kingdom of Ireland, by the four masters from the earliest period to the year 1616*, 3 vols, Dublin.

O'DWYER, PETER **(1981)** *Céli Dé: Spiritual Reform in Ireland, 750-900.* Dublin.

O'FLANAGAN, PATRICK **(1981)** 'Surveys, Maps, and the Study of Rural Settlement Development', in Ó Corráin (1981b).

(1984) 'Landscape of the past', *Peritia* 3: 590-4.

O'GRADY, S.H. **(1926)** *Catalogue of Irish Manuscripts in the British Museum*, Vol. I. London.

(1892) *Silva Gadelica: A Collection of Tales in Irish.* 2 vols., London.

O'HANLON, J., and O'LEARY, E. **(1907)** *History of the Queen's County*, 2 vols., Dublin.

Ó HAODHE, D. **(1978)** ed. and transl., *Bethu Brigte*, Dublin.

O'KEEFE, J. G. **(1905)** *Cáin Domnaig*, ed. *Ériu* 2: 189-214.

O'KELLY, MICHAEL J. (1970) 'Problems of Irish ring-forts', in Moore, 1970: 50-4.

(1989) *Early Ireland: an Introduction to Irish Prehistory.* Cambridge.

O'LEARY, PHILIP (1986) 'Brawl at the Banquet', *Éigse* 21.

O'LOAN, J. (1963-5) 'A History of Early Irish Farming. *Journal of the Department of Agriculture*, Dublin, vol 60 (1963): 178-229; 61 (1964): 242-284; 62 (1965): 131-197.

O'MEARA, JOHN (1982) ed. and transl., Giraldus Cambrensis, *Topographia Hiberniae.* Mountrath (first ed., 1951)

Ó MOGHRÁIN, PÁDRAIG (1944) 'More Notes on the *Buaile*', *Bealoidais* 64: 45-52.

O'RAHILLY, CECILLE (1967), ed. and transl., *Táin Bó Cúalnge, from the Book of Leinster.* Dublin.

(1976), ed. and transl., *Táin Bó Cúalnge, Recension I,* Dublin.

O'RAHILLY, T. F. (1946) *Early Irish History and Mythology.* Dublin.

Ó RAITHBHEARTAIGH (1935) *Genealogical Tracts*, I. Dublin (Irish Manuscripts Commission).

Ó RINNE, STÍOPHAN (1991) *'Dun Aengusa - Daingean no Teampull?'* *Archaeology, Ireland* 5. no, 1: 19-21.

Ó RIORDÁIN, S. P. (1979) *Antiquities of the Irish Countryside* (5th ed., rev. by R. de Valera). London.

ORME, BRYONY (1981) *Anthropology for Archaeologists.* London.

O'SULLIVAN, WILLIAM (1985) 'Insular palaeography: current problems', *Peritia* 4 (1985), pp. 346-59.

OWEN, ANEURIN (1841) *Ancient Laws and Institutes of Wales.*

PATTERSON, NERYS W. (1981) 'Material and symbolic exchange in early Irish clientship', *Proc. Harvard Celt. Coll.*, 1: 43-61.

(1985) 'Kinship law or number symbolism? Models of distributive justice in Old Irish law', *Proc. Harvard Celt. Coll.*, 5: 49-86.

(1988) 'Woman as vassal: gender symmetry in medieval Welsh culture', *Proc. Harvard Celt. Coll.*, 8: 31-45.

(1989) 'Brehon law in the late middle ages: 'antiquarian and obsolete' or 'traditional and functional', *Camb. Med. Celt. Stds.* 17 (Summer): 43-63.

(1990) 'Patrilineal groups in early Irish society: the evidence of the law-tracts', *Bull. Board Celt. Stds.*, 37.

(1991a) 'Gaelic law and the Tudor Conquest of Ireland: the social background to the last recensions of the Prologue to the *Senchas Már*', *Irish Historical Studies*. 27 (May): 1-23.

(1991b) Review Article: 'Archaeology and the historical sociology of Gaelic Ireland, *Antiquity* 65 no. 248: 734-38.

(1991c) *Cattle-lords and Clansmen: kinship and rank in early Ireland*. New York.

(1993) Review Article: 'Prehistoric kinship in northern Europe: comments on Early Irish and Welsh Kinship by T. M Charles-Edwards', *Journal of European Prehistory* 1 no. 2.

(1994) 'Clans are not primordial: pre-Viking Ireland and the modelling of Pre-Roman societies in Northern Europe', in Arnold, B. and Gibson, T. B. (1994).

PENNANT, THOMAS (1774-6), *A Tour in Scotland and Voyage to the Hebrides, mdcclxxii*. Chester.

PETTY, WILLIAM (1719) *Political Survey of Ireland*, 2nd. ed., London.

PHILLPOTTS, BERTHA S. (1913) *Kindred and Clan*. Oxford.

PICARD, J.M. (1982) 'The purpose of Adomnán's *Vita Columbae*', *Peritia* 1: 160-77.

PIGGOTT, STUART. (1958) 'Native economies and the Roman occupation of North Britain' in Richmond 1958, ed.: 1-17

(1968/75) *The Druids*. New York.

(1981) ed., *The Agrarian History of England and Wales* (i).

(1986) 'Horse and Chariot: the Price of Prestige', in Evans, D. Ellis, *et al.* eds, 1986: 25-30.

PLUMMER, CHARLES (1916-36) 'Notes on Some Passages in the Brehon Laws', *Ériu* viii (1916) 127-32; ix (1921) 31-41; x (1936) 113-29.

(1922) ed. and transl., *Bethada Náem nErenn*, 2 vols, Oxford.

(1926) 'On the colophons and marginalia of Irish scribes', *Proc. Brit. Acad.* 12: 11-44.

POKORNY, J. (1954) 'Die Geographie bei Ptolemaios', *Zeit. Celt. Phil.*, 24: 94-120.

POLLOCK, F., and MAITLAND, F.W. (1968) *The History of English Law*, 2 vols., ed. S. F. C. Milsom. Cambridge. (first ed. 1895).

PRICE, LIAM (1963) 'A note on the use of the word *baile* in place-names', *Celtica* 6: 119-26.

PROUDFOOT, V. B. (1961) 'The Economy of the Irish Rath', *Medieval Archaeology* 5: 94-122.

(1970) 'Irish raths and cashels: some notes on chronology, origins, and survivals', *Ulster Journal Archaeology* 33: 37-48.

QUINN, E.G. (1913-76) gen. ed., *Dictionary of the Irish Language based mainly on Old and Middle Irish Materials*. Dublin.

RADCLIFFE-BROWN, A. R. (1952) *Structure and Function in Primitive Society*. London.

RADNER, JOAN (1978) ed. and transl., *Fragmentary Annals of Ireland*. Dublin.

RAFTERY, BARRY (1972) 'Irish hill-forts', in Charles Thomas (1972).

(1976) 'Rathgall and Irish hillfort problems', in Harding (1976).

RAFTERY, JOSEPH (1981) 'Concerning Chronology' in Ó Corráin 1981b: 82-90.

REES, ALWYN, and REES, BRYNLEY (1961) *Celtic Heritage: Ancient Tradition in Ireland and Wales*. New York.

REEVES, W. (1874) *The Life of Saint Columba, founder of Hy, written by Adamnan*. Edinburgh

REEVES-SMYTH, TERENCE, and HAMOND, FRED (1983) eds, *Landscape Archaeology in Ireland*. Oxford. (*Brit. Arch. Rep. Inst., British Ser.*, 116)

RENFREW, COLIN (1987) *Archaeology and Language*. New York.

REYNOLDS, PETER J. (1979) *Iron Age Farm: the Butser Hill Experiment*. London.

RICHMOND, I.A. (1958) ed., *Roman and Native in North Britain*. Edinburgh.

RICHARDS, MELVILLE (1970) 'Places and Persons of the Early Welsh Church', *Welsh History Review* xx: 337-8.

RICHTER, MICHAEL (1988) *Medieval Ireland: the enduring tradition*. Dublin.

ROBERTS, B.K., and GLASSCOCK, R.E. (1983) eds, *Villages, fields and frontiers: studies in European rural settlement in the* medieval and early modern periods. (B.A.R. Int. Ser., 185) Oxford.

ROBINSON, PHILIP (1976) 'Irish settlement in Tyrone before the Ulster Plantation', *Ulster Folklife*, 22: 59-96.

ROSALDO, MICHELLE Z., and LAMPHERE, LOUISE (1974) eds, *Woman, Culture and Society*. Stanford.

ROSS, ANNE (1967) *Pagan Celtic Britain: Studies in Iconography and Tradition*. London.

RUANE, JOSEPH (1992) 'Colonialism and Irish historical development' in Silverman and Gulliver (eds)

RUSSELL, J.C. (1972) 'Population in Europe 500-1500', in C. M. Cipolla, ed., *The Fontana Economic History of Europe: The Middle Ages*. London: 25-70.

RYAN, ALAN (1987) *Property*. Minneapolis.

RYAN, JOHN (1931) *Irish Monasticism: Origins and Early Development*. Dublin.

(1940) ed., *Féil-sgríbhinn Eóin Mhic Néill*. Dublin.

RYAN, MICHAEL (1981) 'Some archaeological comments on the occurrence and use of silver in pre-Viking Ireland' in Scott, ed., 1981: 45-50.

(1988) 'Fine metalworking and early Irish monasteries: the archaeological evidence', in Bradley, ed., 1988: 33-48.

RYDER, M.L. (1981) 'Livestock' in Piggott, ed., 1981: 301-410.

RYNNE, ETIENNE (1967) *North Munster studies*. Limerick.

SAWYER, P.H. (1976), ed., *Medieval Settlement*. London.

(1982) *Kings and Vikings: Scandinavia and Europe, A.D. 700-1100*. London.

(1982b) 'The Vikings and Ireland', in Whitelock, McKitterick and Dumville 1982: 345-61.

SHANKLIN, EUGENIA (1976) 'Donegal's Lowly Sheep and Exalted Cows', *Natural History* LXXXV (No.3).

SHARPE, RICHARD (1979) 'Hiberno-Latin *laicus*, Irish *láech* and the devil's men', *Ériu* 30: 75-92.

(1986) 'Dispute settlement in medieval Ireland: a preliminary enquiry' in Davies and Fouracre: 169-89.

SHAW, LACHLAN (1882) *A History of the Province of Moray*. Glasgow.

SCHEPER-HUGHES, NANCY (1979) *Saints, scholars and schizophrenics*. Berkeley.

SCHNEIDER, D. M., and GOUGH, KATHLEEN (1961) *Matrilineal Kinship*. Berkeley.

SCOTT, B. G. (1970/3) ''Tribes' and 'tribalism' in early Ireland', *Ogam*, tm. 22-25: 197-206.

(1981) ed., *Studies in Early Ireland: essays in honour of M. V. Duignan*. Dublin.

(1983) 'An early Irish law tract on the blacksmith's forge', *The Journal of Irish Archaeology* I: 59-62.

SEEBOHM, FREDERICK (1902) *Tribal Custom in Anglo-Saxon Law*. London.

SILVERMAN, MARILYN, AND GULLIVER, P.H. (1992) eds. *Approaching the Past: historical anthropology through Irish case studies*. New York.

SIMMS, ANNGRET (1988) 'Core and Periphery in Medieval Europe: the Irish experience in a wider context', in Smyth and Wheelan, eds., (1988).

SIMMS, KATHARINE (1975) 'The legal position of Irishwomen in the later middle ages', *The Irish Jurist*, N.S., 10: 96-111.

(1975/6) 'Warfare in the medieval Gaelic lordships', in *The Irish Sword* 12: 98-108.

(1978) 'Guesting and feasting in Gaelic Ireland', *Journ. Roy. Soc. Ant. Ire.*, 108: 67-100.

(1986) 'Nomadry in Medieval Ireland', *Peritia* 5: 379-91.

(1987) *From Kings to Warlords*. Woodbridge.

SINCLAIR, JAMES (1791-9) *Statistical Account of Scotland*. Edinburgh.

SINGER, ALICE (1973) 'Marriage payments and the exchange of people', *Man* 8, no. 1: 80-90.

SJOESTEDT, MARIE-LOUISE (1982), *Gods and Heroes of the Celts*. Berkeley.

SMITH, ROLAND M. (1932), ed. and transl., *The Advice to Doidin*, *Ériu* 11: 66-85.

SMYTH, ALFRED (1975/79) *Scandinavian York and Dublin*, 2 vols. Dublin.

(1982) *Celtic Leinster*. Blackrock.

(1984) *Warlords and Holy Men*. London.

SMYTH, WILLIAM J., and WHELAN, KEVIN (1988), eds, *Common Ground: Essays on the Historical Geography of Ireland*. Cork.

STACEY, ROBIN CHAPMAN (1986) *'Berrad Airechta*: an Old Irish tract on suretyship', in Charles-Edwards, Owen and Walters, 1986: 210-33.
(1991) 'Ties that bind: immunities in Celtic law', *Camb. Med. Celtic. Studs.* 21, Summer 1991.
STEPHENS, N., and GLASSCOCK, R. E. (1970) eds, *Irish Geographical Studies*. Belfast.
STEVENSON, JANE (1990), 'Literacy in Ireland: the evidence of the Patrick dossier in the Book of Armagh', in McKitterick (1990): 11-35.
STOKES, WHITLEY (1862) *Three Irish Glosses*. London.
(1869) ed. *Cormac's Glossary* trans. John O'Donovan. Dublin.
(1890) ed. and transl., *Lives of the Saints from the Book of Lismore*, Oxford (Anecdota Oxoniensia).
(1894) *'Rennes Dindshenchas'*, *Revue Celtiques* XV: 370;373.
STOKES, WHITLEY, AND MEYER, KUNO (1898- 1907) *'Archiv für Celtische Lexicographie*, 3 vols. Halle
STOUT, MATTHEW (1991) 'Ringforts in the South-West Midlands of Ireland', *Proc. Roy. Ir. Acad.* vol. 91, C, no. 8: 202-243.
SWAN, LEO (1983) 'Enclosed ecclesiastic sites and their relevance to settlement patterns of the first millennium A.D.' in Reeves-Smyth and Hamond, eds, 1983: 269-94.
(1988) 'The Early Christian ecclesiastical sites of County Westmeath', in Bradley, ed., 1988: 3-31.
SZARMACH. P.E., and OGGINS, V.D., (1986), eds., *Sources of Anglo-Saxon-Culture*. Kalamazoo.
TANI, YUTAKA (1989), 'The geographical distribution and function of sheep-flock leaders', in Clutton-Brock, ed., 1989: 185-99.
TERRAY, EMMANUEL (1972) *Marxism and 'Primitive Societies'*. New York. (orig. pub. Paris, 1969).
THIRSK, JOAN (1964) 'The Common Fields', Past and Present 29: 3-29.
(1967) ed., *The Agrarian History of England and Wales*, vol iv. London.
THOMAS, CHARLES (1971) *The Early Christian Archaeology of North Britain*. Oxford.
(1972) *The Iron-Age in the Irish Sea Province* (Council of British Arch., Research Report 9). Oxford.

(1976) 'Imported late-Roman Mediterranean pottery in Ireland and western Britain: chronologies and implications, *Proc. Roy. Ir. Acad.* 76 C: 245-55.

THOMPSON, E. A. (1982) *Romans and Barbarians.* Madison.

THURNEYSEN, RUDOLF (1923) '*Aus dem irischen Recht* I' [1. *Das Unfrei-Lehen*], *Zeit. für celt. Phil.* 14: 335-94.

(1925a) '*Aus dem irischen Recht* II' [2. *Das Frei-Lehen*; 3. *Das Fasten beim Pfandungsverfahren*], *ibid* 15: 238-96.

(1925b) '*Aus dem irischen Recht* III' [4. *Die falschen Urteilssprache Caratnia's; 5. Zur Überlieferung und zur Ausgabe der Texte uber das Unfrei-Lehen und das Frei-Lehen*], *ibid.* 15: 302-76.

(1926) *Cóic Conara Fugill: Die fünf Wege zum Urteil. Abhandlungen der preussischen Akademie des Wissenschaften. Jahrgang 1925. Phil.-Hist. Klasse. Nr. 7.* Berlin.

(1927) '*Aus dem irischen Recht* IV' [6. *Zu den bisherigen Ausgaben der irischen Rechtstexte*], *Zeit. fur celt. Phil.* 16: 167-230; *ibid.* 'Nachtragliches': 406-10.

(1928) *Die Bürgschaft im irischen Recht, Abh. preuss. Akad. Wiss., Phil.-Hist. Kl., NR.* 2. Berlin.

(1930) '*Aus dem irischen Recht* V' [7. *Zu Gubretha Caradniad; 8. Zum ursprünglichen Umfang des Senchas Már; 9. Zu der Etymologie von irisch ráth 'Bürgschaft' und zu der irischen Kanonensammlung und den Triaden; 10. Nächtrage zur Bürgschaft*], *Zeit. für celt. Phil.* 18: 353-408.

(1931) *Irisches Recht* I, *Díre. Ein altirischer Rechtstext, II. Zu den unteren Ständen in Irland. Abh. Preuss. Akad. Wiss., Phil.-Hist. Kl. NR.* 2.

(1933) '*Nächtrage zu Irisches Recht*', *Zeit. für celt.Phil.* 19: 346-51.

(1935) '*Das keltische Recht*', *Zeitschrift der Savigny-Stiftung fur Rechtsgeschichte* 55: 81-104; transl. in *Celtic Law Papers*, ed. D. Jenkins. Brussels, 1973: 49-70.

(1936a) '*Cáin Lánamna*', in Binchy (ed.) *SEIL*: 1-80.

(1936b) '*Heirat*' *ibid*: 109-28.

TIERNEY, J. J. (1960) 'The Celtic ethnography of Poseidonius', *Proc. Roy. Ir. Acad.* 60: 189-275.

TROW-SMITH, R. (1955) *A History of British Livestock Husbandry to 1700.* London.

TYMOZKO, MARIA (1985/6) 'Animal Imagery in *Loinges Mac nUislenn*', *Studia Celtica* 20/21: 145-66.

ÜHLIG, HARALD (1971) 'Fields and field systems' in Buchanan, Jones and McCourt, 1971: 93-125.

VAN BATH, SLICHER B. H. (1963) *The Agrarian History of Western Europe, 500 - 1850.* London.

VAN HAMEL, A. G. (1932) *Lebor Bretnach* Dublin.

VAN WIJNGAARDEN-BAKKER, LOUISE H. (1974) 'The animal remains from the Beaker settlement at Newgrange, Co. Meath: First Report', *Proc. Roy Ir. Acad.* 74 C: 313-83.

VENDRYES, J. (1924) *'Imbolc', Revue Celtique* 41: 241-4.

WALSH, PAUL (1948), ed. and transl., *The Life of Aodh Ruadh O Domhnaill*, Part 1 - Text and Translation. Dublin.

WALTERS, D.B. (1986) 'The general features of archaic European suretyship', in Charles-Edwards, Owen, and Walters, 1986: 92-118.

WARNER, RICHARD B. (1976) 'Some observations on the context and importation of exotic materials in Ireland, from the 1st. century B.C. to the 2nd century A.D.', *Proc. Roy. Irish Acad.* 76 C: 267-89.

(1990) 'The 'prehistoric' Irish Annals: fable or history?', *Archaeology, Ireland* 7 no. 1: 7-9

(1988) 'The archaeology of Early Historic Irish kingship', in Driscoll and Nieke, 1988: 47-68.

WASSERSCHLEBEN H. (1885) ed., *Die irische Kanonensammlung*, Leipzig (2nd ed.).

WATERMAN, D.M. (1958) 'Excavations at Ballyfounder Rath, Co. Down,' *Ulster Jrn. Arch.* 21: 39-61.

(1963) 'A Neolithic and Dark Age Site at Langford Lodge, Co. Antrim,' *Ulster Jrn. Arch.* 26: 43-54.

(1971) 'A Marshland Habitation Site near Larne, Co. Antrim,' *Ulst. Jrn. Arch.* 34: 65-76.

WATKINS, CALVERT (1976) 'Sick-maintenance in Indo-European', *Ériu* 27: 21-5.

(1985) *The American Heritage Dictionary of Indo-European Roots* (rev. ed.) Boston.

WATT, JOHN (1972) *The Church in Medieval Ireland.* Dublin.

WEBER, MAX (1951) *The Religion of China: Confucianism and Taoism.* Glencoe (orig. publ, as *Gesammelte Aufsatze zur Religionssoziologie,* 3 vols. Tubingen, 1920-21)
1958 *The Religion of India.* Glencoe. (orig. pub., Tubingen 1920-21)

WHITELOCK, DOROTHY (1981) *History, Law and Literature in 10th and 11th Century England.* London.

WHITELOCK, D., McKITTERICK, R., and DUMVILLE, D. (1982), eds, *Ireland in Early Medieval Europe.* Cambridge.

WHITLOCK, RALPH (1978), *A Calendar of Country Customs.* London.

WILIAM, ALED RHYS (1960), ed., *Llyfr Iorwerth.* Cardiff.

WILLIAMS, CAERWYN, AND FORD, PATRICK (1992) *The Irish Literary Tradition.* Cardiff.

WOOD-MARTIN, W.G. (1886) *Lake Dwellings of Ireland.* Dublin.

INDEX

Aalen, F. H. A., 105, 373, 380
abduction 215, 296
adoption 37, 261, 277, 290, 314, 319
African kinship 26, 289, 388
Agnates 55, 166, 219, 232, 242, 243, 246, 261, 262, 272, 274, 375
agnatic vi, 27, 29, 40, 54-56, 103, 111, 190, 202, 208, 228, 240, 241, 242-246, 249, 256, 257, 259, 260, 281, 292, 297, 315, 321, 335, 337, 356, 375, 377, 378
agriculture 54, 70, 73, 96, 104, 106, 118, 256, 368, 372, 388, 395, 401
Ailill 95, 292, 349
aire 39, 41, 83, 96, 109, 166, 196, 197, 200, 201, 203-205, 207, 219, 223, 227, 251, 256, 278, 290, 330, 332-335, 340, 343, 347, 349-357, 376
aire ard 196, 197, 204, 352-357
aire desó 41, 83, 196, 197, 200, 201, 203, 207, 251, 290, 351, 352
aire échta 196, 197, 204, 251, 343, 347, 350-356
aire forgill 196, 197, 203-205, 353-357
aire tuise 196, 197, 290
aithech 46, 173, 176, 193, 197, 222, 223, 251, 253, 293, 358, 366, 376
aithech fortha 193, 358
aithech-tuatha 46, 173
AL; Ancient Laws of Ireland 6, 7, 9-11, 18-20, 29, 38, 42, 54, 55, 63, 69, 73, 83, 92, 95, 96, 97, 103, 108-111, 135-137, 142, 143, 153, 155, 158, 160, 162-166, 172, 174, 176, 177, 183, 184, 189-194, 198, 201, 209-211, 213-215, 219, 220, 223, 224, 226, 227-231, 245, 246, 250, 252, 253, 260, 261, 264, 266, 267, 269-281, 290, 291, 295, 297, 300, 303-306, 308-310, 312-314, 331, 332, 334, 339, 341-346, 348, 350, 351, 353, 354, 356-358, 390, 392, 397, 399, 400,

402
Alcock, Leslie, 380
ambue 132, 338, 346, 347
ancestor 29, 36, 208, 242, 247, 249
Anderson, J. G. C., 380, 389
Angles 94
Anglo-Saxons 7, 69, 72-77, 80, 91, 92, 95, 96, 106, 107, 109, 111, 120-126, 129, 135-139, 147, 160, 164, 165, 174, 175, 201, 213, 229, 230, 260, 268, 270, 274, 307, 395
annals 4, 5, 22, 36, 52, 95, 102, 123, 146, 171, 252, 367, 388, 392, 394, 400, 403, 408
Annals of Connacht 388
arable 74, 76, 81-83, 91, 92, 96, 100, 105-107, 109, 110, 113, 151, 155, 230, 304, 367, 369
Arensburg, C. M., 380
Arnold, Bettina, ix, 380, 402
assemblies 21, 86, 100, 135, 143-145, 156, 205, 341, 387
Audacht Morainn 44, 62, 205, 392

ballybetagh 93, 170-172, 228, 256
Ballymenone 111, 389
banchomarba 218, 244, 292, 376
Bannerman, J., 48, 49, 172, 380
Barker, Graeme 67, 68, 373, 380
Barrett, G, and Graham, G J., 99, 103, 380
Base-clients 44, 55, 152, 162, 165-168, 172-175, 177, 181, 193, 194, 203, 207, 250, 253, 336, 339, 354, 359
Baumgarten, Rolf, 199, 281, 380
bé cuitchernsa 295, 299, 301
Bechbretha xi, 10, 13, 15, 67, 110, 144, 335, 380, 384
beer 162
Bees; bee-hive 10, 67, 110, 120, 144,

feasts 63, 120, 121, 123, 126, 127, 162, 166, 172, 200, 203, 290, 392
fénechas 50-52
féni 40, 41, 44, 50-52, 191-194, 217, 260, 269, 275, 279, 312-315, 343, 399
fer midboth 176, 196, 197, 213-217, 219, 220, 226, 352, 377, 396
fertilizer 75
FF (Fodla fine) x 17, 18, 24, 27, 29, 40, 45, 49, 54, 62, 68, 73, 92, 94-97, 103, 111, 119, 124, 128-131, 163, 166, 172, 176, 177, 189, 191, 193-195, 210, 211, 214, 215, 220, 221, 225, 227, 230, 243, 246, 250, 251, 259, 260, 262, 267, 272-277, 279, 281, 292, 294, 304, 306, 309, 312, 314, 317, 319, 331-333, 336, 344, 346, 351, 358, 382, 383, 393
fían 26, 47, 69, 83, 97, 98, 122-124, 126, 168, 215, 222, 225, 226, 319, 342, 346, 350, 356
fief xi, 16, 93, 98, 155-158, 161-165, 167-169, 172, 174-177, 182, 200, 201, 212-215, 217, 220, 226, 267, 275, 276, 329, 335, 346, 375, 379
fields 70, 75, 77, 104-108, 110, 111, 136, 167, 231, 403, 406, 408
filid 40, 41, 50, 52, 54, 192, 357
fine v, vi, 9, 16, 17, 29, 32, 40, 54, 55, 58, 62, 97, 103, 119, 127, 142, 166, 173, 184, 186, 193, 194, 196, 198, 208, 209, 212, 214, 215, 217-220, 224, 226-229, 232, 239-248, 250, 251, 254, 256, 257, 259-282, 288-291, 294, 297, 303, 304, 306, 310-316, 319, 321, 328-336, 339, 340, 342-345, 349, 352, 353-355, 357-360, 376, 377, 404
fines 45, 52, 95, 109, 136, 137, 154, 156, 165, 166, 177, 184, 185, 191, 217, 218, 229, 259, 268, 271-273, 275, 279, 294, 328, 333, 338, 339, 341, 344, 345, 356
fintiu 152, 208, 209, 215, 248, 260, 261, 266, 267, 271, 276, 279, 311, 376-378
Fishamble 79
fishing 67, 280, 281

Fitzgerald, Robert, 342, 388
flaith 40, 83, 97, 125, 158, 200, 211, 218, 250, 269, 275, 278, 282, 334, 339, 352, 377, 378
fodder 69, 75, 81, 82, 126, 136, 174
folk 36, 59, 69, 118, 120, 128, 132, 137, 138, 140-144, 202, 265, 341, 387, 389, 391, 392
folud 163, 217, 267, 274, 280
Fomoir 128, 141
food 46, 48, 71, 78, 80, 82-84, 111, 118, 119, 121-127, 130-132, 135, 137, 139, 147, 151, 157, 158, 161, 162, 165, 166, 167, 169, 172, 176, 184, 188-190, 195, 198, 200, 201, 211, 225, 299, 304, 310, 343, 346, 367, 371, 394
Ford, Patrick, 75, 84, 85, 384, 388
forest 47, 64, 71, 82, 83, 90, 96, 111, 118, 125, 126, 137, 350, 360, 367, 369, 371
form 7, 11, 25, 30, 47, 56, 78, 85, 89, 95, 102, 104, 106, 108, 109, 123, 125, 126, 137, 147, 165, 182, 189, 200, 208-211, 223, 240, 275, 294, 295, 318, 319, 334, 342, 346, 355, 376
fosterage 8, 169, 189-191, 196, 220, 242, 243, 250, 261, 275, 276, 297, 306, 316, 359
four lawful women 299
free-clients 157, 159-161, 168, 174, 203, 207, 335, 348, 349
freeman, T.W., 14, 122, 214, 218, 332, 333, 352, 353, 376, 388
fuba and ruba 168, 226, 227, 276
fuidir 40, 97, 152-154, 281, 314, 378

Gaulish 25, 57, 85
gelfhine v, 27, 111, 112, 207, 208, 213, 218, 222-225, 227-229, 232, 239, 242, 244-250, 254, 256, 261, 270, 282, 292, 314, 335, 377, 378
gell 177, 196, 340
gender; sex roles 21-26, 46, 68, 73, 74, 97, 119, 129, 138, 140, 141, 208, 213, 227, 245, 265, 294, 297, 300-308, 314,